ZAGAT®

Connecticut
Restaurants
2010/11

Plus Nearby
New York State
and the Berkshires

LOCAL EDITORS
Lorraine Gengo, John Bruno Turiano, Judith Hausman,
Julia Sexton and Lynn Hazlewood
STAFF EDITOR
Carol Diuguid with John Deiner

Published and distributed by
Zagat Survey, LLC
4 Columbus Circle
New York, NY 10019
T: 212.977.6000
E: conn@zagat.com
www.zagat.com

ACKNOWLEDGMENTS

We thank Susan Cramer, Janet Crawshaw, Jack Dew, Nicholas Gengo-Lehr, Jan Greenberg, Bill Guifoyle, Carrie Haddad, Henry Lehr, Lora Pelton, Robert Seixas, James Sexton, Steven Shukow and Michael Zivyak, as well as the following members of our staff: Josh Rogers (senior associate editor), Brian Albert, Sean Beachell, Maryanne Bertollo, Danielle Borovoy, Jane Chang, Sandy Cheng, Reni Chin, Larry Cohn, Bill Corsello, Alison Flick, Jeff Freier, Curt Gathje, Michelle Golden, Natalie Lebert, Mike Liao, Andre Pilette, Becky Ruthenburg, Art Yaghci, Yoji Yamaguchi, Sharon Yates, Anna Zappia and Kyle Zolner.

The reviews in this guide are based on public opinion surveys. The ratings reflect the average scores given by the survey participants who voted on each establishment. The text is based on quotes from, or paraphrasings of, the surveyors' comments. Phone numbers, addresses and other factual data were correct to the best of our knowledge when published in this guide.

Our guides are printed using environmentally preferable inks containing 20%, by weight, renewable resources on papers sourced from well-managed forests. Deluxe editions are covered with Skivertex Recover® Double containing a minimum of 30% post-consumer waste fiber.

SUSTAINABLE FORESTRY INITIATIVE

Certified Chain of Custody
Promoting Sustainable Forest Management

www.sfiprogram.org

PWC-SFICOC-260

ENVIROINK™

The inks used to print the body of this publication contain a minimum of 20%, by weight, renewable resources.

Contents

Ratings & Symbols

Zagat Top Spot	Name	Symbols		Cuisine	Zagat Ratings			
					FOOD	DECOR	SERVICE	COST

Area, Address & Contact

Z Tim & Nina's ◑ *American*
Litchfield | Litchfield Green (West St.) | 860-555-1234 | www.zagat.com

▽ 23 | 9 | 13 | $15

Review, surveyor comments in quotes

A "former 18th-century stagecoach stop" on the Litchfield Green, this American yanks in both CT Yankees and "staid out-of-staters" with a menu that marries New England classics with Nuevo Latino accents, like a "spicy" pot roast con plantains; though the "fusty Colonial furnishings" fall flat and service is "slow as mid-winter molasses", prices don't "sting" at this "Waspy bastion."

Ratings

Food, Decor and **Service** are rated on the Zagat 0 to 30 scale.

0 – 9	poor to fair
10 – 15	fair to good
16 – 19	good to very good
20 – 25	very good to excellent
26 – 30	extraordinary to perfection
▽	low response	less reliable

Cost

Our surveyors' estimated price of a dinner with one drink and tip. Lunch is usually 25 to 30% less. For unrated **newcomers** or **write-ins,** the price range is shown as follows:

I	$25 and below	E	$41 to $65
M	$26 to $40	VE	$66 or above

Symbols

Z	highest ratings, popularity and importance
◑	serves after 11 PM
⑤	closed on Sunday
Ⓜ	closed on Monday
⊄	no credit cards accepted

About This Survey

This **2010/11 Connecticut Restaurants Survey** is an update reflecting significant developments since our last Survey was published. It covers 925 restaurants in Connecticut (plus nearby New York State and the Berkshires), including 70 important additions. To bring this guide up to the minute, we've also indicated new addresses, phone numbers, chef changes and other major alterations. Like all our guides, this one is based on input from avid local consumers – 4,028 all told. Our editors have synopsized this feedback and highlighted (in quotation marks within reviews) representative comments. You can read full surveyor comments – and share your own opinions – on **ZAGAT.com.**

OUR PHILOSOPHY: Three simple premises underlie our ratings and reviews. First, we've long believed that the collective opinions of knowledgeable consumers are more accurate than the opinions of a single critic. (Consider, for example, that as a group our surveyors bring some 577,000 annual meals' worth of experience to this Survey. They also visit restaurants year-round, anonymously – and on their own dime.) Second, food quality is only part of the equation when choosing a restaurant, thus we ask surveyors to separately rate food, decor and service and report on cost. Third, since people need reliable information in a fast, easy-to-digest format, we strive to be concise and to offer our content on every platform.

ABOUT ZAGAT: In 1979, we started asking friends to rate and review restaurants purely for fun. The term "user-generated content" had not yet been coined. That hobby grew into Zagat Survey; 31 years later, we have over 375,000 surveyors and cover everything from airlines to shopping in over 100 countries. Along the way, we evolved from being a print publisher to a digital content provider, e.g. **ZAGAT.com, ZAGAT.mobi** (for web-enabled mobile devices), **ZAGAT TO GO** (for smartphones) and **nru** (for Android phones). We also produce customized gift and marketing tools for a wide range of corporate clients. And you can find us on Twitter (twitter.com/zagatbuzz), Facebook and other social media networks.

JOIN IN: To improve our guides, we solicit your comments; it's vital that we hear your opinions. Just contact us at **nina-tim@zagat.com.** We also invite you to join our surveys at **ZAGAT.com.** Do so and you'll receive a choice of rewards in exchange.

THANKS: We're grateful to our local editors, Lorraine Gengo, freelance food writer and former editor-in-chief of the *Fairfield County Weekly*; John Bruno Turiano, managing editor of *Westchester Magazine*; Judith Hausman, independent food critic and journalist based in South Salem, NY; Julia Sexton, restaurant critic and food writer; and Lynn Hazlewood, freelance journalist and former editor-in-chief of *Hudson Valley Magazine*. We also sincerely thank the thousands of surveyors who participated – all of our content is really "theirs."

New York, NY
June 9, 2010

Nina and Tim Zagat

What's New

Showing resiliency in the face of a tough economic climate and a high average meal cost ($37.71, compared to $35.25 nationally), many of Connecticut's restaurateurs are doing some recessionary retooling to offer creative yet more cost-conscious dining. But along with the crop of casual new options comes plenty of upscale places, including some glitzy players at the casinos and a spate of sophisticated Latin entries.

BURGERS OR BUST: Given the focus on palatable price points, it's no surprise that the hamburger, that classic comfort favorite, is the main attraction at several newcomers. After shuttering **Fraîche,** his high-end Fairfield New American, chef-owner Marc Lippman debuted **Fraîche Burger,** a gourmet patty purveyor in Downtown Bridgeport's historic Arcade building. In Old Saybrook, chef-owner Jack Flaws closed his upscale cow palace **Jack's Saybrook Steak** and rolled out the gourmet burger-and-dog joint **Jack Rabbit's.** Also new to the genre is Fairfield's **Flipside Burgers & Bar,** which caters to families and happy-hour mavens alike.

MEXICAN GOES UPTOWN: In contrast to the downscaling trend, Connecticut's casual cantinas are being joined by some sophisticated south-of-the-border specialists that command *mucho dinero* by offering hundreds of tequila choices, the freshest high-quality ingredients, tableside preparations of specialty drinks and guacamole and loads of ambiance. At Greenwich's **Lolita Cocina & Tequila Bar,** the vibe is sexy and the Mexican cuisine decidedly haute, and the same is true of West Hartford's stylishly rustic new **Besito.**

MOVERS AND SHAKERS: Among the state's higher-profile arrivals is a new branch of *Top Chef* toque Tom Colicchio's upscale meatery **Craftsteak** in the MGM Grand at Foxwoods, where the craftsmanship is as evident in the sleek, contemporary decor as in the top-notch beef. At the Mohegan Sun casino, TV chef Bobby Flay unveiled an outpost of his NYC eatery, **Bar Americain,** while Westport landed two ambitious newcomers, the New American **Le Farm,** where chef-owner Bill Taibe expands upon the farm-to-table philosophy he honed at **Napa & Co.,** and the Mediterranean **Café Manolo,** a solo turn from the **Barcelona** group's executive chef, Pedro Garzon. Meanwhile, Ignacio Blanco recently exited Norwalk's **Meigas** to open a new branch of New Haven's standout Spaniard, **Ibiza,** in Hamden.

GONE BUT NOT FORGOTTEN: The area saw its share of departures: in Downtown Stamford, Luciano Magliulo closed **Mona Lisa** after 17 years in business, while Margot Olshan shuttered her relatively new **Margot Café & Wine Bar.** Pietro Scotti's **Zest** is no more, although his other Westport venture, the venerable **DaPietro's,** lives on. Chester's **Restaurant du Village** bid adieu, while in South Norwalk, Margherita Aloi's **Goccia** is gone, though her New Canaan Northern Italian, **Aloi,** remains vibrant.

Norwalk, CT
June 9, 2010

Lorraine Gengo

Menus, photos, voting and more – free at ZAGAT.com

Key Newcomers

Our editors' take on the year's top arrivals. See page 184 for a full list.

Bar Americain | *American* | Bobby Flay's bold brasserie goes gambling

Besito | *Mexican* | candlelight and upscale enchiladas

Cafe Manolo | *Med.* | local ingredients and traditional preparations

Craftsteak | *Steak* | a top chef goes top-shelf at Foxwoods

Fraîche Burger | *Burgers* | gourmet patties in Bridgeport

Jack Rabbits | *American* | cheap fun on the run

Le Farm | *American* | foodie cult favorite

Lolita Cocina | *Mexican* | sexy tequila enclave

Pizzeria Molto | *Italian* | artisanal fare and arty decor

Rest. L&E | *French* | upscale French bistro and bar

Rouge Winebar | *Mediterranean* | SoNo sophisticate

Change is in the wind in Connecticut, with several openings and relocations in the works. After 15 years in Westport, Jaime Cooper's beloved **Bonda** has closed up shop with plans to reopen in Fairfield this summer. Stamford's venerable pizza standout **Colony Grill** is out to colonize Fairfield with an outpost, expected to open in early summer. The Florida-based chain **Moe's Southwest Grill** has a branch on the way on Fairfield's Black Rock Turnpike, replacing **Rye Ridge Deli.** In Stamford, the upcoming **Sandella's Flatbread Cafe** will cater to the health-conscious, while **GreenGourmetToGo** is gearing up to offer organic, vegetarian takeout in Bridgeport's Black Rock section. Darien denizens can look forward to getting their neighborhood pub back when **Black Goose Grille,** shuttered in 2008, reopens as **The Goose,** expected any day now. And in West Hartford, they're in hiring mode at **Chipotle Mexican Grill,** to be yet another link in the Denver-based chain.

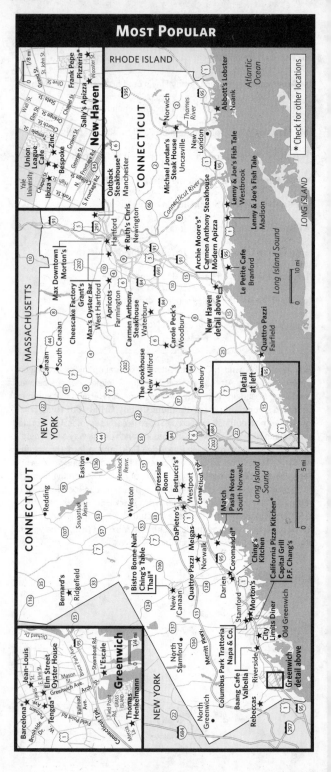

Most Popular

1. Frank Pepe Pizza | *Pizza*
2. Barcelona | *Spanish*
3. Cheesecake Factory | *American*
4. Coromandel | *Indian*
5. Thomas Henkelmann | *French*
6. Morton's | *Steak*
7. Union League | *French*
8. P.F. Chang's | *Chinese*
9. Ruth's Chris | *Steak*
10. Carole Peck's | *American*
11. City Limits | *Diner*
12. Napa & Co. | *American*
13. Jean-Louis | *French*
14. Valbella | *Italian*
15. Ibiza | *Spanish*
16. Capital Grille | *Steak*
17. Tengda* | *Asian*
18. Max Downtown | *Amer./Steak*
19. Abbott's Lobster | *Seafood*
20. Max's Oyster | *Seafood*
21. L'Escale | *French*
22. Le Petit Cafe | *French*
23. Ching's | *Asian*
24. Dressing Room | *American*
25. Rebeccas | *American*
26. Bernard's | *French*
27. Thali | *Indian*
28. Elm St. Oyster | *Seafood*
29. Outback Steak | *Steak*
30. DaPietro's | *French/Italian*
31. Columbus Park | *Italian*
32. Modern Apizza | *Pizza*
33. Bertucci's | *Italian*
34. California Pizza | *Pizza*
35. Pasta Nostra | *Italian*
36. Quattro Pazzi | *Italian*
37. Sally's Apizza* | *Pizza*
38. Bespoke | *Amer./Nuevo Latino*
39. Zinc | *American*
40. Meigas | *Spanish*
41. Match | *American*
42. Grant's | *American*
43. Bistro Bonne Nuit | *French*
44. Michael Jordan's* | *Steak*
45. Archie Moore's | *Pub Food*
46. Lenny & Joe's | *Seafood*
47. Cookhouse | *BBQ*
48. Apricots | *American*
49. Baang Cafe | *Asian*
50. Carmen Anthony | *Steak*

It's obvious that many of the above restaurants are among Connecticut's most expensive, but if popularity were calibrated to price, we suspect that a number of other restaurants would join their ranks. Thus, we have added two pages of Best Buys starting on page 16.

* Indicates a tie with restaurant above

Top Food

28 Thomas Henkelmann | *French*	Coromandel | *Indian*
Ibiza | *Spanish*	Osetra | *Eclectic/Seafood*
Le Petit Cafe | *French*	Sally's Apizza | *Pizza*
Cavey's | *French/Italian*	DaPietro's | *French/Italian*
Jean-Louis | *French*	Thali | *Indian*
27 Bernard's | *French*	Bistro Basque | *French/Spanish*
Carole Peck's | *American*	Piccolo Arancio | *Italian*

28 Thomas Henkelmann | *French*
Ibiza | *Spanish*
Le Petit Cafe | *French*
Cavey's | *French/Italian*
Jean-Louis | *French*

27 Bernard's | *French*
Carole Peck's | *American*
Union League | *French*
Harvest Supper | *American*
Max Downtown | *Amer./Steak*
Valencia | *Venezuelan*

26 Paci | *Italian*
Elizabeth's Cafe | *American*
Woodward House | *American*
Frank Pepe Pizza | *Pizza*
Bistro Bonne Nuit | *French*
Meigas | *Spanish*
Frank Pepe's Spot | *Pizza*
Feng Asian | *Asian*
Métro Bis* | *American*

Coromandel | *Indian*
Osetra | *Eclectic/Seafood*
Sally's Apizza | *Pizza*
DaPietro's | *French/Italian*
Thali | *Indian*
Bistro Basque | *French/Spanish*
Piccolo Arancio | *Italian*

25 Grant's | *American*
Pasta Nostra | *Italian*
SoNo Baking Co. | *Bakery*
Chef Luis | *American*
Capital Grille | *Steak*
La Paella* | *Spanish*
J. Gilbert's | *SW/Steak*
La Zingara | *Italian*
Modern Apizza | *Pizza*
Max's Oyster | *Seafood*
Costa del Sol | *Spanish*
Napa & Co. | *American*
Oliva Cafe | *Med.*

BY CUISINE

AMERICAN (NEW)

27 Carole Peck's
Harvest Supper
Max Downtown
26 Elizabeth's Cafe
Woodward House

AMERICAN (TRAD.)

23 Shady Glen
Vanilla Bean
Woodland
22 Brendan's at the Elms
21 Ted's Montana Grill

BARBECUE

25 Jeff's Cuisine
24 Wilson's BBQ
22 Wood's Pit BBQ
21 Boathouse at Smokey Joe's
Black-Eyed Sally's

BURGERS

24 Burger Bar
23 Plan B Burger Bar
18 City Limits
15 Lucky's
13 Route 22

CHINESE

24 Royal Palace (New Haven)
23 Forbidden City
21 China Pavilion
19 P.F. Chang's
18 Chengdu

CONTINENTAL

24 Grist Mill
Stonehenge
23 Jeffrey's
Woodland
Mill on the River

FRENCH

28 Thomas Henkelmann
Cavey's
Jean-Louis
27 Bernard's
26 Meli-Melo

FRENCH (BISTRO)

28 Le Petit Cafe
27 Union League
26 Bistro Bonne Nuit
25 Café Routier
24 Chez Jean-Pierre

Excludes places with low votes, unless otherwise indicated.

INDIAN

26	Coromandel
	Thali
23	Bangalore
	Bombay
20	Taste of India

ITALIAN

28	Cavey's
26	Paci
	DaPietro's
	Piccolo Arancio
25	Pasta Nostra

JAPANESE

26	Feng Asian Bistro
24	Kazu
	Wasabi Chi
23	Nuage/Fusion
	Miso

MEDITERRANEAN

25	Oliva Cafe
24	John's Café
	Arugula
23	Tapas/Ann
22	Mediterraneo

MEXICAN

22	Wood's Pit BBQ
21	Olé Molé
19	Avenida
18	Villa Del Sol
	Su Casa

PAN-ASIAN

26	Feng Asian Bistro
24	Wasabi Chi
	Ching's
23	Baang Cafe
	Penang Grill

PIZZA

26	Frank Pepe Pizza
	Frank Pepe's Spot
	Sally's Apizza
25	Modern Apizza
	Bru Room at BAR

SEAFOOD

26	Osetra
25	Max's Oyster
24	Max Fish
	Elm St. Oyster
	Liv's Oyster Bar

SPANISH

28	Ibiza
26	Meigas
	Bistro Basque
25	La Paella
	Costa del Sol

STEAKHOUSES

27	Max Downtown
25	Capital Grille
	J. Gilbert's
	Michael Jordan's
24	Ruth's Chris

THAI

23	Little Thai
22	Kit's Thai
	Bangkok Gardens
21	Hot Basil
	King & I

VEGETARIAN

23	It's Only Natural
	Lime
21	Bloodroot
19	Claire's Corner
17	Ahimsa∇

BY SPECIAL FEATURE

BREAKFAST

27	Valencia Luncheria
25	Pantry
	Meli-Melo
23	Aux Délices/Ponzek
	Vanilla Bean

BRUNCH

27	Bernard's
25	La Zingara
22	Roger Sherman Inn
21	Splash
20	Rest./Water's Edge

BUSINESS DINING

28	Thomas Henkelmann
	Cavey's
	Jean-Louis
27	Union League
	Max Downtown

HOTEL/INN DINING

28	Thomas Henkelmann
26	Thali
25	Napa & Co.
	Mayflower Inn
	Michael Jordan's

LUNCH

28 Thomas Henkelmann
   Jean-Louis
27 Bernard's
   Carole Peck's
   Union League

PEOPLE-WATCHING

28 Ibiza
   Jean-Louis
27 Carole Peck's
   Union League
   Max Downtown

RAW BARS

27 Union League
   Max Downtown
25 Max's Oyster
   Water St. Cafe
24 Ralph 'n' Rich's

SINGLES SCENES

26 Feng Asian Bistro
25 J. Gilbert's
   Bru Room at BAR
   Firebox
   Strada 18

WATERSIDE

25 Ondine
24 Grist Mill
   Apricots
23 Abbott's Lobster
   L'Escale

WINNING WINE LISTS

28 Thomas Henkelmann
   Ibiza
   Le Petit Cafe
   Cavey's
   Jean-Louis

BY LOCATION

BRIDGEPORT

25 Tuscany
24 Ralph 'n' Rich's
   Joseph's
21 Two Boots Pizza
   Bloodroot

DANBURY

25 Ondine
23 Café on the Green
   Koo
21 Sesame Seed
18 Chuck's Steak

DARIEN

26 Coromandel
24 Ching's
23 Aux Délices/Ponzek
   Tengda
   Little Thai

FAIRFIELD

26 Frank Pepe Pizza
24 Wilson's BBQ
23 Bangalore
   Saint Tropez Bistro
   Barcelona

GLASTONBURY/ S. GLASTONBURY

25 J. Gilbert's
24 Max Fish

23 Char Koon
   Plan B Burger Bar
   Max Amore

GREENWICH

28 Thomas Henkelmann
   Jean-Louis
25 Rebeccas
   Meli-Melo
24 Elm St. Oyster

HARTFORD

27 Max Downtown
26 Feng Asian Bistro
25 Costa del Sol
   Firebox
   Carbone's

LITCHFIELD COUNTY

27 Carole Peck's
26 Woodward House
25 Oliva
   Mayflower Inn
24 John's Café

MYSTIC

24 Bravo Bravo
23 Azu
22 Capt. Daniel Packer
20 Go Fish
18 Steak Loft

NEW CANAAN

27	Harvest Supper
26	Bistro Bonne Nuit
	Thali
25	Chef Luis
24	Ching's

NEW HAVEN

28	Ibiza
27	Union League
26	Frank Pepe Pizza
	Frank Pepe's Spot
	Sally's Apizza

NORWALK

27	Valencia Luncheria
26	Meigas
	Osetra
25	La Paella
23	Blackstones

OLD SAYBROOK

24	Liv's Oyster Bar
23	Alforno
21	Aspen
18	Cuckoo's Nest
	Zhang's

RIDGEFIELD

27	Bernard's
26	Thali

25	Insieme
24	Stonehenge
	Luc's Café

SOUTH NORWALK

26	Coromandel
25	Pasta Nostra
	SoNo Baking Co.
	Jeff's Cuisine
	Strada 18

STAMFORD

26	Coromandel
25	Capital Grille
	Napa & Co.
	Columbus Park
	Siena

WEST HARTFORD

25	Grant's
	Max's Oyster
	Bricco
24	Arugula
	Harry's Pizza

WESTPORT

26	DaPietro's
24	Tarantino's
	Blue Lemon
23	Bombay
	Dressing Room

Top Decor

28 Thomas Henkelmann	Ralph 'n' Rich's
Woodward House	Capital Grille
27 Mayflower Inn	Dressing Room
26 Union League	Mill on the River
Boulders Inn	Hopkins Inn
25 Copper Beech	Positano's
Paci	Il Palio
Bernard's	Rest./Water's Edge
Feng Asian Bistro	**23** Griswold Inn
Capt. Daniel Packer	Rainforest Cafe
Stonehenge	Ondine
Cobb's Mill Inn	116 Crown
L'Escale	Jean-Louis
Cavey's	Saltwater Grille
Firebox	Max Fish
24 Ibiza	Wasabi Chi
Max Downtown	Bespoke
Chestnut Grille	Napa & Co.
Grist Mill	Hard Rock Cafe
Roger Sherman Inn	Max's Oyster

OUTDOORS

Abbott's Lobster	Edd's Place
Apricots	G.W. Tavern
Bill's Seafood	L'Escale
Boulders Inn	Pond House Café
Costello's	Sono Seaport

ROMANCE

Bernard's	Mayflower Inn
Bespoke	Mill on the River
Chestnut Grille	Ondine
Copper Beech	Stonehenge
Longwood Rest.	Thomas Henkelmann

ROOMS

Bernard's	116 Crown
Brendan's at the Elms	Paci
Grist Mill	Thomas Henkelmann
Mayflower Inn	Todd English's
Morello Bistro	Woodward House

VIEWS

Grist Mill	Positano's
Harbor Lights	Rest./Water's Edge
L'Escale	Sage American
Mill on the River	Splash
PolytechnicON20	Terra Mar

Menus, photos, voting and more – free at ZAGAT.com

Top Service

28	Thomas Henkelmann Woodward House
27	Le Petit Cafe
26	Cavey's Jean-Louis Bernard's Harvest Supper Max Downtown
25	Mayflower Inn Ibiza Capital Grille Union League Ondine Valbella Métro Bis
24	Stonehenge Meigas Insieme DaPietro's Consiglio's

Piccolo Arancio
Tuscany
John's Café
Elizabeth's Cafe
Grant's
Costa del Sol
Diorio
Roger Sherman Inn
Bistro Basque
Tarantino's
Copper Beech
Osetra
Firebox
Carole Peck's

| 23 | Chestnut Grille
Thali
Feng Asian Bistro
Paci
Ralph 'n' Rich's
Luca Rist. |

Best Buys

Everyone loves a bargain, and Connecticut offers plenty of them. All-you-can-eat options are mostly for lunch and/or brunch. For prix fixe menus, call ahead for availability.

ALL YOU CAN EAT

- 26 Coromandel
- 23 Bangalore
- Bombay
- Todd English's
- 21 Splash
- Churrasc. Braza
- 20 Taste of India
- Flanders Fish
- Saltwater Grille
- 19 Squire's
- 18 Abis
- Griswold Inn
- Confetti
- Dakota
- 17 Thai Pan Asian∇

BYO

- 27 Valencia Luncheria
- 25 Chef Luis
- Meli-Melo
- 24 Buon Appetito∇
- 23 Penang Grill
- Little Thai (Greenwich)
- 22 Lenny & Joe's (Madison)
- 21 Hot Basil
- Olé Molé

EARLY-BIRD

- 23 Scribner's
- 21 Saybrook Fish
- 18 Chuck's Steak
- Blue Point B&G∇
- 16 Bull's Bridge Inn
- Putnam House∇

FAMILY-STYLE

- 26 Coromandel
- 22 Boom
- 21 Splash
- Toscana
- 20 Pellicci's
- Eclisse
- 19 Cookhouse
- 18 Chengdu
- 15 Tiger Bowl

PRIX FIXE LUNCH

- 28 Jean-Louis ($29)
- 25 Bin 100 ($30)
- 24 Polpo ($24)
- 23 Saint Tropez Bistro ($15)
- Pacifico ($17)
- 22 Solé Rist. ($14)
- Carmen Anthony Steak ($13)
- Rest. Rowayton ($18)
- La Bretagne ($23)
- 21 Acqua ($14)

PRIX FIXE DINNER

- 26 Meigas ($24)
- 25 Costa del Sol ($25)
- River Tavern ($40)
- Bin 100 ($30)
- 24 Bespoke ($29)
- Shish Kebab/Afghan. ($33)
- 23 Mill on the River ($22)
- 22 Rest. Rowayton ($29)
- Thai Chi Asian Bistro ($25)
- 20 Giovanni's ($33)

PUB GRUB

- 25 Bru Room at BAR
- 20 Eli Cannon's
- 19 John Harvard's
- Wood-n-Tap
- Archie Moore's
- 18 O'Neill's
- 16 Brewhouse
- 15 Mackenzie's
- Southport Brewing

SEAFOOD SHACKS

- 23 Abbott's Lobster
- 22 Lenny & Joe's
- Edd's Place∇
- 20 Lenny's Indian
- Flanders Fish
- 19 Bill's Seafood
- Dolphins Cove∇
- 18 Costello's∇
- Westbrook Lobster
- 16 Sono Seaport

BEST BUYS: BANG FOR THE BUCK

In order of Bang for the Buck rating.

1. Super Duper Weenie
2. Shady Glen
3. Firehouse Deli
4. Layla's Falafel
5. SoNo Baking Co.
6. Jeff's Cuisine
7. Valencia Luncheria
8. Harry's Pizza
9. Lucky's
10. Modern Apizza
11. Vanilla Bean
12. Frank Pepe Pizza
13. Two Boots Pizza
14. Bru Room at BAR
15. Frank Pepe's Spot
16. Plan B Burger Bar
17. American Pie Co.
18. Così
19. Oscar's
20. Little Mark's
21. Burger Bar
22. Claire's Corner
23. Yorkside
24. Meli-Melo
25. Olé Molé
26. Eli Cannon's
27. Tapas/Ann
28. Wilson's BBQ
29. C.O. Jones
30. Zaroka
31. Mystic Pizza
32. China Pavilion
33. Post Corner Pizza
34. Royal Palace (New Haven)
35. Char Koon
36. Rein's NY Deli
37. It's Only Natural
38. Orem's Diner
39. Pot-au-Pho
40. Archie Moore's

BEST BUYS: OTHER GOOD VALUES

Aladdin
Ay! Salsa
Bertucci's
B.J. Ryan's
Boathouse at Smokey Joe's
Bobby Valentine's
Brasitas
Burgers/Shakes
Burke in the Box
Chili Chicken
Colony Grill
Cookhouse
Donovan's & Mackenzie
East-West Grille
Edd's Place
Fat Cat Pie Co.
Fifty Coins
Hanna's
Harry's Bishops Corner
Joe's American
John Harvard's
Kari
King & I
Kit's Thai
La Taverna
Lime
Little Pub
Little Thai
Los Cabos
Lotus
Louis' Lunch
Myrna's
New Deal Steak
Olive Market
Omanel
Osianna
Panda Pavilion
Pasta Vera
Pellicci's
Salsa
Señor Pancho's
Sesame Seed
Southwest Cafe
Stand
Tawa
Thai Pan Asian
Thai Pearl
Two Steps
Vinny's Backyard
Wood-n-Tap

NEARBY NEW YORK'S TOP FOOD

28 | Serevan | *Mediterranean*

27 | Sushi Nanase | *Japanese*
La Panetière | *French*

26 | La Crémaillère | *French*
Arch | *Eclectic*
Big W's Roadside | *BBQ*
Coromandel | *Indian*

25 | Le Château | *French*
John-Michael's | *European*
La Villetta | *Italian*

McKinney & Doyle | *Amer.*
Mulino's | *Italian*
Hajime | *Japanese*

24 | Sonora | *Nuevo Latino*
Sal's Pizza | *Pizza*
Plates | *American*
Bedford Post/Barn | *Amer.*
Tarry Lodge | *Italian*
Morgans Fish | *Seafood*
Spadaro | *Italian*

BY LOCATION

HUDSON VALLEY

28 | Serevan
26 | Arch
Big W's Roadside
25 | McKinney & Doyle
24 | Jaipore Indian

PORT CHESTER

24 | Sonora
Tarry Lodge
23 | Willett House
Piero's
T&J Villaggio

RYE

27 | La Panetière
24 | Morgans Fish
23 | Koo
Frankie & Johnnie's
22 | Watermoon

WHITE PLAINS

27 | Sushi Nanase
25 | Mulino's
24 | Morton's
23 | Aberdeen
Bengal Tiger

Menus, photos, voting and more – free at ZAGAT.com

CONNECTICUT
AND NEARBY
NEW YORK TOWNS
RESTAURANT
DIRECTORY

	FOOD	DECOR	SERVICE	COST

Abatino's *Italian*
21 | 15 | 19 | $30

North White Plains | Super Stop & Shop Ctr. | 670 N. Broadway (Central Westchester Pkwy.), NY | 914-686-0380 | www.abatinosrestaurant.com

For a "night out with the kids" or a "casual lunch", regulars turn to this North White Plains Italian "staple" serving "great garlic pan pizza", "fresh salads" and "ample" pastas all at prices that "won't break the bank"; despite its rather "ordinary" strip-mall setting, it cultivates a "warm atmosphere", thanks in part to a "friendly" staff.

❷ Abbott's Lobster *Seafood*
23 | 15 | 14 | $30

Noank | 117 Pearl St. (Smith Ct.) | 860-536-7719 | www.abbotts-lobster.com

If CT has an "iconic fish shack" it's this Noank mainstay, situated "where the Mystic River meets the ocean" – hence the "fabulous views" and "phenomenally fresh" seafood; "be prepared to queue" for "transcendent lobster rolls" and to stake out a "rustic" "water's-edge picnic table", but beware: crustacean cravers argue there's "no charm to seagulls bombing your meal"; N.B. open May–October.

Aberdeen *Chinese*
23 | 13 | 19 | $32

White Plains | Marriott Residence Inn | 3 Barker Ave. (Cottage Pl.), NY | 914-288-0188

It's the "real deal", sum up surveyors of this "authentic" Cantonese in the White Plains Marriott Residence Inn, where "heavenly dim sum" and "a multitude of fresh seafood" are all ferried to the table by "waiters who know their stuff" ("ask for suggestions and you'll get fantastic dishes not on the menu"); most don't mind its "oddball" location and "tired" decor since it sure "beats going to Chinatown."

Abis *Japanese*
18 | 16 | 19 | $34

Greenwich | 381 Greenwich Ave. (Grigg St.) | 203-862-9100 | www.abis4u.com

"Dependable" is the word on this "kid-friendly" Japanese "standby" in Greenwich proffering "decent" sushi, teriyaki and teppanyaki; the "chefs put on a good show" at the hibachi, so despite complaints of "long-in-the-tooth" decor, it remains "crowded" on weekends.

Abruzzi Trattoria *Italian*
21 | 16 | 20 | $34

Patterson | 3191 Rte. 22 (Rte. 311), NY | 845-878-6800 | www.abruzzitrattoria.com

Patterson locals and "NYC transplants craving good Italian" pile into this "easygoing" "watering hole" for "tasty", "honest food" served by a "solicitous" staff; "reasonable prices" and "comfortable" digs with a "pleasant atmosphere" add to the appeal, although it can get "loud" especially when it's "packed with half the town."

Acqua ⓩ *Mediterranean*
21 | 22 | 19 | $47

Westport | Parker Harding Plaza | 43 Main St. (Post Rd. W.) | 203-222-8899 | www.acquaofwestport.com

"Get a seat overlooking the Saugatuck River" or "cozy up to the bar in front of the warm pizza oven" at this "charming" bi-level

Westporter that attracts a "handsome crowd" with its "high-quality" Med chow and "lovely ambiance"; gourmands gravitate toward the "grilled chicken" and "excellent soufflés", while the $14 "express lunch" downstairs appeals to the budget-minded – and anyone who wants to avoid the "enormous cacophony" at "peak times."

Adriana's *Italian*
| 23 | 16 | 20 | $43 |

New Haven | 771 Grand Ave. (bet. Jefferson St. & Rte. 91) | 203-865-6474 | www.adrianasrestaurant.net

New Havenites hail the "new regime at this old-guard Italian" that "upgraded" the menu a while back with "delicious fried calamari" and the like while preserving its reputation for "excellent" veal dishes – and "holding down costs" to boot; still, a few faultfinders contend "service varies" and bemoan its "tough location" "away from Yale and Downtown"; N.B. a post-Survey renovation may outdate the above Decor score.

Adrienne ⓂＡmerican
| 24 | 22 | 23 | $49 |

New Milford | 218 Kent Rd./Rte. 7 (Rocky River Rd.) | 860-354-6001 | www.adriennerestaurant.com

For a "special dining experience" in the country, surveyors suggest chef-owner Adrienne Sussman's "excellent" New Milford American and its "imaginative", "beautifully presented" fare, including signature game dishes; it's set in a 1774 Colonial that's "lovely in any season" ("fireplace in the winter, patio in summer"), and if some gripe that its "petite portions" are a "tad pricey", the "gracious service" and "romantic" atmosphere win over most.

Ahimsa *Vegan/Vegetarian*
| ▽ 17 | 15 | 21 | $31 |

New Haven | 1227 Chapel St. (Howe St.) | 203-786-4774 | www.ahimsainc.com

With "superb mushroom dishes" and other "interesting", "healthy" fare, this "family-run" "refuge" in Downtown New Haven is out to prove that "tasty" vegan-vegetarian food "isn't an oymoron"; the "spare" decor leaves some cold, however, and even some fans say portions are "sparse for the price" (you may need a "midnight snack"); N.B. a cafe with cafeteria-style seating connects to a more upscale dining room.

AJ's Burgers *American*
| 19 | 15 | 19 | $18 |

New Rochelle | 542 North Ave. (5th Ave.), NY | 914-235-3009 | www.ajsburgers.com

A "throwback to a simpler time", this New Rochelle joint offers a "broad" American menu that "honors the basics" with "great burgers", pizzas and other "comfort foods" served in a skillet (a "clever" touch); despite the frill-free atmosphere, "personable" staffers and "bargain" tabs inspire a steady following.

Akasaka *Japanese*
| ▽ 17 | 14 | 17 | $29 |

New Haven | 1450 Whalley Ave. (Glenview Terr.) | 203-387-4898

This "local sushi spot" in New Haven's Westville section sparks a bit of debate: supporters say it offers "consistently good" fare that's

FOOD | DECOR | SERVICE | COST

"stood the test of time", while detractors declare it's "lost whatever mojo it had"; still, it serves a purpose as a "neighborhood standby" for eat-in or take-out Japanese.

Aladdin ● *Mideastern* ▽ 18 | 12 | 17 | $19

Hartford | 121 Allyn St. (High St.) | 860-278-0202 | www.aladdinhalal.com

For those craving "decent food at 2 AM" in Downtown Hartford, this Middle Eastern is a "solid choice" serving the likes of "well-made" lamb dishes, baba ghanoush and brick-oven pizzas; photos of Syria and Lebanon are what amounts to decor, and no alcohol is served or allowed on the premises.

Alba's ⧄ *Italian* 22 | 19 | 21 | $52

Port Chester | 400 N. Main St. (Rectory St.), NY | 914-937-2236 | www.albasrestaurant.com

"Old-school" dining is alive and well at this "dark", "noisy" Port Chester Northern Italian standby, where the "expertly prepared" fare (like "fabulous Caesar salad" made tableside) and a 300-plus-label wine list are complemented by a "gracious", "pro" staff; yes, it's "a tad expensive", but many insist it's "worth the trip for special occasions."

Alforno *Italian* 23 | 15 | 19 | $30

Old Saybrook | Bennie's Shopping Ctr. | 1654 Boston Post Rd. (bet. Cedar Ln. & Ripley Hill Rd.) | 860-399-4166 | www.alforno.net

"Forget the exterior" – a "nondescript mini-mall off Interstate 95" – and "concentrate on your taste buds" at this "terrific" Northern Italian in Old Saybrook adorned with a 40-ft. mural and "atmospheric" lighting; surveyors swoon over the "best pizza in town" with its "thin-crust crust and excellent homemade sauce", though there's also "amazing pasta Bolognese" and other "solid entrees."

Aloi Ⓜ *Italian* 24 | 20 | 22 | $54

New Canaan | 62 Main St. (Locust Ave.) | 203-966-4345 | www.aloirestaurant.com

"Sit outside on the patio" and you'll "feel like you're in Tuscany" at this "excellent" New Canaan Northern Italian featuring chef-owner Margherita Aloi's "outstanding handmade pastas"; couple that with a "personable staff" and "good wine list" and it's no surprise that the "intimate" indoor space can get "crowded" – and "hardwood floors unfortunately ensure" quite a din.

Altnaveigh Inn ⧄Ⓜ *Continental* ▽ 24 | 26 | 22 | $47

Storrs | Altnaveigh Inn | 957 Storrs Rd. (Spring Hill Rd.) | 860-429-4490 | www.altnaveighinn.com

"If you're in the UConn area" for a "big night out", this Storrs Continental set in a "romantic" 1734 farmhouse inn is the "place to impress"; "outstanding service" complements "delicious" classics like beef Wellington, and though a few fret it's "not the best bang for the buck", the "marvelously warm" atmosphere (could be that four-sided fireplace) melts most hearts.

	FOOD	DECOR	SERVICE	COST

American Pie Company *American*
20 | **15** | **20** | **$21**

Sherman | 29 Rte. 37 Ctr. (Old Greenwoods Ext.) | 860-350-0662
It can "seem like you drive all morning to get there", but nonetheless devotees descend on this "cute" Sherman Traditional American cafe/bakery for "wonderful breakfasts" featuring "generous portions for the price" (hence the "weekend crowds"); there's also "consistent" "heavy-on-the-carbs" lunch and dinner fare dispensed by the "convivial" staff – but just save room for the "marvelous homemade pies" and other "luscious" desserts.

Angelina's *Pizza*
18 | **8** | **18** | **$22**

Westport | Post Plaza | 1092 Post Rd. E. (Morningside Dr.) | 203-227-0865
"There's no decor to speak of" at this "friendly neighborhood" "pizza joint" in a Westport strip mall, but "locals flock" here anyway for "delicious thin-crust" pies and "dependable basics" in "generous servings"; "budget prices" add to the allure for "families with small children" – so if you're not into "crowded and noisy", "do delivery."

Anna Maria's ⓂItalian
18 | **18** | **20** | **$41**

Larchmont | 18 Chatsworth Ave. (Boston Post Rd.), NY | 914-833-0555 | www.annamariascatering.net
"Congenial" owner Anna Maria Santorelli – a former chef to Rudy Giuliani – presides over this "cozy neighborhood place" in Larchmont, where the "comforting" Italian cuisine comes in "substantial" portions; a "disappointed" contingent complains of "uneven" cooking and too "pricey" tabs, but all agree lunch is a "great deal."

Antipasti ⓈItalian
21 | **22** | **18** | **$55**

White Plains | 1 N. Broadway (Main St.), NY | 914-949-3500 | www.antipastiny.com
"Fabulous" small plates, an "extensive" wine selection and a "lively bar scene" lure "foodies" and "singles" to this "cosmopolitan" White Plains Italian set in "sleek" digs with lots of stone and glass detailing; unfortunately, regulars note that "service could be better"; N.B. the above ratings may not reflect a post-Survey chef change.

ⓏApricots *American*
24 | **22** | **22** | **$45**

(aka Ann Howard's Apricots)
Farmington | 1593 Farmington Ave. (Highwood Rd.) | 860-673-5405 | www.apricotsrestaurant.com
Surveyors swear this "venerable" Farmington "favorite" is "worth a trip from anywhere", particularly if you "sit outside by the river in warm weather"; the New American cuisine feels more French in the "formal dining room upstairs", while the "friendly downstairs pub" offers more "reasonably priced" fare, but no matter where you eat, "solicitous waiters" and a "superb wine list" add to the experience.

Arch, The ⓂEclectic
26 | **25** | **26** | **$71**

Brewster | 1292 Rte. 22 (end of I-684), NY | 845-279-5011 | www.archrestaurant.com
You'll be "pampered from start to finish" at this "classy" Brewster "legend", where "simply superlative", "classical" Eclectic cuisine

and "dessert soufflés to die for" are served in a "graceful stone house" exuding "old-world elegance"; sure, tabs are a tad "hefty" (though "Sunday brunch is a steal"), but "put on a coat and tie and spend a few bucks" – "if this doesn't conjure up romance, there's no hope."

☑ Archie Moore's ● *Pub Food*   19 | 14 | 17 | $22

Derby | 17 Elizabeth St. (bet. Main St./Rte. 34 & 3rd St.) | 203-732-3255
Fairfield | 48 Sanford St. (Post Rd.) | 203-256-9295
Milford | 15 Factory Ln. (S. Broad St.) | 203-876-5088
New Haven | 188½ Willow St. (bet. Foster & Orange Sts.) | 203-773-9870
South Norwalk | 77 N. Main St. (bet. Martin Luther King Dr. & Washington St.) | 203-642-3296
Wallingford | 39 N. Main St. (Center St.) | 203-265-7100
www.archiemoores.com

"It's all about the wings" – slathered in a "sauce that's the perfect balance of heat and flavor" – and "cheap beer" at these "nothing-fancy" Traditional Americans that "get the job done while you're watching the game"; "decent" "pub fare" rounds out the menu, but given the "spotty" service and "boisterous" (i.e. "noisy") "college crowd", take "friends you don't have to impress."

Arugula 🅼 *Mediterranean*   24 | 21 | 20 | $39

West Hartford | 953 Farmington Ave. (S. Main St.) | 860-561-4888 | www.arugula-bistro.com

"For a piece of Greenwich Village" on "West Hartford's Restaurant Row", this "small but busy" chef-owned Mediterranean fits the bill, whether it's for "quick nibbles or full dinners" (don't miss the "fabulous flatbreads"); "decent prices" win raves, but evaluators are equivocal about service – it can be "attentive" or "uneven."

Ash Creek Saloon *American*   18 | 16 | 17 | $28

Bridgeport | 2895 Fairfield Ave. (bet. Brewster & Jetland Sts.) | 203-333-2733
Norwalk | 2 Wilton Ave. (Cross St.) | 203-847-7500
www.ashcreeksaloon.com

"Wild West meets the reserved suburbs" at these "family-friendly" "cowboy pubs" rustlin' up "reliable" American grub like "ribs, brisket and burgers" at "reasonable prices"; choose between Norwalk or Bridgeport: while both are "noisy", a few say the latter's "larger", newer Black Rock digs aren't as "rootin' tootin'" as its old locale.

Asiana Cafe *Asian*   20 | 18 | 19 | $35

Greenwich | 130 E. Putnam Ave. (Milbank Ave.) | 203-622-6833 | www.asianacafe.com

"Sushi without the attitude" pleases palates at this "reliable" Greenwich Pan-Asian offering a "little bit of everything" – including "delicious" cooked dishes – on its "reasonably priced" menu; even if a few find it "rather generic" ("where's the character?"), it's "always busy" and "frequently noisy", making "outdoor seating" in warm weather all the more welcome.

	FOOD	DECOR	SERVICE	COST

Asian Kitchen *Asian*
22 | 16 | 18 | $34

(fka Wild Ginger Cafe)

Ridgefield | 461 Main St. (Prospect St.) | 203-431-4588

Picky patrons prefer "anything with mango sauce" at this recently renamed "strip-mall" Pan-Asian in Downtown Ridgefield, though most agree just about "everything" is "fresh and delicious" (including "superior hot-and-sour soup"); a "noisy environment" and service that can feel "rushed" lead some to suggest "get the takeout."

Asian Temptation *Asian*
20 | 22 | 17 | $38

White Plains | City Ctr. | 23 Mamaroneck Ave. (bet. Main St. & Martine Ave.), NY | 914-328-5151 |
www.asiantemptationrestaurant.com

"Thumping dance music" and "modern" decor create a "citylike feel" at this "hip" White Plains enclave presenting an "eclectic mix" of "creative" Asian dishes plus "better-than-average" sushi; despite the "bustling" atmosphere, service can be "sluggish", and alas, it's "too much of a scene" for some – but then upstairs is "more sedate."

Aspen ⓜ *American*
21 | 23 | 19 | $39

Old Saybrook | 2 Main St. (Boston Post Rd.) | 860-395-5888 |
www.aspenct.com

This "sleek" New American in Old Saybrook makes an impression with its "modern" look and "seasonally inspired menu" that uses organic ingredients and – apropos for a "shoreline spot" – includes "varied fish choices"; some find it "slightly costly" and recommend the more "affordable bar menu", or going "for lunch when prices are lower."

Aspen Garden *Eclectic*
15 | 11 | 17 | $26

Litchfield | 51 West St. (bet. Meadow & North Sts.) | 860-567-9477

"Watch the passing parade" from the "large patio" of this "Greek-inflected" "diner-style" eatery on the Litchfield green; "decent" Eclectic cuisine, "reasonable" prices and "quick" service are why "everybody comes", but to some it's just a "million-dollar location with forgettable food" ("dinner = only if you're in a rush"); N.B. a post-Survey renovation may outdate the above Decor score.

Aurora *Italian*
20 | 19 | 18 | $45

Rye | 60 Purchase St. (bet. Elm Pl. & W. Purdy Ave.), NY | 914-921-2333 |
www.auroraofrye.com

A "well-edited menu" of brick-oven pizzas and "satisfying" Tuscan specialties keeps customers contented at this "vibrant" Rye venue sporting French doors that open onto the street in warm weather; though "speedy" service is a plus, critics warn that "poor acoustics" can turn an intimate meal into a "yelling match."

Aux Délices Foods by
23 | 13 | 16 | $27

Debra Ponzek *American/French*

Darien | Goodwives Shopping Ctr. | 25 Old Kings Hwy. N. (Sedgewick Ave.) |
203-662-1136

Greenwich | 3 W. Elm St. (Greenwich Ave.) | 203-622-6644

(continued)

(continued)

Aux Délices Foods by Debra Ponzek

Riverside | 1075 E. Putnam Ave. (Riverside Ave.) | 203-698-1066
www.auxdelicesfoods.com

"When a simple sandwich just won't do", foodies flock to these chef-owned "bakery/delis" in Riverside, Greenwich and Darien for "delish" French–New American entrees and "superb pastries" to take home; a "snooty" vibe and *cher* prices notwithstanding, locals jam the "small seating areas" and "watch the latest fashions on the Size 2" set stroll by.

Avellino's *Italian*

20 | 17 | 20 | $37

Fairfield | 1813 Post Rd. (Mill Plain Rd.) | 203-254-2339 | www.avellinosfairfield.com

Chef-owner Peter Del Franco "rules with a smile and hearty laugh" at his "friendly" Fairfield Italian whose "no-frills decor" doesn't detract from the "generously portioned", "dependable" chow; "but wow! it's loud" shout some; N.B. pizza is now available in-house.

Avenida Ⓜ *Mexican*

19 | 20 | 19 | $44

Greenwich | 339 Greenwich Ave. (Arch St.) | 203-622-1400

"Superb" "boutique margaritas" and "fantastic fresh-made guacamole" are the big enchiladas at this "upscale" Greenwich Mexican, where even the "funky bathrooms" add to the "avant-garde" groove; if the "pricey" entrees don't always measure up to the "trendy" decor, there's always the "lively nighttime scene" to fall back on – though it can be "so loud you can't carry on a conversation."

Aversano's *Italian*

- | - | - | M

Brewster | 1620 Rte. 22 (Rte. 312), NY | 845-279-2233 | www.aversanosrestaurant.com

After a decade running one of Brewster's favorite pizzerias, brothers John and Paul Aversano debuted this well-priced Italian in the space next door where they're turning out a menu of "terrific" classics in a minimalist room; service is "attentive", tabs moderate and it's "getting popular", so "call ahead" to avoid "long waits on weekends."

Avon Old Farms Inn Ⓜ *American*

- | - | - | M

Avon | 1 Nod Rd. (Rte. 44) | 860-677-2818 | www.avonoldfarmsinn.com

This centuries-old Avon inn has reinvented itself with a menu of New American comfort food that's affordable, if not innovative; known especially for its sumptuous brunch buffet, it's also a popular venue for tying the knot (it has several private rooms).

NEW Ay! Salsa Ⓩ⑰ *Pan-Latin*

- | - | - | I

New Haven | 25 High St. (Messina Dr.) | 203-752-0517 | www.aysalsa.net

Chef Franco Gonzalez (ex Roomba) resurfaces in Downtown New Haven with this Pan Latin to-go newcomer specializing in empanadas and Colombian-style arepas (grilled corncakes stuffed with cheese and various choices of meat or fish); it's cash-only and decidedly unfancy, but never mind because it's the food – including decadent tres leches cake – that's the thing here.

	FOOD	DECOR	SERVICE	COST

Azu Restaurant & Bar *American* | 23 | 22 | 20 | $36 |

Mystic | 32 W. Main St. (Water St.) | 860-536-6336 |
www.ckrestaurantgroup.com

Whatever you do, "order the appetizers" (and the "lobster mac 'n' cheese" at lunchtime) at this American "hot spot" in "the middle of Mystic"; "windows that open to the street" and a "lively bar scene" add to the "NYC feel", but it gets "noisy", and though "sardines aren't on the menu", some say "that's how you'll feel."

☑ Baang Cafe & Bar *Asian* | 23 | 20 | 19 | $48 |

Riverside | 1191 E. Putnam Ave. (Neil Ln.) | 203-637-2114 |
www.decarorestaurantgroup.com

"Order a bangarita" and "people-watch" at this Riverside Pan-Asian where the "food is beautiful, but the eye candy is even hotter"; "family-size portions" of the "wonderful" fare (including "crispy spinach" "Popeye would love") are ideal for "sharing with groups", but it's "so loud", some can't "get the baang out of their ears."

Bailey's Backyard *American* | 20 | 17 | 20 | $38 |

Ridgefield | 23 Bailey Ave. (Main St.) | 203-431-0796 |
www.baileysbackyard.com

"Particularly nice when you can sit outdoors", this Ridgefield New American has alfrescans applauding its "friendly service" and "quality" "comfort food"; all agree it's a "highly dependable" choice, even if it won't be "getting any innovation awards"; N.B. the Brookfield branch has closed.

NEW Ballou's Wine Bar *Eclectic* | - | - | - | M |

Guilford | 51 Whitfield St. (bet. Boston & Broad Sts.) | 203-453-0319 |
www.ballouswinebar.com

Coffee, wine and chocolate – a hedonist's bare necessities – are the focus of this Eclectic newcomer located next to the historic Guilford Green, where the lineup of moderately priced light comfort fare includes panini, salads, fondues (both savory and sweet) and assorted cheese plates; the wines, both international and local, are available by the bottle, glass or in flights that arrive in chocolate cordial cups, and there's a cozy fireplace and live music on weekends to provide yet more sensory pleasure.

Bamboo Grill Ⓜ *Vietnamese* | ∇ 21 | 17 | 22 | $29 |

Canton | 50 Albany Tpke./Rte. 44 (Colonial Rd.) | 860-693-4144 |
www.bamboogrillcuisine.com

"Friendly service" is a top draw at this "family-run" Canton Vietnamese serving up "good-quality fish", soups, pancakes and other "cooked-to-order" fare; the small, "casual" space can get "noisy", but the wallet-pleasing BYO policy may take your mind off of that.

Bambou Asian Tapas & Bar *Asian* | ∇ 23 | 21 | 21 | $44 |

Greenwich | The Mill | 328 Pemberwick Rd. (Highview Rd.) |
203-531-3322 | www.bambourestaurant.com

"Tucked away" down by the ol' mill stream in Greenwich's Glenville neighborhood, this "above-average" Pan-Asian is making a splash with

| | FOOD | DECOR | SERVICE | COST |

its "inventive sushi rolls" and tapas-style specialties like "tuna tortilla pizzas"; ask the "gracious" staff for an "outdoor seat near the waterfall", all the better to enjoy this "quiet little spot without attitude."

Bangalore Indian
| 23 | 18 | 22 | $29 |

Fairfield | 1342 Kings Hwy. (Commerce Dr.) | 203-319-0100 | www.bangalorefinedining.com

The "food comes 'spicy' as advertised" at this "reasonably priced" Fairfield find that converts consider "one of the [area's] best Indian restaurants"; even better news: despite "interesting specials", a "lovely atmosphere" and "hospitality galore", you can usually get in "without a wait"; P.S. the $9-and-under lunch boxes are a real "value."

Bangkok Gardens Thai
| 22 | 14 | 18 | $26 |

New Haven | 172 York St. (Chapel St.) | 203-789-8684

With Yale Rep across the street, this "convenient" Thai "hot spot" in Downtown New Haven "can get kind of crowded at theater time", but its "predictably yummy" "cheap student grub" earns applause nevertheless; if contrarians contend it's "not very different" from its "many competitors on nearby blocks", "sit in the atrium room" and you'll see the difference.

Bangkok Thai Thai
| 21 | 9 | 17 | $27 |

Mamaroneck | 1208 W. Boston Post Rd. (Richbell Rd.), NY | 914-833-1200

This "modest", "family-run" Mamaroneck Thai proves "reliable" for "simple, spicy" "home cooking", "cheap" prices and "fast" service; however, considering that the "depressing" digs possess "no ambiance whatsoever", many say "takeout" is the best option.

Bao's Chinese Cuisine Chinese
| - | - | - | M |

White Plains | White Plains Mall | 200 Hamilton Ave. (Cottage Pl.), NY | 914-682-8858

Downstairs from the DMV in the White Plains Mall awaits this cozy Sino enclave; look for Chinese characters on the orange-gold walls as well as on the moderately priced menu, which offers as its signature a split dish of shrimp with honey walnuts and sesame chicken; N.B. parking validated for tabs over $35.

🆕 Bar Americain American
| - | - | - | E |

Uncasville | Mohegan Sun Casino | 1 Mohegan Sun Blvd. (bet. Rtes. 2 & 32) | 860-862-8000 | www.baramericain.com

Leave it to Bobby Flay to add some cosmopolitan glam and sophisticated spice to the roster at Uncasville's Mohegan Sun, where this offshoot of his upscale NYC New American brasserie dwells just off the hotel's lobby; the sexy, dramatically lit setting includes a raw bar, and there are also separate bar and cocktail-lounge spaces.

Barça Spanish
| 20 | 20 | 20 | $42 |

Hartford | Design Ctr. | 1429 Park St. (Bartholomew Ave.) | 860-724-4444 | www.barcahartford.com

For "solid" tapas offered in a "unique" setting, Hartforders head to the "sleek bar and dining room" of this "savvy", if "pricey",

Spanish newcomer in the capital's "revitalized Design Center"; however, issues with sound ("bounces around in the space") and service ("all over the place") make this a "one-visit" experience for a few Barça-loungers.

Z Barcelona Restaurant & Wine Bar *Spanish*

| 23 | 21 | 20 | $41 |

Fairfield | Hi Ho Hotel | 4180 Black Rock Tpke. (Rte. 15) | 203-255-0800
Greenwich | 18 W. Putnam Ave. (Greenwich Ave.) | 203-983-6400
New Haven | Omni Hotel | 155 Temple St. (Chapel St.) | 203-848-3000
South Norwalk | 63 N. Main St. (bet. Ann & Marshall Sts.) | 203-899-0088
NEW Stamford | 222 Summer St. (Broad St.) | 203-348-4800 ◐
West Hartford | 971 Farmington Ave. (Main St.) | 860-218-2100
www.barcelonawinebar.com

"Bring on the sangria" and "to-die-for mojitos" cheer amigos of this "ultrachic" sextet boasting "terrific" vini and "outstanding Spanish tapas" packing "intense" flavors; while the "kickin' bar scene" lures both "upscale singles" "looking for a little action" and "desperate housewives" "dressed for a night on the town", distressed diners dis the "glaringly loud" din and say prices can "add up quickly" (though recessionistas revel in the "half-price wines on Sundays").

Barnacle BBQ & Fish Shack *BBQ/Seafood*

| – | – | – | M |

Mamaroneck | 181 E. Boston Post Rd. (bet. Mamaroneck Ave. & Spruce St.), NY | 914-777-6610 | www.barnaclebbq.com

Smoked-on-premises Texas brisket and St. Louis–style ribs appear alongside mussels in white-wine sauce and almond-crusted salmon at this wood-plank-bedecked Mamaroneck BBQ-seafood arrival; Wednesday night's 'pit meat of the week' prix fixe attracts the budget-conscious, live bands on weekends draw rock-lovers, and come summer, the front and rear decks (the latter with views of Mamaroneck Harbor) entice one and all.

Bar Vivace *Italian*

| ▽ 22 | 19 | 20 | $42 |

Mamaroneck | 213 Halstead Ave. (Mamaroneck Ave.), NY | 914-315-6460

This compact wine bar opposite the Mamaroneck train station is "worth checking out" for its "simple" Italian small plates and housemade pastas, which accompany a "carefully selected" list of *vini*; add "courteous" service, and it's no wonder it's a bona fide area "favorite."

Basso Café Ⓜ *Mediterranean*

| – | – | – | E |

Norwalk | 124 New Canaan Ave. (Bartlett Ave.) | 203-354-6566 | www.bassobistrocafe.com

Norwalk's Broad River neighborhood is home to this Mediterranean whose chef-owner's fusion dishes reflect his dual culinary heritage –

hence, homemade gnocchi with white truffle oil and Venezuelan arepas vie on a menu that includes desserts like panna cotta and tres leches cake; fortunately, a BYO policy makes it easier on the wallet, because entrees are *expensivo*.

Basta *Italian* — 20 | 17 | 19 | $39

New Haven | 1006 Chapel St. (College St.) | 203-772-1715 | www.bastatrattoria.com

Diners may be "squeezed" like the "San Marzano tomatoes" in this "cramped" New Haven Italian's "deep, rich sauce", but "everyone" goes anyway for "excellent" "down-home" fare made from the "freshest possible ingredients" (like line-caught seafood and free-range chicken); then again, a few find the service "lacking" and prices "a little steep."

Beach Café ⓜ *American* — 17 | 20 | 18 | $32

Fairfield | 2070 Post Rd. (Pine Creek Rd.) | 203-254-3606 | www.beachcafefairfield.com

There's "no beach in sight", but you'll still "feel like you're on vacation" at this New American seafooder in Fairfield boasting "Nantucket-style" decor; less transporting is the "slightly pricey" fare (fish tacos, etc.) that's "nothing to write home about", though the "yuppie" scene at the "stunning circular bar" may inspire you to do so.

Beach House ⓜ *Seafood/Steak* — 22 | 23 | 21 | $48

Milford | 141 Merwin Ave. (Abigail St.) | 203-877-9300 | www.beachhousemilford.com

"Excellent beef" and "some of the freshest fish around" join forces in Milford at this "upscale" surf 'n' turfer in a "lovely waterfront setting" on Long Island Sound; a "beautiful" hand-carved oak bar (circa 1848) dominates the "attractive" interior, and there's live jazz on weekends, but all that ambiance comes with a "pricey" tab.

Beach House Café *American* — - | - | - | M

Old Greenwich | 220 Sound Beach Ave. (Arcadia Rd.) | 203-637-0367 | www.beachhousecafe.com

This Traditional American in Old Greenwich cultivates a beachy vibe with black-and-white accoutrements and subtle seawashed accents; like its nearby cousin (Thataway Cafe), it offers a reasonably priced and appropriately sea-centric menu, with fish tacos, crab cakes and lobster rolls making the most waves, though the Sunday brunch and live music (Thursday–Saturday) also have their fans.

Bedford Post, The Barn *American* — 24 | 22 | 19 | $61

Bedford | Bedford Post | 954 Old Post Rd./Rte. 121 (bet. Indian Hill Rd. & Rte. 137), NY | 914-234-7800 | www.bedfordpostinn.com

Popular with the "horsey set", this "bustling" Bedford cafe and bakery co-owned by Richard Gere earns praise for its "inventive" New American breakfasts and lunches based on "local, organic" ingredients and set down in fashionably rustic quarters; yet while the "food is always on the mark", "amateurish" service can be a sore spot, especially given such "pricey" tabs.

Bedford Post, The Farmhouse Ⓜ American — | — | — | VE

Bedford | Bedford Post | 954 Old Post Rd./Rte. 121 (bet. Indian Hill Rd. & Rte. 137), NY | 914-234-7800 | www.bedfordpostinn.com

The more elegant of the dining rooms in co-owner Richard Gere's Bedford Post complex, this ultrapricey New American showcases chef Brian Lewis' haute barnyard cuisine, available à la carte or in a five-course tasting menu; despite the building's origins as an 18th-century farmhouse, Frette linens and a doting staff are among many luxe, modern touches; N.B. dinner only.

Beehive American/Eclectic 17 | 14 | 19 | $31

Armonk | 30 Old Rte. 22 (Kaysal Ct.), NY | 914-765-0688 | www.beehive-restaurant.com

Long an Armonk "mainstay", this "upscale diner" proves a "dependable" pick for well-priced Eclectic–New American eats; service is "pleasant", if "distracted", possibly due in part to the abundance of "children" and "teenagers" often crowding its otherwise "comfortable" quarters; N.B. it closed recently for major renovations (which will outdate the above Decor score), and is slated to reopen in spring 2010.

Bellizzi Italian 15 | 14 | 15 | $24

Larchmont | 1272 Boston Post Rd. (Weaver St.), NY | 914-833-5800 | www.bellizzi.us

One of the "family-friendliest" joints in town, this "boisterous" Larchmont standby is in high demand for "birthday parties", thanks to its "Chuck E. Cheese"-style setting complete with an on-site playroom; the food – "thin-crust" pizzas and Italian standards – is "not memorable", but the wine's "decent enough" and harried parents proclaim "it's worth it just to have the kids occupied."

Bengal Tiger Indian 23 | 18 | 20 | $36

White Plains | 144 E. Post Rd. (bet. Court St. & Mamaroneck Ave.), NY | 914-948-5191 | www.bengaltiger1.com

Known as an "institution, and deservedly so", this decades-old White Plains Indian continues to inspire a "loyal following" with its "diverse" lineup of "wonderfully spiced" dishes set down by a "warmhearted" staff; although its looks are "colorful" and not without "some charm", most find the "kitschy" furnishings in need of an "update."

Bennett's Ⓜ Seafood/Steak 21 | — | 21 | $51

Stamford | 24-26 Spring St. (bet. Bedford & Summer Sts.) | 203-978-7995 | www.bennettsofstamford.com

"If the Rat Pack were still around, you'd find them" at this Stamford "steak and fish house"; those who felt it "could use an update" should know it was revamped post-Survey, and introduced a new menu that augments the old "reliable" surf 'n' turf favorites with some more modern New American dishes, including lots of gluten-free options.

	FOOD	DECOR	SERVICE	COST

Bentara *Malaysian* — 24 | 22 | 21 | $38

New Haven | 76 Orange St. (Center St.) | 203-562-2511 |
www.bentara.com

"Bring a fire extinguisher" to this "classic" "gastronomic adventure" in Downtown New Haven and prepare to use it: the "wonderful" Malaysian fare comes with "lots of spice or none at all" – but just keep in mind that here "hot is *hot*"; "famously slow service" lets you "rub elbows with the Yale hipsters" and admire the "simple but elegant decor" longer.

⧉ Bernard's Ⓜ *French* — 27 | 25 | 26 | $67

Ridgefield | 20 West Ln./Rte. 35 (High Ridge Ave.) | 203-438-8282 |
www.bernardsridgefield.com

"They do everything right" at chef-owner Bernard Bouissou's "*magnifique*" French "gem", the "clear winner in Ridgefield for imagination and taste"; the "excellent food (and it should be for the price)", "superior" wines, "romantic" "country inn" setting and "attentive" service mean most consider it tailor-made for "special occasions"; P.S. Sarah's Wine Bar upstairs has a "bistro feel" and a separate menu.

⧉ Bertucci's *Italian* — 16 | 14 | 16 | $23

Avon | 380 W. Main St. (W. Avon Rd.) | 860-676-1177
Danbury | 98 Newtown Rd. (I-84, exit 8) | 203-739-0500
Darien | 54 Boston Post Rd. (I-95, exit 13) | 203-655-4299
Glastonbury | 2882 Main St. (Griswold St.) | 860-633-2225
Newington | 2929 Berlin Tpke. (Main St.) | 860-666-1949
Orange | 550 Boston Post Rd. (Peck Ln.) | 203-799-6828
Shelton | 768 Bridgeport Ave. (bet. Old Stratford Rd. & Parrott Dr.) |
203-926-6058
Southington | 20 Spring St. (Queen St.) | 860-621-8626
West Hartford | 330 N. Main St. (bet. Pioneer Rd. & Rte. 44) |
860-231-9571
Westport | 833 Post Rd. E. (I-95, exit 18) | 203-454-1559
www.bertuccis.com

"You could make a meal on the hot rolls alone" (some just "wear a big shirt and stuff them in") at these Italian "family feed fests" that also serve "surprisingly good" "thin-crust pizzas" at "fair prices"; then again, saucy types snip that they're mostly "mediocre", with "cafeteria-type" decor, "rushed" service and "too many children running around."

NEW Besito *Mexican* — – | – | – | E

West Hartford | Blue Back Sq. | 46 S. Main St. (Memorial Rd.) |
860-233-2500 | www.besitomex.com

Soft lighting from a wall of candlelit alcoves, cozy, colorfully striped banquettes and a list of tempting tequilas may inspire some to take a cue from the name and blow kisses at their companions while dining at this stylishly rustic West Hartford newcomer; the word is already out about its high-end Mexican cuisine – from guacamole made tableside to the free take-home bag of churros – and lively bar scene, meaning this *cocina* is already packed with amigos.

	FOOD	DECOR	SERVICE	COST

☒ Bespoke *American/Nuevo Latino* | 24 | 23 | 21 | $52

New Haven | 266 College St. (Chapel St.) | 203-562-4644 |
www.bespokenewhaven.com

Chef-owner Arturo Franco-Camacho "never ceases to amaze" at
this "exciting" New Haven Nuevo Latino–New American, where the
food "tastes as good as the patrons look"; "edgy decor that actually
works" and "lovely rooftop dining" are other reasons it's one of the
area's "best places for a classy date" – but just let your "rich boy-
friend" pay the tab.

Big W's Roadside Bar-B-Que Ⓜ *BBQ* | 26 | 7 | 19 | $20

Wingdale | 1475 Rte. 22 (Rock Hill Dr.), NY | 845-832-6200 |
www.bigwsbbq.com

"Meltingly delicious" brisket, "out-of-this-world" ribs and other "di-
vinely inspired" barbecue brings on "serious gluttony" at this "little"
Wingdale pit stop, where "affable" owner Warren Norstein – "Big W
himself" – "proudly" presides as "king of smoke"; even those who
don't care for the "bare-bones" digs declare it's "worth a long drive"
just for the "wonderful takeout", or to picnic beneath a willow when
it's warm; NYC Qs could take lessons here.

Bill's Seafood ⊭ *Seafood* | 19 | 13 | 17 | $25

Westbrook | 548 Boston Post Rd. (Hammock Rd.) | 860-399-7224 |
www.billsseafood.com

The "swooping" seagulls "can be disturbing", but that doesn't stop
budgeteers from "sitting at picnic tables" on the "open-air" deck of
this "riverside" Westbrook "lobster shack"; "mostly fried" seafood
abounds ("clams, shrimp", etc.), which "locals" wash down with
"cold beers" as they listen to live music, which is on tap "nearly every
day"; N.B. cash only.

Bin 100 *Eclectic* | 25 | 22 | 23 | $43

Milford | 100 Lansdale Ave. (Bridgeport Ave.) | 203-882-1400 |
www.bin100.com

"Excellent across the board", the "daring-to-be-different" Eclectic
menu at this "tucked-away find" in Milford melds "multiethnic
fusion" fare like the signature paella Valenciana with a "super"
wine list (some 125 selections by the bottle, 20 by the glass),
"high-quality" service and "classic" decor; never mind if the "strip-
mall location" means you get to "look out to Walgreens from the
main dining room."

Bin 228 Panini & Wine Bar ☒ *Italian* | 23 | 22 | 21 | $31

Hartford | 228 Pearl St. (bet. Ann St. & Service Ct.) | 860-244-9463 |
www.bin228winebar.com

You'll "feel like you're someplace fancier than you actually are"
at this "cozy" Italian in Downtown Hartford overflowing with
"wines by the glass" and staffed by a "knowledgeable" crew to help
guide the vinously challenged; concerned connoisseurs say
"kitchen issues" ("tiny") may be "cramping its creativity", but count
on "tasty panini" and "mostly small plates" of "superb" risotto and
other "light fare."

	FOOD	DECOR	SERVICE	COST

Bistro Basque *French/Spanish* | 26 | 20 | 24 | $42 |

Milford | 13 River St. (bet. Broad & Daniel Sts.) | 203-878-2092 | www.bistrobasqueusa.com

"Better than it has to be", this "reasonably priced" "pearl" in Downtown Milford has wishful thinkers "hoping no one finds out about" its "unique" French-Spanish fare, including "tapas that delight"; its "personal service" extends to the "friendly owner"; P.S. hit the "secluded patio" when the weather's fine.

Ⓩ Bistro Bonne Nuit *French* | 26 | 20 | 22 | $55 |

New Canaan | 12 Forest St. (bet. East & Locust Aves.) | 203-966-5303 | www.culinarymenus.com/bistrobonnenuit.htm

Francophiles almost "expect Edith Piaf to flit through" this "exquisite" bistro, where reservations are needed "to beat New Canaanites to a table" – and it's no wonder, since the "excellent wine list" and "sophisticated food served with aplomb" will leave you "craving cassoulet" for some time; *oui,* "cramped" quarters and "rising prices" are downers, but consider that part of the "Parisian feel."

Bistro Twenty-Two Ⓩ Ⓜ *American/French* | 23 | 24 | 24 | $62 |

Bedford | 391 Old Post Rd. (bet. Lake Ave. & The Farms Rd.), NY | 914-234-7333 | www.bistro22.com

A "model of consistency" after more than 30 years, this "steady" Bedford performer caters to a well-heeled "older crowd" that appreciates its "excellent" French–New American fare and "solicitous" service from a "bygone era"; the "intimate" setting exudes a "low-key elegance" that most maintain is "sure to please", so long as you're not fazed by the "pricey" tabs.

B.J. Ryan's ● *American* | 22 | 18 | 21 | $28 |

Norwalk | 57 Main St. (Hoyt St.) | 203-866-7926 | www.bjryans.com

"Finally, a place in Norwalk" to have a "true *Cheers* experience" beam barflys besotted by this "Irish pub done right"; natch, there's an "expansive list of brews" and "cozy seating" but also a "surprisingly diverse" New American menu with "quality" fare like "bang bang shrimp" and a "top-shelf" burger; P.S. go in "early evening" before the "revelers get there to do Jell-O shots."

Black-Eyed Sally's BBQ & Blues Ⓩ *BBQ* | 21 | 19 | 19 | $28 |

Hartford | 350 Asylum St. (bet. Ann & High Sts.) | 860-278-7427 | www.blackeyedsallys.com

"Let the good times roll" at this "bluesy" Cajun-barbecue joint that injects a "little bit of the South into buttoned-down Hartford" – just "keep your napkin handy" while feasting on "fried oysters, ribs" and other "finger-lickin'" fare; with "outstanding" live bands and "Big Easy"-ish decor, it's hard not to have a "real good night", unless it's quiet conversation you're after.

Blackstones Steakhouse *Steak* | 23 | 21 | 22 | $56 |

Norwalk | 181 Main St. (Plymouth Ave.) | 203-840-9020

Though it's in an "odd mall-ish location", carnivores crow that this Norwalk steakhouse is "better" than some of the big-name cow palaces, and "without the noise or pretense"; "excellent" slabs come out "perfectly cooked" in "enjoyable" environs, but frugal types gripe that "everything's à la carte and pricey."

Blazer Pub ⊅ *Pub Food*

| 22 | 11 | 18 | $21 |

Purdys | 440 Rte. 22 (Rte. 116), NY | 914-277-4424 | www.theblazerpub.com

Devotees "dare you to find a better burger" than the one at this "been-around-forever" Purdys pub where the "big, juicy" patties are paired with "diet-killing fries" and ice-cold beer; despite the "divey" decor, it's "usually packed" with a motley mix of "bikers", "investment bankers" and "lithe women in riding gear", though the "friendly" staff keeps the "crowds" in check; N.B. cash only.

Bloodroot Ⓜ *Vegan/Vegetarian*

| 21 | 14 | 15 | $24 |

Bridgeport | 85 Ferris St. (Harbor Ave.) | 203-576-9168 | www.bloodroot.com

"Throw on your Birkenstocks" – you'll need them while "busing your own tray" at this "crunchy" Bridgeport "time capsule of '70s feminism" where the women "cook for you but don't serve you"; chow down on "lovingly prepared" vegan-vegetarian cuisine so "flavorful you don't miss the meat", though even if you do, it's hard to argue with its "on-the-water" locale.

BLT Steak *Steak*

| 23 | 24 | 21 | $72 |

White Plains | Ritz-Carlton Westchester | 221 Main St. (bet. Church St. & Rennaissance Sq.), NY | 914-467-5500 | www.bltsteak.com

"Fabulous steaks" and "outrageous" Gruyère popovers are the hallmarks of this "chic" NYC chophouse import in White Plains' Ritz-Carlton hotel, inhabiting a "modern" space with an open kitchen; add in "astute" servers, and most find this "suburban substitute" "lives up to its reputation", though an "underwhelmed" minority feels stung by "astronomical" tabs.

Blue Ⓩ *American*

| 19 | 20 | 18 | $51 |

White Plains | 99 Church St. (Hamilton Ave.), NY | 914-220-0000 | www.bluewhiteplains.com

It's not NYC, but it "comes close" say supporters of this "hip" White Plains Downtowner with a "Manhattan Uptown vibe", thanks to "excellent strong cocktails", "Asian-inflected" New American fare and "inviting" azure-hued digs; however, "earsplitting" acoustics, "overpriced" items and "not-up-to-snuff" service have skeptics snapping it's "not as special as it wants to be."

Blue Dolphin Ristorante Ⓩ *Italian*

| 23 | 13 | 20 | $34 |

Katonah | 175 Katonah Ave. (Jay St.), NY | 914-232-4791 | www.thebluedolphinny.com

Though it looks like a "little diner" from the outside, this "quirky" Katonah canteen conjures up a "trip to Capri" with its "generous portions" of "simple" Southern Italian classics "done very well"; it's a "tight fit" in the dining room, but an "engaging" staff keeps the mood "convivial", and prices are a "great value" too; N.B. "come early" or prepare to wait.

Blue Lemon *American* — 24 | 20 | 23 | $45

Westport | Sconset Sq. | 15 Myrtle Ave. (Post Rd.) | 203-226-2647 |
www.bluelemonrestaurant.com

Chef-owner Bryan Malcarney does a "terrific job with his New American creations" – check out the "exquisite" Dover sole special on Mondays for proof – at this "sophisticated yet unpretentious" "gem" near the Westport Country Playhouse; the setting may be "tight" (you may need to ask the "exceptional" staff "for a shoehorn when you order"), but most would agree "you leave feeling anything but blue"; N.B. check out the new $23 prix fixe offered Tuesday–Thursday.

Blue Pearl Ⓢ Ⓜ *American/Fondue* — 20 | 22 | 20 | $37

New Haven | 130 Court St. (Orange St.) | 203-789-6370 |
www.thebluepearlnewhaven.com

"Twentysomething hipsters" head to this New Haven "modern oasis" to "chat over drinks" – "creative cocktails" are the "real star of the show here" – and share "sweet and savory fondues" that come in "tasty" combos; some find the food "just ok" and say the "trendy" decor "seems to be trying too hard", but the "bubbly atmosphere" pleases most.

Blue Point Bar & Grill *American* — ∇ 18 | 19 | 18 | $34

Stratford | 2415 Main St. (E. Broadway) | 203-375-2583

It's the bar that is the big draw at this Stratford New American, so if you're in the mood to "watch a game and chat with locals" while sampling "slightly upscale appetizers" and "pricey but yummy drinks", you are bound to find it "enjoyable"; otherwise, the "only thing blue here" may be those bummed by "inconsistent" food and service.

Boathouse *American* — 16 | 20 | 18 | $37

Lakeville | 349 Main St./Rte. 44 (Walton St.) | 860-435-2111 |
www.boathouseatlakeville.com

"Prep school kids' families" and locals alike drop anchor at this "popular" Lakeville American, where the "attractive" "boat decor" and "beautiful location" make more waves than the "perfectly acceptable but uninspired" fare, including "steaks, burgers, seafood" and even "surprisingly tasty sushi"; the jury is still out regarding the service, however: some say it's "friendly and efficient", while others insist it's "spotty."

Boathouse at Smokey Joe's *BBQ* — 21 | - | 15 | $22

Stamford | 1308 E. Main St./Rte. 1 (Weed Ave.) | 203-406-0605 |
www.smokeyjoesribs.com

"Tasty", "no-b.s." BBQ that "won't break the bank" is still the heart and soul of this Stamford rib joint, but following a recent (post-Survey) renovation and expansion, it now also boasts a full-service surf 'n' turf room on its second floor; the "cafeteria-style" downstairs remains "perfect for families" and "great for takeout", while the more polished upstairs offers moderately priced steaks, fish, salads and some 'cue options.

	FOOD	DECOR	SERVICE	COST

Bobby Q's Barbeque & Grill *BBQ*   19 | 15 | 17 | $29

Westport | 42 Main St. (Post Rd.) | 203-454-7800 |
www.bobbyqsrestaurant.com

It may be the "last restaurant you'd ever expect to find" in chichi Westport, but this "kid-friendly" BBQ joint dishing out "large portions" of pulled pork and ribs "hits all the right notes" with the 'cue crowd (and at "fair prices"); still, a few saucy sorts say the chow's "mediocre" and gripe about "inexperienced" service and "sparse" decor; P.S. the "summer rooftop music is a big draw."

Bobby Valentine's Sports Gallery Café ❶ *American*   15 | 16 | 16 | $23

Stamford | 225 Main St. (Washington Blvd.) | 203-348-0010 |
www.bobbyv.com

Packed with "memorabilia to the ceiling" and "rowdy" crowds glued to a "zillion TVs", this Stamford American "sports fan's dream" offers "cheap pitchers" and "standard pub fare" ("can you say deepfried?") in "portions suitable only for the cholesterally tolerant"; critics cry foul over the "incredible noise" and "tired" decor, suggesting maybe "Bobby should stick to managing baseball" – though all appreciate that "it's not unusual" to see the namesake former Mets honcho "puttering around the place."

Bogey's Grille & Tap Room *American*   16 | 14 | 18 | $30

Westport | 323 Main St. (Canal St.) | 203-227-4653 |
www.bogeyswestport.com

For a "casual night out" Downtown, this "friendly", "low-key" hangout offers Westporters "popularly priced" Traditional American fare like "great burgers" and 'sandwedges' "named in golfese" (e.g. the Ben Hogan tuna melt); but non-duffers dis the "tacky golf theme" and fault "dated decor and food."

Bombay *Indian*   23 | 14 | 19 | $30

Westport | 616 Post Rd. E. (bet. Crescent & Rayfield Rds.) |
203-226-0211 | www.fineindiandining.com

See review in The Berkshires Directory.

🆕 Bombay Olive *American/Indian*   - | - | - | M

West Hartford | 450 S. Main St. (New Britain Ave.) | 860-561-3000 |
www.bombayolive.com

Housed in a former IHOP, this affordable West Hartford newcomer seeks to please as many palates as possible, offering Indian cuisine with a smattering of American, Nepalese and Persian grill dishes, all of which can be had à la carte or buffet-style; once inside its A-frame abode, the decor is appropriately subcontinental.

Bond Grill *Asian*   ∇ 18 | 18 | 18 | $29

Norwalk | 250 Westport Ave. (bet. Lovatt St. & Vollmer Ave.) |
203-840-0610 | www.asianbistrogroup.com

Even James Bond would appreciate the "imaginative sushi", "courteous staff" and "entertaining hibachi room" antics complete with "chefs throwing food in the air" at this Norwalk Pan-Asian; despite "upscale, modern decor", it's a bit "hard to get away from the strip-mall feel", but most agree it's "worth it."

Boom Restaurant American
22 | 20 | 20 | $42

Old Lyme | 90 Halls Rd. (Rte. 95) | 860-434-0075 🅢
Westbrook | Brewer's Pilots Point Marina | 63 Pilot's Point Dr. (Rte. 1) | 860-399-2322
www.boomrestaurant.net

Your choice: eat outside on a "delightful" deck "overlooking a marina" in Westbrook or in Old Lyme's "strip-mall location"; either way, these "understated" New Americans please with their "small-bite" menus offering the likes of "to-die-for scallops" and fish 'n' chips; P.S. vets warn the seasonal watersider can be a "bit difficult to find."

❏ Boulders Inn Ⓜ American
22 | 26 | 23 | $58

New Preston | The Boulders Inn | 387 E. Shore Rd./Rte. 45 (Rte. 202) | 860-868-0541 | www.bouldersinn.com

"You'll win a lot of points if you take someone special" to this "worth-the-drive" New Preston Contemporary American set in a "romantic" 1890 inn; the "unsurpassed" patio view of "stunning Lake Waramaug" goes down as easily as the "fine" food and "excellent service", and though it may "feel like you're miles from civilization", the "pricey" tab will bring reality home; N.B. except for holiday weekends, it's closed in winter.

Boxcar Cantina Southwestern
20 | 18 | 18 | $34

Greenwich | 44 Old Field Point Rd. (Prospect St.) | 203-661-4774 | www.boxcarcantina.com

Tequila-istas swear by the "get-a-ride-home" margaritas at this "crowded" Greenwich cantina whose "high-end" SW fare made from "locally grown" ingredients where possible is a "cut above typical tacos"; "rustic decor" and a "family atmosphere" make this a "kiddy palace" before 8 PM, so "go on the later side" lest your conversation be "drowned out by small screaming children."

Brasitas Pan-Latin
- | - | - | M

Norwalk | 430 Main Ave. (bet. Creeping Hemlock Dr. & Valley View Rd.) | 203-354-7329
Stamford | 954 E. Main St. (Lincoln Ave.) | 203-323-3176
www.brasitas.com

It's "hard to go wrong with any dish" at these "lively" Norwalk-Stamford Pan-Latins whose plethora of *platos* pack flavors from Mexico, Colombia, Brazil and Spain; even the "plantain chips and salsa served with meals are addictive" – and go down well with the mojitos and margaritas fueling the "fun, fun, fun" vibe.

Brass City Bistro Continental
- | - | - | E

Waterbury | 812 Hamilton Ave. (Rte. 84) | 203-574-2489

This chef-owned Waterbury standby makes customers an offer they can't refuse with its signature veal Godfather (a breaded cutlet in a red-wine tomato sauce with mozzarella) from an Italian-leaning Continental menu; the black-and-gold color scheme provides plenty of bada bing, and you can expect the bill to amount to lotsa ka-ching.

Bravo Bravo ▯ *Italian*

24 | 19 | 21 | $46

Mystic | Whaler's Inn | 20 E. Main St./Rte. 1 (Holmes St.) | 860-536-3228 | www.bravobravoct.com

"Snag a window seat" for a "view of the passing boats" (and "tourists") at this "trendy-as-Mystic-gets" Italian in the Whaler's Inn; "top-class cuisine" like the signature *zuppa de pescado* and "wonderful housemade bread" ensures there's "rarely an empty table", so don't be surprised if the "festive" crowd gets a bit "noisy"; P.S. it's the "older sister of Olio and Azu."

Brazen Fox ◑ *American*

15 | 17 | 16 | $29

White Plains | 175 Mamaroneck Ave. (bet. Maple Ave. & E. Post Rd.), NY | 914-358-5911 | www.thebrazenfox.com

The barkeeps "pour a pint with a smile" at this spacious, split-level White Plains watering hole attracting hordes of "working stiffs" with a "fantastic" lineup of brews and "classic" vintage-style decor kicked up by a multitude of flat-screen TVs; it's "quite popular", but judging from the "bland" Traditional American grub, "one doesn't exactly go for the food."

Brendan's at the Elms ▯ *American*
(fka Elms Restaurant & Tavern)

22 | 21 | 22 | $52

Ridgefield | The Elms Inn | 500 Main St./Rte. 35 (Gilbert St.) | 203-438-9206 | www.brendansattheelms.com

"Thoughtfully prepared" Traditional American cuisine is at the heart of this "cozy", "elegant" 1799 Colonial in Downtown Ridgefield; whether you choose to chow down in the "formal dining rooms" ("a little stuffy" for some), on the covered porch or in the "more casual tavern room" ("marvelous in the winter with a fire blazing" and "more reasonable prices"), the "food is equally good."

Brewhouse *American*

16 | 18 | 16 | $27

South Norwalk | 13 Marshall St. (N. Main St.) | 203-853-9110 | www.sonobrewhouse.com

If "pretzel rolls and beer are all you need", this "pleasant" Traditional American near Norwalk's aquarium "delivers", plus the "kiddies" "enjoy identifying the country flags"; but while the "copper kettles and pipes" decor strikes some as "cute", foes froth that it's "dated" (especially since it "doesn't micro-brew" on-site), while others deem the chow merely "acceptable"; N.B. check out the new Sunday brunch buffet.

Bricco *Italian*

25 | 23 | 23 | $40

West Hartford | 78 LaSalle Rd. (Farmington Ave.) | 860-233-0220 | www.billygrant.com

"Awesome pasta specials", "sophisticated entrees with an Italian flair" and "standout desserts" emanate from the "open kitchen" of Billy Grant (among "West Hartford's best chef-owners"), which explains why surveyors continue to exclaim "this one's a keeper"; "attentive" staffers manage the "bustling" scene "well", but "sometimes the wait is awful", as it accepts reservations for "large parties" only (six-plus).

	FOOD	DECOR	SERVICE	COST

Brickhouse 🅼 *Italian*
| | - | - | - | M |

Derby | 90 Pershing Dr. (Division St.) | 203-732-0600 |
www.brickhousederby.com

Get down at this Derby Italian, which on weekends serves its moderately priced steak and seafood in two-four time with a revolving selection of live music (karaoke, piano and vocals, live bands and DJs), and dancing is an option too; surrounded by 200-plus images of celebrities, diners can hope for some of that star quality to rub off.

Brie & Bleu 🅂🅼 *French*
| | ▽ 24 | 16 | 19 | $28 |

New London | 84 Bank St. (Golden St.) | 860-437-2474 |
www.brieandbleu.com

New Londoners are finding their whey Downtown to this "charming" "cheese shop bistro" "attached to a remarkable wine store"; nibblers nosh on a "limited" menu of "excellent" "salads, soup and panini" in its "cramped" interior, though the "harbor-view deck" ("perfect for watching sub races on the Thames!") is a better in-season option.

Brix 🅂🅼 *French/Italian*
| | ▽ 19 | 19 | 19 | $36 |

Cheshire | 1721 Highland Ave./Rte. 10 (Fieldstone Ct.) | 203-272-3584 |
www.brixct.com

A "standout" in a "dull eating environment", this "upscale" Cheshire French-Italian pleases fans who report "wonderful" pastas and "flavorful" meat and fish dishes "worth going out of your way for"; then again, cynics claim people think it's "good only because no one else is."

Brooklyn's Famous Subs & Pasta *Diner*
| | 15 | 15 | 19 | $19 |

White Plains | 51 Court St. (bet. Main St. & Martine Ave.), NY |
914-422-0115 | www.brooklynsfamous.com

"Egg creams", sub sandwiches and other assorted Americana are on offer at this "kitschy" 1950s-themed coffee shop in Downtown White Plains, which also slings a "solid burger"; parents praise the "quick" service, "low prices" and "kid-friendly" vibe, though ultimately most maintain the grub's "nothing special."

Bru Room at BAR ● *Pizza*
| | 25 | 17 | 16 | $22 |

New Haven | 254 Crown St. (bet. High & York Sts.) | 203-495-1111 |
www.barnightclub.com

"Who woulda thought to put mashed potatoes" on a pizza? wonder those wowed by this "secret contender in the constant battle" for New Haven's premier pie; however, the airy, brewerylike space "gets louder" as the "young, fun" crowd washes down that "fantastic" 'za with "world-class" brews, so "don't expect to have an intimate conversation."

Bugaboo Creek Steak House *Steak*
| | 15 | 17 | 15 | $27 |

Manchester | Buckland Hills Plaza | 1442 Pleasant Valley Rd. (I-84) |
860-644-6100 | www.bugaboocreeksteakhouse.com

"Animatronic taxidermy" and other "kitschy" Canada-themed decor elements await at this Manchester chain link that serves

| | FOOD | DECOR | SERVICE | COST |

up "standard" burgers and steaks "at the mall"; most all "kids will love" sharing a meal with a "talking moose", and adults who find it "reminiscent of a theme park ride" can always reach for the "decent beverage" menu.

Bull's Bridge Inn *American*
16 | 15 | 19 | $35

Kent | 333 Kent Rd./Rte. 7 (Bull's Bridge Rd.) | 860-927-1000 | www.bullsbridge.com

Particularly appealing "after dashing through the snow on a cold day" in Kent, this "no-frills" Traditional American set in a 1762 inn gets "packed" with locals enjoying "ample portions" of "decent" "meat-and-potatoes" fare; if the "rustic" decor, "early-bird specials" and salad bar don't appeal, there's always the view of the "landmark" covered bridge nearby.

Buon Amici *Italian*
19 | 15 | 21 | $38

White Plains | 238 Central Ave. (Tarrytown Rd.), NY | 914-997-1399 | www.buonamicirestaurant.com

Oft "overlooked", this "unassuming" White Plains Italian is a find for "hearty" "red-sauce" fare "prepared with care" and delivered by a "friendly" staff that's "willing to bend over backward" for you; trendsetters yawn at the "ho-hum" beige digs and "no-surprises" menu, but all appreciate the "affordable" prices.

Buon Appetito Ⓜ *Italian*
▽ 24 | 10 | 19 | $32

Canton | 50 Albany Tpke./Rte. 44 (Secret Lake Rd.) | 860-693-2211

There's "enough garlic to scare off a few monsters" in the "consistently excellent" entrees at this chef-owned Canton Italian, but go ahead, "order the garlic bread" as well; the BYO policy "ensures an affordable meal", and though there's "zero atmosphere", the vibe is so "friendly" it won't seem to matter.

Burger Bar & Bistro *Burgers*
24 | 15 | 18 | $23

South Norwalk | 58 N. Main St. (bet. Ann & Marshall Sts.) | 203-853-2037 | www.burgerbarsono.com

"Forget your arteries" when ordering the "hard-to-beat" burgers at this "cool" South Norwalk "treasure", especially if you also want to enjoy the "worth-the-visit" fries smothered in "cheese and truffle oil"; "crayons keep kids entertained", but it's mostly "hipsters after 8 PM", many of whom shrug off the "stale" bovine decor and sometimes "sloooowww service"; N.B. a post-Survey expansion may outdate the above Decor score.

Burgers, Shakes & Fries Ⓩ ⌧ *Burgers*
- | - | - | I

Greenwich | 302 Delavan Ave. (New Lebanon Ave.) | 203-531-7433 | www.burgersshakesnfries.com

The name of this "tiny place" in Greenwich says it all, so expect "tasty, moist" burgers customized with a "ton of toppings", "thick, delicious shakes" and "great fries"; "sit at the butcher-block counter or take it home" (it only seats 20), and bring cash, though "super reasonable prices" mean the no-credit-card policy isn't much of a bother.

	FOOD	DECOR	SERVICE	COST

Burke in the Box ⓂAmerican   - | - | - | I

Ledyard | Foxwoods Resort Casino | 39 Norwich Westerly Rd./Rte. 2 (bet. Mains Crossing & Preston Plains Rd.) | 800-369-9663 | www.foxwoods.com

Celebrity chef David Burke has fun with food – including his signature 'cheeseburkers', Kobe dogs and fries with Asiago cheese and truffle oil – at this Foxwoods outpost of his playful New American in NYC's Bloomingdale's; pinstripe packaging and colorful custom-designed boxes put an upscale spin on takeout (eating in is also an option), and you can pay with casino points.

Butterfly Chinese *Chinese*   15 | 13 | 17 | $25

West Hartford | 831 Farmington Ave. (Lancaster Rd.) | 860-236-2816 | www.butterflyrestaurantct.com

Fans insist "you won't be disappointed" at this "old-style" West Hartford Chinese with "really special specials" and "even karaoke"; others aren't so sure, citing "bland" fare that "delivers the expected" and "traditional" decor that doesn't "encourage lingering" ("it's not the '70s anymore, time to redecorate").

Cafe Allegre Ⓜ*Italian*   20 | 21 | 20 | $48

Madison | Inn at Lafayette | 725 Boston Post Rd. (Wall St.) | 203-245-7773 | www.allegrecafe.com

Sure, some find it a "little stuffy", but this "lovely" chef-owned Italian in the "landmark" Inn at Lafayette is *the* "place to see and be seen" in Madison – especially if you want to see "locals" chow down on "reliable" "old-world eats" like veal scaloppine; "friendly service" is another lure, though a few find "prices a little high" for portions "a little small."

Cafe Goodfellas *Italian*   21 | 17 | 21 | $44

New Haven | 758 State St. (Bradley St.) | 203-785-8722 | www.cafegoodfellas.com

"Mobster movies" "constantly" play on the TV screens and Sinatra and Dino croon at this "always-busy" Southern Italian "joint" in New Haven dishing up "big portions" of "decent" basics; detractors declare all that "bada-bing"-ing is "annoying", and even a few fans fret that it's "a bit pricey."

Cafe Livorno Ⓩ*Italian*   20 | 17 | 19 | $45

Rye | 92 Purchase St. (Purdy Ave.), NY | 914-967-1909

Amid "glitzier options" in "upper-crust" Rye, this "comfortable" Northern Italian proves a "dependable" pick for moderately priced specialties served in "quiet", "intimate" surroundings; it's a little "stuffy" to some, though the wine and martini bar upstairs make an "atmospheric" perch for a drink.

Cafe Lola *French*   - | - | - | E

Fairfield | 57 Unquowa Rd. (bet. Post & School Rds.) | 203-292-8014 | www.cafelolarestaurant.com

A couple of lovebirds, chef Henri Donneaux (ex Le Figaro Bistro, La Panetière) and wife Ivanina, co-own this cozy, pricey Fairfield French bistro named after their *très* bohemian imaginary muse; one room takes you to Paris with shabby-chic decor and another channels Provence with bench seats mounded with country-floral cushions, while the mussels Madras, steak au poivre and other classics complemented by impressive wines transport the taste buds.

NEW Café Manolo ⬛Ⓜ *Mediterranean* — | — | — | E

Westport | 8 Church Ln. (State St.) | 203-227-0703 | www.cafemanolo.com

Chef-owner Pedro Garzon (ex Barcelona) honors his grand-uncle at this namesake Mediterranean newcomer, which replaces Zest in the old bank vault in Downtown Westport; the below-street-level space has an airy upscale bistro feel and now features a cheese display and food bar, while the cuisine showcasing local ingredients is matched with a global wine list; N.B. a tip for wallet-watchers: everything on the menu can be ordered as a small plate.

Cafe Mirage ⬛ *Eclectic* 21 | 11 | 20 | $40

Port Chester | 531 N. Main St. (Terrace Ave.), NY | 914-937-3497 | www.cafemirageny.com

Set in a "funky, former gas station" in Port Chester, this midpriced Eclectic eatery whips up "solid" "comfort food" alongside more "inventive" dishes, all served in portions "enormous" enough to ensure "leftovers"; the "cavernous" dining room is "not much to look at", but the staff works hard to please and plus it's "open late" on weekends.

Cafe Mozart *Coffeehouse* 17 | 14 | 16 | $25

Mamaroneck | 308 Mamaroneck Ave. (Palmer Ave.), NY | 914-698-4166

"Decadent desserts" beckon at this Mamaroneck European cafe favored for a "cup of joe" and a "light bite" after a movie, or a "leisurely" Sunday brunch; it has an "old-fashioned" "college campus" coffeehouse vibe, helped along by live guitar and piano on weekends.

Café on the Green *Italian* 23 | 22 | 23 | $47

Danbury | Richter Park Golf Course | 100 Aunt Hack Rd. (Mill Plain Rd.) | 203-791-0369 | www.cafeonthegreenrestaurant.com

"Don't let the venue turn you off", because this "excellent" Danbury Northern Italian on the Richter Park Golf Course scores points for its "wonderfully diverse menu" ("don't leave without having the bananas Foster"), "top-notch" service and "spectacular sunset views"; if a few faultfinders single out "spotty quality" and a "hard-to-find" locale, most agree it's "well worth the effort"; N.B. there's now live music on Saturday nights.

Café Roma ⬛ *Italian* ▽ 22 | 21 | 19 | $38

Bridgeport | 269 Fairfield Ave. (bet. Broad & Harrison Sts.) | 203-333-0055 | www.caferomarestaurant.com

"Brick walls, gaslights, high ceilings" and artwork inspired by the movie *Roman Holiday* add to the "comfortable" atmosphere at this "small" Bridgeport Northern Italian appreciated for its fresh pastas and "excellent veal and duck"; it's a bit "like eating at grandmom's" – only with tabs that can be a bit "pricey."

	FOOD	DECOR	SERVICE	COST

Café Routier French

| 25 | 22 | 23 | $44 |

Westbrook | 1353 Boston Post Rd. (bet. Burdick & Goodspeed Drs.) |
860-399-8700 | www.caferoutier.com

"You might consider a second home" in "out-of-the-way" Westbrook
once you sample the "immensely satisfying" fare at this "charming"
French bistro where "everything works", including "camp-style trout
and steak frites"; add in an "adventurous" wine list, "attentive" service and a "convivial" atmosphere (ok, it can get a little "loud"), and
it's no surprise partisans proclaim "you always leave pleased."

Café Silvium ⊠ Italian

| - | - | - | M |

Stamford | 371 Shippan Ave. (Park St.) | 203-324-1651 |
www.cafesilvium.com

Brotherly love abounds at this Southern Italian stalwart in Stamford
whose chefs/co-owners are siblings and "friends with everyone";
handmade pastas in "large portions" are the standouts (particularly
the signature cavatelli), and staffers are "savvy" enough to keep the
tiny, "always-packed" dining room happy and feeling that the "wait
is worth it."

Café Tavolini Italian

| ∇ 19 | 15 | 17 | $36 |

Bridgeport | 3074 Fairfield Ave. (bet. Fox & Morehouse Sts.) |
203-335-1111 | www.cafetavolini.com

Supporters of this "intimate" Bridgeport Italian "highly recommend"
it for "well-prepared" classics served in "lively" environs; a few are
less charmed, citing "drowned-in-sauce pastas" and decor featuring
"Sinatra and *Sopranos* pictures" as well as "multiple big-screen TVs"
("tacky"), but "nice outdoor dining in season" is a plus.

⊠ California Pizza Kitchen Pizza

| 16 | 12 | 14 | $23 |

Farmington | Westfarms Mall | 3 Westfarms Mall (New Britian Ave.) |
860-561-1027
Ledyard | Foxwoods Resort Casino | 39 Norwich Westerly Rd./Rte. 2
(bet. Mains Crossing & Preston Plains Rd.) | 860-859-2912
Stamford | Stamford Town Ctr. | 230 Tresser Blvd. (Town Center Dr.) |
203-406-0530
www.cpk.com

Expect to see "all of your friends with their kids" at these "cheerful"
"suburban" outlets where a "harried" staff shuttles "relatively
healthy chain food" like "interesting salads" and a "wide variety" of
pizzas with "creative toppings"; though "affordable" tabs keep them
constantly "packed", purists are aghast at the "bland", "bready" pies –
maybe "California should leave the pizza making to New York."

⊠ Capital Grille, The Steak

| 25 | 24 | 25 | $62 |

Stamford | Stamford Town Ctr. | 230 Tresser Blvd. (Canal St.) |
203-967-0000 | www.capitalgrille.com

"Everything a steakhouse ought to be", this "upscale" Stamford chain
link lures "buttoned-down" "power" players with "flavorful", "artfully presented" chops; the "low-lit, dark-wood" digs and "attentive"
service are "ideal for a special occasion or a business dinner", so although the bille can be "expensive", "you get what you pay for" here.

	FOOD	DECOR	SERVICE	COST

☑ Captain Daniel Packer Inne *Eclectic* | 22 | 25 | 23 | $39 |

Mystic | 32 Water St. (Noank Rd.) | 860-536-3555 |
www.danielpacker.com

"Sit by the fire" upstairs in the "romantic dining area" or "hang with locals in the basement pub" – aka "the coziest bar" in Mystic – at this "rustic" Eclectic set in a "superbly restored Colonial" inn; whatever floor you choose, expect "solid" fare from the "different menus", though frugal types tout the "lively" tavern as the better "deal."

Carbone's Ristorante ☒ *Italian* | 25 | 20 | 23 | $46 |

Hartford | 588 Franklin Ave. (bet. Goodrich & Hanmer Sts.) |
860-296-9646 | www.carboneshartford.com

"They'll make you a meal you won't refuse" at this "iconic" "family-run" Hartford Northern Italian whose "old-school" "21 Club vibe" is matched by a "traditional" menu that includes "everything from antipasto to amaretto apéritifs" – with "showy" "tableside" preparations (salads, desserts) to boot; if upstarts call it a "has-been", most maintain it "never fails to please."

Carmen Anthony Fishhouse *Seafood* | 21 | 20 | 20 | $48 |

Avon | The Shops at River Pk. | 51 E. Main St./Rte. 44 (Rte. 10) |
860-677-7788
Wethersfield | 1770 Berlin Tpke./Rte. 515 (Pawtuckett Ave.) |
860-529-7557
Woodbury | 757 Main St. S./Rte. 6 (Middle Quarter Rd.) |
203-266-0011
www.carmenanthony.com

This "stylized" "fish-and-potatoes" chainlet may be "nothing out of the ordinary", but it's "solid" according to those hooked on its "delicious chowder", "delightful" lobster rolls and "made-to-perfection martinis"; still, some finatics fret over "spotty" service and kinda "boring" fare they consider "too expensive for what you get."

Carmen Anthony Steakhouse *Steak* | 22 | 20 | 22 | $52 |

New Haven | 1 Audubon Bldg. | 660 State St. (Audubon St.) | 203-773-1444
Waterbury | 496 Chase Ave. (Nottingham Terr.) | 203-757-3040
www.carmenanthony.com

For "steaks the way they should be", beef eaters in Waterbury and New Haven cut a trail to these "quintessential" chophouses "good for working dinners" or "taking the family for a night out"; but the "Manhattan-caliber" prices don't add up for those who gripe about "mediocre" meat served in an "old-fashioned atmosphere."

☑ Carole Peck's | 27 | 20 | 24 | $49 |
Good News Cafe *American*

Woodbury | Sherman Village Plaza | 694 Main St. S./Rte. 6 (Rte. 64) |
203-266-4663 | www.good-news-cafe.com

It's "a godsend in the bleak landscape of CT restaurants" exult enthusiasts of this Woodbury New American whose namesake chef "uses locally grown organic foods" to create "cuisine for cultivated palates" in "fresh, delicious" ways (e.g. "wonderful onion rings that go with anything"); patrons part ways over the "funky" art, which some call "quirky" and others say "might improve if they threw plates of spaghetti on it"; N.B. closed Tuesdays.

Carrabba's Italian Grill *Italian*

19 | 18 | 19 | $33

Manchester | 31 Red Stone Rd. (Buckland St.) | 860-643-4100 | www.carrabbas.com

The "next best thing to a 'real' Italian restaurant" is this "reliable" Manchester chain link where "large portions" of "fairly inexpensive", "not watered-down" grub comes in "homey" digs; while some report "inconsistent" service and quality that "varies from franchise to franchise", the overall word here is "satisfying."

Cascade Mountain Winery & Restaurant Ⓜ *American*

16 | 17 | 17 | $40

Amenia | 835 Cascade Mountain Rd. (Flint Hill Rd.), NY | 845-373-9021 | www.cascademt.com

A "destination" for oenophiles, this seasonal "lovely winery" in Dutchess County offers tastings of its 12 varieties on a "breathtaking" "mountaintop"; a "limited menu" of Traditional American eats is deemed simply "so-so" and service in the "basic" country-style space sometimes spotty, but brunch on the deck in summer is "a delight."

Caseus Ⓢ *Eclectic*

- | - | - | M

New Haven | 93 Whitney Ave. (Trumbull St.) | 203-624-3373 | www.caseusnewhaven.com

New Havenites say this "friendly bistro" serving Eclectic fare with a French flair "fills a void" in the East Rock neighborhood; standouts include "mac 'n' cheese made from the riches of the adjoining" fromagerie and the "chocolate pot de crème"; N.B. no dinner served Monday–Tuesday when the space is used for cheese/wine/beer classes and events.

Cava Wine Bar & Restaurant *Italian*

23 | 22 | 22 | $48

New Canaan | 2 Forest St. (East Ave.) | 203-966-6946 | www.cavawinebar.com

It's "always a treat to go underground" at this "imaginative" "basement" New Canaan Northern Italian that "feels like a wine cellar" and offers an "impressive selection" of vinos to boot; if the "cozy" setting can get "a bit noisy", the "delicious" chow (including "housemade pastas worth the calories") and "attentive" service mean most fuhgeddaboudit.

☑ Cavey's Restaurants Ⓢ Ⓜ *French/Italian*

28 | 25 | 26 | $60

Manchester | 45 E. Center St. (Main St.) | 860-643-2751 | www.caveysrestaurant.com

At this two-in-one "treasure" in Manchester, you're in for a "memorable dining experience" whether you choose the "special occasion"–worthy downstairs French or the "less formal", "more affordable" street-level Italian; the "delicious" duo shares "sophisticated" service, a "wonderful" 20,000-bottle wine cellar (with "options in different price ranges") and an "ambiance conveying warmth and luxury."

	FOOD	DECOR	SERVICE	COST

Cedars ❶ *Steak* — 21 | 20 | 22 | $55

Ledyard | Foxwoods Resort Casino | 39 Norwich Westerly Rd./Rte. 2 (bet. Mains Crossing & Preston Plains Rd.) | 860-312-4252 | www.foxwoods.com

For a "break from the hustle and bustle of the casino", Foxwoods denizens duck into this "reliable" Ledyard option where the "usual steakhouse fare is done well"; better go "before hitting the slots or tables", though, since "prices are based on the assumption you won"; N.B. smokers hit the jackpot with a lounge of their own.

Central Steakhouse ⓈⓂ *Steak* — 23 | 22 | 19 | $49

New Haven | 99 Orange St. (bet. Center & Chapel Sts.) | 203-787-7885 | www.centralsteakhouse.com

"Prime beef", just a "hint of Asian fusion" and an "extensive wine list" make this Downtown New Haven "sleeper" an "intriguing alternative to your dad's steakhouse"; romantics suggest eating in the "beautiful wine cellar" for an "intimate" meal with "someone special", though the less-enthralled cite "lackluster" service and those "Manhattan prices."

Centro Ristorante & Bar *Italian/Mediterranean* — 19 | 18 | 18 | $33

Fairfield | 1435 Post Rd./Rte. 1 (bet. Sanford St. & Unquowa Rd.) | 203-255-1210
Greenwich | The Mill | 328 Pemberwick Rd. (Glenville Rd.) | 203-531-5514
www.centroristorante.com

Use your noodle and "stick with a simple salad or bowl of pasta" at these Med-Northern Italians, "reliable standbys" where you're encouraged to "draw on the tablecloth" (the "walls are covered with framed doodles"); for a "casual night out with family" ("kiddie city", anyone?), they're "easy on the lira", even if longtimers lament they're "just not what they used to be"; P.S. dine alfresco "overlooking a waterfall" in Greenwich and "right by the gazebo" in Fairfield.

Char Koon *Pacific Rim* — 23 | 14 | 19 | $24

South Glastonbury | Nayaug Shopping Ctr. | 882 Main St./Rte. 17 (Water St.) | 860-657-3656 | www.charkoon.com

This "almost-too-small" chef-owned Pacific Rim specialist in South Glastonbury is "still a favorite" with reviewers who rate it their "Asian of choice" for "consistently delicious" eats; an "underdone", "uncomfortable" dining room, however, has some suggesting "do takeout"; N.B. Middletown's Forbidden City is its younger sibling.

Chat 19 *American* — 18 | 16 | 18 | $36

Larchmont | 19 Chatsworth Ave. (Boston Post Rd.), NY | 914-833-8871 | www.chat19.net

There's "always a buzz" at this "lively" Larchmont bistro boasting an "inventive" American menu as well as "excellent" martinis; "moderate" prices keep it "crowded" with "families" in the early evening, making way for "quite the bar scene" later on – either way, it's "extremely noisy"; N.B. a post-Survey redecoration may outdate the Decor score.

	FOOD	DECOR	SERVICE	COST

Chatterley's *American* ▽ 20 | 18 | 20 | $36

New Hartford | 2 Bridge St. (Rte. 44) | 860-379-2428 |
www.chatterleysct.com

"Townies and out-of-towners" alike tuck into midpriced New
American cuisine "that's a cut above typical tavern fare" at this
"charming" chef-owned "little hideaway" in a circa-1773 New
Hartford building; "pretty flowers" and a "lively" patio make it "especially nice in the summer."

☑ Cheesecake Factory *American* 18 | 18 | 17 | $30

Hartford | 71 Isham Rd. (Raymond Rd.) | 860-233-5588 ◑
White Plains | The Source | 1 Maple Ave. (Bloomingdale Rd.), NY |
914-683-5253
www.thecheesecakefactory.com

It's a "suburbanite" "mob scene" at these "lines-out-the-door" chain
links where the "endless" American options arrive in equally "colossal" portions; despite "ordinary" settings, "spotty" staffing and "lots
of commotion", these "well-oiled machines" are so "busy, busy,
busy" that they're best accessed "off-hours" to avoid a "long wait."

Chef Antonio *Italian* 16 | 13 | 19 | $34

Mamaroneck | 551 Halstead Ave. (Beach Ave.), NY | 914-698-8610
This well-priced Mamaroneck Southern Italian has "been around
forever" (or at least since 1960), thanks in part to its "warm",
"homey" feel and "ample portions" that signal "good value"; in spite
of the rather "ordinary" fare, it's a "pleasant place that meets modest expectations" for a "family" meal.

Chef Luis ☒ *American* 25 | 16 | 22 | $45

New Canaan | 129 Elm St. (bet. Main & Park Sts.) | 203-972-5847 |
www.chefluis.net

Chef-owner Luis Lopez "names his creations after regulars" at this
"tiny" (28 seats) New Canaan "gem" offering "prepared-to-
perfection" New American cuisine with a Latin "flair"; the "BYO policy eases up the bill quite a bit" – and if you forget to pack a bottle,
"there's a liquor store across the street."

Chengdu *Chinese* 18 | 14 | 18 | $26

West Hartford | 179 Park Rd. (Oakwood Ave.) | 860-232-6455
"Well-prepared" "crispy duck and other Sichuan dishes" served
family-style in "huge portions" make this "unpretentious" Chinese a
"safe bet" for West Hartforders; still, aesthetes say the "pedestrian"
decor is more "geared to the Friendly's crowd."

Chestnut Grille at the 24 | 24 | 23 | $52
Bee & Thistle Inn ☒ Ⓜ *American*

Old Lyme | Bee & Thistle Inn | 100 Lyme St./Rte. 1 (I-95, exit 70) |
860-434-1667 | www.beeandthistleinn.com

"Fireplaces glowing with candles" make this "romantic old inn"
(circa 1756) even more "appealing" to lovebirds who make the
"pleasant drive" to "pretty" Old Lyme for "weekend getaways"; but you
can "take your mother" as well, since a "delectable" New American

	FOOD	DECOR	SERVICE	COST

menu, "afternoon teas" and "impeccable service" make it a "winner all-around"; N.B. dinner Wednesdays–Saturdays only.

Chez Jean-Pierre *French*

24	21	22	$50

Stamford | 188 Bedford St. (Broad St.) | 203-357-9526 | www.chezjeanpierre.com

It feels like "Paris in Downtown Stamford (unlikely as that seems)" at this bistro boasting a "small menu without a bad item on it", featuring mostly "classic" dishes like coq au vin; chef-owner Jean-Pierre Bars "takes care of customers personally", whether they're eating alfresco or in the "quaint" dining room, and oenophiles pour in on Sunday evenings when "all the wine is half-price."

NEW Chili Chicken *Chinese/Indian*

-	-	-	I

Stamford | 19 High Ridge Rd. (Bedford St.) | 203-977-0400 | www.chilichickenct.com

Lovers of esoteric cuisines are making a beeline for this new Stamford hot spot serving Indo-Chinese food, which traces its origins to India's urban areas and, like Malaysian cooking, features lots of curries and other aggressively seasoned dishes, as well as momos (Tibetan-style dumplings); lined with banquettes and hung with calming Eastern-inspired art, its cozy dining room is already fillling up fast, especially during the $8 all-you-can-eat buffet lunch – possibly the best bargain in town.

China Pavilion *Chinese*

21	17	19	$24

Orange | 185 Boston Post Rd. (Lindy St.) | 203-795-3555 | www.chinapavilion.net

As far as its "authentic" Chinese cuisine is concerned, fans say this Orange "favorite" has "always been at the top of its game", but after a renovation not too long ago it's "quite jazzy" now as well; the less enthusiastic shrug "it serves a purpose" ("family meals" among them) but there's "nothing special here."

∑ Ching's Kitchen *Asian*

24	17	19	$38

Darien | 971 Post Rd. (Center St.) | 203-656-2225

∑ Ching's Table *Asian*

New Canaan | 64 Main St. (Locust Ave.) | 203-972-8550 | www.chingsrestaurant.com

"Still wonderful after all these years", this "imaginative" New Canaan Pan-Asian and its Darien offshoot draw an "upscale crowd" for "amazing dishes" (with "prices to match") so "tasty" the "flavors jump out at you"; the "fun atmosphere can get rambunctious", but "if you can look past the noise", "waiters who rush you" and the "kids Connecticut couples can't seem to leave at home", they're a "must" when you need a "fusion fix."

Chocopologie Cafe *Dessert*

-	-	-	M

South Norwalk | 12 S. Main St. (Washington St.) | 203-854-4754 | www.chocopologie.com

"Beware, you may enjoy the generous entrees so much" you won't have room for the "exquisite desserts" at this Euro-style cafe in SoNo that's also an ultratrendy retail outlet for "world-class" choco-

| | FOOD | DECOR | SERVICE | COST |

latier Fritz Knipschildt; choose from "salads, savory crêpes" and heartier fare like short ribs, then top it off with the house specialty coffee.

Christopher Martins *Continental*   20 15 21 $34

New Haven | 860 State St. (bet. Clark & Humphrey Sts.) | 203-776-8835 | www.christophermartins.com

For "local color" and "surprisingly good" Continental chow, New Havenites "count on" this "quality neighborhood haunt" in Yale's "grad ghetto"; "cheerful" service and "reasonably priced" fare like rack of lamb get high marks, but detractors declare the "noisy bar" and "face-lift"-ready decor don't make the grade.

Chuck's Steak House *Steak*   18 13 17 $35

Branford | 377 E. Main St. (I-95) | 203-483-7557
Danbury | 20 Segar St. (bet. Lake & Park Aves.) | 203-792-5555
Darien | 1340 Boston Post Rd. (I-95, exit 11) | 203-655-2254
Rocky Hill | 2199 Silas Deane Hwy. (I-91, exit 24) | 860-529-0222
Storrs | 1498 Stafford Rd./Rte. 32 (Rte. 44) | 860-429-1900
West Haven | 1003 Orange Ave. (Tuthill St.) | 203-934-5300
www.chuckssteakhouse.com

"Step back in time" – think "Nixon administration" – and order a "hunk of meat" "with confidence" at this "family-friendly" "chestnut" of a steakhouse chain, where content carnivores salute the "huge" salad bar, "delicious bread" and "reasonable prices"; the less-impressed mete out a tougher judgment, saying it's "hit-or-miss" with "tired" interiors "so dark you can't see the food"; N.B. the Branford and Storrs branches offer a Margarita Grill Mexican menu.

Churrascaria Braza Ⓜ *Brazilian*   21 17 19 $39

Hartford | 488 Farmington Ave. (Sisson Ave.) | 860-882-1839 | www.hottomatos.net

"Bring your appetite and an empty stomach" to this bi-level Brazilian steakhouse in Hartford where as fast as you can say "carnivore's delight", "friendly" waiters "bombard you" with a "dozen kinds of roast meat"; while some say "it's heaven", others groan it's just "too much food" to tolerate in one sitting.

Cinzano's *Italian*   19 17 20 $32

Fairfield | 1920 Black Rock Tpke. (Stillson Rd.) | 203-367-1199 | www.cinzanosrestaurant.com

The "owner makes you feel like you're home" at this "muraled" family-run Italian in Fairfield where you'll "definitely leave full" thanks to "can't-go-wrong" cuisine served in "huge portions at fair prices"; snobs sniff there's "nothing special on the menu", but most agree it's a "dependable" place for a "nice" evening out.

Ⓩ City Limits Diner *Diner*   18 15 17 $26

Stamford | 135 Harvard Ave. (I-95, exit 6) | 203-348-7000
White Plains | 200 Central Ave. (bet. Harding Ave. & Tarrytown Rd.), NY | 914-686-9000
www.citylimitsdiner.com

There's "something for a whole family of picky eaters" at the Livanos family's "tony" Stamford–White Plains diner duo, where the "fancied-up" "feel-good" fare includes "breakfast any time of the day", "terrific burgers" and "fabulous" "giant desserts"; the "kitschy '50s"-style settings are perennially "packed", so be prepared for plenty of "hustle and bustle" and "spotty service."

Claire's Corner Copia   *Vegetarian*   19 | 11 | 14 | $18

New Haven | 1000 Chapel St. (College St.) | 203-562-3888 | www.clairescornercopia.com

"Your mother would be proud" that you're dining at this "classic" "'60s throwback" in New Haven offering an "unbelievable selection" of "self-serve" kosher-vegetarian dishes – including "unbeatable" soups and "Lithuanian coffeecake worth its weight in gold"; however, upstarts argue that the food "looks tastier than it is (how do they do this?)" and wish it "would start serving recipes from this century."

Cobble Stone ◑   *American*   15 | 13 | 15 | $29

Purchase | 620 Anderson Hill Rd. (bet. Lincoln Ave. & Purchase St.), NY | 914-253-9678 | www.cobblestone-thecreek.com

Once a Prohibition-era speakeasy, this Purchase Traditional American is now a "quick-bite" staple for nearby nine-to-fivers, "college students" and folks seeking "dinner before a show at SUNY"; it's "not fine dining", but it works for a "burger and a beer", and besides – "the price is right."

ⓩ Cobb's Mill Inn Ⓜ   *American*   18 | 25 | 20 | $46

Weston | 12 Old Mill Rd. (Rte. 57) | 203-227-7221 | www.cobbsmillinn.com

"Ducks and swans play" outside the windows of this "romantic" Traditional American "hideaway" housed in a 1770 Weston mill with "fabulous waterfall views" and "fireside dining"; alas, a fair number knock "uninteresting" food that "never seems to measure up" to the "amazing" atmosphere, suggesting it's "better just to go for drinks."

C.O. Jones   *Californian/Mexican*   16 | 13 | 15 | $19

New Haven | 969 State St. (Edwards St.) | 203-773-3344 | www.c-o-jones.com

Statues of Mexican 'tequila gods' set the tone at this New Haven "hangout" where the "enormous", "deliciously potent" margaritas ensure that "any of the Cal-Mex food offerings" will seem "perfectly serviceable"; some argue that "fresh and healthy doesn't have to equate to limp and bland", but it's "noisy and crowded" nonetheless.

Colony Grill ◑⊟   *Italian*   - | - | - | I

Stamford | 172 Myrtle Ave. (bet. Elm & Frederick Sts.) | 203-359-2184

Second home to Stamford softball leaguers, firefighters and police officers, this neighborhood "institution" serves "darn good" ultra-thin-crust pizzas that provide a delicious crunch without spilling the pie's toppings (like the "killer hot oil"); draft beer comes in frosty mugs, and though the surroundings "leave much to be desired", locals can't help but "love" the place all the same; N.B. cash only.

Ⓩ Columbus Park Trattoria Ⓢ *Italian* | 25 | 19 | 22 | $44 |

Stamford | 205 Main St. (Washington Blvd.) | 203-967-9191 |
www.columbusparktrattoria.com

Owner Maria Marchetti makes the pasta "fresh each morning" and
"boy, does it show" at this "old world–style" Stamford Italian, which
dishes up "nearly flawless" food (including "amazing" osso buco)
coupled with "impeccable" service; sure, it's "pricey" and can get a
"little cramped", but most agree the "only complaint is when the
meal is over."

Confetti Ⓜ *Italian/Seafood* | 18 | 11 | 18 | $37 |

Plainville | 393 Farmington Ave. (Ashford Rd.) | 860-793-8809 |
www.idineconfetti.com

Admittedly, there's "not much competition" in Plainville, but con-
federates of this "crowd-pleasing" Italian-style seafooder salute
"ample portions" of "reasonably priced" fare served by a "friendly"
staff; nitpickers note the "interior needs updating" and advise aim-
ing for the "spacious patio" when possible.

Consiglio's *Italian* | 25 | 20 | 24 | $39 |

New Haven | 165 Wooster St. (bet. Brown St. & Depalma Ct.) |
203-865-4489 | www.consiglios.com

Paesani "make it a point to stop in" this family-run New Haven "favorite" for "traditional" "Italian with a capital I", meaning "delicious"
dishes ("go for the lobster ravioli"), "excellent" service and, natch,
"old-style white tablecloths"; just "don't forget your wallet, because
the bill can be hefty."

Ⓩ Cookhouse, The *BBQ* | 19 | 14 | 17 | $29 |

New Milford | 31 Danbury Rd./Rte. 7 (Sunny Valley Rd.) |
860-355-4111 | www.thecookhouse.com

"When you want to get your meat on", take your 'cue from the "reasonably priced" pulled-pork sandwiches ("hog heaven") and "terrific"
ribs at this "homey" New Milford haven; "the portions are so large
you may have to be rolled out", but a few foes say the chow "should
be better", and the "uneven" service and "no-decor" digs don't help.

Copacabana Ⓜ *Brazilian* | ▽ 23 | 17 | 23 | $44 |

Port Chester | 29 N. Main St. (Westchester Ave.), NY | 914-939-6894 |
www.copacabanaportchester.com

Those in the mood for a "meatfest" head to this Port Chester Brazilian
BBQer where "incredible quantities" of "tender" skewered cuts are
ferried by a "friendly" staff in handsome wood-lined quarters; add in
a "plentiful" salad bar, and even though it's not inexpensive, the all-
inclusive prices are considered a "bargain" for what you get.

Ⓩ Copper Beech Ⓜ *American* | 24 | 25 | 24 | $65 |

Ivoryton | Copper Beech Inn | 46 Main St. (Johnny Cake Rd.) |
860-767-0330 | www.copperbeechinn.com

If "you can't get romantic here, you *can't* get romantic" chide champions of this "elegant" New American in a "charming" Ivoryton inn;
with "bound-for-glory" chef Tyler Anderson now on board, it "has it

all going for it", including "superb" food and service, though an out-voted few maintain it's "overpriced"; P.S. dodge the dining room's jacket-suggested policy at Brasserie Pip, a "less expensive" on-site bistro open seven days a week.

Coppia Ristorante Ⓜ *Italian* ▽ 24 | 17 | 24 | $41

Fairfield | 937 Post Rd. (Benson Rd.) | 203-254-7519 |
www.coppiafairfield.com

"Delicious" food, "passionate" service and a "jovial, welcoming pro-prietor" make this "cool little" Northern Italian in a "hidden" location one of "Fairfield's best-kept secrets"; the addition of a "charming in-door garden" not long ago has added "more room", though some still gripe about a "lack of ambiance."

Corner Bakery *Bakery* ▽ 23 | 18 | 20 | $34

Pawling | 10 Charles Colman Blvd. (Main St.), NY | 845-855-3707 |
www.mckinneyanddoyle.com

Tucked into the entrance of Pawling's McKinney & Doyle, its parent eatery, this "cute, homey" cafe turns out "terrific" "new and old fa-vorites" like "wonderful baked goods", salads, sandwiches and such; though "always crowded", the vibe's "friendly" and prices "moderate", even if you get carried away and end up "leaving with five pounds of cookies."

Ⓩ Coromandel *Indian* 26 | 18 | 22 | $34

Darien | Goodwives Shopping Ctr. | 25-11 Old Kings Hwy. N.
(Sedgewick Ave.) | 203-662-1213

Orange | 185 Boston Post Rd. (Lindy St.) | 203-795-9055

South Norwalk | 86 Washington St. (bet. Main & Water Sts.) |
203-852-1213

Stamford | 68 Broad St. (Summer St.) | 203-964-1010

New Rochelle | 30 Division St. (bet. Huguenot & Main Sts.), NY |
914-235-8390

www.coromandelcuisine.com

"Like dining first-class on the night train to Mumbai", these "top-notch" Indians take "lovers of exotic comfort food" on a "tour of the subcontinent" while managing to "outclass others" of their ilk with "standout culinary artistry" and "stellar service"; the weekend buffet brunches are a "steal" – just "don't let the dated decor scare you off."

Così *Sandwiches* 15 | 11 | 11 | $15

Avon | 385 W. Main St. (Dale Rd.) | 860-678-8989

Darien | 980 Post Rd. (Center St.) | 203-655-0335

Greenwich | 129 W. Putnam Ave. (Dayton Ave.) | 203-861-2373

West Hartford | 970 Farmington Ave. (bet. Lasalle Rd. & Main St.) |
860-521-8495

Larchmont | Ferndale Shopping Ctr. | 1298 Boston Post Rd. (Weaver St.),
NY | 914-834-9797

New Rochelle | North Ridge Shopping Ctr. | 77 Quaker Ridge Rd.
(North Ave.), NY | 914-637-8300

Rye | 50 Purchase St. (Elm Pl.), NY | 914-921-3322

www.getcosi.com

This "modern sandwich" chain is all about the "fresh-baked" flatbread that's the "addictive" foundation for its "creative" concoctions;

maybe it's "a little pricey for what you get" and the staff "seems minimally interested in working there", but that doesn't keep fans from "coming back" (the WiFi and "free samples" don't hurt either).

Costa Brava *Mediterranean*
22 | 18 | 23 | $40

Norwalk | Tower Plaza Shopping Ctr. | 120 New Canaan Ave. (Bartlett Ave.) | 203-849-5905 | www.costabravact.com

"Forget the decor" and "drab" "strip-mall" setting and "focus on the paella" and "astounding", "affordable" wine list at this "excellent" Norwalk Mediterranean; the "treats-you-like-family" owner is usually there overseeing the "warm and inviting" service.

Costa del Sol Ⓜ *Spanish*
25 | 19 | 24 | $40

Hartford | Costa del Sol Plaza | 901 Wethersfield Ave. (Eaton St.) | 860-296-1714 | www.costadelsolrestaurant.net

"Please! be adventurous and try something other" than the "fabulous paella" (perhaps the "mariscada in salsa verde") beg boosters of this "wonderful" family-run Spanish in South Hartford; it's "off the beaten path" and a "little pricey", but "consistent quality and a friendly staff" make it a "repeat visit" for most.

Costello's *Seafood*
∇ 18 | 17 | 14 | $27

Noank | 145 Pearl St. (Noank Shipyard) | 860-572-2779 | www.costellosclamshack.com

"How can you have Abbott's without Costello's?" quip aficionados of this "unfussy" seasonal seafooder in Noank (and "cousin" to the lobster shack "down the road") where locals "go for their fry fix"; however, "ok" service and "blah" food have some sniping that the "best things about it are the [waterfront] views" and BYO policy, which "keeps costs down."

Country House Ⓜ *American/Steak* (fka Steakhouse 22)
∇ 20 | 19 | 21 | $38

Patterson | 2693 Rte. 22 (¼ mi. north of Haviland Hollow Rd.), NY | 845-878-9877 | www.steakhouse-22.com

Patterson denizens in search of Traditional American "comfort food" head to this "solid performer" (which changed its name but nothing else post-Survey), where "good" steaks and other mid-priced eats come in "plentiful" supply; a "friendly atmosphere" prevails in the three dining rooms, although "in fair weather, it's best on the deck", overlooking "stunning" scenery and "fantastic sunsets."

Coyote Blue Tex Mex Cafe Ⓜ *Southwestern*
23 | 19 | 21 | $28

Middletown | 1960 Saybrook Rd. (Aircraft Rd.) | 860-345-2403 | www.coyoteblue.com

"Watch out for the margaritas" – "so strong" "they recommend no more than two" – at this "solid" Southwestern in Middletown where the likes of shrimp quesadillas, burritos and tacos are all *"muy delicioso"*; it's "off the beaten track" but not undiscovered, so a "small capacity" means "waits can be long."

Coyote Flaco *Mexican*
∇ 21 | 18 | 20 | $30

Bridgeport | 694 Brooklawn Ave. (Capitol Ave.) | 203-338-0808 Ⓜ

(continued)

Coyote Flaco

Hartford | 635 New Britain Ave. (Mountain St.) |
860-953-1299 🅜
Mansfield Center | 50 Higgins Hwy. (Stafford Rd.) | 860-423-4414
New Rochelle | 273 North Ave. (Huguenot St.), NY |
914-636-7222 🅜
Port Chester | 115 Midland Ave. (bet. Armett St. & Weber Dr.), NY |
914-937-6969
www.mycoyoteflaco.com
See review in The Berkshires Directory.

NEW Craftsteak *Steak*   – | – | – | E

Ledyard | MGM Grand at Foxwoods | 240 MGM Grand Dr.
(Norwich Westerly Rd.) | 860-312-7272 |
www.mgmatfoxwoods.com
Everything about Top Chef Tom Colicchio's steakhouse in the
Foxwoods Resort Casino is finely crafted, from the sleek, contemporary decor fashioned from Brazilian walnut, bronze and
leather to the hunks of top-drawer beef (including the signature
Japanese Wagyu); as to be expected given its vaunted provenance
and tony locale, this newcomer is priced for high rollers and
expense-account beneficiaries.

Creek, The *American*   ▽ 17 | 16 | 20 | $40

Purchase | 578 Anderson Hill Rd. (bet. Lincoln Ave. & Purchase St.),
NY | 914-761-0050 | www.cobblestone-thecreek.com
"Convenient" "after a concert at SUNY", this "friendly" Purchase
New American stands out for its "well-prepared" fare "in an area
where restaurants are scarce"; soothing water views add to the appeal of the "warm" wood-paneled digs, though some suggest it's "a
little overpriced for what it is."

NEW Crooked Shillelagh *Irish*   – | – | – | M

Branford | 576 Main St. (Monroe St.) | 203-481-0348 |
www.crookedshillelagh.com
Emerald Isle expats and others linger over bangers 'n' mash and signature Guinness stew at this Branford newcomer named for a legendary walking stick; there are 16 tap beers to accompany the
affordable Celtic comfort food, plus flags from County Leitrim and
photos of Irish landscapes to have you singing 'Danny Boy' in no
time; N.B. live music on weekends and a $28.50 couples' prix fixe din-
ner Tuesday–Thursday are added draws.

Croton Creek Steakhouse &   20 | 19 | 19 | $57
Wine Bar *Steak*

Croton Falls | 4 W. Cross St. (Rte. 22), NY | 914-276-0437 |
www.crotoncreek.com
This "chic" "boutique steakhouse" in Croton Falls sears "good"
meats and pairs them with "inventive" sauces and "luscious" sides
in a "sophisticated" tavern setting with exposed-brick walls and mahogany accents; though service is "personable", a few find the overall package falls short of the "Manhattan" prices.

	FOOD	DECOR	SERVICE	COST

Cucina Modo Mio *Italian* — — — M

Westport | 5 Bridge Sq. (Riverside Ave.) | 203-557-4826 |
www.cucinamodomio.com

A "tiny outpost overlooking the Saugatuck River", this Westporter serves "tasty" Italian cuisine and fine seafood "from the fish store below"; seating is tight, but it's worth the wait given the reasonable prices (e.g. the two-course prix fixe lunch for $9.99).

Cuckoo's Nest *Mexican* 18 17 16 $25

Old Saybrook | 1712 Boston Post Rd. (Rte. 166) | 860-399-9060 |
www.cuckoosnest.biz

Loyalists of this "popular" Cajun-Mexican "barn" in Old Saybrook swear by its "reasonably priced" fajitas and other "tasty, simple" fare, not to mention "deep-fried ice cream" and "great sangria"; even so, a few still slam "slow" service and grub that's "standard at best."

Curtis House *American* ▽ 16 17 20 $32

Woodbury | 506 Main St. S./Rte. 6 (Rte. 64) | 203-263-2101 |
www.curtishouseinn.com

"Creaky floorboards" mimic the "older" clientele at this "steady-as-ever" Traditional American set in a 1754 Woodbury house and featuring a "simple menu" "unchanged in decades"; the four-course prix fixe dinners (starting at $16.95) may be a "great value", but critics contend you'd best like "cafeteria food, including Jell-O for dessert."

NEW DaCapo's Italiano Ristorante *Italian* — — — M

Avon | 5 E. Main St. (bet. Old Farms Rd. & Rte. 44) | 860-677-5599

Yes, there were already plenty of Italian options in Avon, but word is that this newcomer stands out with thin-crust, brick-oven pizzas, signature spaghetti pomodoro, mussels fra diavolo and such served in generous portions at reasonable rates; the exposed-brick walls and vintage photos of local scenes lend a homey feel.

Da Giorgio Ⓜ *Italian* ▽ 20 17 21 $46

New Rochelle | Quaker Ridge | 77 Quaker Ridge Rd. (North Ave.), NY | 914-235-2727 | www.dagiorgiorestaurant.com

The fare "far surpasses" the strip-mall locale at this "dependable" New Rochelle Italian; service is "friendly" and the mood "pleasant", so even if some eaters are irked by "uneven" cooking, "lots of regulars" "highly recommend" it.

Dakota Steakhouse *Steak* 18 17 19 $34

Avon | 225 W. Main St./Rte. 44 (Rte. 202) | 860-677-4311 |
www.steakseafood.com
Rocky Hill | 1489 Silas Deane Hwy. (I-91) | 860-257-7752 |
www.dakotarockyhill.com

See review in The Berkshires Directory.

Ⓩ DaPietro's Ⓩ *French/Italian* 26 20 24 $65

Westport | 36 Riverside Ave. (Post Rd.) | 203-454-1213 |
www.dapietros.com

"Reservations are a must" at this "fabulous" 28-seat Westport "shoebox" where for more than two decades "master chef" Pietro

Scotti's "outstanding" French–Northern Italian cuisine and "excellent wine list" have provided "memorable experiences for true foodies"; some surveyors find the "intimate" atmosphere "romantic", but critics carp about a "dining room built for Lilliputians" and prices that are so "high" they should include "a limousine ride home."

David Burke Prime *Steak* ▽ 27 | 24 | 26 | $68

Ledyard | Foxwoods Resort Casino | 39 Norwich Westerly Rd./Rte. 2 (bet. Mains Crossing & Preston Plains Rd.) | 860-312-8753 | www.davidburkeprime.com

From celebrity chef David Burke, this player at Ledyard's Foxwoods Resort Casino offers some of the "best dry-aged steaks" around in a "tasteful" setting that's "fitting" for a meatfest; however, "leave the craps table after winning" if you want to eat here: it's "so expensive."

David Chen *Chinese* 18 | 15 | 17 | $28

Armonk | 85 Old Mt. Kisco Rd. (Rte. 128), NY | 914-273-6767 | www.davidchens.com

Loads of Armonk eaters have a "soft spot" for this local "institution", an "old reliable" for a "wide selection" of "suburban-standard" Chinese dishes set down in a "pleasant", "family-friendly" setting; perhaps it's "nothing to write home about", but it meets the need "when you have no energy to cook" – "and they deliver" too!

DiNardo's Ⓜ *Italian* 19 | 15 | 19 | $40

Pound Ridge | Scott's Corners | 76 Westchester Ave. (Trinity Pass Rd.), NY | 914-764-4024 | www.dinardos.net

Supporters "stick with the pizzas" and other "classics" like linguine marinara and meatball wedges at this Italian "old-timer" whose split setup offers a "choice between family and formal seating"; though detractors declare it "too expensive for what you get", given the "lack of options" in posh Pound Ridge, it remains "busy" most nights.

Diorio Ⓩ *American/Italian* 24 | 22 | 24 | $48

Waterbury | 231 Bank St. (Grand St.) | 203-754-5111 | www.diorios.com

The "patrons are just as interesting" as the "top-notch" Northern Italian–New American cuisine at this "classic power-broker spot" in Waterbury, where the tin ceilings and "bankers' booths" "bring you back in time"; "attentive service" adds to the "old-school" vibe, which carries over into the "great bar" and its "unique" acid-etched mirrors.

Dish Bar & Grill *American* 20 | 22 | 18 | $41

Hartford | 900 Main St. (Pratt St.) | 860-249-3474 | www.dishbarandgrill.com

Depending on whom you ask, the "high-tech", "are-we-really-in-Hartford?" decor at chef-owner Bill Carbone's "swanky" New American is either "exciting" and "enjoyable" or "cold" and "cavernous"; likewise, supporters say its "modern take on comfort food" (e.g. "deconstructed" lobster pot pie) and "hip bar scene" are "welcome" Downtown, but foes fault "slow" service and chow that "lacks wow" at "NYC prices."

	FOOD	DECOR	SERVICE	COST

Dock & Dine Seafood
15 | 16 | 17 | $31

Old Saybrook | Saybrook Pt. (College St.) | 860-388-4665 |
www.dockdinect.com

"Pull up your yacht or dingy" ("or car") and enjoy the "gorgeous views
of the Connecticut River" from this veteran Old Saybrook seafooder
serving "moderately priced" "standard shore fare", including fish 'n'
chips and crab cakes; alas, a mutinous crew complains "it's a crying
shame" such "marginal" grub has to share that "divine" location.

Doc's Trattoria Ⓜ Italian
21 | 21 | 20 | $40

Kent | 9 Maple St. (Main St.) | 860-927-3810 | www.docstrattoria.com
Though it moved a couple of years back to "handsome", bigger digs
in the "quaint town of Kent", this "longtime favorite" is still offering
the "same excellent" Italian fare (particularly the "can't-be-beat"
pizzas) and "friendly service"; if a few fans miss the old BYO policy
("it's less of a value now"), most toast the "attractive" bar and "good
wine list"; P.S. "dine on the terrace and all's right with the world."

Dolphins Cove Marina Seafood
∇ 19 | 14 | 15 | $29

Bridgeport | Dolphins Cove Marina | 421 Seaview Ave. (Newfield Ave.) |
203-335-3301 | www.dolphinscovect.com

"Everyone goes for the lobsters" and the "nice view" from the
harborside patio of this large, Portuguese-inflected Bridgeport seafooder; "it is what it is" – a "place for the masses", but "nothing
fancy for sure."

Donovan's & Mackenzie American
- | - | - | I

South Norwalk | 138 Washington St. (bet. S. Main & Water Sts.) |
203-354-9451 | www.donovanssono.com

It closed a few years back, but this venerable SoNo saloon's faithful
fans came right back when it reopened in its original digs in 2009; on
offer is the same affordable Traditional American fare (burgers, salads, etc.) as before, and also in evidence are the vintage boxing pictures and gleaming Victorian-style bar that dominates the dining
room – though it now vies for attention with 10 flat-screen TVs.

Dragonfly Ⓩ Eclectic
∇ 20 | 22 | 20 | $36

Stamford | 488 Summer St. (Spring St.) | 203-357-9800 |
www.dragonflyloungect.com

The "Goth" decor sets the tone for this "inventive" Downtown
Stamford Eclectic whose architectural flourishes come from old
churches and make you feel as if you're "walking onto a movie
set"; "medieval" atmosphere aside, it's a place to "impress out-
of-towners" with "unique" tapas (Kobe beef meatballs, etc.),
"well-made" drinks and "dessert nachos" to complement the "live
music" Thursday–Saturday.

Drescher's Ⓩ German
∇ 22 | 21 | 23 | $35

Waterbury | 25 Leavenworth St. (bet. Grand & Main Sts.) |
203-573-1743 | www.dreschers.com

In its present location since 1982, this "charming", "casual" stomp-
ing ground in Waterbury features "good German fare" (as well as

Continental cuisine) and a chef-owner who "makes you feel welcome"; Tiffany lamps, vaulted tin ceilings and turn-of-the-century murals add to the "old-world" vibe.

☑ Dressing Room ⓜ *American*   23 | 24 | 22 | $59

Westport | 27 Powers Ct. (Compo Rd.) | 203-226-1114 | www.dressingroomhomegrown.com

Admirers "miss seeing" restaurant co-founder Paul Newman "stroll in for lunch" at this "cheerful", "barnlike" New American that's "cheek by jowl" to widow Joanne Woodward's Westport Country Playhouse, but they're still cheering chef Michel Nischan's "delectable" "organic" fare made with "local ingredients"; "exorbitant prices" for "oh-so-small portions" get many a thumbs-down – but a new, more affordable 'gastropub' small-plates menu should quiet the catcalls.

du Glace Bistro & Patisserie ⓜ *French*   - | - | - | E

Deep River | 158 Main St. (bet. River & Village Sts.) | 860-526-2200 | www.duglacebistro.com

Deep River denizens rave about this unpretentious chef-owned French bistro whose menu includes classics like coq au vin and sautéed calf's liver in bacon-cream sauce; the ambiance is decidedly Parisian, with hand-painted murals in the style of Toulouse-Lautrec, and an adjacent patisserie adds to the bonhomie.

Duo ☒ *European/Japanese*   23 | 21 | 20 | $47

Stamford | 25 Bank St. (Atlantic St.) | 203-252-2233 | www.duoeurojapanese.com

"This island of innovation and flavor" in Downtown Stamford seeks to "impress discerning palates" with "food prepared in two different styles" – Japanese and European – served "on the same plate"; bonuses include an "extensive sake list", "sleek" decor and a "friendly staff that doesn't rush you out the door"; the downside: the "tiny portions" can seem "a little like elf food."

East Side Restaurant ⓜ *German*   20 | 20 | 21 | $33

New Britain | 131 Dwight St. (bet. East & Fairview Sts.) | 860-223-1188 | www.eastsiderestaurant.com

"Wear silly hats and sing German drinking songs" ("hoy! hoy! hoy! with every 32-ounce draft") at this New Britain veritable "Deutschland" complete with beer garden; the "soup to dessert" meal deals include "huge portions of filling food" like sauerbraten so "you never leave hungry" – no wonder mug-wielders wail "it's *wunderbar!*"

East-West Grille ⓜ *SE Asian*   ▽ 23 | 14 | 18 | $23

West Hartford | 526 New Park Ave. (Oakwood Ave.) | 860-236-3287 | www.eastwestgrille.com

The "funky diner setting" and Southeast Asian menu "don't really go together", but "where else are you gonna get Laotian food" in West Hartford ponder partisans of this "excellent" chef-owned "family spot" that "won't break the bank"; mornings are similarly "quirky", as "good" American-style breakfasts are served by a "congenial" staff.

	FOOD	DECOR	SERVICE	COST

Eclisse *Italian* | 20 | 15 | 19 | $36 |

Stamford | Harbor Sq. | 700 Canal St. (bet. Henry & Market Sts.) |
203-325-3773 | www.eclissestamford.com

Even if you "go with a big group", "you're guaranteed to over-order"
at this Stamford "family-style Italian" that serves up "hearty yet
tasteful" "basic Italian" in "huge", "reasonably priced" portions; a
few shrug it's "just ok", but those who felt the decor needed "a
spruce up" should know it was remodeled recently (post-Survey).

Edd's Place Cuisine to Go *Deli* | ▽ 22 | 14 | 18 | $17 |

Westbrook | 478 Boston Post Rd. (Hammock Rd.) | 860-399-9498
Get "back to nature while you eat" at this Westbrook deli-cum-
seafooder, a chef-owned "shack with a view" of the Menunketesuk
River, "marshlands and wildlife"; order at the counter – from barbecue ribs and clam chowder to "grandma's homemade desserts" –
then grab a seat "in the gazebo or at a picnic table" and wait for the
"friendly, fast" staff to deliver the goods; N.B. it's BYO.

Edo Japanese Steakhouse *Japanese/Steak* | 20 | 16 | 19 | $34 |

Port Chester | Pathmark Shopping Ctr. | 140 Midland Ave. (Weber Dr.),
NY | 914-937-3333 | www.edohibachi.com

Scores of families frequent this teppanyaki-style Japanese steakhouse in Port Chester where the "theatrics" of the "entertaining
chefs" and their flying foodstuffs outshine the "run-of-the-mill"
fare; prices are "not cheap", and the "multitude of birthday parties"
going on makes it "too loud" for some – perhaps they "should have
an adult section" as well; P.S. come "prepared to wait."

Egane *Korean* | ▽ 20 | 13 | 20 | $34 |

Stamford | 135 Bedford St. (Broad St.) | 203-975-0209
"Play with your food and have it still be delicious" at this Downtown
Stamford "Korean bistro" offering diners "a culinary adventure with
their own hibachis", i.e. do-it-yourself barbecue; sushi and "attentive
service" are other draws, but it's still "never as crowded as it should
be"; N.B. a spruce-up not long ago may outdate the Decor score.

80 West *Seafood* | 19 | 21 | 18 | $47 |

White Plains | Renaissance Hotel | 80 W. Red Oak Ln. (Westchester Ave.),
NY | 914-696-2782 | www.80westrestaurant.com

"Business travelers" rely on this "pleasant" entry in the White Plains
Renaissance Hotel featuring a "worthwhile" breakfast buffet and
"tasteful" seafood dishes at lunch and dinner; yet, even in spite of its
handsome setting with floor-to-ceiling windows affording "splendid" wooded views, nonguests claim they're "disappointed" by the
experience, citing "weak" service and "mediocre" grub.

NEW Elaine's
Healthy Choice *Soul Food/Vegetarian* | - | - | - | I |

New Haven | 117 Whalley Ave. (bet. Orchard & Sperry Sts.) |
203-773-1897 | www.elaineshealthychoice.com

Expect a warm welcome from chef-owner Elaine and her kin at
this brightly lit soul fooder, where the Jamaican fare is 100%

vegan (meatless curried chicken bites are a specialty), prodigiously portioned and modestly priced; though there are other vegetarian options in Downtown New Haven, this newcomer has found its niche and its 10 seats are generally filled, so takeout may be the way to go; N.B. no alcohol; closed Saturdays.

Elbow Room *American*   18 | 16 | 17 | $30

West Hartford | 986 Farmington Ave. (Main St.) | 860-236-6195 | www.elbowroomct.com

It's "all about the scene" at this West Hartford "mainstay", particularly on the "wonderful rooftop patio" "in the summer"; otherwise, vets diverge on the "New American comfort food" ("inventive" vs. "inconsistent"), and while some say a "lively staff" contributes to an "easy atmosphere", a few cynics snarl that "snotty twentysomethings" are "slow" getting grub to the table.

Elements Bistro *American*   - | - | - | M

West Hartford | 1128 New Britain Ave. (bet. Grove & Princeton Sts.) | 860-233-8125 | www.elements-bistro.com

Despite its strip-mall locale, this eatery in West Hartford's Elmwood section provides a sophisticated setting with warm, butterscotch-colored walls and dark-wood accents, and draws the after-work crowd for specialty martinis mixed by bartenders who know their business; the eclectic, reasonably priced New American offerings – gourmet burgers, chili, pastas – also have a following, but it's the bar scene that's really the thing here.

Eli Cannon's ●Ⓜ *American*   20 | 19 | 18 | $24

Middletown | 695 Main St. (Grand St.) | 860-347-3547 | www.elicannons.com

"Be brave, be bold" and be ready to make decisions at this "loud" Traditional American in Middletown, because there's a "dizzying array of beers", "truckload" of hot sauces and menu full of "classic bar food" to choose from; it's all set amid "offbeat" 'trailer park fusion' decor, leading some to suggest they'd "rather not see this place in daylight."

Elizabeth's Cafe at   26 | 18 | 24 | $51
Perfect Parties *American*

Madison | 885 Boston Post Rd. (bet. Scotland Ave. & Wall St.) | 203-245-0250 | www.perfectparties.com

"From its take-out origins", this "casual" Madison New American has blossomed into an "absolute gem" with "delicious", "imaginative dishes" and "excellent Sunday brunches"; "cottagey antiques and castoffs" create a "charming" (if "tight") space that's "homey but stylish", and while it's still the local "savior when you need catered food in a hurry", there's "one caveat: it ain't cheap"; N.B. closed Tuesdays.

🅩 Elm Street Oyster House *Seafood*   24 | 16 | 20 | $48

Greenwich | 11 W. Elm St. (Greenwich Ave.) | 203-629-5795 | www.elmstreetoysterhouse.com

"Thank goodness it *finally* takes reservations!" a while back cheer champions of this "comfortably disheveled" seafooder, a "teeny-

tiny" "hideaway" from the "pretense of most Greenwich eateries";
"awesome oysters" and "fish so fresh you'll think it jumped into the
frying pan" have fans "coming back", despite "cramped" conditions
and a decibel level so high you need "a headset and cell phone to talk
to your dining partner."

El Tio *Mexican*
▽ | 24 | 12 | 20 | $22

New Rochelle | 25 Anderson St. (bet. Le Count Pl. & North Ave.), NY |
914-633-8686
Port Chester | 143 Westchester Ave. (bet. Broad & Pearl Sts.), NY |
914-939-1494

These "well-priced" Mexican nooks in New Rochelle and Port Chester
dish out "spicy and tasty" specialties from the Jalisco region alongside
tacos, enchiladas and other crowd-pleasing favorites in "huge portions"; "cramped" digs come with the territory, and servers are "not
entirely English speaking", but they're "friendly" spots nonetheless.

Emilio Ristorante Ⓜ *Italian*
23 | 18 | 23 | $55

Harrison | 1 Colonial Pl. (bet. Harrison Ave. & Purdy St.), NY |
914-835-3100 | www.emilioristorante.com

Boosters "never get bored" of the "old-fashioned" cooking at this
"pricey" Harrison Italian also favored for its "colorful" antipasti selections, "outstanding" wines and "wonderful" staff; though its
"stately" Colonial edifice remains the same, renovations have
spruced up the interior, cementing its standing as a "go-to-place"
for "expense-account" dinners and other "special occasions."

Emma's Ale House *American*
- | - | - | M

White Plains | 68 Gedney Way (Mamaroneck Ave.), NY |
914-683-3662 | www.emmasalehouse.com

This White Plains Traditional American is basically a well-dressed
pub with a brick-backed bar and pictures of its namesake – the
owner's canine – everywhere; burgers, chicken pot pie and other
comfort favorites are the fare of choice, while friendly barkeeps
administer rotating drafts.

Encore Bistro Français *French*
22 | 17 | 21 | $44

Larchmont | 22 Chatsworth Ave. (Boston Post Rd.), NY | 914-833-1661 |
www.encore-bistro.com

A "home-away-from-home" for Larchmont locals, this "charming"
bistro "brings one back to Paris" with "satisfying" French fare served
in a "cozy" (if "noisy") setting decked out with red leather booths
and vintage posters; add in "affordable" prices, and the majority
maintains it's "casual" enough for everyday, and yet "cute" enough
for a "date."

Enzo's *Italian*
18 | 14 | 20 | $42

Mamaroneck | 451 Mamaroneck Ave. (Halstead Ave.), NY | 914-698-2911

Chef-owner Luciano Savone "always makes you feel welcome" at
this "down-to-earth" Mamaroneck mainstay that's been dishing out
"traditional" "red-sauce" fare for nearly 30 years; despite the "generic" decor, it retains a "mom-and-pop feel" with a "comfortable"
ambiance and an abundance of "locals" filling up the dining area.

	FOOD	DECOR	SERVICE	COST

Eos Greek Cuisine *Greek*

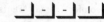

| - | - | - | M |

Stamford | 490 Summer St. (bet. Broad & Spring Sts.) | 203-569-6250 | www.eosgreekcuisine.com

Greek staples – souvlaki, moussaka, etc. – come in sleek environs at this upscale Downtown Stamford spot, where you can order the *saganaki* (flaming cheese) appetizer for a little added drama; the modern space features clean lines, hardwood floors and a white, wavelike bas-relief frieze along the main wall, adding up to a pleasantly sophisticated atmosphere.

Épernay Bistro 🗷 *American*

| - | - | - | I |

Bridgeport | 272 Fairfield Ave. (bet. Broad St. & Lafayette Circle) | 203-334-3000 | www.epernaybistro.com

Set behind a 1915 facade and near theaters and museums, this stylish eatery with an exposed-brick interior offers Bridgeporters a "good place for a rendezvous", if only to partake in the daily wine-by-the-glass specials; hungry sorts should pore over the menu, though, as chef-owner Peter Wroe uses organic, locally grown ingredients in his American dishes, and emulates European sensibilities by making his own charcuterie; N.B. there's live jazz on Friday nights.

Ernesto Ⓜ *Italian*

| 21 | 14 | 20 | $36 |

White Plains | 130 W. Post Rd. (Maple Ave.), NY | 914-421-1414

"Solid" pizzas and pastas lead the menu at this White Plains Italian; in spite of "uninspired" decor, a "friendly" staff that "knows your preferences" makes it "worth seeking out" for "takeout" or a casual meal.

Esca *Italian*

| - | - | - | E |

Middletown | 437 Main St. (Washington St.) | 860-316-2552 | www.escact.com

The moniker means 'lure', and it's the 300-strong wine list that baits the hook at this family-run Middletown Italian, where the *vini* are stored in a cave behind the bar and go down well with dishes including signature risottos and grilled calamari; its elegant space featuring lots of marble and granite puts the emphasis on romance, which, along with the wine, may be why it's considered great for a date.

España Ⓜ *Spanish*

| 20 | 19 | 20 | $47 |

Larchmont | 147 Larchmont Ave. (Boston Post Rd.), NY | 914-833-1331 | www.espanatapas.com

"Barcelona" comes to Larchmont via this venue rolling out "real-deal" Spanish cooking – from "terrific tapas" to "savory paella" – backed by an "extensive" list of wines and cocktails; "high prices" aside, its "pretty" setting and "knowledgeable" staff have most hailing it as a "nice" option in the area.

Euro Asian *Asian*

| 21 | 19 | 19 | $39 |

Port Chester | The Waterfront at Port Chester | 30 Westchester Ave. (bet. Townsend St. & Traverse Ave.), NY | 914-937-3680 | www.euroasianrestaurant.com

"Well-located" near the Port Chester multiplex for a pre- or post-movie meal, this Asian emporium supplies "fresh sushi" and a "va-

"riety" of fusion dishes all plated to look "pretty to the eye"; it owes its "slightly upscale" atmosphere to "attractive" wood-lined decor adorned with pops of vivid color and a "pleasant" staff providing "attentive" service.

NEW Eveready Diner ● Diner | 19 | 17 | 18 | $21 |

Brewster | 90 Independence Way (Dykeman Rd.), NY | 845-279-9009 | www.theeverearydiner.com

An offshoot of an "iconic" Hyde Park diner, this Brewster arrival (which opened post-Survey) features the same "bible-size menu" of "comfort" fare in "Flintstonian portions", "fair prices" and a "hearty dose of kitsch" to keep things "hopping"; it's all "done well", with the "quintessential" experience including a "happy staff", "cherry cokes" and other "amazing soda fountain" treats, plus it's open round the clock on weekends.

Evergreens Ⓜ American | ▽ 25 | 22 | 24 | $41 |

Simsbury | Simsbury Inn | 397 Hopmeadow St./Rte. 10 (Rte. 185) | 860-651-5700 | www.simsburyinn.com

For a "typical New England" dining experience, surveyors suggest this "cozy", "white-tableclothed" Traditional American offering a seasonal menu in the Simsbury Inn; it's "elegant yet affordable", particularly the $25.95 all-you-can-eat champagne brunch buffet on Sundays.

Fat Cat Pie Co. Pizza | 23 | 15 | 19 | $26 |

Norwalk | 9-11 Wall St. (bet. High & Knight Sts.) | 203-523-0389 | www.fatcatpie.com

The "top-shelf" wines and "fabulous cheeses" elicit as many purrs as the "yummy" "ultra-thin-crust pizzas" (with "Penzeys spices on the table" for extra oomph), "huge salads" and "delish" charcuterie at this "worth-hunting-for" Norwalk "hangout"; it's one "cool" Cat, though some get their dander up over "spacey servers" and a "cavernous" interior that encourages "a lot of noise."

☒ Feng Asian Bistro Asian | 26 | 25 | 23 | $47 |

NEW Canton | Shoppes at Farmington Valley | 110 Albany Tpke. (bet. Lovely St. & Secret Lake Rd.) | 860-693-3364
Hartford | 93 Asylum St. (bet. Main & Trumbull Sts.) | 860-549-3364
www.fengrestaurant.com

Downtown Hartford "really needed something like this" "stunning" Pan-Asian "paradise" declare devotees, who say that "everything" – "from the sushi to the Kobe beef" – is "fresh and full of flavor"; coupled with "awesome drinks", "solicitous service" and "sleek, modern" decor (banquettes, polished wood, stainless steel), it's no surprise it can be "expensive", but few fuss; N.B. the Canton offshoot opened post-Survey.

Ferrante ● Italian | 20 | 20 | 19 | $51 |

Stamford | 191 Summer St. (Broad St.) | 203-323-2000 | www.ferranterestaurant.com

Locals consider this "upscale Italian" a "solid" member of the Stamford dining scene, given its "expansive menu" – including the signature

	FOOD	DECOR	SERVICE	COST

risotto con funghi – and "excellent service"; "well-spaced tables make conversation possible", and while the large oak bar and bounty of fresh flowers add to the "wonderful atmosphere", penne-pinchers warn "you'd better rob a bank before you go."

Field, The *American* | 17 | 19 | 21 | $32

Bridgeport | 3001 Fairfield Ave. (Gilman St.) | 203-333-0043 | www.fieldrestaurant.com

Whether it comes from the "nice fireplace" or "personable staff", the "warm" atmosphere is what stands out at this "beautiful" Bridgeporter, "part of the Black Rock [neighborhood] renaissance"; though the Traditional American fare gets mixed marks ("some very good food, some so-so"), most dig the "hopping" bar and "wonderful bands" on weekends.

Fifty Coins *American* | 14 | 12 | 15 | $25

New Canaan | 26 Locust Ave. (bet. Forest & Main Sts.) | 203-972-3303
Ridgefield | 426 Main St. (Big Shop Ln.) | 203-438-1456
www.fiftycoinsrestaurant.com

"Stick to simple menu items" advise veterans of this "family-friendly" pair of equestrian-themed Traditional Americans in Ridgefield and New Canaan; while the "standard pub fare" (burgers, sandwiches) is "affordable" and the drinks "strong", neigh-sayers sigh "if you love noise, kids and mediocre food, this is the place for you."

55° *Italian* | - | - | - | E

Fairfield | 55 Miller St. (bet. Boston Post Rd. & Carter Henry Dr.) | 203-256-0099 | www.55winebar.com

Unlike its cozy, cavelike New Canaan sibling (Cava Wine Bar & Restaurant), this Downtown Fairfield Italian is all about wide-open spaces, with a multilevel dining area, cathedral ceilings and an expansive outdoor patio; still, housemade pastas like tagliatelle with broccoli rabe and fennel sausage bear a family resemblance, as does its focus on interesting by-the-glass wines.

59 Bank *American* | 18 | 17 | 17 | $34

New Milford | 59 Bank St. (bet. Main & Railroad Sts.) | 860-350-5995 | www.jamrestaurantgroup.com

It may be "nothing fancy", but this "reliable" American in New Milford serves up "particularly good" flatbread pizzas, burgers and "creative salads" from a "moderately priced" menu with "a lot of variety"; contrarians can't get past the "sparse decor" and deem the fare merely "passable", though the happening bar scene and live music on weekends compensate.

Fin *Japanese* | 22 | 11 | 19 | $28

Fairfield | 1253 Post Rd. (Benson Rd.) | 203-255-6788
Stamford | 219 Main St. (Washington Blvd.) | 203-359-6688

"Melt-in-your-mouth sashimi" and "inventive specialty rolls" at "affordable prices" are what you'll find at these "unpretentious" chef-owned Japanese spots in Fairfield and Stamford; you may have to "squeeze into" "tight accommodations" in a "nondescript room", but once there, the "pristine fish" experience is frequently fintastic.

| | FOOD | DECOR | SERVICE | COST |

Z Firebox *American* | 25 | 25 | 24 | $46 |

Hartford | Billings Forge | 539 Broad St. (bet. Capitol Ave. & Russ St.) | 860-246-1222 | www.fireboxrestaurant.com

So "hot", yet so "chill": this "farm-to-table" New American in Downtown Hartford's Billings Forge complex has boosters buzzing, as much for its "masterful" "seasonal fare" derived mostly from "organic, local ingredients" as its "breathtaking decor" (including the "funky" bar's 30-ft. vaulted ceiling) and "attentive service"; true, it's "a bit off the beaten path", but since "you really can't go wrong" once you arrive, "don't let the location keep you away."

Firehouse Deli *Deli* | 21 | 11 | 17 | $15 |

Fairfield | 22 Reef Rd. (Post Rd.) | 203-255-5527 | www.firehousedelifairfield.com

The "menu reads like a novel" and the "yummy sandwiches" are "longer than your forearm" at this "classic" Fairfield deli set in an "old firehouse" with a "spacious patio" and a recently added selection of beer and wine; "friendly" staffers "whisk you in and out" (a good thing, since "half the town" seems to be in line), and though it's "a little pricey", most leave feeling "more than satisfied."

First & Last Tavern *Italian* | 20 | 18 | 18 | $27 |

Avon | 26 W. Main St./Rte. 44 (Simsbury Rd.) | 860-676-2000
Guilford | 535 Boston Post Rd. (Goose Ln.) | 203-458-1400 Ⓜ
Hartford | 939 Maple Ave. (bet. Freeman & Linnmoore Sts.) | 860-956-6000
Middletown | 220 Main St. (College St.) | 860-347-2220
Plainville | 32 Cooke St. (New Britain Ave.) | 860-747-9100
www.firstandlasttavern.com

"Delicious" "brick-oven" pizzas topped with "amazing ingredients" drive pie-zani to these "family-friendly" Italians that also win props for "freshly baked" bread and "basic" red-sauce items such as the "giant entree of sausage peppers"; though some shrug it's "neither exciting nor disappointing", "prompt" service and "huge" portions add to the overall "good value."

f.i.s.h. Ⓜ *Seafood* | 21 | 16 | 18 | $45 |

Port Chester | 102 Fox Island Rd. (Grace Church St.), NY | 914-939-4227 | www.fishfoxisland.com

"Greenwich preppies", "ex-Manhattanites" and other fin fans convene at this "off-the-beaten-path" Port Chester seafooder famed for "seriously fresh" fish dishes "with a twist" like spicy tuna flatbread and lobster fra diavolo; given the "noisy", "minimalist" interior, many say they "prefer it in summer", when you can "sit out on the deck" and take in the "evening breezes" and "pretty water views"; P.S. order before 6:30 PM, and they'll throw in a "complimentary bottle of wine."

NEW Flaggstead Smokehouse *BBQ* | - | - | - | M |

Farmington | 1085 Farmington Ave. (Forest Park Dr.) | 860-674-6028 | www.flaggsteadsmokehouse.com

Goods from the smoker (pork ribs, brisket, sausage, chicken) are slapped on a butcher paper–lined tray, paired with the usual sides (beans, slaw, creamed corn, potato salad, cornbread) and served with beer or lemonade at this new Farmington BBQ joint; it's Texas-style bliss, whether you eat inside among the saddles and sombreros or out on the wooden porch; N.B. closes at 8 PM; BYO for wine.

Flanders Fish Market & Restaurant *Seafood*

20 | 13 | 18 | $28

East Lyme | 22 Chesterfield Rd. (Rte. 1) | 860-739-8866 | www.flandersfish.com

A "local favorite" in East Lyme, this seafooder/retailer serves up "basic preparations" of fin fare "worth licking the plate clean" for as well as some of the "freshest fish around" at "reasonable prices"; "cheery" service and a "family" atmosphere help offset decor that a few peg as "one step down from the mall", while the "helpful" market staff is always ready with "numerous suggestions for the asking."

NEW Flipside Burgers & Bar *Burgers*

- | - | - | M

Fairfield | 1125 Post Rd. (bet. Beach & Unquowa Rds.) | 203-292-8235 | www.flipsiderestaurant.com

Fairfield is flipping for this newcomer's freshly made burgers (beef, chicken or veggie), fries, shakes and such, which are big draws for families as well as happy-hour mavens who belly up to the semicircular bar for signature martinis; large booths, lots of TVs and an outdoor patio make this an all-season locals' place.

Flood Tide *Continental/Eclectic*

▽ 21 | 24 | 21 | $45

Mystic | Inn at Mystic | 3 Williams Ave./Rte. 1 (Denison Ave./Rte. 27) | 860-536-8140 | www.innatmystic.com

"First-rate" Continental-Eclectic cuisine, including "memorable" Sunday brunches, and "old-time tableside service" make this "white-tablecloth" Mystic destination a "great place for a romantic dinner"; the staff "treats you like a king and queen" ("generous pours by the bartender help" too) in the "elegant setting" highlighted by "wonderful" views of the harbor and a "still-great piano bar" on weekends.

Foe, An American Bistro Ⓜ *American*

22 | 19 | 21 | $42

Branford | 1114 Main St. (Veto St.) | 203-483-5896 | www.foebistro.com

"Make a friend" of this "attractive" Branford New American where "sublime" seafood succotash and other "fresh, imaginative" dishes are "nicely served" by a "courteous" staff in a "warm", "lovely" environment; aficionados aver the "pleasantly decorated space" is an "improvement from its previous location" and "seems to have energized the entire experience."

Fonda La Paloma *Mexican*

18 | 15 | 18 | $33

Cos Cob | 531 E. Putnam Ave. (Orchard St.) | 203-661-9395 | www.fondalapaloma.com

Many folks are fonda this "white-tablecloth Mexican" that's been "in Cos Cob for decades", serving up "solid" fare that's "close to authentic" and "great sangria"; "friendly" service and a "family"-oriented atmosphere help make it a "rewarding" experience, even if some complain the room looks as if it "hasn't been redecorated in 30 years."

Forbidden City Bistro *Chinese*

| 23 | 23 | 20 | $38 |

Middletown | 335 Main St. (Court St.) | 860-343-8288 |
www.forbiddencitybistro.com

"Not your daddy's Chinese", this Middletown purveyor of Middle Kingdom cuisine (and sibling of Glastonbury's Char Koon) "stands out" with its "distinctive menu" full of "many tempting selections", complemented by "superb wines" and "excellent martinis" and served in "chic, trendy" surroundings; the only knock is on the service, which can be "inconsistent."

42 Ⓜ *American*

| 22 | 26 | 22 | $87 |

White Plains | Ritz-Carlton Westchester | 1 Renaissance Sq., 42nd fl. (Main St.), NY | 914-761-4242 | www.42therestaurant.com

The "knockout views" are "something to behold" at this aerie atop the Ritz-Carlton in White Plains, a "luxurious", "modern" setting showcasing chef-owner Anthony Goncalves' "forward-thinking" New American creations; however, many express "disappointment" at the "inconsistent quality", not to mention service that's sometimes "below what you would expect" at these prices.

Foster's Ⓢ *American*

| 17 | 17 | 17 | $41 |

New Haven | 56-62 Orange St. (Crown St.) | 203-859-6666 |
www.fostersrestaurant.com

Located in New Haven's Ninth Square neighborhood, this "super-chic, super-sleek" sanctuary from co-owner/chef David Foster features "upscale New American comfort food" served in a setting steeped in "bamboo tabletops", "modern sculptures and white sheets adorning the walls and ceiling"; still, while devotees dub the grub "delicious" and "inventive", the less-impressed "want it to be better than it is."

NEW Fraîche Burger Ⓢ *Burgers*

| - | - | - | I |

Bridgeport | The Arcade | 997 Main St. (bet. Fairfield Ave. & John St.) | 203-870-8392 | www.fraicherestaurants.com

With a nod to the current economy, chef-owner Marc Lippman (of Fairfield's erstwhile Fraîche) gets on the burger bandwagon with this affordable newcomer located in Downtown Bridgeport's newly renovated, historic Arcade building; the beef, chicken and salmon patties come with battered fries, sodas and beer, and with 49 seats it's as amenable to those who like to eat in as it is for takeout.

Frankie & Johnnie's Steakhouse Ⓜ *Steak*

| 23 | 20 | 21 | $65 |

Rye | 77 Purchase St. (bet. Purdy & W. Purdy Aves.), NY | 914-925-3900 | www.frankieandjohnnies.com

"Suburban carnivores" claim this Rye spin-off of an NYC chophouse lives up to its Midtown counterpart with "succulent" steaks, "traditional sides" and an 800-plus-label wine list "that makes you giddy"; set in an "elegant" former bank building, it hosts a "see-and-be-seen" crowd of "investment bankers" and "politicians" who remain unfazed by the typically "expensive" prices.

	FOOD	DECOR	SERVICE	COST

☒ Frank Pepe Pizzeria *Pizza*   26 | 11 | 15 | $20

Fairfield | 238 Commerce Dr. (bet. Berwick Ct. & Brentwood Ave.) | 203-333-7373

Manchester | 233 Buckland Hills Dr. (bet. Buckland & Deming Sts.) | 860-644-7333

New Haven | 157 Wooster St. (Brown St.) | 203-865-5762

NEW Uncasville | Mohegan Sun Casino | 1 Mohegan Sun Blvd. (bet. Rtes. 2 & 32) | 860-862-8888 ●

www.pepespizzeria.com

"Bury me with a slice in my hand" declare devotees of this New Haven "pinnacle of pizzerias" and its offshoots, voted Most Popular in the Connecticut Survey for its "always perfect fresh tomato" pizzas, "transcendent" white clam pies and other offerings on a menu that "hasn't changed in 85 years because it hasn't had to"; cognoscenti caution that service can be "bipolar when it gets crowded", which it often is, and the waits can be "intolerable" – but all the same to most it's "worth it anytime."

Frank Pepe's The Spot Ⓜ *Pizza*   26 | 10 | 15 | $20

New Haven | 163 Wooster St. (Brown St.) | 203-865-7602 | www.pepespizzeria.com

The "lines are usually shorter and the pace a little less rushed" at this "no-frills" "original location" of New Haven's pizza "standard-bearer", serving the "same delicious" pies as the "parent across the alley"; some find the "interior a little bleak" and say "don't expect to be pampered", but in the end, "your stomach won't be disappointed."

Fratelli *Italian*   21 | 15 | 22 | $36

New Rochelle | East End Shopping Ctr. | 237 E. Main St. (Stephenson Blvd.), NY | 914-633-1990 | www.fratellirestaurantnewrochelle.com

Regulars relish "well-prepared" Italian "basics" and "nice wines" at this moderately priced "old-time" eatery in New Rochelle; its "strip-mall" locale notwithstanding, it's the "real" deal, where "owners who make you feel like family" create an experience that's a "cut above" the competition.

Fuji Mountain *Japanese*   17 | 15 | 19 | $38

Larchmont | 2375 Boston Post Rd. (Deane Pl.), NY | 914-833-3838

Following the "suburban Benihana" "formula", this Larchmont Japanese offers up "typical hibachi fare" cooked tableside by "knife-twirling" chefs in a "crowded", "smoky" atmosphere; it's a "blast" for the "kids" – and a favorite for "birthday parties" – but once the smoke clears, some patrons are peeved by "expensive" tabs (which were reportedly lowered post-Survey).

Gabrielle's *American*   21 | 20 | 21 | $45

Centerbrook | 78 Main St. (Westbrook Rd.) | 860-767-2440 | www.gabrielles.net

Located in the "lovely little town" of Centerbrook, this New American small-plates specialist seems to "want to be a NYC eatery" with its "creative menu", "professional" (if "sassy") service and "pretty" decor in a "comfortable" "old house", where "fabulous live jazz" livens up the "lovely" Sunday brunch; while skeptics find it merely "good, but not remarkable", others tout it as a "reliable" option "if you're in the neighborhood."

Gates   Californian/Mediterranean
18 | 18 | 19 | $33

New Canaan | 10 Forest Rd. (bet. East & Locust Aves.) | 203-966-8666 | www.culinarymenus.com/gates.htm

"Some things never change", and that includes the "diverse menu" at this "colorful" New Canaan Cal-Med "institution" that attracts everyone from "financiers and families" to "ladies who lunch" (and brunch); sure, its "reasonably priced" fare – salads, "burgers, fries", etc. – isn't "super-inventive", but after more than 30 years on the scene, it "must be doing something right"; N.B. there's now live music on weekends.

Gavi   Italian
17 | 15 | 18 | $48

Armonk | 15 Old Rte. 22 (Rte. 22), NY | 914-273-6900 | www.gavirestaurant.com

"Convenience" is key at this Armonk Italian where the "basic" dishes are "well done", if "nothing special"; detractors dub it "inconsistent" and "overpriced" (especially the "specials", which require a "second mortgage") and say that service "lacks a personal touch", though the busy "bar scene" is a selling point for some.

Geronimo   Southwestern
17 | 20 | 16 | $37

New Haven | 271 Crown St. (High St.) | 203-777-7700 | www.geronimobarandgrill.com

An interior with a "true Santa Fe feeling", a heated outdoor patio and "tons of tequila" tantalize tipplers who gather 'round the "crowded, rowdy" watering hole at this "upscale" player on the "New Haven scene"; if some say it "succeeds more as a bar than a restaurant", you'll still find "ok" Southwestern fare "with surprising ambition" on the menu, albeit with "spotty service" on the side.

Gervasi's   Italian
- | - | - | E

White Plains | 324 Central Ave. (Tarrytown Rd.), NY | 914-684-8855 | www.gervasis.com

That old Mulino's man, chef John Gervasi, has gone out on his own with this White Plains Italian; the heavily curtained, carpeted dining room with chandeliers and colorful wall-to-ceiling murals sets a formal mood for dining on rich dishes like shrimp wrapped in phylo dough, black-and-white lobster ravioli and chicken scarpariello, accompanied by a globally diverse array of vino.

Ginban Asian Bistro & Sushi   Asian
- | - | - | M

Mamaroneck | 421 Mamaroneck Ave. (Spencer Pl.), NY | 914-777-8889 | www.ginbanasianbistro.com

Elaborate sashimi plates and evocatively named sushi rolls ('banana mama', 'spicy girl') star on the extensive menu at this Mamaroneck Asian from restaurateur Andy Lin (also of White Plains' Asian Temptation); there's also plenty of hot stuff, like Thai coconut curry and grilled mango shrimp, cooked to order – giving you just enough time to admire the black-lacquered furniture and blue-lit bar.

	FOOD	DECOR	SERVICE	COST

Ginger Man *American* | 17 | 18 | 18 | $32 |

Greenwich | 64 Greenwich Ave. (Putnam Ave.) | 203-861-6400 |
www.gingermangreenwich.com
South Norwalk | 99 Washington St. (bet. Main & Water Sts.) |
203-354-0163 | www.gingermannorwalk.com
The "eye candy" and "lively bar scene" trump the "hearty" "pub
grub" at these "upmarket" Traditional Americans, and that's just
fine with lagerheads frothing over the "excellent beer selection" –
100-plus bottles in the newer South Norwalk locale – and "cozy" vibe;
Greenwichers take note: "shoot for the back room" and its "fireplace"
to escape the "noise", then settle in – service can be "s-l-o-w."

Giorgio's 🅼 *Italian* | ▽ 23 | 13 | 20 | $55 |

Port Chester | 64 Merritt St. (Ellendale Ave.), NY | 914-937-4906
Ever "steady", this longtime Italian proffers "traditional" Northern-
style fare like veal chops and pasta primavera in an "off-the-beaten-
path" Port Chester locale; though "concerned" service promotes an
"intimate" feel, the less-charmed claim its "tired" blue-and-brown
decor crosses the line from "old-world" into just plain "old."

Giovanni's *Steak* | 20 | 16 | 20 | $46 |

Darien | 2748 Boston Post Rd. (I-95, exit 9) | 203-325-9979 |
www.giovannis.com
"Giovanni always gives you a hearty meal" at his "old-fashioned"
Italian steakhouse, and if you order the prix fixe dinner, you'll also
get "unbelievable bang for the buck"; too bad aesthetes say the interior is "tired" even in spite of an upgrade not too long ago, though
its "pretty setting overlooking the water" in Darien goes a long way.

Globe Bar & Grill *American* | 15 | 18 | 16 | $42 |

Larchmont | 1879 Palmer Ave. (Chatsworth Ave.), NY | 914-833-8600 |
www.globegrill.com
For "a casual night out", Larchmont locals select this "neighborhood" New American proffering "simple pizzas" and burgers in a
"nicely decorated" minimalist milieu; it also hosts a "great singles
scene" centered around the well-stocked bar, but critics claim that's
no consolation for "ordinary" fare and "indifferent" service.

Gnarly Vine ◑🅼 *American* | ▽ 19 | 18 | 24 | $31 |

New Rochelle | 501 Main St. (bet. Lawton St. & Norman Rockwell Blvd.),
NY | 914-355-2541 | www.thegnarlyvine.com
New Rochelle is home to this intimate American-style enoteca offering an "interesting" lineup of 30 wines by the glass alongside
"nice little tapas dishes" like Sicilian meatballs, oysters and artisanal cheese platters; it's "popular with the ladies", thanks in part to a
"welcoming" vibe that offers refuge from rowdier bars nearby.

Go Fish *Seafood* | 20 | 18 | 19 | $36 |

Mystic | Olde Mistick Vill. | 26 Coogan Blvd. (Rte. 27) | 860-536-2662 |
www.gofishct.com
"As the name implies", this "big, modern spot near the Mystic shopping village" is "heavy on fresh seafood", including offerings from a

"wonderful sushi bar" that some find a "better choice than the regular menu"; hedgers deem the fare "good but not spectacular", and the "loud" "warehouse" setting doesn't wow everyone, while the conscientious find it "difficult to eat fish in such close proximity to an aquarium."

Golden Rod *Asian* | 20 | 12 | 15 | $27 |

New Rochelle | 55 E. Main St. (Premium Point Rd.), NY | 914-235-6688

A "diverse" lineup of "fresh-tasting" "Chinese, Thai and Japanese" selections awaits at this New Rochelle Pan-Asian that's also appreciated for its "decent value for the dollar"; given its "unassuming" beige-and-bamboo looks, "you don't go for the atmosphere" – thankfully "the food comes out fast" and "takeout travels well" too.

Gold Roc Diner ◗ *Diner* | 12 | 9 | 15 | $18 |

West Hartford | 61 Kane St. (Oakwood Ave.) | 860-236-9366

"The neon lights call to all night owls" who "count on" this 24/7 "greasy spoon" in West Hartford dishing out "grub" that's "a little above average"; if some observe the "servers are less than happy to be there" and the digs are strictly "diner standard", stoics shrug "you could do worse."

Grand ⊠Ⓜ *American* | 18 | 21 | 17 | $41 |

Stamford | 15 Bank St. (Summer St.) | 203-323-3232 | www.stamfordgrand.com

"James Bond wannabes" can be spied sipping "after-work" martinis at this "sleek" Stamford New American "known more for its bar scene than its food", though the "inventive menu" (e.g. truffled mac 'n' cheese) – if not the "pretentious" staffers – has its fans; just "eat early and leave before the crazies come in" to dodge the "loud" *"Night at the Roxbury"* vibe.

Ⓩ Grant's *American* | 25 | 22 | 24 | $46 |

West Hartford | 977 Farmington Ave. (Main St.) | 860-236-1930 | www.billygrant.com

Devotees declare Billy Grant is "a god" who "has taken comfort food to a new level" at his West Hartford New American (sibling of Bricco) offering "top-notch, creative" fare and "fantastic" desserts served by a "perceptive staff"; if a few deem the decor "a bit pretentious", others find the setting "elegant" and "comfortable", and though tabs may be "pricey", most agree it's "worth it."

Graziellas *Italian* | 17 | 13 | 17 | $41 |

White Plains | Esplanade White Plains Hotel | 95 S. Broadway (E. Post Rd.), NY | 914-761-5721 | www.graziellasny.com

Surveyors seeking "old-fashioned" Italian fare head to this "tried-and-true" mainstay in the Esplanade White Plains Hotel serving standards like penne alla vodka; despite the "Downtown convenience" and "relatively modest" tabs, critics call it "unexciting", with "nothing to complain about", but "nothing to brag about either."

	FOOD	DECOR	SERVICE	COST

Great Taste *Chinese* ▽ 27 | 23 | 27 | $28

New Britain | 597 W. Main St. (Corbin Ave.) | 860-827-8988 |
www.greattaste.com

Sinophiles "go early and often" to this New Britain "treasure" for the "best Chinese food in CT", including an "impressive presentation" of Peking duck (with "pancakes prepared tableside") and other "first-rate" dishes, served by an "accommodating" staff in a "kid-friendly" setting; though it's usually "packed on weekends", the "place buzzes with efficiency" "under the watchful eye of the owner."

Greenwich Tavern *American* - | - | - | M

Old Greenwich | 1392 E. Putnam Ave. (Ferris Dr.) | 203-698-9033 |
www.greenwichtavern.net

Chef/co-owner Rafael Palomino (Sonora) has reinvented his Old Greenwich crowd-pleaser as this American tavern featuring items like mini BLTs and sliders that encourage sharing, as well as a few of his old signature favorites including crawfish risotto and braised short ribs; the decor is much the same, but has been given a more casual feel to match the lower prices; N.B. the valet-only parking sometimes spells a wait when you're ready to leave.

Grist Mill *Continental* 24 | 24 | 23 | $46

Farmington | 44 Mill Ln. (Garden St.) | 860-676-8855 | www.thegristmill.net

"If you can't win her heart here, quit trying" counsel cognoscenti who commend this "lovely" Continental "on the Farmington River" with a "splendid view of the old mill" and the falls; while the menu features "a number of consistent winners" (including the signature Dover sole) that are "always fresh and well presented", for many the "romantic setting" alone is "worth the price."

Griswold Inn *American* 18 | 23 | 19 | $43

Essex | Griswold Inn | 36 Main St. (Scholes Ln.) | 860-767-1776 |
www.griswoldinn.com

This "jolly" Essex inn (circa 1776) is "as quaint as they come", with a "cozy, historic setting" that makes it a "great place for out-of-towners who want the old New England experience"; there's "nice variety" on the Traditional American menu, including a "fabulous hunt breakfast", and the "wine bar with an excellent happy hour" and live "music on most nights" help create an "ambiance that can't be beat."

Gusano Loco *Mexican* 19 | 12 | 18 | $31

Mamaroneck | 1137 W. Boston Post Rd. (Richbell Rd.), NY | 914-777-1512

"Simple, yet tasty" Mexican cooking is the soul of this "casual" Mamaroneck eatery tended by an "eager-to-please" staff; its bare-bones decor gets a boost from patio seating, while "low prices" please wherever you sit.

Gus's Franklin Park *Seafood* 20 | 11 | 18 | $41

Harrison | 126 Halstead Ave. (1st St.), NY | 914-835-9804

A "Harrison tradition", this long-standing seafooder (circa 1931) "hasn't changed in years, and that's a good thing" insist those fond of its "retro" mahogany-trimmed setting and "warm", "family-oriented" service; it's a "tight" squeeze in the oft-crowded dining room, but the payoff is "excellent" lobster, "simply prepared" fish and other "honest" grub all presented in "big portions"; N.B. no reservations, so come early or be "ready to wait."

G.W. Tavern *American* | 20 | 22 | 21 | $37 |

Washington Depot | 20 Bee Brook Rd./Rte. 47 (bet. Blackville Rd. & Calhoun St.) | 860-868-6633 | www.gwtavern.com

By George, this "classic tavern" (circa 1850) in "rustic" Washington Depot "just oozes Americana" – or so say the "locals and weekenders" who "curl up by the fireplace" near its "beautiful bar" or dine on the "patio overlooking the Shepaug River"; other pluses include traditional "comfort fare" that's "surprisingly good" and "not over-priced (too much)", plus "live music on weekends."

NEW Haiku ◑ *Asian* | - | - | - | M |

White Plains | 149 Mamaroneck Ave. (bet. E. Post Rd. & Maple Ave.), NY | 914-644-8887 | www.haikuasianbistro.com

Though the name of this new White Plains cousin of Mamaroneck's Haiku Asian Bistro & Sushi Bar is shorter, the space is larger – and sleeker too, with a glowing blue wall and an ample bar area, plus a hip techno backbeat; its winning formula features midpriced Pan-Asian noodles, dumplings, curries and more, as well as many original specialty sushi rolls.

Haiku Asian Bistro & Sushi Bar *Asian* | 23 | 18 | 20 | $34 |

Mamaroneck | 265 Mamaroneck Ave. (Prospect Ave.), NY | 914-381-3200 | www.haikuasianbistro.com

"Impeccably fresh sushi" plus "terrific" Pan-Asian plates "perfect for sampling" make this "modern", midpriced Mamaroneck outpost "worth frequenting" according to fans who also consider it a solid bet for "takeout"; the "pretty" stone-and-lacquer setting is "frequently overcrowded", so expect a "hectic" vibe along with service that borders on "rushed."

Hajime Ⓜ *Japanese* | 25 | 15 | 20 | $42 |

Harrison | 267 Halstead Ave. (Harrison Ave.), NY | 914-777-1543

Acolytes of "masterful" chef Sam Takahashi say his Harrison Japanese "rivals NYC and Tokyo" with "superb" sushi served in "simple" environs; "portions are small" and "service is somewhat indifferent", but those who "could eat here every day" insist "the food alone is worth it."

Halstead Avenue Bistro *American* | 18 | 13 | 20 | $40 |

Harrison | 123 Halstead Ave. (1st St.), NY | 914-777-1181 | www.halsteadbistro.com

Expect "a wide variety" of New American specialties at this candlelit Harrison bistro where the "gray-haired crowd" shows up Sundays–Thursdays for a "reasonable" three-course prix fixe ($24.95); service is "cordial", though some suggest the "dark", "cramped" setting "leaves a lot to be desired" – perhaps it's "time for a spruce-up."

	FOOD	DECOR	SERVICE	COST

Hamilton Inn *Eclectic*

▽ 21 | 22 | 22 | $45

Millerton | 67 Main St. (Park St.), NY | 518-789-9399 |
www.thehamiltoninn.com

The "epitome of country dining" declare devotees of this "welcoming"
"old-timer" set in one of "quaint" Millerton's Victorian houses; a
"steady hand prevails in the kitchen", turning out Eclectic fare with
"thoughtful, creative touches", all delivered by an "attentive staff" in a
candlelit room with a "cozy" fireplace, or on the porch come summer.

Hanami *Japanese*

- | - | - | M

Clinton | 114 E. Main St. (Liberty St.) | 860-664-9268 |
www.hanamiclinton.com

Maybe the decor's not cutting-edge, but this midpriced Clinton
Japanese keeps the knives flying at its crowd-pleasing hibachi grill;
those who aren't in the mood for flying food can choose from a wide
range of cooked entrees, sushi, sashimi and bento boxes.

Hanna's Mideastern ⊠ *Lebanese*

▽ 22 | 13 | 19 | $22

Danbury | 72 Lake Ave. (bet. Abbott Ave. & Lawncrest Rd.) | 203-748-5713

For "fab" "authentic" Lebanese fare, head to this "no-frills" nook in
an "unassuming Danbury strip mall"; if its "small, dark" interior dis-
pleases, no problem: the "store next door means you can take it with
you" – just remember to "pick up some extra hummus."

Harbor Lights *Mediterranean/Seafood*

20 | 22 | 20 | $48

Norwalk | 82 Sea View Ave. (bet. East Ave. & 1st St.) | 203-866-3364 |
www.harborlightsrestaurant-ct.com

Whether you take in the "beautiful harbor views" from the "enclosed
porch" or "sit out on the deck and watch the boats", the "scenery is
divine" at this Norwalk waterfronter, where Mediterranean-inspired
seafood is served by a "solicitous" staff; if there's a bit of debate
over the food ("well prepared", "fabulous" raw bar vs. "underwhelming"), there's no question that the "lovely location" keeps
folks "coming back."

Harborside Bar & Grille *American*

15 | 14 | 15 | $28

Stratford | 946 Ferry Blvd. (Bridgeport Ave.) | 203-375-3037 |
www.harborsidebargrill.com

In "warmer months", it's "nice to enjoy lunch or dinner on the deck"
of this "casual" Stratford American with a "beautiful view of the
Housatonic River"; critics may dismiss the food as "ordinary", but
that doesn't prevent the place from becoming "a twentysomething party central" at night, thanks to a "great happy hour with
half-price appetizers."

Hard Rock Cafe ◑ *American*

15 | 23 | 17 | $31

Ledyard | Foxwoods Resort Casino | 39 Norwich Westerly Rd./Rte. 2
(bet. Mains Crossing & Preston Plains Rd.) | 860-312-7625 |
www.hardrock.com

An "iconic part of the tourist landscape", this rock 'n' roll-themed
American chain was "cool in the '80s" but many feel it's "past its sell
date", citing "mundane" grub, "haphazard" service and "way too

loud" acoustics; despite a "surprisingly decent burger" and all that "fun music memorabilia", some opt to "buy the T-shirt" from this Foxwoods Resort Casino outpost instead.

Harney & Sons *Tearoom* | 21 | 22 | 21 | $21 |

Millerton | Railroad Plaza | 13 Main St. (bet. N. Center St. & N. Elm Ave.), NY | 518-789-2121 | www.harney.com

A "tea-lover's delight", this "tiny" Millerton cafe offers "the best" brews "this side of the pond", as well as "excellent scones", sandwiches, "delicate salads" and other "light" lunch- or teatime fare; sippers enjoy the "calm" atmosphere and "respectful" service in its "charming" room or on the terrace, while those who prefer it to-go select "interesting blends" from the adjacent "pretty shop."

Harry's Bishops Corner Ⓜ *Pizza* | - | - | - | I |

West Hartford | 732 N. Main St. (Albany Ave.) | 860-236-0400 | www.harrysbc.com

It's no longer affiliated with Harry's Pizza, the beloved West Hartford pie-maker, but this Bishops Corner outpost continues to produce Napoletana-style thin-crust creations that are both crispy and chewy in texture and topped with seasonal delights; bonus: eat in at one of the granite-topped tables and enjoy an affordable bottle of wine.

Harry's Pizza *Pizza* | 24 | 14 | 18 | $20 |

West Hartford | West Hartford Ctr. | 1003 Farmington Ave. (bet. Lasalle Rd. & Woodrow St.) | 860-231-7166 | www.harryspizza.net

"The smell of olive oil and spices" lures you into this West Hartford pizzeria known for its "wonderfully fresh thin-crust" pies, "amazing" house salad dressing you can buy "by the bottle" and "free ices that ensure you won't leave with garlic breath"; the "eager staff aims to please" and the atmosphere is "pleasant", even if some surveyors find the "wooden benches" and "marble-topped tables" a bit "sterile."

Harvest, The Ⓜ *Continental* | ▽ 22 | 26 | 22 | $47 |

Pomfret | 37 Putnam Rd. (Woodstock Rd.) | 860-928-0008 | www.harvestrestaurant.com

"Set in an old farmhouse" in Pomfret with "picture-perfect outdoor charm" and offering "consistently good" fare and "downhome" service, this "classic" Continental works for an "impressive dinner", "celebrating something special" or just a "night out with a loved one"; in any event, most agree it's a "gem" in this "Quiet Corner of Connecticut."

⊿ Harvest Supper ⊠Ⓜ *American* | 27 | 20 | 26 | $56 |

New Canaan | 15 Elm St. (Main St.) | 203-966-5595

The "tiny, tempting" dishes "salute the seasons" and "burst with flavor" at this "classy" New Canaan New American that's "like being in Manhattan", which makes sense since it's owned by NYC restaurateurs Jack and Grace Lamb (she's also the "gracious" hostess); chef Michael Campbell's menu is "inventive" "without making diners

	FOOD	DECOR	SERVICE	COST

squeamish" and so "delicious" "you'll want to order everything", but those with "slender wallets" might want to show restraint.

Hawthorne Inn *American*

| 18 | 14 | 19 | $40 |

Berlin | 2421 Berlin Tpke. (Toll Gate Rd.) | 860-828-3571 | www.hawthorne-inn.com

This "classic icon" (circa 1945) is "the place for prime rib" in Berlin crow carnivores who also commend the other "reliable" Traditional American eats, "served up in hearty portions" by a "motherly" staff in a "quaint, inviting" setting – the kind of "place your grandparents would go to for their anniversary"; modernists, though, translate that into "tired" fare and "outdated" decor.

Heirloom *American/Continental*

| – | – | – | E |

New Haven | Study at Yale Hotel | 1157 Chapel St. (bet. Park & York Sts.) | 203-503-3919 | www.studyhotels.com

Ensconced within The Study boutique hotel at Yale, this dapper eatery is outfitted with hardwood floors, clean lines and leather chairs; the cuisine from chef John Nordin (a Todd English protégé) is similarly contemporary (Continental–New American), with a focus on regional fare such as New England clam chowder and New Haven spaghetti with veal meatballs.

Hidden Vine 🗷 Ⓜ *Italian*

| – | – | – | M |

Newington | 1052 Main St. (bet. Cedar St. & Market Sq.) | 860-667-8463 | www.hiddenvinewinebar.com

Hiding in plain sight in Newington's Market Square is this moderately priced Italian eatery specializing in homemade gnocchi, manicotti and lighter fare made to be paired with selections from a global wine list; in its cozy interior, one room resembles a wine cave, another is dominated by a leather-and-suede banquette and there's also a tasting area for bimonthly classes and wine dinners – not to mention a patio that's in the works.

Hopkins Inn Ⓜ *Austrian*

| 20 | 24 | 21 | $49 |

New Preston | Hopkins Inn | 22 Hopkins Rd. (½ mi. west of Rte. 45 N.) | 860-868-7295 | www.thehopkinsinn.com

"Eat out on the patio" and soak in the "spectacular views" of Lake Waramaug from this family-run New Preston "institution" where "courteous" servers in dirndls lug "large portions" of "Austrian specialties" to table; devotees deem the Wiener schnitzel and such "excellent", but the less-impressed shrug "ho-hum" and wonder "can we get into this century and revamp the menu?"; N.B. closed January–mid-March.

Horse & Hound Inn *American*

| ▽ 16 | 14 | 16 | $36 |

South Salem | 94 Spring St. (Main St.), NY | 914-763-3108 | www.thehorseandhoundinn.com

Set in a converted stagecoach stop in South Salem, this "rustic" American has a "neighborhood feel" that makes it "good for a burger" or a beer at the bar "on a winter's day"; however, "disappointed" patrons lament that's it's not as ambitious as it once was – given the building's "history and character", it "has so much potential."

	FOOD	DECOR	SERVICE	COST

Hostaria Mazzei *Italian*   21 | 20 | 20 | $55

Port Chester | 25 S. Regent St. (Westchester Ave.), NY | 914-939-2727 | www.hostariamazzei.com

The "wood-fired oven" is "put to delicious use" pumping out pizzas, meats and "wonderful fish" at this "upscale" Port Chester Italian set in "spacious" digs "quiet" enough for conversation; a "cordial owner" boosts the "inviting" ambiance, but alas, the prices are "too expensive" for some; N.B. it closed recently for major renovations (which will outdate the above Decor score), and is slated to reopen in spring 2010.

Hot Basil Thai Café Ⓜ *Thai*   21 | 17 | 19 | $28

West Hartford | 565 New Park Ave. (Talcott Rd.) | 860-523-9554 | www.hotbasilcafe.com

It's a "little place that packs a punch" proclaim proponents of this West Hartford BYO Thai serving "excellent" hot basil stir fry, "outstanding drunken noodles" and more, although a few who can't "get enough burn" say dishes "need more spice"; "don't be deceived by the storefront setting" – the interior is "tasteful" and "romantic."

Hot Tomato's *Italian*   21 | 20 | 20 | $36

Hartford | 1 Union Pl. (Asylum St.) | 860-249-5100 | www.hottomatos.net

"Garlic city" is what fans dub this "hopping" Hartford Italian "near the civic center" popular for its "incredible cheesy garlic bread" and "memorable" house pasta specials at prices that are "quite reasonable"; it's a "casual" place with "great people-watching" and a "fun-loving staff" that "treats you like family", though critics caution the room can get "very noisy."

Hunan Larchmont *Chinese/Japanese*   16 | 11 | 16 | $27

Larchmont | 1961 Palmer Ave. (West Ave.), NY | 914-833-0400 | www.hunanlarchmont.com

"Classic Cantonese" cooking comes in "abundant" quantities at this "not exciting", but always "reliable" Chinese in Larchmont that's been "packing them in" for almost two decades; apart from an "exotic fish tank", there's not much to look at, but service is "quick" for both eat-in and delivery; N.B. there's also a four-seat sushi bar.

Iannelli's *Italian*   19 | 11 | 14 | $30

White Plains | 359 Mamaroneck Ave. (Livingston Ave.), NY | 914-683-1313 | www.iannellisrestaurant.com

A no-brainer for a casual dinner or a "quick lunch", this "down-to-earth" White Plains "pizza place" turns out solid pies and "hearty" Italian standards like heros and lasagna; those who have faulted it for its "crowded", "lackluster" quarters should know that a fancy inside-outside rooftop dining area was created post-Survey and may outdate the above Decor score.

ⓏIbiza Ⓢ *Spanish*   28 | 24 | 25 | $53

New Haven | 39 High St. (bet. Chapel & Crown Sts.) | 203-865-1933 | www.ibizanewhaven.com

(continued)

Z NEW Ibiza Tapas *Spanish*

Hamden | 1832 Dixwell Ave. (Robert St.) | 203-909-6512 |
www.ibizatapaswinebar.com

New Haven's "premier Spanish" "might as well be in a little villa in Spain" attest amigos agog over the "exquisite", "authentic" cuisine, including a weeknight $59 six-course tasting menu "worth fasting for"; the "well-coordinated" staff "manages to be both meticulous and warm" in the "comfortable, spare" contemporary space, all of which makes it an "experience to savor – and especially to repeat"; N.B. the Hamden branch opened post-Survey.

NEW Il Castello Ⓜ *Italian*   – | – | – | M

Mamaroneck | 576 Mamaroneck Ave. (Waverly Ave.), NY | 914-777-2200

Old-school flourishes are on display at this Mamaroneck Italian arrival where gracious staffers de-bone whole branzini and prepare Caesar salads tableside, and the cozy room flaunts rich woods and chandeliers; somewhat surprisingly given this level of service and atmosphere, the prices for the classic-leaning fare tilt toward moderate; N.B. the 300-strong wine list features labels from The Boot and California.

Il Falco Ⓢ *Italian*   22 | 18 | 23 | $49

Stamford | 59 Broad St. (bet. Franklin & Summer Sts.) | 203-327-0002 |
www.ilfalco.com

Oenophiles and "housemade" pasta lovers alike say "*grazie* very much" to the owners of this Stamford "standard bearer for fine Italian dining", whose "vast wine cellar" holds 2,000-plus vinos (many at "fair" prices); less toast-worthy: the "old-world" decor, which some suggest "could use a face-lift."

Il Palio Ⓢ *Italian*   23 | 24 | 21 | $47

Shelton | Corporate Towers | 5 Corporate Dr. (Bridgeport Ave.) |
203-944-0770 | www.ilpalioct.com

While it may "look like a bank" from the outside, the "beautifully decorated interior" of this "Italian gem in a corporate park" in Shelton resembles an "authentic Tuscan" villa, where "wonderful" "rustic" fare is served by a "knowledgeable" staff in an "upscale atmosphere"; while some complain about the "NY prices", others insist it's "well worth the money."

Il Sogno *Italian/Mediterranean*   – | – | – | M

Port Chester | 316 Boston Post Rd. (S. Regent St.), NY | 914-937-7200 |
www.ilsognony.com

The team behind this Port Chester Italian-Med is chef/co-owner Jimmy Resulbegu (whose résumé includes Manhattan's San Pietro) and co-owner Rafael Palomino of Sonora fame; an interior of stone, hardwood floors and white tablecloths sets a subdued backdrop for such signatures as risotto with cream of white truffles and chicken martini, a Parmesan-coated breast dipped in a lemon and white wine sauce (it's not on the menu, so ask); N.B. a 200-plus Italo-centric wine list is also offered.

	FOOD	DECOR	SERVICE	COST

Imperial Wok *Chinese/Japanese* | 18 | 15 | 17 | $28 |

North White Plains | 736 N. Broadway (bet. McDougal Dr. & Palmer Ave.), NY | 914-686-2700

An "overwhelming" array of "flavorful" Chinese and Japanese dishes is presented in "plentiful portions" at this North White Plains place set in "pleasant", if slightly "shabby" digs; "a wok on the wild side they're not", but prices "won't break the bank" either, so most consider them a "staple" in the suburban repertoire.

Inn at Newtown *American* | 19 | 21 | 19 | $40 |

Newtown | Inn at Newtown | 19 Main St./Rte. 25 (Church Hill Rd.) | 203-270-1876 | www.theinnatnewtown.com

Some "love the Main Street view" from the main dining room of this "homey" New American housed in an "idyllic" Newtown inn, while others find it "more fun" to dine in the "less formal pub", but either way the "huge burgers" are a "favorite"; as for service, opinions range from "prompt and knowledgeable" to "service? what service?"

☑ Insieme Ristorante ☒ *Italian* | 25 | 13 | 24 | $51 |

Ridgefield | 103 Danbury Rd. (bet. Copps Hill Rd. & South St.) | 203-894-8141

He's "always there", so be sure to "chat with owner Sal Scala about what he likes on the menu" of "delightful" Italiana at his "hole-in-the-wall" in a Ridgefield shopping center; you'll have to contend with "tight quarters" and "unsuitably inexpensive" decor, but "it's worth it" for the food, "remarkably attentive" service and "thoughtful wine list."

Irving Farm | 20 | 16 | 15 | $17 |
Coffee House *Coffeehouse/Sandwiches*

Millerton | 44 Main St. (Dutchess Ave.), NY | 518-789-2020 | www.irvingfarm.com

This Millerton "hot spot" "with a cool factor" serves "delicious homemade soups", "satisfying" sandwiches, breads, pastries and 39 varieties of famously "excellent" coffee, making it "a good choice" for "locals and city folk" alike; it's right next to the Millerton Moviehouse, and on Fridays and Saturdays it's open for dinner too.

Isabelle et Vincent ☒ *Bakery/French* | - | - | - | M |

Fairfield | 1903 Post Rd. (bet. Bungalow Ave. & Granville St.) | 203-292-8022 | www.isabelleetvincent.com

The aroma of Valrhona chocolate and freshly baked croissants wafts across the threshold of this tiny patisserie in Downtown Fairfield, where seventh-generation chocolatier Vincent and his wife, Isabelle, carry on the culinary traditions of their native Strasbourg, France; cakes for every occasion, breads and quiches can be ordered to go or enjoyed at the communal table by the fireplace; N.B. closes at 5 PM.

It's Only Natural *Health Food* | 23 | 18 | 21 | $27 |

Middletown | Main Street Mkt. | 386 Main St. (bet. Baylis Ct. & Washington St.) | 860-346-9210 | www.ionrestaurant.com

"It isn't hard to eat your veggies" at this "reasonably priced" Middletown health food haunt that's "been around forever" (since

1972) serving "inventive vegetarian, vegan" and macrobiotic dishes, with wines to go with them, and groupies gush "every bite is surprising and delicious"; the service is "friendly" and the "attention-grabbing" "local artwork" gracing the walls adds to the "counterculture" mood.

🆕 Jack Rabbit's *American*

`- | - | - | I`

Old Saybrook | 254 Main St. (bet. Maynard Rd. & Sheffield St.) | 860-510-0048 | www.jackrabbitsburgers.com

After closing his high-end steakhouse, Jack's Saybrook Steak, chef-owner Jack Flaws is appealing to the masses with this Old Saybrook gourmet burger-and-dog joint, which, if all goes as planned, will be the first link of a New England chain; its signature sliders come in six-packs, while 'dirty' wings range in spiciness from G-rated to triple-X, setting a playful tone that matches the retro '50s decor.

Jaipore Royal Indian *Indian*

`24 | 20 | 20 | $34`

Brewster | 280 Rte. 22 N. (3 mi. off I-684, exit 8), NY | 845-277-3549 | www.fineindiandining.com

A "tantalizing" variety of "perfectly seasoned" Indian cuisine "fit for a rajah" is the draw at this Brewster "gem" set in a "rambling Victorian" house; a "willing staff" and a "bargain buffet" of specialties are other reasons it's been "a crowd-pleaser for years."

Jasmine *Chinese/Japanese*

`15 | 12 | 14 | $24`

Westport | 60 Charles St. (I-95, exit 17) | 203-221-7777 | www.jasminerestaurant.com

"Dependable" Chinese and Japanese "comfort food" and a "bargain" lunch buffet make this "old-school" eatery in Westport a "great spot to bring the family"; maybe skeptics find "nothing exciting" here, but "kids love the fish tank", and the "quick" home delivery strikes some as nothing short of "amazing."

Jasper White's Summer Shack *Seafood*

`21 | 16 | 19 | $39`

Uncasville | Mohegan Sun Casino | 1 Mohegan Sun Blvd. (Sandy Desert Rd.) | 860-862-9500 | www.summershackrestaurant.com

"Take a gambling break and enjoy" this "family-friendly" Mohegan Sun seafooder, an outpost of the popular Cambridge, MA-based "clam shack" serving a "large selection" of "New England classics" (including signature "pan-roasted lobster") at prices that are "reasonable for the casino"; the "big, bright" digs can get "crowded and noisy", but proponents promise the fare will "quickly make you forget your losses."

🗾 Jean-Louis 🗾 *French*

`28 | 23 | 26 | $83`

Greenwich | 61 Lewis St. (bet. Greenwich Ave. & Mason St.) | 203-622-8450 | www.restaurantjeanlouis.com

Chef-owner Jean-Louis Gerin helps you "discover taste buds you never knew you had" at his "first-rate" Greenwich French, where the "imaginative, adventurous" cuisine is complemented by a "beautifully appointed dining room" and the "most courteous service imaginable"; *oui*, you may need "to get that second mortgage" or have "someone else pick up the tab", but for a "special occasion" the experience will be "hard to duplicate anywhere" ("including NYC").

Jeffrey's *American/Continental*
| 23 | 19 | 22 | $44 |

Milford | 501 New Haven Ave. (Old Gate Ln.) | 203-878-1910 | www.jeffreysofmilford.com

"Even after a change in ownership", regulars report having the "same positive experience" at this "lovely" New American-Continental in Milford where "excellent fish selections", "good steaks and chops" and more are "professionally served" in a "romantic" setting enhanced by views of the marshes and garden; while a few dismiss it as "nothing special", it's a "favorite" of many who like to "dine in a civil manner."

Jeff's Cuisine Ⓜ *BBQ/Southern*
| 25 | 9 | 20 | $18 |

South Norwalk | South Norwalk Plaza | 54 N. Main St. (bet. Ann & Marshall Sts.) | 203-852-0041 | www.jeffscuisine.com

"If your soul needs sustenance", respondents recommend the "phenomenal" ribs, "outstanding" veggies and other "down-home" victuals at this South Norwalk Southern BBQ joint where chef-owner Jeff Esaw is "always open to chatting and trading recipes"; fashionistas may frown at the "dingy environs", but no one's complaining about the "huge portions" or "low prices", and for "takeout, it's awesome."

J. Gilbert's *Southwestern/Steak*
| 25 | 20 | 23 | $44 |

Glastonbury | 185 Glastonbury Blvd. (Main St.) | 860-659-0409 | www.jgilberts.com

A "steakhouse without an attitude", this Glastonbury outpost of a national chain "can hang with the best of NYC and Chicago" boast boosters bullish on its "excellent" Southwestern-style steaks and "seafood that's every bit as good"; while the setting sparks a bit of debate ("classy" vs. "no warmth"), an "extremely professional staff" wins most over.

Joe's American Bar & Grill *American*
| 16 | 17 | 16 | $28 |

Fairfield | 750 Post Rd. (Eliot Pl.) | 203-319-1600 | www.joesamerican.com

Aimed at the average Joe, this Traditional American chain outpost is a "staple for Fairfield families and college kids" who gravitate toward its "serviceable" "burgers, salads and ribs" at "reasonable prices"; but critics take aim at "prepackaged" food "with no oomph" served by a "clueless" staff.

John Harvard's Brew House *American*
| 19 | 18 | 18 | $27 |

Manchester | 1487 Pleasant Valley Rd. (Buckland Ave.) | 860-644-2739 | www.johnharvards.com

It's all about the "constantly changing menu of craft brews" at this "no-frills" brewpub franchise in Manchester where the "typical" American menu is outperformed by the "nice suds selection" (after a few pints "you can convince yourself you made it into Harvard"); it's "executed with much more style than you'd expect" – and for a "decent price."

John-Michael's Ⓜ European | 25 | 25 | 26 | $59 |

North Salem | Purdys Homestead | 100 Titicus Rd. (Rte. 22), NY | 914-277-2301 | www.johnmichaelsrestaurant.com

"Talented" chef-owner John-Michael Hamlet creates a "treasure" in the country with this remake of the historic Purdys Homestead in North Salem, serving his "divine" European cuisine in a "quaint" setting that's especially "cozy" "when they have the fireplaces going"; yes, prices are "high", but the "gracious" service and setting make for "perfect" "special-occasion" supping.

John's Café American/Mediterranean | 24 | 19 | 24 | $47 |

Woodbury | 693 Main St. S./Rte. 6 (Rte. 64) | 203-263-0188 | www.johnscafe.com

Insiders say this "small, sometimes unnoticed" Woodbury New American–Med is a "must go" thanks to "outstanding" fare (much of it made from local organic produce) and a "killer wine list"; even for a "secret" it can be "crowded and loud", though the "friendly staff" and "warm" vibe blunt complaints.

Joseph's Steakhouse Steak | 24 | 20 | 23 | $58 |

Bridgeport | 360 Fairfield Ave. (Lafayette Blvd.) | 203-337-9944 | www.josephssteakhouse.com

As you'd expect from a place whose namesake is a Peter Luger alum, this "old-school" "gem" "brings home the bacon" – and "humongous" hunks of "prime beef" "cooked to perfection" – to Downtown Bridgeport; if a few shrug it's "just ok", most surveyors insist it's "all that you'd expect" from a "top-quality" steakhouse – "with prices to match."

Kalbi House Korean | 20 | 11 | 18 | $34 |

White Plains | 291 Central Ave. (Wilson St.), NY | 914-328-0251

The namesake kalbi (marinated short ribs) are a "must" at this "no-frills" Korean "BBQ joint" in White Plains where the cook-your-own format makes it "fun for families or groups" (there are also some Japanese dishes); maybe it's "not up to Flushing standards", but it's more "convenient", and "eager" staffers and moderate tabs are certainly appealing.

Karamba Café Cuban/Pan-Latin   ▽ | 20 | 11 | 19 | $19 |

White Plains | 185 Main St. (Court St.), NY | 914-946-5550 | www.karambacafe.com

Chowhounds craving "authentic", inexpensive Pan-Latin dishes like "savory stewed chicken", rice and beans and sweet plantains find them at this "best-kept-secret" in White Plains whose culture-spanning menu also boasts a "great Cuban sandwich"; the environs are absolutely bare-bones, but service is "friendly" and devotees don't "go for the decor" anyhow; N.B. takeout is also an option.

Kari Malaysian   ▽ | 23 | 18 | 23 | $25 |

New Haven | 1451 Whalley Ave. (Glenview Terr.) | 203-389-1280

The "bamboo musical instruments", "masks and poster art" on the walls of this "friendly" Malaysian belie its New Haven "strip-mall" locale, as does its "consistently excellent" fare like curry chicken; besides, it's "nice to go to a place that isn't Downtown", and even better when it's affordable.

Karuta *Japanese*   ▽ 21 | 16 | 19 | $28

New Rochelle | North Ridge Shopping Ctr. | 77 Quaker Ridge Rd. (North Ave.), NY | 914-636-6688

New Rochelle residents in search of a quick "sushi fix" seek out this Japanese "standby" slicing up a variety of "fresh" fish at "reasonable" prices; despite its strip-mall locale, it has a "neighborhood" feel, thanks in part to a "welcoming" owner who seemingly is "always on premises."

Kazu *Japanese*   24 | 19 | 21 | $37

South Norwalk | 64 N. Main St. (West Ave.) | 203-866-7492 | www.kazusono.com

Fish "so fresh it's still flappin'" and "inventive" chefs who double as "magnets – they draw people back all year" – make this "swanky" Japanese "crowd-pleaser" the place where "sushi begins and ends" in South Norwalk; "tasty" "cooked dishes" and bento boxes fill out the midpriced menu, so the "energetic" crowd (including "lots of young families") has plenty to choose from.

Kicho *Japanese*   ▽ 17 | 15 | 20 | $38

Bedford Hills | 352 N. Bedford Rd. (Hill St.), NY | 914-666-3332

Opinions are split over this Bedford Hills Japanese set in "spacious" environs in a converted "country home" with outdoor seating in warm weather; pros praise the "innovative sushi combinations", "nice portions" and "good-value" pricing, while cons contend that "quantity tops quality", concluding the "ordinary" fare is best left for "takeout."

King & I Ⓜ *Thai*   21 | 15 | 19 | $28

Bridgeport | Beardsley Park Plaza | 545 Broadbridge Rd. (Huntington Tpke.) | 203-374-2081

Fairfield | 260 Post Rd. (Shoreham Village Dr.) | 203-256-1664
www.kingandict.com

All the "smells whet your appetite" at these "reasonably priced" twin Thais in Bridgeport and Fairfield proffering "authentic", "tasty" fare (including "lots of vegetarian and fish choices") served by "friendly staffers" who "guide you" through the menu; still, they're a puzzlement to some who "want to like them more", while a few dis the "strip-mall" settings.

Kiosko *Mexican*   - | - | - | I

Port Chester | 220 Westchester Ave. (bet Grove & Oak Sts.), NY | 914-933-0155 | www.kioskorestaurant.com

The mole poblanos and huaraches – corn tortillas topped with salsa, cheese and steak, that is – are the signatures at this Port Chester storefront purveying an inexpensive and interesting lineup of regional Mexican specialties throughout the day; the decor is simple but homey, and enlivened by the array of margaritas and sangrias on offer.

	FOOD	DECOR	SERVICE	COST

Kira Sushi *Japanese*

| | 21 | 13 | 17 | $36 |

Armonk | Armonk Town Ctr. | 575 Main St. (School St.), NY | 914-765-0800

Armonk "sushi mavens" say this neighborhood Japanese standby "stacks up" against the competition with "generous portions" of "fresh", "high-quality" fish all "presented nicely" in "plain", strip-mall surroundings; tabs are "not too pricey" either, but longtimers warn that overly "prompt" servers sometimes "hurry you through the meal."

Kisco Kosher *Deli*

| | 19 | 11 | 15 | $22 |

White Plains | 230 E. Post Rd. (bet. Mamaroneck Ave. & S. B'way), NY | 914-948-6600 | www.kiscokosher.com

Noshers in need of a "pastrami fix" head to this White Plains delicatessen where "quality" smoked meats are piled into "colossal", "overstuffed" sandwiches served in surroundings with "no decor – except the Yankee game on TV"; true, maybe the tastes "will never rival the old days" on the "Lower East Side", but diehards insist that for the area, "it's as good as it gets."

Kit's Thai Kitchen *Thai*

| | 22 | 11 | 18 | $24 |

Stamford | Turn of the River Shopping Ctr. | 927 High Ridge Rd. (Cedar Heights Rd.) | 203-329-7800 | www.kitsthaikitchen.com

"If you're fit to be Thai'd", this "fortunate find" – "one of North Stamford's few ethnic food fixes" – features "mouthwatering drunken noodles" and other "authentic" dishes; the "line can be out the door" for a table in its "tiny" strip-mall digs (look for the "ghastly" "yellowish-green" facade) and seating on the "lovely terrace" is also "limited", leading surveyors to suggest "takeout as the best bet."

Kobis Japanese Steak House *Japanese*

| | 19 | 19 | 19 | $34 |

Fairfield | 451 Kings Hwy. E. (bet. Jennings Rd. & Shepard St.) | 203-610-6888

Shelton | 514 Bridgeport Ave. (bet. Todd Rd. & Woodland Park) | 203-929-8666

www.kobisrestaurant.com

Get set for an "adventure" at these "consistent" Japanese steakhouses in Fairfield and Shelton where it's "fun watching the chefs perform" and the koi cavort in indoor ponds; most find the food "good" (if a bit "pricey"), though impatient types warn the "wait for hibachi can be long" – and so can everything else, thanks to service that's "a little lacking."

Koji *Japanese*

| | ▽ 19 | 15 | 17 | $29 |

Hartford | 17 Asylum St. (Main St.) | 860-247-5654 | www.hellokoji.com

"Who doesn't love meat on a stick?" ponder partisans of the "tasty" yakitori (and sushi) at this Hartford Japanese, a "hip" "hot spot" where the "lively clientele" knocks back "low-cost" "sake-tinis" and appetizers during the "best happy hour around"; it gets "loud" as it gets late, so "try it on a weeknight" when it's less "busy."

	FOOD	DECOR	SERVICE	COST

Kona Grill *American/Asian* `17` `19` `15` `$33`
Stamford | Stamford Town Ctr. | 230 Tresser Blvd. (Greyrock Pl.) |
203-324-5700 | www.konagrill.com
Sip with the "hip crowd" during this Downtown Stamford chain link's
"reverse happy hours", when the "indoor/outdoor bar" becomes a
"happening singles scene"; savvy surveyors who'd rather hook up
with food suggest the "creative appetizers" and "flavorful sushi" as
good bets on its "hit-or-miss" American-Asian menu, and though
most dig the "pleasant decor", some say it seems like "every waiter
is working his first day on the job."

Koo *Japanese* `23` `19` `18` `$49`
Danbury | 29 E. Pembroke Rd. (Hayestown Rd.) | 203-739-0068
Ridgefield | 470 Main St. (Prospect St.) | 203-431-8838
Rye | 17 Purdy Ave. (2nd St.), NY | 914-921-9888
A "cool" clientele convenes at these Westchester and Connecticut
Japanese outfits where "jazzy sushi rolls" and "inventive" mains are
matched with creative cocktails and sake in modern, "upscale" environs; proponents proclaim they "deliver the goods", though a minority grouses that "too-pricey" tabs and occasionally "slow"
service detract from an otherwise "on-the-mark" experience.

Kotobuki Ⓜ *Japanese* `23` `12` `19` `$35`
Stamford | 457 Summer St. (bet. Broad & North Sts.) | 203-359-4747 |
www.kotobukijapaneserestaurant.com
The "friendly" staffers really "know what they're doing" at chef-
owner Masanori Sato's long-standing Stamford Japanese, which
hooks "sushi-lovers" with the "freshest fish in town"; factor in the
"reasonable prices", and it's no wonder fans keep returning to this
"unassuming" storefront "again and again", shrugging off the
"almost depressing decor."

Kudeta *Asian* `21` `23` `20` `$41`
New Haven | 27 Temple St. (N. Frontage Rd.) | 203-562-8844 |
www.kudetanewhaven.com
There's "a lot going on" at this "trippy" New Haven Asian fusion,
from a "dazzling array" of "delicious" "food with a twist" to "cutting-
edge decor" featuring "lights in a constant state of flux" and "relent-
less techno music"; some wish the proprietors would just "tone it
down a notch" (particularly those "expensive prices"), but "friendly,
unintrusive" service makes it all go down easier.

Kujaku *Japanese* `17` `13` `16` `$36`
Stamford | 84 W. Park Pl. (Summer St.) | 203-357-0281 |
www.kujakustamford.com
"If you like knife-throwing", this "convenient" Downtown Stamford
Japanese puts on a "fun" "hibachi show" and offers "relatively inexpensive sushi" to boot; however, critics deem the decor "early-attic"
and the experience "good for the kids . . . and that's about it."

Kumo *Japanese* ▽ `22` `22` `18` `$30`
Hamden | 218 Skiff St. (Whitney Ave.) | 203-281-3166

(continued)

Kumo

New Haven | 7 Elm St. (State St.) | 203-562-6688
www.kumojapaneserestaurant.com

"If you want a knife show" at a "hibachi grill", these Japanese performers in Hamden and New Haven are "fun, particularly if you bring kids or have a lot to drink" (plus there's "good sushi at great prices"); one thing that doesn't cut it, however, is the "variable service."

La Bocca *Italian*

| 22 | 19 | 20 | $53 |

White Plains | Renaissance Corporate Ctr. | 8 Church St.
(bet. Hamilton Ave. & Main St.), NY | 914-948-3281 |
www.laboccaristorante.com

"Traditional" Italian cooking gets "modern" twists at this Downtown White Plains spot set inside the Renaissance Corporate Center in a "cozy" space with stone-and-tile decorative touches; yes, it's expensive, but "warm" service from "congenial" host-owner Tony Spiritoso imparts a "welcoming" vibe, and oenophiles toast the "moderate" selections on the wine list.

La Bretagne 🗷 *French*

| 22 | 16 | 23 | $52 |

Stamford | 2010 W. Main St. (bet. Harvard Ave. & Havemeyer Ln.) |
203-324-9539 | www.labretagnerestaurant.com

"It's been around since the Pilgrims" (well, 1976), but this "classic" Stamford French still dishes up "wonderful" standards like duck à l'orange – "expertly carved tableside" by an "attentive" staff; but whippersnappers whine that the "old-style" ambiance, "tired" decor and sea of "blue hair" would "make your grandmother feel young."

La Crémaillère 🅼 *French*

| 26 | 26 | 26 | $82 |

Bedford | 46 Bedford-Banksville Rd. (Round House Rd.), NY |
914-234-9647 | www.cremaillere.com

"La crème de la crème" of Bedford, this longtime "charmer" pampers guests with "professional" service and "delectable" "classic French" feasts set down in an "enchanting" country-elegant setting; prices aren't recession-friendly, but "rich" regulars and "special-occasion" celebrators find it "worth every penny"; N.B. jackets suggested.

La Cuisine Café, Market & Catering 🅼 *American*

| - | - | - | M |

Branford | 750 E. Main St. (Goldsmith Rd.) | 203-488-7779 |
www.lacuisine.net

This Branford New American cafe from caterer Ben Bloom produces "good sandwiches" (including a mean signature Cuban) and is a "fun spot for lunch" (breakfast too), although its better half may be the market, "which gives you the chance to taste the food at home"; N.B. no hot chow available after 3 PM.

Lady Luck *Pub Food*

| - | - | - | M |

Bridgeport | 2931 Fairfield Ave. (Jetland St.) | 203-572-0372 |
www.ladyluckblackrock.com

Park City denizens feel fortunate to have this New American arrival to the Black Rock area, both for its creative pub food (as in Buffalo chicken egg rolls) and its back-room bands; the vibrant, retro-chic setting is tattoo-themed, with a long stainless-steel bar catering to imbibers looking to watch the game; N.B. its weekly Acoustic Kegs & Eggs is one of Bridgeport's few Sunday brunch options.

Laguna *Italian*
19 | **17** | **18** | **$36**

White Plains | 189 E. Post Rd. (Waller Ave.), NY | 914-428-3377 | www.lagunasignature.com

Red-sauce fanciers frequent this White Plains staple that's "always a solid choice" for "huge", "family-style" portions of "above-average" Italiana; cheery posters of Italy grace Venetian-plastered walls, while the "busy, bustling" atmosphere "makes for a good time", especially for "groups."

La Herradura *Mexican*
- | **-** | **-** | **M**

NEW **Mamaroneck** | 406 Mamaroneck Ave. (Spencer Pl.), NY | 914-630-2377

New Rochelle | 1323 North Ave. (Northfield Rd.), NY | 914-235-3769

New Rochelle | 563 Main St. (Center Ave.), NY | 914-235-2055

These New Rochelle Mexicans, with a sibling that arrived recently on Mamaroneck's theater-and-restaurant row, are popular choices for enchiladas, fajitas and other south-of-the-border standards offered at moderate cost; decorations including horseshoes (as the name translates), cacti and sombreros add to the fiesta feel – as do the free-flowing margaritas, *naturalmente*.

NEW Lalo's *Mexican*
- | **-** | **-** | **I**

Hartford | 860 Maple Ave. (Chapman St.) | 860-956-4762

This Mexican newcomer in Hartford's South End recently reopened after going dark for a while as it was awaiting its liquor license; it's firing on all cylinders now, meaning patrons who venture here can order a cerveza with their enchiladas and fajitas, at very reasonable prices to boot.

La Manda's ⊄ *Italian*
18 | **6** | **14** | **$28**

White Plains | 251 Tarrytown Rd. (Dobbs Ferry Rd.), NY | 914-684-9228

It's a "throwback to a bygone era" at this White Plains Italian "institution" that "hasn't changed in 50 years" with "charmingly dingy decor" and "longtime waitresses" lending it a certain "nostalgic" appeal; expect pizza plus all the "classics, done well" and well priced, just "don't try anything fancy" – vets advise you stick with "anything in gravy" or their "incomparable" pork chops with peppers.

Lansdowne *Pub Food*
- | **-** | **-** | **M**

New Haven | 179 Crown St. (bet. Church & Temple Sts.) | 203-285-3939 | www.lansdownect.com

On weekends, this New Haven watering hole's long, polished wood bar is packed, as are the booths sporting flat-screen TVs, while the dance floor is going full-tilt boogie; its popularity is due in part to the drinks and Traditional American pub grub that are generously served at moderate rates.

FOOD | DECOR | SERVICE | COST

La Paella ⓜ *Spanish*

25 | 18 | 23 | $38

Norwalk | 44 Main St. (Burnell Blvd.) | 203-831-8636 | www.lapaellatapaswinebarrestaurant.com

"The name says it all" (yes, the "paella is excellent"), but the "small plates shine in a big way" too at this "intimate" Norwalk Spanish serving "flavorful" fare paired with an "extensive wine list"; adding to the "homey" vibe is Jaime Lopez, the "gracious" chef-owner who ensures you "enjoy a fine meal that's easy on the wallet."

La Panetière *French*

27 | 27 | 27 | $80

Rye | 530 Milton Rd. (Oakland Beach Ave.), NY | 914-967-8140 | www.lapanetiere.com

"Impeccable" sums up this "refined" Rye "grande dame" where "exquisite" New French creations are backed by a "voluminous" (900-label) wine list; "meticulous attention to detail" shows in its "superior" service that "never fails to impress" and "gracious" flower-filled setting, so "if you want to break the bank for a memorable dinner", don a jacket and do it here.

La Piccola Casa *Italian*

▽ 20 | 13 | 22 | $48

Mamaroneck | James Fenimore Cooper Hse. | 410 W. Boston Post Rd. (Fenimore Rd.), NY | 914-777-3766 | www.lapiccolacasa.com

This Mamaroneck casa pleases patrons with "nicely prepared" Northern Italian specialties from a menu offering "plenty of options"; the "staff works hard" to keep the mood "relaxed" – an easier job now that the quarters are no longer so *piccola* following a move to roomier digs.

Larchmont Tavern *American*

17 | 13 | 16 | $26

Larchmont | 104 Chatsworth Ave. (bet. Boston Post Rd. & Palmer Ave.), NY | 914-834-9821 | www.larchmonttavern.com

"Local charm" abounds at this longtime Larchmont "favorite" – "affectionately known as The LT" – slinging "authentically greasy tavern food" like burgers and roast-beef sandwiches since 1933; on the downside, some lament that the "noisy" TVs in the dining area upset the otherwise "hospitable" vibe.

La Riserva *Italian*

▽ 18 | 13 | 18 | $47

Larchmont | 2382 Boston Post Rd. (Deane Pl.), NY | 914-834-5584 | www.lariservarestaurant.com

On the scene since 1977, this "family-run" Larchmont Italian still attracts "lots of regulars" for "consistent" Northern-style fare served by "longtime" staffers who greet patrons "by name"; yet, in spite of its "big following", even fans find the "tired" decor could use sprucing up.

La Taverna ⓜ *Italian*

22 | 16 | 22 | $37

Norwalk | Broad River Shopping Ctr. | 130 New Canaan Ave. (I-95, exit 15) | 203-849-8879

They "always treat you like family" at this Norwalk Northern Italian, where the "humble setting" and "generous portions" of orecchiette with meatballs makes you feel "like you're eating in grandma's kitchen"; though it "doesn't look like much from the outside", most agree it's a "fun place" with "fair prices."

La Tavola ⊠ *Italian*
- | - | - | E

Waterbury | 702 Highland Ave. (bet. Bennett & Wilkenda Aves.) | 203-755-2211 | www.latavolaristorante.com

Chef-owner Nicola Mancini's signature braised veal shank and handmade pastas have won over Italian cuisine lovers, making this Waterbury's table-to-be-seen-at; with sexy dark wood and warm lighting, it's an ideal date place, so make a reservation, dress your best and pack your platinum plastic.

Latin American Cafe *Cuban*
∇ 20 | 10 | 18 | $26

White Plains | 134 E. Post Rd. (Mamaroneck Ave.), NY | 914-948-6606 | www.latinamericanmenu.com

When you can't get to "Havana or Miami", there's always this "no-frills" Downtown White Plains Cuban cooking up "tasty, authentic" fare like roast pork, beans and rice; though it's favored for "takeout", in back there's a "cozy" dining area staffed by a "friendly" crew – it's certainly "not fancy", but at least the "price is right"; N.B. it serves beer and a short list of wines from California, Chile and Spain.

La Villetta ⊠ *Italian*
25 | 17 | 23 | $58

Larchmont | 7 Madison Ave. (N. Chatsworth Ave.), NY | 914-833-9416

Father and son team Francesco and Pasquale Coli are behind this "wonderful" "neighborhood Italian" that "shines" in Larchmont thanks to "beautifully prepared" pastas, "excellent" seafood dishes and desserts that are "hard to skip"; despite "steep" pricing, it earns points for its "intimate" atmosphere and service that's especially "personable" – "go a few times, and they remember you."

Layla's Falafel *Lebanese*
23 | 5 | 17 | $14

Fairfield | 2088 Black Rock Tpke. (Stillson Rd.) | 203-384-0100
Stamford | 936 High Ridge Rd. (Cedar Heights Rd.) | 203-461-8004
www.laylasfalafel.com

The "atmosphere is nothing to write home about", but few seem to care when it comes to this "family-run" Lebanese duo in Fairfield and Stamford; the "lovingly made" fare includes "excellent chicken shawarma" and some of the area's "best hummus and tabbouleh" at "can't-be-beat" prices – but with "just a few tables", many say it's "better as takeout."

La Zingara *Italian*
25 | 21 | 22 | $47

Bethel | 8 P.T. Barnum Sq. (Greenwood Ave.) | 203-744-7500 | www.lazingararistorante.com

"Get your map and find your way" to this Italian "charmer" in "tiny" Bethel, where surveyors say there's "never an off night" because the "chef is always on" (check out the "superb" duck pappardelle); if it gets "noisy" inside, you can retreat to the "romantic" "covered patio", a "beautiful" spot to enjoy "terrific" Sunday brunches ($26) with jazz and "all-you-can-drink Bellinis" and Bloody Marys; N.B. closed Tuesdays.

	FOOD	DECOR	SERVICE	COST

Lazy Boy Saloon ● *Pub Food*
17 13 14 $24

White Plains | 154 Mamaroneck Ave. (bet. E. Post Rd. & Maple Ave.),
NY | 914-761-0272 | www.lazyboysaloon.com

A "huge selection of beer" (over 40 on tap, nearly 500 by the bottle)
is the main selling point of this White Plains pub also purveying
"better-than-average" grub like burgers and wings, just in case "you
need to fill your stomach"; it's a "noisy" scene, with crowds of
"twentysomethings" and the "big game" on TV adding to the
"sports-bar" vibe.

Le Château Ⓜ *French*
25 28 26 $72

South Salem | 1410 Rte. 35 (Rte. 123), NY | 914-533-6631 |
www.lechateauny.com

Set in a "luxurious" Tudor-style mansion with "breathtaking
views" of the valley, this "expensive" South Salem enclave is a "favorite" for "first-class" "traditional" French cuisine served by a "gracious staff"; it's a bit "dated" to some, but admirers insist it's the
ultimate "place to impress" for a "grown-up, dress-up night out";
N.B. jackets suggested.

NEW Le Farm ⓈⓂ *American*
- - - E

Westport | 256 Post Rd. E. (bet. Campo Rd. & Imperial Ave.) |
203-557-3701 | www.lefarmwestport.com

Chef-owner Bill Taibe (ex Napa & Co.) raises the bar again at this
pricey Westport New American where his farm-to-table approach
now encompasses unique relationships with local growers plus
12 acres of his own on which he's growing rare veggies; surprising the palate seems to be the goal of the ever-evolving menu –
as in the signature dessert, cornbread with candied bacon and
maple chile gelato – while simpatico service and modern farmhouse
decor heighten the experience; N.B. with only 34 seats, reservations
are a must.

Le Figaro Bistro de Paris *French*
20 20 18 $52

Greenwich | 372 Greenwich Ave. (Grigg St.) | 203-622-0018 |
www.figarogreenwich.com

Greenwichers start behaving like Parisians – "two kisses, please" –
at this "wonderfully authentic" "French outpost" where "all the classics are done well", including pommes frites and *"magnifique"*
croque monsieurs; the "pleasant atmosphere" can turn "noisy",
however, and some turn up their noses at "impersonal service" and
prices that are less bistro and more *"gastronomique* wonder."

Le Fontane Ristorante Ⓜ *Italian*
20 19 19 $42

Katonah | 137 Rte. 100 (Rte. 139), NY | 914-232-9619 |
www.lefontane.net

Owner-host Antonio Abbate "brings smiles to every table" at this
"warm" Katonah Italian offering "good value" with its "enjoyable", if "run-of-the-mill", Southern-style fare; the setting is "casual", but those who find the Tuscan-style tiled dining room in
need of an "update" take solace under the awning in the pretty
garden come summer.

	FOOD	DECOR	SERVICE	COST

Legal Sea Foods *Seafood* | 19 | 17 | 18 | $41 |

White Plains | City Ctr. | 5 Mamaroneck Ave. (bet. Main St. & Martine Ave.), NY | 914-390-9600 | www.legalseafoods.com

"Beyond-fresh" fish that would "make Neptune proud" is the bait at this White Plains link of the "family-friendly", Boston-based seafood chain, and though the "straightforward" menu is "not very adventurous", the food's "skillfully prepared"; "midtier" pricing, "can-do" service and that "famous New England clam chowder" make up for the "sterile" setting and "off-putting" crowds with "too many kids."

Lemon Grass *Thai* | 19 | 16 | 20 | $26 |

West Hartford | 7 S. Main St. (Farmington Ave.) | 860-233-4405

"If you like Thai" and "great value", fans say "you could not do better" than this West Hartford "hole-in-the-wall" offering an "extensive menu" of "simple" dishes that allow "flavors to shine through"; then again, an almost equal number of surveyors disagree, citing "so-so food in a dated setting", but a "pleasant staff" works in its favor.

⊠ Lenny & Joe's Fish Tale *Seafood* | 22 | 11 | 17 | $23 |

Madison | 1301 Boston Post Rd./Rte. 1 (Hammonasset Connector) | 203-245-7289

Westbrook | 86 Boston Post Rd. (bet. Grove Beach Rd. & Linden Ave.) | 860-669-0767

www.ljfishtale.com

"Snobs, keep out" of these "hectic" "seafood shacks" with "fabulous lobster rolls" and "well-prepared but simple" "fried fish standards" that are "reasonably priced"; Westbrook offers "table service", a "broader menu" and a bar, while the adventuresome "rough it" at the BYO Madison branch with its "counter service", "paper plates" ("don't expect to impress your date") and seasonal "carousel" that "kids love."

Lenny's Indian Head Inn *Seafood* | 20 | 16 | 17 | $30 |

Branford | 205 S. Montowese St. (2 mi. south of Main St.) | 203-488-1500 | www.lennysnow.com

It finally accepts plastic, meaning you no longer have to "bring cash" to enjoy this "classic" Branford fish house's "basic lobster dinners" and "ample portions" of "fried" clams, scallops and oysters covered in a "light, crispy coating", all served by a "friendly" staff; longtimers lament it's "gotten pricey", though, and the "wait in summer can be forever" in "noisy surroundings."

Leon's *Italian* | - | - | - | E |

New Haven | 501 Long Wharf Dr. (Water St./Rte. 1) | 203-562-5366 | www.leonsrestaurant.com

This venerable New Haven Italian has been serving up a version of chef-owner Edward Varipapa's signature gypsy chicken and roasted rack of lamb since 1938, but it's become a bit more atmospheric following a recent move to the former Rusty Scupper space on Long Wharf Drive, overlooking the Sound; a $20 early-bird special and live music on weekends are further enticements.

	FOOD	DECOR	SERVICE	COST

☑ Le Petit Cafe ⓜ *French*   28 | 23 | 27 | $55

Branford | 225 Montowese St. (Main St.) | 203-483-9791 |
www.lepetitcafe.net

"Personable" chef-owner Roy Ip "turns out exquisite French food" "presented elegantly" in his "sophisticated", "tiny" Branford bistro, including "homemade truffle butter on warm bread" so "sublime" you'll "want to sneak into the kitchen and take some home"; even better, the "extraordinary" "four-course prix fixe menu" ($48.50) is an "unbelievable bargain", leading a legion of loyalists to declare it's "one of the best meals you'll eat on the shoreline – at any price."

Le Provençal Bistro *French*   23 | 19 | 21 | $49

Mamaroneck | 436 Mamaroneck Ave. (bet. Mt. Pleasant & Palmer Aves.), NY | 914-777-2324 | www.provencalbistro.com

Everything "a bistro should be", this "delightful" Mamaroneck French earns praise for its "approachable" menu of "heartwarming" fare, "excellent wines" and "inviting" atmosphere; it can be "costly", but it pays off with "warm" service and a "wonderful spirit" that makes it a "keeper"; P.S. the all-you-can-eat mussels special (Sundays–Wednesdays) is "the big bargain" here.

☑ L'Escale *French*   23 | 25 | 21 | $65

Greenwich | Delamar Hotel | 500 Steamboat Rd. (I-95, exit 3) | 203-661-4600 | www.lescalerestaurant.com

It's the "attractive scenery (both the clientele and water views)" that cops the top props at this "l'upscale" French in Greenwich's "luxury" Delamar Hotel, where the "old-money-meets-hedge-fund" set "feels like royalty" sitting outdoors savoring the signature seafood bouillabaisse or "wonderful" brunch; "feh" say dissatisfied sorts who find the food "overpriced" and "over-fussy" and the "singles crowd" "a bit much."

Lime *Health Food*   23 | 10 | 20 | $29

Norwalk | 168 Main Ave. (Center Ave.) | 203-846-9240 | www.limerestaurant.com

Despite its "awesome Gorgonzola steak" and "well-prepared fish dishes", this Norwalk "hangout for the healthy set" is an "easy-on-the-wallet" "vegetarian's delight" too, with "tasty stir fry" ("not just tofu") and "delicious" soups and salads; "small, unattractive" and "cramped", however, it's "not a place for claustrophobes."

NEW Limoncello ⓜ *Italian*   - | - | - | E

Mamaroneck | 974 E. Boston Post Rd. (Stuart Ave.), NY | 914-630-2311 | www.limoncellony.com

The historic 19th-century Mamaroneck stagecoach stop that was last Tollgate Steakhouse has been revamped into this upscale Italian; a sun-colored, striped awning beckons diners into a warm setting featuring multiple rooms on two levels, plus a bar and lounge, all sporting Venetian plaster and Carrera marble and offering signatures like sausage-sprinkled rigatoni Calabrese and arancini (Sicilian deep-fried rice balls).

Little Kitchen *Asian*
| 22 | 20 | 18 | $32 |

Westport | Compo Acres Shopping Ctr. | 423 Post Rd. E. (N. Compo Rd.) |
203-227-2547

You can "live large" on "heavenly shrimp dumplings" and other
"creative" comestibles from the "ever-changing menu" at this
chef-owned Westport Pan-Asian that's "little in name only";
you'll need to "keep an eye out" to find its "strip-mall" locale, which
belies the interior's "beautiful" decor "with food plated to match";
just beware of prices that even some supporters call "expensive
for the portions."

Little Mark's Big BBQ *BBQ*
| 20 | 11 | 19 | $20 |

Vernon | 226 Talcottville Rd. (north of Dobson Rd.) | 860-872-1410 |
www.littlemarksbbq.com

This "no-frills" BBQ joint in Vernon "hits the mark" with *Flintstones*-
sized beef ribs and melt-in-your-mouth onion rings" ("bring lots of
Wet-Naps") at "bargain prices"; sure, the "decor is a bit lacking",
but as non-aesthetes aver, "you can't eat atmosphere"; N.B. serves
beer and wine only.

Little Mexican Cafe ◐ *Mexican*
| 22 | 12 | 18 | $23 |

New Rochelle | 581 Main St. (Centre Ave.), NY | 914-636-3926 |
www.littlemexicancafe.com

Enthusiasts adore this funky New Rochelle "gem of a Mexican cafe"
where the "authentic" eats – like "wonderful" tortas – are made
from "fresh ingredients" and served with "terrific margaritas"; despite its "simple" setting on an "ungentrified" block, regulars keep
returning to sample the "cheap" *comida*.

NEW Little Pub *Pub Food*
| - | - | - | I |

Ridgefield | 59 Ethan Allen Hwy. (Rte. 102) | 203-544-9222 |
www.littlepub.com

Bargain-hunters are beating a path to the Branchville section of
Ridgefield, where this newcomer right next to the train station offers
Euro-style pub staples like fish 'n' chips and shepherd's pie, plus a
few trendier items like ahi tuna tacos, many priced under $10; fur-
ther endearments are the 45-strong beer list (including a gluten-
free option), organic wines and a cozy atmosphere enhanced by a
couple of fireplaces – no wonder its 38 seats are always filled.

Little Thai Kitchen *Thai*
| 23 | 15 | 19 | $30 |

Darien | 4 West Ave. (Boston Post Rd./Rte. 1) | 203-662-0038
Greenwich | 21 St. Roch Ave. (Gerry St.) | 203-622-2972
NEW Little Buddha *Thai*
Stamford | 2270 Summer St. (Bridge St.) | 203-356-9166
Thai Spice *Thai*
Norwalk | 345 Main Ave. (Linden St.) | 203-846-3533
www.littlethaikitchen.com

"It's clearly the food that's brought success" to these "tiny, terrific"
and "reasonably priced" Thais, whose "amazing pad Thai" and other
"authentic" fare have boosters boasting that it's like "eating in
Bangkok"; they're a "little cramped", making them "excellent for

takeout", but if you opt to eat on-premises you'll find the service "fast and friendly"; N.B. the Stamford branch opened post-Survey.

Liv's Oyster Bar *Seafood*

24 | 23 | 21 | $44

Old Saybrook | 166 Main St. (Maplewood St.) | 860-395-5577 | www.livsoysterbar.com

With its "wonderful setting in an old movie theater" (1930) in a supporting role, this "chic" chef-owned Old Saybrook standout wins applause as a "step up in sophistication from the standard shoreline fish house"; the signature "seared local scallops" and, natch, "excellent fresh oysters" highlight a "thoughtfully conceived menu" with "reasonable prices", ample compensation to the few who boo "spotty service" and "deafening noise levels"; N.B. closed Tuesdays.

NEW Lolita Cocina & Tequila Bar ● *Mexican*

- | - | - | E

Greenwich | 230 Mill St. (bet. Henry & Water Sts.) | 203-813-3555 | www.lolitamexican.com

Candle-enhanced dark-and-decadent decor sets the sexy mood at this Greenwich newcomer, where the decidedly haute Mexican dishes are bursting with *sabor,* as in enchiladas stuffed with orange-ancho-glazed lobster, and come in *muy grande* portions; to wash it all down there are some 150 varieties of tequila, as well as margaritas made tableside from a rolling cart stocked with freshly squeezed juices – no wonder early discoverers are wishing they could kept this *cocina* a secret.

Long Ridge Tavern *American*

14 | 19 | 17 | $37

Stamford | 2635 Long Ridge Rd. (Rte. 104) | 203-329-7818 | www.longridgetavern.com

The "roaring fireplace"-enhanced "cozy atmosphere", 50-ft. bar and "live music" on weekends are the lures of this "classic tavern" "where old (and I do mean old) friends meet to eat" in the "back country of Stamford"; alas, even some supporters say the "hit-or-miss" American "comfort food" doesn't do the setting justice, and "off service doesn't help."

Longwood Restaurant ⓜ *American*

▽ 18 | 20 | 20 | $56

Woodbury | Longwood Country Inn | 1204 Main St. S. (bet. Mansion House Rd. & Woodside Circle) | 203-266-0800 | www.longwoodcountryinn.com

It's in the state's antiques capital, so it's fitting that this Woodbury New American is in a "lovely historic building" (circa 1789); still, with food that's "not too fussy or overwrought", "friendly service" and a "serene" garden setting, some seem mystified as to "why it doesn't get more buzz"; N.B. the all-you-can-eat Sunday brunch is $30.

L'Orcio ⓜ *Italian*

23 | 20 | 20 | $47

New Haven | 806 State St. (bet. Eld & Pearl Sts.) | 203-777-6670 | www.lorcio.com

"Old-world peasant Italian" fare that's "sophisticated but not self-conscious" draws those "who care about food" to this "warmly appointed" New Haven row house; the chef-owner's "amazing" pastas (there are as many as nine types made daily) are complemented by "flavorful sauces", but detractors dis "so-so service" and "NYC prices" – which may be easier to shrug off on the "lovely" "garden patio with twinkling lights."

Los Cabos *Mexican*

| 17 | 13 | 17 | $26 |

Norwalk | 36 Westport Ave. (East Ave.) | 203-847-5711 | www.loscabosmexicanfood.com

"Texas-sized Mexican food" (as in "huge servings" "that'll fill up just about anyone") is the kind of "affordable" fare you'll find at this colorful Norwalk hacienda; some enjoy the meandering mariachis, but others shout "just let me enjoy my chimichanga!", while enimigos classify the cuisine as suitable only "for extreme gringos."

Lotus 🗷 🅼 *Vietnamese*

| ∇ 23 | 16 | 18 | $24 |

Vernon | 409 Hartford Tpke. (Merline Rd.) | 860-871-8962

"Top-notch Vietnamese" in Vernon seems unlikely, but this family-run "place fills up fast" thanks to "reasonable prices" and "well-prepared fare" like Saigonese pancakes and spicy soups; so "be prepared to wait for a table" even though it's in "the middle of nowhere."

Lotus Thai Restaurant & Bar *Thai*

| ∇ 20 | 16 | 18 | $24 |

Stratford | Station House Sq. | 2505 Main St. (Broadbridge Ave.) | 203-386-1563 | www.lotusct.com

Don't expect the "usual" at this "charming little" Thai across the street from the Stratford train station, but rather red curry chicken and avocado duck dishes that are "fresh, spicy" and "always good"; still, some say it doesn't live up to a "location that seems to have potential."

Louis' Lunch 🗷 🅼 🚭 *Burgers*

| ∇ 24 | 15 | 14 | $11 |

New Haven | 261-263 Crown St. (bet. College & High Sts.) | 203-562-5507 | www.louislunch.com

If a "basic burger" could be considered a "historical icon", then this "classic dive" in New Haven may well be "its birthplace"; accidentally invented in 1900, the "original hamburger" consists of "excellent ground beef seared in an ancient flame-broiling contraption and served on toast"; a few faultfinders say to expect "maddening crowds" and meals served "with a big side of attitude"; N.B. cash only.

Luca Ristorante Italiano 🗷 *Italian*

| 24 | 21 | 23 | $55 |

Wilton | 142 Old Ridgefield Rd. (Godfrey Pl.) | 203-563-9550 | www.lucaristoranteitaliano.com

"Throw the diet out for the evening" and "order the special pasta" or signature osso buco with a bottle from the "spectacular wine list" at this "romantic" Wilton Italian; it "tries hard to win you over" with "top-notch" food and service ("and usually succeeds"), but just "be prepared to pay New York prices."

🆕 Lucky Lou's Bar & Grill *American*

| – | – | – | M |

Wethersfield | 222 Main St. (Church St.) | 860-257-0700 | www.luckylousbarandgrill.com

Inventive burgers, finger foods and American comfort classics with a twist (think lobster mac 'n' cheese) can be had at affordable prices in Old Wethersfield's beautifully refurbished, circa-1787 Standish House; the more casual downstairs includes a lively bar and flat-screens throughout, while the upstairs offers more formal dining and a pleasant view of historic Main Street.

Lucky's *Diner*   15 | 18 | 16 | $17
Stamford | 209 Bedford St. (bet. Broad & Spring Sts.) | 203-978-0268 | www.luckysrestaurant.net

"Ask your waiter for some nickels for the jukebox", then order the "burger and fries" – and "don't forget the shake!" – at this "cute" *"Happy Days"*-style diner in Downtown Stamford; a "kid-friendly" vibe and "reasonable" prices "seal the deal" for families, but foes fret over "questionable" service and "mediocre" food ("made me feel unlucky"); N.B. staffers sing and dance on weekends.

Luc's Café ⊠ *French*   24 | 20 | 19 | $42
Ridgefield | 3 Big Shop Ln. (bet. Bailey Ave. & Main St.) | 203-894-8522 | www.lucscaferestaurant.com

The "wall clock only displays European time" at this "cozy slice of France" in Ridgefield, but no one's complaining, since the "excellent" French "bistro standards", "understated" decor and "lovely owner" work in tandem to "transport you to Paris"; if there's "not enough elbow room" and the "noisy atmosphere" vexes some – for most it's still a "wonderful place to dine with friends."

Luna Pizza *Pizza*   20 | 12 | 15 | $21
Glastonbury | 88 Hebron Ave. (bet. Main St. & New London Tpke.) | 860-659-2135
Simsbury | Simsbury Commons | 530 Bushy Hill Rd. (Rte. 44) | 860-651-1820 | www.lunapizzasimsbury.com
West Hartford | 999 Farmington Ave. (LaSalle Rd.) | 860-233-1625 | www.lunapizzact.com

Moonstruck stalwarts "love" the "cracker-thin crust" and "large selection" of "generous toppings" on the "excellent" pies at this "casual" trio of "family pizza joints"; still, some say it's just "ok", and "rounding out your meal" with other items is tough unless you're at the cafe in Simsbury, which boasts an extended menu and bar.

Lusardi's *Italian*   24 | 20 | 23 | $57
Larchmont | 1885 Palmer Ave. (bet. Chatsworth Ave. & Weaver St.), NY | 914-834-5555 | www.lusardislarchmont.com

"Ah, perfection" sigh admirers of Larchmont's "elegant but affable" "classic", which weaves "terrific" housemade breads, pastas and Italian-Med mains with "smooth" service; it's "steps above" the standard joint, though some mutter that the intimate rooms (one sporting a fireplace) can get "noisy" and overly "crowded" – to the extent there may be "waits on Saturday nights, even with reservations."

Mackenzie's Grill Room ❷ *Pub Food*   15 | 13 | 16 | $28
Old Greenwich | 148 Sound Beach Ave. (Webb Ave.) | 203-698-0223 | www.mackenziesgrillroom.com

"Locals" make tracks to this "classic neighborhood tavern" convenient to the Old Greenwich train station for "reliable" burgers, ribs and other "well-priced pub food"; "live entertainment" and the "always-special Oktoberfest" abet an already "convivial atmosphere", so most find it easy to overlook the "cliché decor."

Made In Asia *Asian*
21 | 18 | 20 | $31

Armonk | 454 Main St. (bet. Annadale St. & Orchard Dr.), NY | 914-730-3663 | www.madeinasiarestaurant.com

"Creative" Pan-Asian cuisine is the forte of this Armonk eatery dispensing dishes from "Japan, China, Vietnam, Thailand and Malaysia" in "spacious" environs decorated with statuary and opera masks; though servers can be "overwhelmed" when the crowds hit, they're usually "accommodating", especially to kids.

Maestro's *Italian*
∇ 16 | 8 | 16 | $30

New Rochelle | 1329 North Ave. (Quaker Ridge Rd.), NY | 914-636-6813 | www.maestrosit.com

Lots of New Rochelle families frequent this "neighborhood" Italian "joint" for pizzas and "plentiful" portions of "red-sauce" fare, all at "inexpensive" rates; it's nothing fancy, but regulars report it's a godsend "when you don't feel like cooking."

Mamma Francesca *Italian*
16 | 15 | 18 | $32

New Rochelle | 414 Pelham Rd. (bet. Meadow Ln. & Town Dock Rd.), NY | 914-636-1229 | www.mammafrancesca.com

New Rochelle's "City Hall cronies" congregate at this "suburban" Italian "hangout" for "huge bowls of pasta" served in "comfortable", "low-key" surroundings with a view of the marina; service is "accommodating" too, so even if many maintain it's only "mediocre", it remains a "standby" in the area.

Mancuso's *Italian*
∇ 18 | 14 | 18 | $31

Fairfield | 601 Kings Hwy. E. (Fairchild Ave.) | 203-367-5359 | www.mancusos-restaurant.com

"Good value and big portions" attract Fairfielders to this chef-owned Italian known for its "homestyle" take on dishes like chicken scarpariello, frutti di mare and pizza; the "comfortable" if "bland" setting is abetted by an "eager-to-please" staff, though some snap that the youthful "servers show their lack of experience."

Mango's Bar & Grille *Caribbean*
∇ 19 | 19 | 20 | $29

Branford | 988 Main St. (Park Pl.) | 203-483-7700 | www.mangosbarandgrille.com

"You feel as if you're on an island" at this chef-owned Branford Caribbean where the "yummo" "sweet potatoes" ("smashed" or fried) and "cute atmosphere" make the biggest waves; there's a "little bit of everything on the menu", from "good burgers" to "more elegant fare" like macadamia nut-crusted tuna, but it's all rather "ordinary", leading some to suggest "I can cook as well as them."

Manna Dew *Eclectic*
24 | 19 | 21 | $40

Millerton | 54 Main St. (Center St.), NY | 518-789-3570

You'll find "foodies at the tables and Bud drinkers at the bar" in this "congenial", "cosmopolitan" Millerton "oasis" turning out "excel-

	FOOD	DECOR	SERVICE	COST

lent" Eclectic fare based on local ingredients (including some from the garden in back); other attractions include an "amazing assortment of beers" and a "stellar wine list", "competent, efficient" service in an "intimate" space and live music on weekends.

Marc Charles Steakhouse ⊠ *Steak* ▽ 28 | 21 | 26 | $60

Armonk | La Quinta Hotel | 94 Business Park Dr. (Bedford Rd.), NY | 914-273-2700 | www.marccharlessteakhouse.com

From the Opus 465 folks comes this "high-end" steakhouse in the Armonk La Quinta Hotel catering to an expense-account crowd with cowboy cuts and porterhouses, all customizable with sauces and rubs (or a whole lobster tail, should you choose); for less-expensive bites, the lounge offers sandwiches and salads alongside stiff cocktails.

Marianacci's ⊠ *Italian* ▽ 20 | 15 | 18 | $47

Port Chester | 24 Sherman St. (S. Regent St.), NY | 914-939-3450 | www.marianaccis.com

Local customers have been "counting on" this Port Chester Italian and its "well-prepared" renditions of "old-style" dishes for 60 years; despite the steady hand in the kitchen, given the somewhat "high prices", some wish they'd "spruce up" its "dated" green-and-white interior.

Mario's Place *Italian/Steak* 19 | 13 | 18 | $35

Westport | 36 Railroad Pl. (Riverside Ave.) | 203-226-0308

The "club without dues rolls on and on" ("nothing has changed here since 1967, and it's perfect") say loyalists of this "legendary" Italian across from Westport's train station; "locals predominate", and they come for "prime rib and chops" served in "super-human portions" at prices "you can't beat with a stick"; only an outsider would see it as "nothing special", but some do.

Marisa's Ristorante *Italian* 18 | 16 | 18 | $38

Trumbull | 6540 Main St. (bet. Rte. 25 Connector & Stonehouse Rd.) | 203-459-4225 | www.marisastrumbull.com

This "busy" Trumbull Italian draws a crowd for its monthly "comedy club" and "noisy" "party environment"; the food's "good" if "not fancy" (some would say only "ok"), but some reviewers get riled over the dining room's "distracting decor", citing "crazy red chairs in a barnlike setting."

Market Restaurant *American* 23 | 23 | 21 | $57

Stamford | 249 Main St. (bet. Clark St. & Washington Blvd.) | 203-348-8000 | www.marketstamford.com

"Manhattan comes to Stamford" at this "trendy" New American, where "expertly prepared" cocktails complement the seasonal "innovative culinary mix" – including "incredible" desserts like "mini ice cream cones" – and a "sleek interior" helps attract "young professional" types; however, a few find the service "lacking", and even ascetics who assert "we should *all* be on a diet" decry portions they find "ridiculously small" and "overpriced."

	FOOD	DECOR	SERVICE	COST

Mary Ann's *Tex-Mex* | 17 | 11 | 16 | $29

NEW **Stamford** | 184 Summer St. (bet. Broad St. & Tresser Blvd.) | 203-323-8900

Port Chester | 275 Boston Post Rd. (bet. Olivia & S. Regent Sts.), NY | 914-939-8700

www.maryannsmexican.com

"Addictive chips and salsa" are the highlight of this Port Chester spin-off of an NYC cantina, where the rest of the Tex-Mex eats are "decent", if nothing special; still, given "cheap" prices and child-friendly atmosphere, customers "count on it" for an easy meal with the "kids"; N.B. the Stamford branch opened post-Survey.

Masala *Indian* | - | - | - | E

Hartford | 391 Main St. (Capitol Ave.) | 860-882-0900

At this "upscale" Hartford Indian, "well-prepared and interesting regional dishes" like lobster masala showcase "fragrant sauces"; if some say "its aim is higher than its execution", at least the "lovely Downtown space" with exposed-brick walls adorned with saris is a standout.

Z Match *American* | 24 | 22 | 21 | $49

South Norwalk | 98 Washington St. (bet. Main & Water Sts.) | 203-852-1088 | www.matchsono.com

"There's no match for this" "always-evolving" New American in South Norwalk, where co-owner/chef Matt Storch's "inventive" touch is evident "from appetizer to dessert"; take note that the "Manhattan-type atmosphere" comes with "Manhattan-level prices" – and a "cool" crowd nursing "fancy drinks" that can really ratchet up the decibel level.

Matsumoto *Asian* | - | - | - | M

Larchmont | 158 Larchmont Ave. (Addison St.), NY | 914-834-2833

A worthy successor to Larchmont's erstwhile neighborhood Japanese vet, Marimo, this eatery expands on the sushi-bar theme with Asian fusion specialties like tuna pizza; a trickling water wall and a screen of green bamboo make handsome backdrops for lunch and dinner fare that's as strikingly plated as it is priced to move.

NEW **Matthew's** **M** *American* | - | - | - | E

Unionville | 55 Mill St. (S. Main St.) | 860-673-7373 | www.matthews-restaurant.com

Nestled on the western bank of the Farmington River by the Steel Bridge, this upscale Unionville newcomer pampers patrons with an eclectic American menu that's heavy on seafood but also includes the likes of beef Wellington; a patio provides a view of the water and the local artwork on the dining room walls changes monthly, meaning the eyes are entertained along with the palate.

Max-a-Mia *Italian* | 24 | 19 | 21 | $39

Avon | 70 E. Main St. (Waterville Rd./Rte. 10) | 860-677-6299 | www.maxrestaurantgroup.com

At this "Avon outpost of the ever-growing Max group", "suburban sophisticates" go "casual" with "creative" brick-oven pizzas and

	FOOD	DECOR	SERVICE	COST

other "terrific" Italian fare; "families" at the tables and "singles" at the "hot-spot bar" create plenty of "deafening" "hustle and bustle" – which the "well-trained staff" can assuage with "quick" service.

Max Amore Ristorante *Italian*
23 | 21 | 22 | $39

Glastonbury | The Shops at Somerset Sq. | 140 Glastonbury Blvd. (Main St.) | 860-659-2819 | www.maxrestaurantgroup.com
"One of the more reasonably priced members of the Max chain", this "comfortable" "'place to be' in Glastonbury" plies its "fashionable" fans with "dependable", "creative yet down-to-earth" Northern Italian cuisine; "hospitable" servers add to the "boisterous" atmosphere, which can get downright "noisy" when the "strong drinks" and wine start flowing.

☑ Max Downtown *American/Steak*
27 | 24 | 26 | $53

Hartford | City Place | 185 Asylum St. (bet. Ann & Trumbull Sts.) | 860-522-2530 | www.maxrestaurantgroup.com
Considered by connoisseurs to be the "crown jewel of the Max group", this "Downtown Hartford power spot" "consistently delivers" "heaven on a plate" in the form of "awesome steaks" and "terrific" New American fare coupled with "inspired cocktails" and "fine wines"; "top-notch service" "without snobbery" and "elegant" yet "comfortable" environs are two more reasons why it's "totally worth" the "pricey" tabs.

Max Fish *Seafood*
24 | 23 | 23 | $48

Glastonbury | 110 Glastonbury Blvd. (bet. Main St. & Naubuc Ave.) | 860-652-3474 | www.maxrestaurantgroup.com
Glastonbury's "sophisticated fish house" nets finatics with "consistently superb", "pricey" seafood that includes "ever-changing" raw-bar selections; the staff and "built-to-be-green" kitchen "hum with efficiency", but "as with others in the Max chain", the "aesthetically pleasing" space – comprising the "casual, white-tiled" Shark Bar and the "dimly lit", "white-tablecloth dining room" – "gets loud during busy times."

☑ Max's Oyster Bar *Seafood*
25 | 23 | 23 | $50

West Hartford | 964 Farmington Ave. (S. Main St.) | 860-236-6299 | www.maxrestaurantgroup.com
"Often filled to the max", this "sublime" seafooder in West Hartford features a "loud", "happening" bar where "yupscale singles" slurp "exotic" cocktails and a "grand choice of oysters"; in the dining area, burgundy booths help create a "Rat Pack"-like atmosphere, while "attentive" staffers "guide you to what's best" among the "expensive", "extra-fresh" fish; P.S. "outdoor dining in the summer is a plus."

☑ Mayflower Inn & Spa *American*
25 | 27 | 25 | $73

Washington | The Mayflower Inn & Spa | 118 Woodbury Rd./Rte. 47 (Rte. 199) | 860-868-9466 | www.mayflowerinn.com
"Dress your best here, folks, otherwise you'll feel like the help" at this "over-the-top" "dining experience" in Washington's "plush" Relais & Châteaux inn/spa, where "pampering and primping" meet

FOOD DECOR SERVICE COST

"outstanding" New American cuisine; an "attentive" staff makes you "feel royal" in the "exquisite surroundings", and while a few find all the fuss "too precious for words" and the menu "in need of some spark", the majority says it's worth the "astronomic prices" for a "treat with all the frills."

McKinney & Doyle
Fine Foods Cafe Ⓜ *American*   25 | 18 | 23 | $38

Pawling | 10 Charles Colman Blvd. (E. Main St.), NY | 845-855-3875 | www.mckinneyanddoyle.com

"Patrons wait cheerfully" for a table at this "happening" Pawling "treasure" showcasing chef-owner Shannon McKinney's "exciting twists" on New American fare and "amazing" "fresh-baked breads"; the "on-the-ball staff" serves "with a smile" in the "whimsical", "country-style" room, while "value for money" explains the "crowds in this tough economy"; P.S. you "can't beat the brunches."

Mediterranean Grill *Mediterranean*   19 | 19 | 20 | $46

Wilton | Stop & Shop Plaza | 5 River Rd. (Old Ridgefield Rd.) | 203-762-8484 | www.mediterraneangrillwilton.com

"Close your eyes" and the "flavorful, well-prepared" Mediterranean cuisine at this "reliable favorite" will have you thinking "you're on the Riviera" – instead of a "nice patio" in a Wilton "strip mall"; the "lovely" ambiance and "big-city" service continue inside, though a few disenchanted diners snarl about "stellar price tags" for a place that "doesn't live up to its reputation."

Mediterraneo *Mediterranean*   22 | 19 | 19 | $48

Greenwich | 366 Greenwich Ave. (Grigg St.) | 203-629-4747 | www.mediterraneoofgreenwich.com

"Delicious" fish and thin-crust pizza come out of the brick oven at this "lovely" Mediterranean on Greenwich's "main drag", where there's "good people-watching" from the "outdoor seating"; "whimsical" decor and a "pleasant" staff add to the "overall fun experience", though some subtract points for "expensive" prices and an "uncomfortable noise level" (you better "like screaming at people").

Meetinghouse
Food and Spirits Ⓜ *American*   18 | 16 | 17 | $38

Bedford Village | 635 Old Post Rd./Rte. 22 (Court Rd.), NY | 914-234-5656 | www.meetinghouserestaurant.com

"Mobs" of moviegoers gather at this "homey" Bedford bistro whose proximity to the Playhouse also makes it a "quick-bite" "standby" for "pre- or post-theater" meals of burgers and other New American fare; "spotty" service is a sore spot, and the unimpressed suspect that "location" may be its biggest asset.

⊠ Meigas *Spanish*   26 | 22 | 24 | $57

Norwalk | 10 Wall St. (bet. High & Knight Sts.) | 203-866-8800 | www.meigasrestaurant.com

"Superb", "creative" Spanish cuisine and "an equally outstanding wine list" are conveyed by "gracious", "experienced" servers at this Norwalk "sophisticate" – and while it's "not cheap", the $64-per-couple, 10-course tapas tasting proves to be a relatively economical option; some aesthetes "can't get away from the feeling" that they're "in an office building", but the majority finds the "lovely setting" "suitable for both business and romance."

Mei Tzu Asian Cuisine *Asian*   - | - | - | M

East Windsor | 4 Prospect Hill Rd. (Main St.) | 860-254-5797 | www.meitzu.com

Korean, Thai, Vietnamese and sushi are the stars of the far-reaching Pan-Asian menu presented at this East Windsor venture; moderate prices encourage experimentation, while comfy furnishings and Buddhist imagery promote relaxation.

Meli-Melo Crêperie *French*   25 | 11 | 18 | $22

Greenwich | 362 Greenwich Ave. (Fawcett Pl.) | 203-629-6153 | www.melimelogreenwich.com

"Squeeze yourself" into this "teeny-tiny" Greenwich French "favorite" for "fab crêpes" that come in "tons of choices", "incredible" daily soup specials and "delicious homemade sorbets"; "great prices" are another reason devotees discount the "elbow-to-elbow seating" and "funky" atmosphere ("not for the pretentious") – now if only "it could expand next door . . ."

Melting Pot *Fondue*   18 | 18 | 19 | $49

Darien | 14 Grove St. (bet. Brook & Day Sts.) | 203-656-4774
White Plains | 30 Mamaroneck Ave. (bet. Main St. & Martine Ave.), NY | 914-993-6358
www.meltingpot.com

"Change-of-pace" mavens and "do-it-yourself" types are fond of this "novel" fondue franchise for its "interactive" approach, i.e. the chance to "cook your own dinner"; the "long, slow meals" make it appropriate for "first dates" or "large crowds", but while the morsels are "tasty", you'll "end up spending a lot of money" for them (and "leave smelling like oil").

Meson Los Españoles Ⓜ *Spanish*   ▽ 23 | 18 | 24 | $44

White Plains | 135 E. Post Rd. (bet. Court St. & Mamaroneck Ave.), NY | 914-428-8445 | www.mesonlosespanoles.net

For a "quiet, romantic evening" surveyors select this "old-fashioned" White Plains Spaniard specializing in "tasty" tapas, "ample" helpings of paella and other "authentic" Iberian plates; its "lovely", "low-lit" ambiance gets a lift from "personable" service and the addition of guitar players and occasional flamenco dancers on weekends.

Metric Bar & Grill *Eclectic*   - | - | - | M

Bridgeport | 39 Cannon St. (bet. Broad & Main Sts.) | 203-576-6903 | www.themetricbarandgrill.com

Next to the federal courthouse in Downtown Bridgeport resides this chef-owned bistro that "delights" those who've discovered it with a midpriced menu exhibiting Italian, Thai and "Caribbean flair", among other "interesting" Eclectic influences; the exposed-brick environment features works by local artists and "attentive" service.

	FOOD	DECOR	SERVICE	COST

☑ Métro Bis ☒ American `26` `21` `25` `$47`

Simsbury | Simsburytown Shops | 928 Hopmeadow St./Rte. 10
(bet. Massaco St. & Plank Hill Rd.) | 860-651-1908 | www.metrobis.com
Chef-owner Christopher Prosperi is Simsbury's "epicurean star", and
his "cozy" New American bistro boasts a "loyal following" that returns
often to sample the "creative", locally sourced fare; its strip-mall
setting is "not ideal", but if you can get over that, you're in for a
"gourmet" "meal with superb service" (and it's only "a little pricey").

☑ Michael Jordan's Steak House Steak `25` `22` `22` `$62`

Uncasville | Mohegan Sun Casino | 1 Mohegan Sun Blvd. (bet. Rtes. 2 &
32) | 860-862-8600 | www.michaeljordansteakhouse.com
Only a "good day at the table" can fund a "big night out" at this
Mohegan Sun Casino eatery co-owned by it namesake "basketball
wiz" – but "you get what you pay for", namely "fantastic" chops
"cooked to perfection", "generous portions" of "tasty sides" and
"excellent wines"; completing the "classic steakhouse" picture are
"masculine" decor and an "attentive staff."

Michael's Trattoria ☒ Italian `▽ 23` `18` `21` `$36`

Wallingford | 344 Center St. (Main St.) | 203-269-5303 |
www.michaelstrattoria.com
"Great" Northern Italian fare produced in hearty portions makes this
venue a commendable choice in Wallingford; sure, you've "seen better
decor", but when you factor in a chef-owner who often greets his
guests and "live music in the bar" Thursday–Saturday, it's no wonder
"it's getting harder and harder to get a table" in the "tight quarters."

Mighty Joe Young's Steak `16` `19` `17` `$45`

White Plains | 610 W. Hartsdale Ave. (Dobbs Ferry Rd.), NY |
914-428-6868 | www.mightyjoeyoungs.com
"College buddies" hit the "meat market" at the bar while kids ogle the
"game heads on the walls" at this "kitschy", "theme-park" steakhouse in White Plains thriving in "noisy", "hectic" digs; after a 2008
chef and menu change, surveyors report a "downhill" slide, insisting
the "lackluster" eats ultimately don't live up to the "expensive" tabs.

Mill on the River Continental `23` `24` `21` `$35`

South Windsor | 989 Ellington Rd./Rte. 30 (Beldon Rd.) | 860-289-7929 |
www.themillontheriver.com
The Continental fare served at this "enchanting old mill" in South
Windsor is "delightful", but its views of a pond and gazebo are downright "swoon"-worthy; though it has that "banquet/wedding feel" (it
hosts its share of both), "value" prices make it appropriate for "frequent" "casual meals at the bar" and "awesome Sunday brunches."

NEW Milonga Argentinean/Italian `-` `-` `-` `E`

North White Plains | 577 N. Broadway (Fisher Ln.), NY | 914-358-1444 |
www.milongarestaurant.com
Argentina meets Italy in North White Plains at this new, elegantly
appointed wine-and-tapas place where Latin-leaning small plates
(empanadas, quesadillas, ceviche) pair with mojitos and South

American vino in a deep-red, TV-bedecked bar; the more formal dining room proffers a comprehensive, pricey, Italo-heavy menu listing something to please everyone in the usually quiet crowd.

Miso *Japanese*

23 | 22 | 21 | $38

New Haven | 15 Orange St. (bet. Crown & George Sts.) | 203-848-6472 | www.misorestaurant.com

"Perfectly executed" "sushi and sashimi" have loyalists lauding this "cool" New Haven Japanese, although the cooked "specialties are much more than an afterthought"; "relaxed and spacious", the setting gives you a "feeling of dining out, not just eating out", but beware: you'll leave with "a dent in your pocket."

⚡ Modern Apizza Ⓜ *Pizza*

25 | 11 | 17 | $19

New Haven | 874 State St. (Humphrey St.) | 203-776-5306 | www.modernapizza.com

"In the great New Haven pizza debate", aficionados insist this stalwart (since 1934) offers "more choices and shorter lines"; many feel the thin-crust pies "made the old-world way" and "laden" with "delicious toppings" are, like the competition's, "fantastic", just as service is similarly "average" and the setting is equally "plain."

Modern Restaurant & Pizzeria *Italian*

21 | 10 | 18 | $25

New Rochelle | 12 Russell Ave. (Main St.), NY | 914-633-9479 | www.modernrestaurantandpizzeria.com

"Modern, it ain't", but this New Rochelle "hole-in-the-wall" is a "find" for "thin-crust" pizzas fired in an old-fashioned brick oven plus "comforting" Southern Italian standards; prices are a "good value" too, so as long as you "don't expect atmosphere", you'll leave "satisfied."

🆕 Molly Spillane's *American*

16 | 15 | 19 | $28

Mamaroneck | 211 Mamaroneck Ave. (Prospect Ave.), NY | 914-899-3130 | www.mollyspillanespub.com

This sister to the Eastchester sports bar Mickey Spillane's opened in Mamaroneck post-Survey, perfect for "drinks and a quick nosh"; it offers much the same inexpensive American "grill standards" as its big brother, served amid satellite TVs blaring the big game.

Morello Bistro *Italian*

- | - | - | E

Greenwich | 253 Greenwich Ave. (W. Elm St.) | 203-661-3443 | www.morellobistro.com

Since taking over Gaia's stunning digs in a former Greenwich Avenue bank, this eatery has made its mark with Italian-leaning bistro fare like sautéed branzino and roasted veal chops and a wine list featuring some 750 vinos from around the globe; while they sip and sup, diners can ogle the dramatic amber-tiled arched ceilings, exposed brick, atmospheric mezzanines and large, lively bar.

Morgans Fish House *Seafood*

24 | 22 | 22 | $60

Rye | 22 Elm Pl. (bet. Purchase St. & Theodore Fremd Ave.), NY | 914-921-8190 | www.morgansfishhouse.net

A "well-heeled" "yuppie" crowd fills this "flashy" Rye seafooder that "rivals Manhattan" with its "first-class" fish, "innovative cocktails" and "modern" aquamarine-and-glass decor exuding a "SoHo" feel; service is beyond "accommodating", but be prepared for "splurge"-worthy pricing, along with "noisy" acoustics.

☑ Morton's The Steakhouse *Steak*   24 | 21 | 23 | $68

Hartford | 852 Main St. (Asylum St.) | 860-724-0044
Stamford | UBS Investment Bank | 377 N. State St. (Elm St.) | 203-324-3939
White Plains | 9 Maple Ave. (Bloomingdale Rd.), NY | 914-683-6101
www.mortons.com

"Consistency abounds" at this "old-school" steakhouse chain pairing "well-prepared" chops that fairly "hang off the plate" with "seriously powerful martinis"; "arm-and-a-leg" pricing comes with the territory, along with a "Saran-wrapped presentation" of raw meats (accompanied by an instructional "recitation" by the waiter) – a "shtick" that many find "tired."

Mo's New York Grill Ⓜ *American*   21 | 19 | 21 | $58

New Rochelle | 14 Memorial Hwy. (bet. Huguenot & Main Sts.), NY | 914-632-1442 | www.mosnewyorkgrill.com

"Any Yankee fan would love" this "upscale" New Rochelle American by All-Star pitcher Mariano Rivera and serving "well-presented" steaks and chops in "masculine" wood-trimmed environs decorated with "cool" memorabilia; indeed, it's "worth it" just for the "chance to see Mo" in the flesh; N.B. post-Survey, prices were taken down and more seafood and pasta were added to the menu.

Mulino's of Westchester ❶☒ *Italian*   25 | 23 | 24 | $65

White Plains | 99 Court St. (Quarropas St.), NY | 914-761-1818 | www.mulinosny.com

"Power-lunchers" and "special-occasion" celebrants convene at this "glitzy" White Plains Italian for "ambitious, upscale" meals served by a staff that's always "a whisper away"; granted, it's "expensive", but "worth paying the extra cash" given touches like "complimentary antipasti" and a "waterfall"-equipped garden; P.S. it's "especially beautiful at Christmas" when they "go all out" on the decorations.

Murasaki *Japanese*   ▽ 19 | 14 | 16 | $36

West Hartford | 23 LaSalle Rd. (Farmington Ave.) | 860-236-7622 | www.murasakijapaneserestaurant.com

This "cramped" "keyhole of a space" in a "convenient" West Hartford locale "fills up fast" with devotees of "fine sushi", tempura and other Japanese fare – no wonder it's been around for two decades now; still, even those who appreciate how "fresh" everything is "wish the prices were cheaper."

Myrna's Mediterranean Bistro *Mideastern*   21 | 12 | 20 | $30

Stamford | 866 E. Main St. (N. State St.) | 203-325-8736 | www.myrnas.com

You're "part of the family" at this Stamford Middle Eastern, whose devotees are "hooked" on its "welcoming" vibe and "absolutely delicious" "classics like hummus and tabbouleh", followed by "mouthwatering baklava"; a post-Survey expansion may outdate the above

	FOOD	DECOR	SERVICE	COST

Decor score – and hopefully addressed complaints about decor that was "not too pretty."

Mystic Pizza *Pizza*

| 17 | 14 | 16 | $20 |

Mystic | 56 W. Main St. (Bank St.) | 860-536-3700

Mystic Pizza II *Pizza*

North Stonington | 209 Providence-New London Tpke./Rte. 184 (Norwich Westerly Rd.) | 860-599-3111
www.mysticpizza.com

"Those stuck in the '80s" (and on Julia Roberts) "must stop" at this "reasonably priced" Mystic "tourist trap" or its North Stonington tie-in to check out the "movie memorabilia everywhere" and dig into "average" pizzas served by "cute waitresses" in 'Slice of Heaven' T-shirts; even those who find them as "cheesy" as the pies recommend going "at least once to say you did it."

Z Napa & Co. *American*

| 25 | 23 | 21 | $56 |

Stamford | Courtyard Marriott Hotel | 75 Broad St. (bet. Bedford & Summer Sts.) | 203-353-3319 | www.napaandcompany.com

Known for its "farm-to-fork philosophy", this "transporting" Stamford New American has won raves from respondents for its "terrific", "ever-evolving menu", "amazing cheese selection" and "wall of wine"; yes, it's in a Courtyard Marriott, but "don't let the location" or "uneven service" dissuade you, because devotees declare it's almost a "pleasure to spend money here"; N.B. the recent (post-Survey) departure of founding chef Bill Taibe places the above Food rating in question.

Napoli Sul Fiume *Italian*

| ∇ 16 | 18 | 18 | $49 |

Westport | 5 Riverside Ave. (Post Rd. W.) | 203-221-5000 | www.napolisulfiume.com

"Sit outside" and take in the "beautiful view" of the Saugatuck River to get the best from this waterside Westport Italian with an ever-changing name; while the staff is generally "eager to please", it may be impossible to gratify those who consider the fare "way too expensive" and "lacking soul."

NEW Nat Hayden's Real Pit Barbecue *BBQ*

| - | - | - | M |

Windsor | 226 Broad St. (Maple Ave.) | 860-298-8955 | www.haydensrealbbq.com

This new Windsor pit stop has become an instant hit both with locals and itinerant BBQ mavens, who come for succulent pulled pork, tender St. Louis–style ribs and the requisite Southern sides (don't pass on the pepper-jack grits); friendly owners make eating here all the more enjoyable, but given that it has but 20 seats, takeout may be the best option.

Nautilus Diner ◗ *Diner*

| 15 | 10 | 16 | $23 |

Mamaroneck | 1240 W. Boston Post Rd. (bet. Richbell Rd. & Weaver St.), NY | 914-833-1320

A "vast" array of "typical" diner offerings – "good coffee", "huge desserts" – are done well at this 24/7 Mamaroneck mainstay whose "bright", "bustling" interior is also a prime source of weekend "schmoozing"; prices are gentle and "service comes with a smile", so no wonder it's "popular" with both "kids" and the "senior set."

Nessa *Italian*

20 | 18 | 18 | $50

Port Chester | 325 N. Main St. (Horton Ave.), NY | 914-939-0119 | www.nessarestaurant.com

A "surprising oasis in the back end of Port Chester", this Italian sets a "sultry" scene with low lighting and sheer curtains and a "sophisticated" "cityesque" atmosphere populated with "pretty people"; service can be "less than helpful", but the food is "tasty" and "portions are huge" – all nice touches to offset the "Manhattan prices."

New Deal Steakplace *Steak*

∇ 14 | 13 | 17 | $25

Westbrook | 704 Boston Post Rd. (Eckford Ave.) | 860-399-0015

Some surveyors deem the steaks served at this "casual" Westbrook beef emporium "decent", others claim they "lack flavor", but value-seekers contend it "really is a deal"; the design scheme is strictly "suburban bland", but the atmosphere is "kid-friendly", so parents aren't complaining.

Niko's Greek Taverna *Greek*

20 | 15 | 20 | $33

White Plains | 287 Central Ave. (Aqueduct Rd.), NY | 914-686-6456 | www.nikostaverna.com

"You're always treated like a regular" at this "amiable", "inexpensive" White Plains taverna known for its "fresh, clean-flavored" Hellenic specialties presented in "huge portions"; its "popularity" makes for "tight quarters" inside, so the roomy patio is especially appealing in summer – you might actually "think you're in Greece", "if only they could get some sailboats to go by on Central Avenue."

Nino's *Italian*

18 | 14 | 20 | $40

South Salem | 355 Rte. 123 (Glen Dr.), NY | 914-533-2671 | www.ninos123.com

Set in a "cavernous" Colonial home, this South Salem Italian caters to a "neighborhood" crowd with "basic" red-sauce fare and "thin-and-crispy" pizzas; it's a "local hangout" – no more no less – with "friendly" servers and "reasonable prices" adding to the appeal.

Nino's ⊠ *Italian*

19 | 15 | 18 | $43

Bedford Hills | 13 Adams St. (Rte. 117), NY | 914-864-0400 | www.ninosrestaurant.us

This Bedford Hills haunt dispenses "basic" Italian (think brick-oven pizzas and pastas) from a wide-spanning menu that offers "something for everyone"; in spite of occasional service missteps, "reasonable prices" and "inviting" environs overcome any shortcomings.

Noda's Japanese Steakhouse *Japanese*

19 | 13 | 20 | $34

White Plains | White Plains Mall | 200 Hamilton Ave. (Dr. Martin Luther King Ave.), NY | 914-949-0990 | www.nodarestaurant.com

"Friendly" chefs who are "real characters" man the "hibachi-style" cooktops at this White Plains Japanese, a no-brainer for "children's

FOOD DECOR SERVICE COST

birthdays" or for anyone in the mood to "have fun at dinner"; there's also "fresh" raw fish available at the 30-seat sushi bar, but detractors say no matter where you wind up, the joint "needs refurbishing."

NEW No. 9 🗷 🅼 American — | — | — | E

Millerton | Simmons' Way Village Inn | 53 Main St. (bet. Dutchess & N. Maple Aves.), NY | 518-592-1299

Chef Tom Cocheo (formerly of Ancram's shuttered, offbeat Bottle Tree) has taken over the dining room of Simmons' Way Village Inn in Millerton, serving somewhat pricey French-accented New American fare alongside a few Austrian specialties like Wiener schnitzel and cod strudel; the Victorian setting of its previous incarnation, Martha's, has been renovated into a pretty provincial bistro with gold-and-sage decor, softly lit by candles and sconces.

North Star American 23 | 21 | 23 | $48

Pound Ridge | 85 Westchester Ave. (Pine Dr.), NY | 914-764-0200 | www.northstarny.com

It's "quite the scene" at this "hip" "hangout" in otherwise sleepy Pound Ridge where "imaginative" New American cooking comes together with "terrific" wines and cocktails in "upscale-casual" quarters with an abundance of stacked stone; some say the atmosphere suffers from "too much SoHo", but a "warm" staff redeems for fans who "keep coming back"; N.B. live bands on Thursday nights.

Nuage French/Japanese 23 | 18 | 23 | $60

Cos Cob | Mill Pond Shopping Ctr. | 203 E. Putnam Ave. (bet. Sinawoy Rd. & Suburban Ave.) | 203-869-2339 | www.nuagerestaurant.com

French-Japanese cuisine "done deliciously", an "ample" wine list and "polished" service earn kudos from Cos Cobians at this chef-owned venue "popular with couples" due to its "romantic" "candlelit environment"; "wonderful tasting menus" sate foodies, but numbers-crunchers calculate the "price is too high for what it is": a "strip-mall Asian fusion" place.

Octagon Seafood/Steak ∇ 26 | 26 | 27 | $60

Groton | Mystic Marriott Hotel & Spa | 625 North Rd. (I-95) | 860-326-0360 | www.waterfordgrouprestaurants.com/octagon

"No steak aficionado" should miss this "unlikely" stop in "the middle of nowhere" – the Mystic Marriott in Groton, to be exact – because the chops are "done to perfection" and taste "amazing" (they're "pricey", but "well worth it"); also to be found in its "upscale" digs are "delicious" seafood, a "tremendous" wine list, "amazing breakfasts" and "courteous, professional" service.

Old Heidelberg German 20 | 17 | 18 | $36

Bethel | 55 Stony Hill Rd./Rte. 6 (McNeil Rd.) | 203-797-1860 | www.restaurantheidelberg.com

"If it's *oma*'s cooking you're looking for", head to this "value"-priced German in Bethel for "hearty, satisfying, old-country" fare served amid "Bavarian decor" "with a refreshing lack of kitsch"; a "great beer selection" keeps the crowds "boisterous", especially in the biergarten and during the "fantastic Oktoberfest celebration."

	FOOD	DECOR	SERVICE	COST

Old Lyme Inn *American* | 20 | 22 | 20 | $48

Old Lyme | Old Lyme Inn | 85 Lyme St. (I-95) | 860-434-2600 | www.oldlymeinn.com

"Take a table by the fireplace" in the casual Tap Room, settle in for a more formal, "romantic" meal in the "pleasantly appointed" Winslow Dining Room or "sit outside" on the terrace "when weather permits" at this "nicely restored" 1840 Old Lyme inn offering "well-prepared" Traditional American fare via an "accommodating" crew; but whichever "quiet" environment you choose, don't forget to "bring your wallet" – and call ahead in winter, when hours vary.

Olé Molé 🅜 *Mexican* | 21 | 11 | 17 | $20

Darien | 1020 Post Rd. (bet. Brook & Day Sts.) | 203-202-7051
Southport | 3381 Post Rd. (Spruce St.) | 203-319-7400
Stamford | 1030 High Ridge Rd. (Olga Dr.) | 203-461-9962
www.olemole.net

"*Olé* indeed!" bellow boosters of these "tiny", "first-rate" Mexicans in Stamford, Southport and Darien beloved for "spicy, crunchy, fall-apart" pork tacos, "homemade salsas" and "anything with mole sauce"; most agree the trio "works best as takeout"; N.B. BYO except for Southport, which serves alcohol.

Olio Bar & Restaurant *American* ∇ | 24 | 18 | 20 | $43

Groton | 33 Kings Hwy. (Rte. 1) | 860-445-6546 | www.olioct.com

"An exciting adventure in eating" awaits at this Groton purveyor of "delicious, modern" New American cuisine in "smart, urban-chic" digs (they're maybe too "minimalist" since "skinny folks" might find the benches "uncomfortable"); it's often quite "noisy", but "ask for the smaller dining room for a little more quiet."

Oliva Cafe 🅜 *Mediterranean* | 25 | 20 | 23 | $47

New Preston | 18 E. Shore Rd./Rte. 45 (Church St.) | 860-868-1787

The "Moroccan-inspired dishes are exceptional" at this "cozy" Med in New Preston, where the "wonderful chef-owner and his wife" have turned a converted Colonial into a "local treasure"; vets say opt for the second floor or "lovely" "three-season" patio; P.S. "well-chosen wine list" aside, BYOers are subject to a relatively "low corkage fee."

Olive Market 🅜 *Spanish* | - | - | - | M

Georgetown | 19 Main St. (Redding Rd./Rte. 107) | 203-544-8134

This intimate Spanish-inspired cafe inside an old-fashioned cheese shop and specialty market is one of the reasons Georgetown's on the radar of more foodies these days; the Pan-Latino influence includes Cuban sandwiches, as well as signature lamb chops with organic greens and chorizo and fig crostini; a tapas menu is served from 6 PM to closing Thursday–Saturday.

Oliver's Taverne *American* ∇ | 13 | 12 | 12 | $26

Essex | 124 Westbrook Rd./Rte. 153 (Bokum Rd.) | 860-767-2633 | www.oliverstavern.com

"If you're in the mood" for "loud music" and "a rowdy crowd", come on down to this Essex bar/eatery with pool, sports playing on "big

TVs" and "pretty dull decor"; if hunger strikes, remember to "keep it simple" when choosing from the large, inexpensive American menu – and still, "don't expect too much."

Olive Tree Ⓜ *American* ▽ 19 | 20 | 20 | $39

Southbury | 137 E. Hill Rd. (bet. Country Club Ln. & Lakeview Dr.) | 203-263-4555 | www.theolivetreesouthbury.com

"Large portions" of "interesting" American fare is the deal at this "charming" old house in Southbury; though the setting may be "a bit stuffy", most say that "relaxing meals" are the norm, whether in one of "multiple rooms" with "golf-course views" or on the "spacious patio."

Omanel *Portuguese* ▽ 22 | 11 | 18 | $30

Bridgeport | 1909 Main St. (bet. Commercial & Grand Sts.) | 203-335-1676

Afishionados aver "no one does seafood like the Portuguese", making this veritable "secret in Bridgeport" a "real find" for traditional dishes like pork and clams and paella served in portions that "assure leftovers"; the heavily Iberian clientele doesn't mind that the decor "hasn't changed in decades", since neither seemingly have the prices.

❷ Ondine *French* 25 | 23 | 25 | $66

Danbury | 69 Pembroke Rd./Rte. 37 (Wheeler Dr.) | 203-746-4900 | www.ondinerestaurant.com

Chef-owner Dieter Thiel "never disappoints!" exclaim enthusiasts of this "old-school" Danbury French, where an "outstanding" staff serves "beautifully prepared" dishes like roast duckling; *amis* attest that the $59 "prix fixe" is a "bargain", and if some cite "stuffy" surroundings, others say "get past that and enjoy the elegance."

O'Neill's Pub & Restaurant *Pub Food* 18 | 18 | 20 | $29

South Norwalk | 93 N. Main St. (bet. Ann & Pine Sts.) | 203-838-0222 | www.oneillsono.com

A "personable owner" who regales customers with "stories from across the pond", "friendly" servers and bartenders who keep the "cold Guinness" flowing create the "genuine" feel at this Irish pub in South Norwalk; though the cheap grub is "nothing to write home about", it's "good" enough, especially given the overall "cozy" vibe.

116 Crown ❍ *Eclectic* 23 | 23 | 21 | $37

New Haven | 116 Crown St. (bet. Church & Orange Sts.) | 203-777-3116 | www.116crown.com

The "ultracool" bar "is reason enough to try" this New Haven Eclectic whose "inventive drinks" (including "wonderful martinis") and "delicious small plates and charcuterie" make it an "outstanding place for foodies and boozies alike"; an "unabashedly trendy design" adds to the "exciting vibe", but take note: you'll pay "steep prices" to take it all in; N.B. 21-and-unders must be accompanied by parents.

121 Restaurant & Bar *American* 21 | 18 | 19 | $44

North Salem | 2 Dingle Ridge Rd. (Rte. 121), NY | 914-669-0121 | www.121restaurant.com

"Long waits" attest to the popularity of this midpriced North Salem tavern boasting a "city-ish atmosphere" amid "cozy country" furnishings with a working fireplace and a "lovely porch" for summer; its "sophisticated" New American menu and "welcoming" vibe keep it "packed" most nights, though the scene's a bit "deafening" for some, especially at the "busy" bar.

121 Restaurant @ OXC Ⓜ American   23 | 23 | 20 | $42

Oxford | Waterbury-Oxford Airport | 7 Juliano Dr. (Christiansan St.) | 203-262-0121 | www.121atoxc.com

Aviation buffs who descend on this "upscale airstrip eatery" don't mind its "out-of-the-way" Oxford locale because it's "fun" "watching planes land" while indulging in "unexpectedly good" New American cuisine ("from pizza to a fine meal"); a "happening" bar adds to the "enjoyable" vibe, but the sound-sensitive warn it can be a "little loud at peak times."

122 Pizza Bistro *Italian/Pizza*   19 | 17 | 19 | $28

Stamford | 122 Broad St. (Bedford St.) | 203-348-1232 | www.122pizza-bistro.com

Expect a "wide variety" of thin-crust pizzas and daily specials at this "cozy", "family-owned" Italian across from the mall in Downtown Stamford; if a few feel the chow "lacks kick", proponents point out that "moderate prices", "friendly service" and a "convivial" atmosphere make it a "good place for a quick bite" before the movies.

Opus 465 *American*   16 | 15 | 17 | $42

Armonk | 465 Main St. (Orchard Dr.), NY | 914-273-4676 | www.opus465.com

At this "relaxed" Armonk respite, you can count on "solid" American cooking that encompasses everything from big salads to burgers and meatloaf; some suggest it's "best for lunch", though judging from the "packed bar on weekends", evenings hold appeal as well – especially on Wednesday–Saturday nights when there's live music.

Orem's Diner ➊ *Diner*   16 | 12 | 17 | $19

Wilton | 167 Danbury Rd./Rte. 7 (Wolfpit Rd.) | 203-762-7370 | www.oremsdiner.com

They "come for the comfort food and leave in a coma" quip connoisseurs of this "busy" "Wilton mainstay" (open since 1921) where the "menu goes on for pages" and the "reliable", "reasonably priced" breakfasts "draw long lines"; nonetheless, a fair share say it's "just a diner" and wonder "why does it keep popping up on the radar?"

Oscar's *Deli*   19 | 8 | 15 | $17

Westport | 159 Main St. (bet. Elm St. & Parker Harding Plaza) | 203-227-3705

Main Street shoppers "meet their friends for lunch" at this "NY deli" in "upscale Westport" for "quality" kosher-style sandwiches, "homemade soups" and the like; it "looks like something out of the '50s" (1948 to be precise) and there's sometimes "attitude" at the counter, but that only adds to its "authenticity"; P.S. nice weather brings "limited outdoor seating."

Osetra ⓜ *Eclectic/Seafood*

26	21	24	$51

Norwalk | 124 Washington St. (bet. Main & Water Sts.) | 203-354-4488 |
www.osetrasono.com

Norwalk gourmands enthuse "whether you go with the small plates or the large plates, just go" to this "minimalist, cozy" seafood-centric Eclectic from Todd English protégé David Nevins, who turns "unusual" "flavor combos" into "culinary masterpieces"; "knowledgeable, friendly" staffers are on hand to "guide" you, and though it's pricey, such is the cost of "awesome."

Osianna ⓩ *Mediterranean*

-	-	-	M

Fairfield | 70 Reef Rd. (Sherman St.) | 203-254-2070 | www.osianna.com
The maize-colored walls, exposed wood beams and linens billowing from the ceiling evoke a seaside taverna ("like you're at home in Greece") at this "bright, cheery" Mediterranean in Downtown Fairfield; standouts from the "big menu" include the signature grilled fresh octopus and whole fish, while the two-course prix fixe lunch ($12) and three-course dinner ($21) make it all more affordable.

Osteria Applausi ⓩ *Italian*

23	17	21	$51

Old Greenwich | 199 Sound Beach Ave. (Arcadia Rd.) | 203-637-4447 |
www.osteriaapplausi.com

"It's like sitting down to Sunday dinner with the family" at this "terrific" Old Greenwich Italian (cousin to Columbus Park) – as long as your family can get a "second mortgage to pay the bill"; "superb housemade pastas" and a "friendly" staff take the edge off of "expensive" prices, though some "wish the ambiance were warmer."

ⓩ Outback Steakhouse *Steak*

16	13	16	$31

Danbury | 116 Newtown Rd. (I-84) | 203-790-1124
Manchester | 170 Hale Rd. (Slater St.) | 860-648-2900
Newington | 3210 Berlin Tpke. (Deming St.) | 860-666-0002
New London | 305 N. Frontage Rd. (bet. Briggs & Colman Sts.) |
860-447-9205
North Haven | 345 Washington Ave. (bet. Temple & Wadsworth Sts.) |
203-985-8282
Orange | 132 Marsh Hill Rd. (Rte. 95) | 203-795-0700
Shelton | 698 Bridgeport Ave. (Old Stratford Rd.) |
203-926-3900
Southington | 817 Queen St. (Aircraft Rd.) | 860-276-9585
Wilton | 14 Danbury Rd. (bet. Fawn Ridge Ln. & Heathcoate Rd.) |
203-762-0920
White Plains | 60 S. Broadway (Bloomingdale Rd.), NY |
914-684-1397
www.outback.com

"Meat lovers on a budget" report that this "midtier", Aussie-themed chophouse chain provides terrific "bang for the buck", not to mention "basic" steaks and "hefty sides" (the famed bloomin' onion supplies "a week's worth of calories" in a single serving); it's "not known for subtlety" – starting with the "overly friendly, chat 'n' squat" service – but when you "don't want to splurge", it's a "decent" enough option.

☑ Paci ⒮Ⓜ *Italian*

26 | 25 | 23 | $62

Southport | 96 Station St. (Pequot Ave.) | 203-259-9600 |
www.pacirestaurant.com

"Impressed" surveyors "haven't seen a slowdown in the economy" at
this "steeply priced" Italian in a converted Southport train station, as
it's always filled with folks enjoying the "outstanding", "inventive" fare
and "large variety of wines"; the "modern", brick-lined downstairs
"with a big clock projection" is quite "open" (hence, it "can get loud"),
while the upstairs is more "intimate" and the "barroom is cozy."

Pacifico *Nuevo Latino/Seafood*

23 | 19 | 21 | $46

New Haven | 220 College St. (Crown St.) | 203-772-4002 |
www.pacificorestaurants.com

Real "creativity" abounds in chef-owner Rafael Palomino's "beautifully
presented" Nuevo Latino fare starring "lots of spicy" seafood at this
New Haven haunt, which is somewhat "expensive but worth it"; "colorful ocean" decor and "attentive" staffers fashion a "welcoming environment", while "terrific drinks" make it "best if you're not the driver."

Palmer's Crossing *American*

18 | 16 | 19 | $43

Larchmont | 1957 Palmer Ave. (Larchmont Ave.), NY | 914-833-3505 |
www.palmerscrossing.com/

Opinions are split on this Larchmont "locals'" spot serving "mid-
range" New Americana in an "open, airy" window-lined room that's
"upscale", yet still comfy enough to "hang out with friends"; pros
praise the "simple dishes" that "hit the spot", but cons contend the
"pedestrian" fare "should be better" given the price.

Panda Pavilion *Chinese*

16 | 12 | 18 | $25

Fairfield | Fairfield Shopping Pk. | 923 Post Rd. (I-95, exit 22) |
203-259-9777

Greenwich | 420 W. Putnam Ave. (bet. Harold & Melrose Aves.) |
203-869-1111 | www.panda3gw.com

Depending on whom you talk to, this Greenwich-Fairfield Chinese duo
is either a "cut above" other area options or just "another Pan-Asian
that doesn't ring my chimes"; in either case, the Decor score suggests
they may be best for "takeout and delivery", which can be "crazy fast."

Pantry, The ⒮Ⓜ *American*

25 | 15 | 18 | $25

Washington Depot | 5 Titus Rd. (Rte. 47) | 860-868-0258

"Zabar's in the country" is how fans describe this Washington
Depot New American, where "area celebrities" and "foodies" flock
for "excellent" breakfast and lunch fare, which is served at tables
surrounded by "store shelves full of gourmet foods and kitchen
items" or as takeout; weekends can be "zoo-ish", but the staff is "always friendly" and "accommodating"; N.B. closes at 6 PM.

Papacelle ⒮ *Italian*

- | - | - | E

Avon | 152 Simsbury Rd./Rte.10 (Rte. 44) | 860-269-3121 |
www.papacelle.com

The chefs are brothers and their mother is the maitre d' at this pricey
Avon Italian, where the staff works to make you feel like one of the

family; housemade pastas and a signature rabbit dish are done Tuscan-style, and the decor features the warm colors of that region.

Papaya Thai & Asian BBQ *Thai* | 20 | 19 | 18 | $33 |

South Norwalk | 24 Marshall St. (N. Water St.) | 203-866-8424 | www.papayathai.com

"Well-spiced", "reasonably priced" Thai dishes, including some barbecued specialties, are "promptly served" at this South Norwalk eatery "eclectically decorated" with palm trees and wood carvings; "fun drinks" from the thatched-roofed tiki lounge bait adults, but since it's "near the aquarium", "it's always full of kids."

Paradise Bar & Grille *American* | 13 | 18 | 14 | $35 |

Stamford | Stamford Landing | 78 Southfield Ave. (I-95, exit 7) | 203-323-1116 | www.paradisebarandgrille.com

"It's all about the sunsets" at this New American located "next to a marina" at Stamford Landing, which fans tout as the "most happening place" around for "drinks" on a "balmy summer eve"; critics lament, however, that the "forgettable" fare "served indifferently" "doesn't match the waterfront view" – or the "high prices."

Pascal's ☑ *French* | 20 | 19 | 21 | $47 |

Larchmont | 141 Chatsworth Ave. (Palmer Ave.), NY | 914-834-6688

"Gallic charm" pervades this "reliable", "family-run" Larchmont venue that's an "easy choice" for "traditional French" bistro cooking; the "warm, homey" setting "isn't Paris, but close", and a "reasonable", "not-to-be-missed" prix fixe makes it a hot ticket for "older" types.

Pasquale Ristorante II ☑ *Italian* | 21 | 15 | 20 | $40 |

Port Chester | 2 Putnam Ave. (N. Main St.), NY | 914-934-7770 | www.pasqualeristorante.com

"Sinatra" on the speakers sets the tone at this "inviting", "old-world" Italian in Port Chester offering "great value" with its "generous portions" of "delicious" "red-sauce" fare; the staff is "attentive" and the tableside touches "make you feel special", so the only downside is lackluster looks that could "use sprucing up."

☒ Pasta Nostra ☒☑ *Italian* | 25 | 15 | 20 | $54 |

South Norwalk | 116 Washington St. (bet. Main & Water Sts.) | 203-854-9700 | www.pastanostra.com

"If you can get into" this South Norwalk Italian, you're in for "*stupendo*" fare that "changes weekly" based on "seasonally available ingredients and chef Joe Bruno's imagination" (he "knows what he's doing", but he's got "peculiarities" – "try making substitutions" at your own peril); the "diligent, long-employed staff" helps pair the "wonderful wines", and while the whole shebang is "expensive", it's "worth it", even if it comes with "not much atmosphere."

Pasta Vera *Italian* | 21 | 14 | 17 | $34 |

Greenwich | 48 Greenwich Ave. (W. Putnam Ave.) | 203-661-9705 | www.pastavera.com

"Order pastas with any sauce you want" at this "understated Italian" in Downtown Greenwich, a "local favorite" with a "friendly, casual"

FOOD | DECOR | SERVICE | COST

atmosphere and a "staff that bends over backward to please"; "one of the few bargains to be had on the Avenue", it "draws a big lunch crowd", although it tends to be "forgotten at dinner", thanks perhaps to the "take-out counter in front" that does "booming business."

Pastorale Bistro & Bar Ⓜ French   24 | 22 | 23 | $48

Lakeville | 223 Main St./Rte. 44 (Lincoln City Rd.) | 860-435-1011 | www.pastoralebistro.com

"Well-prepared" French bistro fare that "warms you from the inside out" and "lovely wines" are served by a "marvelous", "attentive" staff at this Lakeville Gallic housed in a "creaky but charming old Colonial" with two appealing upstairs dining rooms, a "lively bar" and a "pleasant" terrace; toss in a "comfortable, inviting" atmosphere and it all adds up to a "delightful" experience.

Patrias Restaurant Peruvian/Spanish   ▽ 20 | 13 | 20 | $37

Port Chester | 35½ N. Main St. (bet. Adee St. & Westchester Ave.), NY | 914-937-0177 | www.patriasrestaurant.com

"South America meets Spain" at this "quaint", colorful Port Chester nook proffering Peruvian plates like ceviche alongside tapas and a sprinkling of Colombian dishes; backed by a "gracious" crew, it's an "informal" place that gets "packed on the weekends" and is made more convivial by liberal "pitchers of sangria."

Pat's Kountry Kitchen American   14 | 11 | 14 | $20

Old Saybrook | 70 Mill Rock Rd. E. (Boston Post Rd./Rte. 1) | 860-388-4784 | www.patskountrykitchen.com

"En route to the shore", this "touristy" Old Saybrook spot is a "good place to stop" for Traditional American breakfast, lunch and dinner fare that's "reasonably priced" if "ordinary" (only the "famous" "clam hash is worth going out of the way for"); the "kitschy", "diner-like" space is "crowded" with Teddy bears, perhaps making it best if you've got the "grandchildren" in tow.

Pazzo Italian Café Italian   23 | 17 | 19 | $32

Glastonbury | 60 Hebron Ave. (bet. Main St. & New London Tpke.) | 860-657-3447 🅰

Rocky Hill | 377 Cromwell Ave. (New Britian Ave.) | 860-721-8888 www.pazzoitaliancafe.net

"Notable for its excellent pastas and killer desserts" doled out in "huge portions", this "old-style" Glastonbury Italian now boasts a full bar (bye-bye, BYO policy); the "homey" interior and "nice patio" make it a "real gem" for "casual lunches and suppers"; N.B. the Rocky Hill branch opened post-Survey.

Pellicci's Italian   20 | 12 | 18 | $30

Stamford | 96-98 Stillwater Ave. (bet. Alden & Spruce Sts.) | 203-323-2542 | www.pelliccis.com

The "owner greets you at the door" of this "casual, loud", 60-plus-year-old Stamford Italian, where the "classic red-sauce" cooking is "consistent" (the "baked chicken takes the prize"), the portions are "huge" and the "price is right"; while some gripe that it's "lost a little of its luster" and find the "late '50s Brooklyn decor" "unattractive", *paesani* proclaim it "worth repeat visits", especially if you're "bringing the whole clan."

Penang Grill *Asian*   23 | 14 | 19 | $30

Greenwich | 55 Lewis St. (Greenwich Ave.) | 203-861-1988

Asiana Cafe's "teeny" Pan-Asian sibling off Greenwich Avenue turns out "quick but tasty" takes on "all types of Asian cuisines" that are "fresh" and "served steaming hot" by a "likable" staff in a "casual", "bare-bones" setting; the prices are deemed "incredibly reasonable" and it's "BYO to boot", making it one of the "best values in the area."

Peniche Tapas ☒ *Spanish*   22 | 22 | 21 | $46

White Plains | 175 Main St. (Court St.), NY | 914-421-5012 | www.penichetapas.com

"Hopping" and "high-decibel", this White Plains tapas stop from chef Anthony Goncalves rolls out "absolutely delicious" Portuguese-Spanish bites that "hit the right balance between authentic and modern"; it earns praise for both its "hip" looks with communal seating and "friendly service", though there are a few gripes about "pricey" tabs that "can really add up."

Peppercorn's Grill ☒ *Italian*   25 | 21 | 22 | $47

Hartford | 357 Main St. (bet. Buckingham St. & Capital Ave.) | 860-547-1714 | www.peppercornsgrill.com

"Passionate" chef/co-owner Dino Cialfi juxtaposes "traditional" Italian preparations with "delicious bursts of whimsy" at this "bright spot in Downtown Hartford"; the "attentive, knowledgeable staff" abets the venue's reputation as a "completely reliable" part of the "pre-theater routine" – although a few bean-counters calculate it's an "overpriced" one.

Peppermill Steak & Fish House *Seafood/Steak*   18 | 14 | 16 | $32

Stratford | Ramada Inn | 225 Lordship Blvd. (Watson Blvd.) | 203-870-8445 | www.peppermillstratford.com

This standby in Stratford's Ramada Inn offers "not fancy" yet "solid" steak and seafood alongside an "adequate salad bar", all "at fair prices"; "bummers" include just "ok service", "no atmosphere whatsoever" and, for whippersnappers, the fact they "will almost certainly be surrounded by old people."

Peppino's Ristorante *Italian*   19 | 16 | 19 | $34

Katonah | 116 Katonah Ave. (Jay St.), NY | 914-232-3212 | www.peppinosristorante.com

"It's not fancy", but supporters swear they're "never disappointed" by this Katonah Italian dishing out "traditional" Northern-style dinners in a "kitschy" setting in a converted train station; low prices and "welcoming" service keep the regulars "returning", often for takeout.

☒ P.F. Chang's China Bistro *Chinese*   19 | 18 | 17 | $33

Stamford | Stamford Town Ctr. | 230 Tresser Blvd. (bet. Atlantic St. & Greyrock Pl.) | 203-363-0434

(continued)

(continued)

P.F. Chang's China Bistro

West Hartford | West Farms Mall | 322 W. Farms Mall (New Britain Ave.) | 860-561-0097

White Plains | Westchester Mall | 125 Westchester Ave. (Bloomingdale Rd.), NY | 914-997-6100

www.pfchangs.com

Expect "major hustle-bustle" at these "noisy" Chinese chain links where the "sanitized", "mass-produced" menus "aren't really authentic" yet do "appeal to most palates"; no one minds the "spotty" service and "ersatz" Sino decor since they "have the formula down" – starting with "nothing-fancy" prices and an overall "fun" vibe.

Pho Mekong *Thai/Vietnamese* ▽ 20 | 11 | 17 | $25

Westport | 1849 Post Rd. E. (bet. Bulkley Ave. N. & Hulls Hwy.) | 203-255-2900

Hankerings for "authentic Thai" and Vietnamese vittles are satisfied in Westport at this "well-run family operation" proffering an "extensive menu" with inexpensive price points; the "friendly" servers welcome "big groups as well as kids", and while it's "not the best" you'll ever have, it yields "no complaints" either.

Piccolo Arancio ⑤ *Italian* 26 | 22 | 24 | $45

Farmington | 819 Farmington Ave./Rte. 4 (Main St./Rte. 10) | 860-674-1224 | www.piccoloarancio.com

"Loyal followers" "enjoy la dolce vita" at this "high-end" Farmington Italian where "efficient, thoughtful" staffers serve "wonderful appetizers", "fantastic pastas" and more alongside "impressive wines"; if some find the "decor a bit flat", even more deem it "chichi" and make it a go-to for both "business meetings" and "special occasions."

Piero's Ⓜ *Italian* 23 | 10 | 21 | $40

Port Chester | 44 S. Regent St. (bet. Ellendale Ave. & Franklin St.), NY | 914-937-2904

"Everything is made from scratch" at this "old-fashioned" Italian in Port Chester where "nice portions" and "warm" owners ensure "you always leave stuffed and happy"; forget the "dingy", "crowded" digs, because the payoff is "excellent" cooking at "decent" prices.

Pizzeria Lauretano Ⓜ *Pizza* ▽ 26 | 15 | 20 | $23

Bethel | 291 Greenwood Ave. (Grassy Plain St.) | 203-792-1500

"Exquisitely thin, crispy crusts", "great sauce" and "top-notch" toppings are the "awesome" components of this Bethel strip-maller's "imaginative" Neapolitan pizzas, which are offered beside "incredible soups", "innovative salads" and other Italian selections; if it irks you that the "tables are close together and it gets crowded", you can always call ahead and get it to go.

NEW Pizzeria Molto *Italian* – | – | – | E

Fairfield | 1215 Post Rd. (Old Post Rd.) | 203-292-8288 | www.pizzeriamolto.com

This *molto* trendy newcomer by the Fairfield train station specializes in Italian tapas (including artisanal mozzarellas), fried artichokes and gourmet pizzas, but it's the striking black walls, red-leather booths and 36-ft. white-marble bar that garner the most oohs and aahs; expect loud acoustics and long waits for a table.

Plan B Burger Bar *Burgers* | 23 | 17 | 18 | $23 |

Glastonbury | 120 Hebron Ave. (bet. Main St. & New London Tpke.) | 860-430-9737
Simsbury | 4 Railroad St. (bet. Phelps Ln. & Station St.) | 860-658-4477
West Hartford | 138 Park Rd. (bet. Beverly Rd. & Kingston St.) | 860-231-1199
www.planbtavern.com

Prepare to be "ruined for any other burger" when you order one of the "insanely good", "inventive", sometimes "unusual" patties proffered at this tavern trio, which also offers "over 100 types of beer" including "fantastic microbrews"; it's "often crowded", but the "knowledgeable" staff is "accommodating", and the "small outdoor seating" areas are bonuses.

Plates Ⓜ *American* | 24 | 21 | 22 | $62 |

Larchmont | 121 Myrtle Blvd. (Murray Ave.), NY | 914-834-1244 | www.platesonthepark.com

"Imaginative" chef-owner Matthew Karp is behind this Larchmont "gem" where his "whimsical" New American creations – e.g. whiskey-glazed chicken and "homemade Ring Dings" – are matched with "boutique wines" in an "inviting" setting that oozes "sophistication"; the staff is "eager to please", so while some raise eyebrows at "pricey" tabs, most maintain "it'll set you back, but it's worth it."

Plum Tree *Japanese* | 21 | 18 | 21 | $36 |

New Canaan | 70 Main St. (Locust Ave.) | 203-966-8050 | www.plumtreejapanese.com

Bring your "finatic friends" to this New Canaan Japanese where the "fresh sushi doesn't clip the wallet as much as some"; it also gets a shout out for "friendly" service and decor that was "improved" not too long ago, which includes a rock and bamboo garden, but a few critics carp there are too many "kids running around."

Polpo *Italian* | 24 | 21 | 20 | $66 |

Greenwich | 554 Old Post Rd. (W. Putnam Ave.) | 203-629-1999 | www.polporestaurant.com

"You're bound to see a celebrity or two" at this "*bellissimo*" Greenwich Italian known for its "delicious" grilled octopus and other "wonderful seafood" dishes, served in a "clubby" setting peopled by "'in' crowd" types, including a large "financial services" contingent; gripes abound about "loud, loud, loud" acoustics, a "haughty" staff that "favors regulars" and "incredibly steep" prices – but the fact that it's generally "crowded" speaks for itself.

PolytechnicON20 Ⓩ *American* | ▽ 28 | 24 | 28 | $55 |

Hartford | Hartford Steam Boiler Bldg., 20th fl. | 1 State St. (Columbus Blvd.) | 860-722-5161 | www.ontwenty.com

"Serious gourmets" break bread with folks "made of money and time" at this weekday-lunch favorite atop Hartford's Steam Boiler

	FOOD	DECOR	SERVICE	COST

Building for chef Noel Jones' "amazing", "imaginative" cuisine, now offered at dinner on Thursdays and Fridays; the contemporary setting is notable for its "incredible views", while "well-orchestrated" service and a "solid wine list" are two more facets that make it a "not-to-be-missed experience."

Pond House Café Ⓜ American `22` `20` `18` `$32`

West Hartford | Elizabeth Pk. | 1555 Asylum Ave. (bet. Golf & Sycamore Rds.) | 860-231-8823 | www.pondhousecafe.com

When "lunching with the ladies", there may be no more "lovely spot" in West Hartford than this "charming" New American located pondside in Elizabeth Park, especially on the patio "in spring and summer when the roses are in bloom"; the "fair prices" asked for the "solid fare" seem even more so considering it's BYO; N.B. evening hours are abbreviated in winter.

Ponte Vecchio Italian ▽ `20` `20` `21` `$38`

Fairfield | The Brick Walk | 1275 Post Rd. (bet. Beach & Unquowa Rds.) | 203-256-1326 | www.pontevecchiofairfield.com

"Familiar like a pair of slippers", this Fairfield strip-mall Italian offers "solid" cookery served by "attentive, young" staffers in a space that's "nicer inside than it looks from the outside"; "reasonable prices" are de rigueur, but "lots of choices" of "delicious" $8-and-under lunch items make it "one of the best values" around for midday repasts.

Porter House American `18` `17` `18` `$31`

White Plains | 169 Mamaroneck Ave. (E. Post Rd.), NY | 914-831-5663 | www.porterhousebar.com

"Another great pub" in an area of many, this White Plains watering hole appeals to twentysomethings and the "after-work crowd" with "excellent burgers" and other "decent" American grub that goes down well with pours from the fine draft beer selection; "reasonable" tabs and "on-top-of-it" service are additional draws, and the vibe is "friendly" too.

Portofino Pizza & Pasta Italian `22` `8` `17` `$18`

Goldens Bridge | A&P Shopping Ctr. | Rtes. 22 & 138 (Anderson Ln.), NY | 914-232-4363

The slices alone "can practically feed a family" at this Goldens Bridge Italian famed for its "gargantuan" pizza and "hearty" red-sauce standards that "won't break your wallet"; despite "friendly" order-at-the-counter service, its "hectic" strip-mall setting with "limited seating" makes a strong case for "takeout."

Portofino's ⊄ Italian `21` `16` `21` `$36`

Wilton | 10 Center St. (Ridgefield Rd.) | 203-761-9115 | www.portofinoswilton.com

"Hit the ATM" before you "bring the family" to this "cash-only" Italian in Wilton, where the "price is right" for "dependable" "Sicilian pizza" and "interesting specials", complemented by "generous pours" of vino; although the "service is still good", critics say it's often "crowded and noisy" in the "dark" digs, and plastic-lovers say the credit card ban "has gotten old."

	FOOD	DECOR	SERVICE	COST

Positano's *Italian*

| | 22 | 24 | 22 | $51 |

Westport | 233 Hills Point Rd. (Compo Hill Ave.) | 203-454-4922 |
www.positanoswestport.com

Yes, the Southern Italian fare is "wonderful", but it's the "multimillion-dollar views" of Long Island Sound that command the "pricey" fees at this "pretty", "romantic" venue on "lovely" Compo Beach; indeed, it's such a "rare dining experience" in Westport, even those who cop to being "slightly disappointed" find themselves "going again and again."

Post Corner Pizza *Pizza*

| | 19 | 11 | 17 | $20 |

Darien | 847 Boston Post Rd. (Mansfield Ave.) | 203-655-7721 |
www.postcornerpizza.com

Fans of this "Darien institution" surmise it "may have invented" those "tasty" "square-cut" Greek-style pizzas, but it also gets props for its "amazing" salads and "delicious" gyros; "fast service" and a "family-friendly manner" have made it a "popular neighborhood gathering place" "for over 30 years", but the kid-averse caution "go after 8 PM if you don't want local soccer teams crawling all over you."

Posto 22 *Italian*

| | - | - | - | M |

New Rochelle | 22 Division St. (bet. Huguenot & Main Sts.), NY |
914-235-2464 | www.posto22.com

Homemade pastas and pizzas are the focus of this midpriced Italian in New Rochelle also boasting an extensive list of wines by the glass; its low-lit interior has a rustic feel with a tile floor, warm yellow walls and white tablecloths adding to the inviting ambiance.

Pot-au-Pho ⊠ *Vietnamese*

| | 20 | 10 | 14 | $19 |

New Haven | 77 Whitney Ave. (bet. Grove & Trumbull Sts.) |
203-776-2248

At this New Haven Vietnamese, the "cavelike dining room" sports "absent decor", the "young staff" borders on "negligent" and the prices are "just ok" – but those shortcomings don't deter the "student crowd" from "cramming" it for "wonderful soups", "tasty entrees" and bubble tea that's a real "treat."

Primavera *Italian*

| | 23 | 23 | 23 | $51 |

Croton Falls | 592 Rte. 22 (bet. Birch Hill & Deans Corner Rds.), NY |
914-277-4580 | www.primaverarestaurantandbar.com

The "terrific" Northern Italian–Med menu gets a boost from an "endless list" of nightly specials at this "handsome", "elegant" Croton Falls standby; "perhaps it's a bit overpriced", but a "professional" staff "attending to your slightest need" ensures a "pleasurable" experience all around.

Prime 16 *Pub Food*

| | - | - | - | M |

New Haven | 172 Temple St. (Chapel St.) | 203-782-1616 |
www.prime16.com

Yalies hail the 'poor student' lunch special (organic beef on brioche for five bucks) as well as the half-price beers at happy hour at this new Downtown New Haven burger bar; gourmet patties, along with 20 taps loaded with IPAs, ambers, ales, lagers and stouts, are the prime reasons its wood-accented dining room is always filled to the brim.

Puket Café *Thai*

- | - | - | M

Wethersfield | 1030 Silas Deane Hwy. (bet. Maple & Mill Sts.) | 860-529-6590 | www.puketcafe.com

It "looks unimpressive from the outside", but there's a "wonderful surprise" waiting within this Wethersfield Thai: "authentic" fare served in "ample portions" at "value" prices; "nicely decorated" digs rife with bamboo, fresh-cut flowers and "attentive" staffers add up to a wholly "pleasant dining experience."

Putnam House Restaurant & Tap Room *American*

∇ 16 | 18 | 19 | $34

Bethel | 12 Depot Pl. (Greenwood Ave.) | 203-791-1852 | www.theputnamhouse.com

Housed in a restored 1852 mansion, this midpriced Traditional American in Bethel offers "everything from burgers to bisque" in a casual taproom, Victorian-style dining areas and on a "cozy" patio; too bad the "standard fare" "doesn't live up to the lovely" setting, which leads some to just "come here for the beer."

Q Restaurant & Bar *BBQ*

20 | 11 | 15 | $26

Port Chester | 112 N. Main St. (bet. Adee St. & Willette Ave.), NY | 914-933-7427 | www.qrestaurantandbar.com

"Putting an end to the rumor that you can't get good 'cue in these parts" is this "three-napkin" BBQ pit in Port Chester featuring "fall-off-the-bone ribs", "delish pulled pork" and "tasty brisket", all washed down with boutique beers and bourbons; maybe there's "not much Southern hospitality" in the order-at-the-counter service or "quasi-cafeteria setup", but tabs are "cheap", the vibe "kid-friendly" and the handwashing stations pure "genius" – "roll up your sleeves and dig in."

☒ Quattro Pazzi Ⓜ *Italian*

22 | 17 | 19 | $38

Fairfield | 1599 Boston Post Rd. (bet. Reef Rd. & Ruane St.) | 203-259-7417
Norwalk | Oak Hills Pk. | 165 Fillow St. (Charles Marshall Dr.) | 203-855-1800
www.quattropazzi.com

"Low-key but chic", these chef-owned Italians are famous for "*ab-bondanza* portions" of "outstanding" "fresh pasta" at "reasonable prices"; Fairfield frequenters don't mind its "coziness", "crowds" and "constant clatter" and insist "it's always worth the wait" (though the "no-reservations policy" is a "hassle"); the larger, sportier Norwalk locale is "on a golf course", where an "exceptional deck" makes for "flavorful" alfresco feasts.

Rainforest Cafe *American*

11 | 23 | 15 | $26

Farmington | Westfarms Mall | 500 Westfarms Mall (New Britian Ave.) | 860-521-2002 | www.rainforestcafe.com

"Appease the kids" at this "jungle"-themed chain link in Farmington, a "gimmicky" franchise where the "mediocre" Traditional American grub is overshadowed by its "Disney-like animatronics" and faux thunderstorms; "jet-plane noise levels", "so-so service" and rather "expensive" tabs come with the territory, though after a "couple of drinks, it seems more parent-friendly."

Ralph 'n' Rich's *Italian*
24 | 24 | 23 | $43

Bridgeport | 815 Main St. (bet. N. Frontage Rd. & State St.) | 203-366-3597 | www.ralphnrichsct.com

"With Ralph in the kitchen and Rich overseeing the dining room", this "beautiful" "old-school" Italian "across from the Barnum Museum" in a "revitalized" part of Downtown Bridgeport "just keeps getting better"; the "interesting menu" has "something for everyone", and an "attentive" staff ensures that the "moderately priced" dishes arrive "hot and on time"; P.S. there's weekend entertainment in the "lively" bar.

Rangoli *Indian*
▽ 24 | 18 | 23 | $35

New Rochelle | 615 Main St. (Maple Ave.), NY | 914-235-1306 | www.rangoliindiancuisine.com

"Solid" subcontinental cooking draws fans to this New Rochelle Indian run by a "wonderful" family; maybe the dimly lit setting is "not as intimate as the old location", but "aim-to-please" service bolsters the overall "worthwhile" experience, with the bargain-priced $9.95 lunch buffet sealing the deal.

Rani Mahal *Indian*
▽ 23 | 16 | 21 | $28

Mamaroneck | 322-323 Phillips Park Rd. (bet. E. Prospect Ave. & Spencer Pl.), NY | 914-835-9066 | www.ranimahalny.com

Though "hidden away" off the beaten path in Mamaroneck, this modestly priced Indian "stands out" for its "ambitious" lineup of "creative", "flavorful" dishes and a "bargain" lunch buffet; it's not fancy, but it earns praise for its "soothing" ambiance thanks to white-linen tablecloths, fresh flowers and a "sweet" staff providing "polite and efficient service."

Rasa *Indian*
(fka Chola)
20 | 14 | 18 | $35

Greenwich | 107-109 Greenwich Ave. (Lewis St.) | 203-869-0700 | www.rasagreenwich.com

"Tucked away on the back of Greenwich Avenue" – and "upstairs" at that – this "hard-to-find", recently renamed Indian "gets the spices and shades of spices" just right; its Decor score may not be very impressive, but the good news is the relatively "expensive" fare "stands up well to delivery."

Ray's Cafe *Chinese*
19 | 7 | 15 | $28

Larchmont | 1995 Palmer Ave. (Parkway St.), NY | 914-833-2551
Rye Brook | Rye Ridge Shopping Ctr. | 176 S. Ridge St. (bet. Crescent Pl. & Ellendale Ave.), NY | 914-937-0747

These Larchmont–Rye Brook Sino siblings specialize in "better-than-average" Shanghainese items at "reasonable" rates; despite "spotty" service and "unappealing", "out-of-the-'70s" decor, they "never seem hurting for customers", but regulars suggest "takeout" or the "less frantic" Rye Brook satellite and its "easier parking."

	FOOD	DECOR	SERVICE	COST

☒ Rebeccas ☒Ⓜ *American*   25 | 20 | 22 | $79

Greenwich | 265 Glenville Rd. (bet. Pemberwick & Riversville Rds.) |
203-532-9270 | www.rebeccasgreenwich.com

At his Greenwich "foodie mecca", Reza Khorshidi's New American
menu "abounds with nonpareil culinary delights" such as "heaven-
sent" foie gras dumplings in black truffle broth, and his wife, Rebecca,
"runs a tight ship"; you can "rub elbows with the super-elite" in the
"ultramodern" (read: "very minimal") space, but nitpickers note it can
get "excruciatingly noisy", and as one might expect from the "parking lot full of hedge-fund trophy cars", the "prices are over the top."

Red Barn *American*   17 | 19 | 19 | $41

Westport | 292 Wilton Rd./Rte. 33 (Merritt Pkwy., exit 41) |
203-222-9549 | www.redbarnrestaurant.com

"Do brunch" ("and don't eat the day before") bellow boosters of this
"family-run" Traditional American set in a "sprawling old" "antiques-
filled" barn "right off the Merritt Parkway" in Westport; but despite
an across-the-board bump in Survey scores, a cadre of critics still
call this a "tired" "grande dame" that's "more of a blue-hair special
than a fine-dining experience."

Red Lotus *Thai*   20 | 13 | 19 | $32

New Rochelle | 227 Main St. (Stephenson Blvd.), NY | 914-576-0444 |
www.redlotusthai.com

A "storefront sleeper" in New Rochelle, this "congenial" Thai supplies "mouthwatering" noodles and curries in "modest" red quarters
staffed by "gracious" servers; the budget-focused find it "pricey" for
the genre, but better Asian options are "scarce" in the area.

Red Plum *Asian*   - | - | - | E

Mamaroneck | 251 Mamaroneck Ave. (bet. Palmer & Prospect Aves.),
NY | 914-777-6888 | www.redplumrestaurant.com

From the owners of Mamaroneck's Toyo Sushi, this next-door Pan-
Asian sports spiffy, mod decor (accented with glossy wooden tables
and red-and-black accoutrements), which echoes the contemporary menu, a selection of sushi and cooked fare; the upscale cocktails, wines and champagnes also are aligned with the eatery's
upmarket ambitions – likewise the prices.

Red Rooster Drive-In ⊅ *Burgers*   18 | 10 | 15 | $13

Brewster | 1566 Rte. 22 (Rte. 312), NY | 845-279-8046

"Juicy burgers, crispy fries", "chili dogs", "thick shakes" – "all the
good stuff" of a "roadside drive-in" is on offer at this bang-for-the-
buck Brewster "landmark" (since 1964); seating inside is scarce, so
most grab their grub and eat it "alfresco" at picnic tables, then fol-
low it up with a round of "mini golf" at the adjacent course.

Rein's NY Style Deli-Restaurant ● *Deli*   22 | 11 | 17 | $22

Vernon | Shops at 30 Plaza | 435 Hartford Tpke./Rte. 30 (bet. Dobson &
Merline Rds.) | 860-875-1344 | www.reinsdeli.com

"NYers trapped in Connecticut" appreciate this "always mobbed"
"Jewish deli" and aren't reined in when it comes to ordering "crunchy

	FOOD	DECOR	SERVICE	COST

garlic pickles", "all-day breakfasts" and "piled-high sandwiches"; plus, the "convenient" Vernon venue means it's a "perpetual" "pit stop" for NYC-Boston travelers, who dismiss the "nondescript" decor ("all the charm of a bus depot") and "wait for a table" like everyone else.

Reka's Thai
18 | 14 | 18 | $34

White Plains | 2 Westchester Ave. (Main St.), NY | 914-949-1440 | www.rekasthai.com

"Hostess with the mostest" Reka Souwapawong "loves to mingle with the customers" at her White Plains Thai supplying "basic" Siamese standards; though cynics cite "tired" decor and "underwhelming" cooking, partisans praise the overall "pleasant" experience.

Restaurant at Rowayton
Seafood Seafood
22 | 20 | 20 | $48

Rowayton | 89 Rowayton Ave. (bet. Crockett St. & Logan Pl.) | 203-866-4488 | www.rowaytonseafood.com

At this "busy, busy" Rowayton "find", noshing at tables "overlooking Five Mile River" "somehow makes the seafood taste fresher", though the "adjacent [fish] market" is the true cause; and while "lobster ravioli" and other "well-prepared" dishes have "locals" saying it's "a keeper", a few landlubbers lament that given the "awesome view", it's "only as good as it has to be" – and "pricey" at that.

Restaurant at Water's Edge American
20 | 24 | 20 | $48

Westbrook | Water's Edge Resort & Spa | 1525 Boston Post Rd. (bet. Knothe Hill & Little Stannard Beach Rds.) | 860-399-5901 | www.watersedge-resort.com

Buffeteers beam over the "fabulous" Sunday brunch at this New American seafooder in Westbrook's Water's Edge Resort & Spa, whose "lovely" view of Long Island Sound "sweeps you away into another world"; indeed, while some insist the "pleasant" atmosphere makes "any shortcomings forgivable", the less-charitable say "overpriced", "mediocre food" can lead to a "disappointing" experience.

NEW Restaurant L&E and
French 75 Bar French
- | - | - | E

Chester | 59 Main St. (Maple St.) | 860-526-5301 | www.restaurantfrench75bar.com

To Chester's former Restaurant du Village space comes this antiques-bedecked arrival from chef Everett Reid and his wife, Linda, the founders of Nantucket's highly rated American Seasons (which they no longer own); upscale New French fare emphasizing seasonal New England ingredients is on offer in the main bistro, either in a tasting menu or small-plate format, and in the bar there are burgers, moules frites and such to accompany the cocktails and wine.

Ristorante Luce Italian
22 | 20 | 21 | $48

Hamden | Mt. Carmel Shopping Ctr. | 2987 Whitney Ave. (Ives St.) | 203-407-8000 | www.ristoranteluce.net

For "wonderful meatballs served with a dollop of fresh ricotta" and "generous portions" of other "reliably good" fare, look for this family-run Italian "tucked off Route 10" in Hamden; "lovely decor" and "courteous" service" complete the picture; P.S. the "can't-be-topped wine list" features 1,000-plus bottles.

River Bistro Ⓜ *Spanish* ▽ 19 21 19 $41

New Milford | 300 Kent Rd./Rte. 7 (Boardman Rd.) | 860-355-4466 | www.riverbistro.net

The "talented" chef-owner's "scintillating" tapas and "superb" paella have fans fawning at this New Milford Mediterranean-Spanish bistro with a "lovely" setting overlooking the Housatonic River; skeptics, though, find it "overpriced" and "nothing special" "except for the view" of the historic Boardman Bridge; N.B. also closed Tuesdays.

River Cat Grill *American* 22 21 20 $41

Rowayton | 148 Rowayton Ave. (bet. McKinley St. & Wilson Ave.) | 203-854-0860 | www.rivercatgrill.com

Whether it's sitting by the "fireside in the winter" or on the "little summer patio", Rowayton locals "love" their "cool cat on the river" and its "diverse", "quality" New American dishes; weekend "live music" is a "real draw", but it's the "cougar-hunting" that's "pure entertainment" when this "charmer" morphs into "the second-chance saloon."

River House *American* 16 20 17 $44

Westport | 299 Riverside Ave. (bet. River Ct. & Sylvan Ln.) | 203-226-5532 | www.riverhousewestport.com

Surveyors enjoy "watching the skullers or ducks skim past" this Westport Traditional American on the banks of the Saugatuck River and applaud a "warm atmosphere" and "improved service"; but many maintain the "view's better than the chow", so "bring someone worth talking to, because you won't have much to say about the food."

River Tavern *American* 25 23 21 $51

Chester | 23 Main St. (Rte. 148) | 860-526-9417 | www.rivertavernchester.com

Chef-owner Jonathan Rapp's "sense of adventurous fun" permeates this "informal but innovative" New American in the "little town of Chester", where "fresh, top-quality ingredients" are used to "wonderful" effect for a menu that's "always changing" (daily, in fact) and enhanced by a "superior wine list"; though the "cramped but cozy" quarters can get a bit "noisy" and a few fret about "aloof" servers, fans find it near "perfect every time."

Rizzuto's Wood-Fired Pizza *Italian* - - - M

Bethel | 6 Stony Hill Rd. (Sky Edge Dr.) | 203-790-4444
NEW **West Hartford** | 111 Memorial Rd. (S. Main St.) | 860-232-5000
NEW **Westport** | 540 Riverside Ave. (Bridge St.) | 203-221-1002
www.rizzutos.com

This trio of upscale pizzerias began in Bethel with a display kitchen, counter seating and a wood-fired oven, a winning formula replicated at the new West Hartford and Westport outposts, which, in addition to a range of Italian dishes, offer amenities like a raw bar and retail market selling fresh pastas, sauces and artisanal breads; know that the decibel levels can be on the high side, especially when the premises are packed with kids.

NEW Roasted Peppers *American*   – | – | – | M

Mamaroneck | 320 Mamaroneck Ave. (Spencer Pl.), NY | 914-341-1140 |
www.roastedpeppersny.com

At this casual, midpriced new Mamaroneck eatery, a trio of chefs previously at Sam's of Gedney Way prepares New American plates like red snapper tacos, beer-braised beef short ribs and, surprise, signature stuffed roasted peppers two ways; cappuccino-colored tables and mustard-and-exposed-brick walls comprise the simple yet appealing decor, and sidewalk seating beckons when the weather cooperates; N.B. check out the long list of specialty drinks.

NEW Rocco's Italian Kitchen *Italian*   – | – | – | M

New Canaan | 36 Pine St. (Cherry St.) | 203-966-2200 |
www.roccosct.com

Homestyle Neapolitan cooking – eggplant parm, ravioli, etc. – is what you'll find at this family-friendly Italian arrival to a New Canaan strip mall, where roomy tables, polished wood and tin ceilings lend an old-school-NY feel; add to that brick-oven pizzas and an approachable international wine list, and you've got an already-popular neighborhood haunt.

Roger Sherman Inn Ⓜ *Continental*   22 | 24 | 24 | $56

New Canaan | Roger Sherman Inn | 195 Oenoke Ridge/Rte. 124 (Holmewood Ln.) | 203-966-4541 | www.rogershermaninn.com

Set in a "beautiful" circa-1783 country house, this New Canaan Continental is a "lovely" choice for a "quiet, romantic dinner for two" and "meets all expectations for a special occasion" as well; most feel it "hits all the right notes" with its "charming dining rooms", "well-prepared" fare (especially at "fantastic" Sunday brunch) and live music on weekends, but a few still find its "old New England inn" vibe a touch "stuffy."

NEW Rouge Winebar *Mediterranean*   – | – | – | M

South Norwalk | 88 Washington St. (Main St.) | 203-354-4781 |
www.rougewinebar-ct.com

Its Parisian-sounding moniker is deceiving, because the Med fare at this savvy South Norwalk newcomer reflects the heritage of the Greek family that owns it (along with Harbor Lights across town); its 20-plus wines by the glass complement a variety of meze, as well as signature lobster risotto, allowing diners to either graze or feast within its posh storefront setting featuring exposed brick and, yes, *rouge* accents; N.B. dinner only.

Route 22 *Pub Food*   13 | 16 | 14 | $26

Stamford | 1980 W. Main St. (Alvord Ln.) | 203-323-2229
Armonk | 55 Old Rte. 22 (Kaysal Ct.), NY | 914-765-0022
www.rt22restaurant.com

A "favorite" among the "five-year-old" set, these "loud", "kitschy" auto-themed joints in Armonk and Stamford sling burgers that are a "cut above fast food" and presented in mini cardboard cars; yet in spite of "cute" settings decked out in "early-20th-century Americana", doubters declare them "too costly" given the "distracted" service and "average" grub – "if you don't have kids", "keep on driving."

Royal Palace *Chinese* — 24 | 15 | 21 | $26
New Haven | 32 Orange St. (Crown St.) | 203-776-6663 | www.ctmenusonline.com/rp.htm
"Royal, indeed!" exclaim enthusiasts of this long-standing "family-owned crowd-pleaser" in New Haven where "you can choose from three menus" (standard Sino-American "staples", plus "authentic" fare written in Chinese and its translation); you may "not be impressed with the decor", but with grub this "exotic", "delicious and surprising", you probably won't care.

Royal Palace *Indian* — 20 | 13 | 17 | $32
White Plains | 77 Knollwood Rd. (Dobbs Ferry Rd.), NY | 914-289-1988 | www.royalpalacecuisines.com
Loyal subjects say it's all about the "extensive" buffet available for both lunch and dinner (the latter offered only Monday–Thursday) at this White Plains Indian where the food is "authentic" and "delicious"; alright, it may be "basic in the atmosphere department", but few mind since you can dine well for "only a few rupees" here.

Rraci ⓢ *Italian* — - | - | - | M
Brewster | 3670 Rte. 6 (bet. Branch & Thomas Rds.), NY | 845-278-6695
The "classic Italian" cooking at this slightly "expensive" but "always-crowded" Brewster "favorite" is the "best for miles around" according to boosters of its "terrific" housemade pastas, "superb risottos" and "real waiters" to deliver it; the dining rooms are done up in "sophisticated", "old-world" style, with "red velvet, dark wood" and dim lights that most find "soothing and comfortable", while "weather permitting", the bright, stone patio is "like another place entirely."

RSVP Ⓜ⇗ *French* — ▽ 29 | 16 | 25 | $71
West Cornwall | 7 Railroad St. (Rte. 128) | 860-672-7787
"Given that there are only eight tables" and "regulars treat it like a club", it's "next to impossible" to "get a reservation" at this "deliciously unpretentious" chef-owned French in West Cornwall; your "persistence is well worth it", though, to sample the "sublime" seven-course, $75 prix fixe "feasts" – a "bargain at twice the price" insiders insist, and "BYO" makes it even better; N.B. dinner only Friday through Sunday and no credit cards accepted.

Ruby's Oyster Bar & Bistro *Seafood* — 21 | 19 | 19 | $47
Rye | 45 Purchase St. (Smith St.), NY | 914-921-4166
Rye's "beautiful people" turn out in force at this "hopping" piscatorial palace where "tasty" plates of "pristine seafood" abound and the "sexy" "Moulin Rouge" vibe "feels like the city"; an "active bar scene", communal tables and "sharp young servers" enhance the "festive" atmospherics, and though it's "a bit pricey", nobody minds since the place just "makes you feel good."

	FOOD	DECOR	SERVICE	COST

Rue des Crêpes *French*

∇ 15 | 20 | 19 | $24

Harrison | 261 Halstead Ave. (Harrison Ave.), NY | 914-315-1631 | www.ruedescrepes.com

Francophiles feel "transported to Paris" by the sweet and savory crêpes at this "charming" Harrison bistro that's "fun for dessert" and for Sunday brunch; a "relaxed", "accommodating" vibe and "value" pricing bolster the appeal, though aside from the namesake comestibles, a few "weren't happy with the other selections."

⑂ Ruth's Chris Steak House *Steak*

24 | 20 | 22 | $62

Newington | 2513 Berlin Tpke./Rte. 515 (Kitts Ln.) | 860-666-2202 | www.ruthschris.com

"Have your cardiologist on speed dial" when you dig into the "massive mounds of marbled meat" at this "dependably excellent" Newington chain link; "polished service" and a "corporate" ambiance make you feel as if you're "living high on the cow", but those "butter-slathered steaks" go down easier if you're "on an expense account" – otherwise you may join those who deem it "overpriced and under-good."

Rye Grill & Bar *Eclectic*

- | - | - | M

Rye | 1 Station Plaza (on 1st St., off Purdy Ave.), NY | 914-967-0332 | www.ryegrill.com

After an extensive makeover, this multilevel Rye Eclectic now occupies 14,000 sq. ft. of space, with four distinct dining areas, two bars, fireplaces and a wraparound front porch; downstairs is rather raucous, with a communal table and booths filled with families enjoying sliders, quesadillas and other moderately priced fare, while the nautically themed second floor is slightly more subdued.

Rye Roadhouse *Cajun/Creole*

18 | 14 | 17 | $32

Rye | 12 High St. (bet. Clinton & Maple Aves.), NY | 914-925-2668 | www.theryeroadhouse.com

"Down-home cooking" is the name of the game at this "funky" Rye roadhouse delivering "authentic" Cajun-Creole fare like boiled crawfish alongside not-so-authentic dishes like fried mac 'n' cheese; foes find the food "marginal", but the charmingly "rustic" atmosphere (it's a "hoot") still makes it "worth a visit."

Sage American Grill *Seafood/Steak*

20 | 21 | 20 | $43

New Haven | 100 S. Water St. (Howard Ave.) | 203-787-3466 | www.sageamerican.com

If "wonderful views" are a "primary" concern, this surf 'n' turfer's "spectacular setting" "right on New Haven Harbor" delivers, plus it's a "beautiful location to sip drinks on the balcony"; "large, delicious portions" of "steak, seafood and lamb", "live entertainment" and a "welcoming staff" ("even when mobbed") add to the appeal.

Sagi ⓩ *Italian*

- | - | - | M

Ridgefield | 23 Catoonah St. (Main St.) | 203-431-0200 | www.sagiofridgefield.com

Chef-owner Bianca DeMasi Occhino, who hails from Calabria, brings her flair for homemade pasta and spins on regional Italian

FOOD | DECOR | SERVICE | COST

cuisine to this Ridgefielder whose standouts include fresh ravioli, tagliatelle and a house special ricotta gnocchi; the family pitches in here, with her airline pilot husband selecting the reasonably priced wines and oldest daughter waiting tables.

Saint Tropez Bistro Francais *French*

| 23 | 22 | 23 | $46 |

Fairfield | 52 Sanford St. (off Post Rd.) | 203-254-8094 | www.saint-tropez-bistro.com

"Start eating the bouillabaisse and you'll forget there's anything else on the menu" at this "elegant place for a splurge" in Downtown Fairfield; happily, respondents report that the other "French bistro fare" is equally "outstanding", including *"trés bon"* sweetbreads, and the "colorful mural" makes you "feel as if you're sitting in Provence"; P.S. the adjacent "'O' Bar is a relaxing place for drinks."

Sakura *Japanese*

| 21 | 17 | 20 | $38 |

Westport | 680 Post Rd. E. (Hills Point Rd.) | 203-222-0802 | www.sakurarestaurant.com

"Flames shoot up and knives twirl" at this Westport "institution"-cum-"birthday party central", an "always-packed" "family favorite" whose "solid" "hibachi room" can be a "real factory"; the grill-averse can choose more "relaxing environments" for "fresh", "dependable" sushi and other "traditional" Japanese fare ("i.e. tempura"); just be prepared for an "expensive" tab and staffers who "seem to rush you out the door."

☑ Sally's Apizza Ⓜ⇗ *Pizza*

| 26 | 9 | 11 | $21 |

New Haven | 237 Wooster St. (bet. Olive & Warren Sts.) | 203-624-5271 | www.sallysapizza.net

"Rude service", "no atmosphere" and "stunningly long and slow lines" in which "regulars can cut in front of everyone else" - "it's all part of the experience" at this "classic" "New Haven pizza joint"; those in-the-know say you learn to "manage your expectations", because the "amazing" "fresh mozzarella" pies with "thin, charred, lightly seasoned crust" are "worth it"; foes simply say "forget it"; N.B. cash only.

Salsa Ⓜ⇗ *Southwestern*

| ▽ 23 | 11 | 22 | $22 |

New Milford | 54 Railroad St. (Bank St.) | 860-350-0701

"You could walk by 50 times and miss" this "tiny storefront" in New Milford serving "top-flight", "creative" Southwestern fare "that tastes homemade", thanks to "fresh ingredients"; there's "not much ambiance" in its "unassuming" digs, but the staff is "friendly" and "helpful", and the "marvelous" eats alone are "worth the trip"; N.B. cash only.

Sal's Pizza ⇗ *Pizza*

| 24 | 7 | 13 | $15 |

Mamaroneck | 316 Mamaroneck Ave. (Palmer Ave.), NY | 914-381-1022

Renowned for its "legendary pizza" and "all-day-every-day long lines", this "sizzling" Mamaroneck "main drag" pizzeria supplies cheesy "works of art" in a "little hole-in-the-wall" setting; they don't take reservations or credit cards, and service is "brusque" ("unless you're a pretty girl"), but ultimately the pies are so "perfecto" that no one cares; P.S. the gelateria next door provides "much needed extra seating."

Saltwater Grille *American*   20 | 23 | 17 | $46

Stamford | 183 Harbor Dr. (off Shippan Ave.) | 203-391-6500 | www.saltwatergrille.net

"Amazing views of the harbor" and "lots of outdoor dining space" make this "out-of-the-way" New American on Stamford's "beautiful Shippan Point" a "go-to summer" destination, while a "cozy fireplace upstairs" adds to its winter appeal; it recently (post-Survey) introduced a new menu focused singularly on seafood, which may outdate the above Food score; P.S. its "fresh and inventive" Sunday brunch is considered "one of the best around."

Sam's of Gedney Way *American*   17 | 16 | 18 | $37

White Plains | 52 Gedney Way (bet. Mamaroneck Ave. & Old Mamaroneck Rd.), NY | 914-949-0978 | www.samsofgedneyway.com

Folks "hankering for something familiar" tuck into "hearty" comfort chow from the "no-surprises" menu of this White Plains American that's been a neighborhood resource since 1932; though a tad "run-of-the-mill" for sophisticated sorts, it's "busy seven days a week" given its "comfortable" "pubby vibe" and "reasonable prices."

Sardegna Ⓜ *Italian*   21 | 17 | 22 | $44

Larchmont | 154 Larchmont Ave. (Addison St.), NY | 914-833-3399 | www.sardegnany.com

Surveyors seeking "something different" hail this Larchmont Italian "gem" where "unusual", "toothsome" dishes like malloreddus (a shell-shaped pasta) and various game preparations offer a "refreshing change" from the usual red-sauce suspects; its "relaxed" service is overseen by an ever-present owner who "maintains high standards", even if a few find the rust-and-gold decor on the "nondescript" side.

Saybrook Fish House *Seafood*   21 | 17 | 20 | $34

Rocky Hill | 2165 Silas Deane Hwy. (bet. Harbor View Dr. & Joiners Rd.) | 860-721-9188 | www.saybrookfishhouserestaurants.com

"Giant portions" of "well-prepared" fin favorites "rule the day" at this Rocky Hill seafooder, where the "salad bowl is bottomless" and the white paper tablecloths are disposable; if a few former fans fret it's "living on its rep from days gone by", they're outnumbered by proponents who praise the "pleasant staff and reasonable prices."

Schoolhouse at Cannondale Ⓜ *American*   – | – | – | E
(aka Cannondale)

Wilton | 34 Cannon Rd. (Seeley Rd.) | 203-834-9816 | www.schoolhouseatcannondale.com

Housed in one of Wilton's most treasured historic buildings (an 1872 schoolhouse overlooking the Norwalk River), this intimate New American's focus is on farm-fresh produce that's locally grown, with chef-owner Tim LaBant contributing to the bounty with his own gardens; expect a decidedly French slant to the weekly evolving menu that showcases the best the season has to offer; N.B. also closed Tuesdays.

	FOOD	DECOR	SERVICE	COST

Scoozzi Trattoria & Wine Bar Ⓜ *Italian*   22 | 21 | 21 | $42

New Haven | 1104 Chapel St. (York St.) | 203-776-8268 | www.scoozzi.com

It's "next door to Yale Rep" in New Haven's "cultural center", but it's the "innovative", "reliably excellent" food that's in the spotlight at this "upscale" Northern Italian; a "solid wine list" and "Sunday jazz brunch" are other star attractions, but most save their loudest ovations for the "wonderful" "alfresco dining in the courtyard."

Scribner's *Seafood*   23 | 16 | 20 | $40

Milford | 31 Village Rd. (Hawley Ave.) | 203-878-7019 | www.scribnersrestaurant.com

Even "landlubbers" are "pleasantly surprised" at this longtime sea-fooder in Milford, whose "standout rack of lamb" shares menu space with "homemade desserts" and "as-fresh-as-it-gets" fish prepared with "some new twists" (as in the "signature Gorgonzola swordfish"); the "affordable wine selection" is a plus, inasmuch as you won't be drinking in the "nonexistent atmosphere."

Seamen's Inne   ▽ 19 | 20 | 20 | $36
Restaurant & Pub *American/Seafood*

Mystic | Mystic Seaport | 105 Greenmanville Ave. (Rossie Pentway) | 860-572-5303 | www.seamensinne.com

"Spectacular views" bring this "old-fashioned" American seafooder "up a notch", a good thing since it's "part of Mystic Seaport" and often "overrun by tourists"; still, the midpriced food is "pretty good", and the "no-nonsense, classic New England service" adds to the "casual" vibe; P.S. there's "music on weekends."

Seaside Johnnie's *Seafood*   13 | 17 | 14 | $38

Rye | 94 Dearborn Ave. (Forest Ave.), NY | 914-921-6104 | www.seasidejohnnies.com

"Killer views" of Long Island Sound are the main attraction at this "informal" seasonal seafooder set on Rye's Oakland Beach; however, even though it can "feel like a vacation if you go at sunset", the "mediocre" fried food and "harried" service from "off-duty students" lead cynics to call it a "waste of an amazing location."

Seasons Japanese Bistro *Japanese*   20 | 15 | 19 | $35

White Plains | 105 Mamaroneck Ave. (Quarropas St.), NY | 914-421-1163 | www.seasonsjapanesebistro.com

Patrons "pop in" to this "unassuming" White Plains Japanese for "fresh sushi" and a "decent selection" of midpriced entrees well-suited to "business lunches" or an "easy" dinner; the less-impressed call it "average", but even critics concede it "does the job" for a "quick" bite.

Señor Pancho's *Mexican*   17 | 17 | 19 | $25

Litchfield | 7 Village Green (Greenwoods Rd.) | 860-567-3663
Southbury | Union Sq. (Main St. S.) | 203-262-6988
Waterbury | 280 Cheshire Rd. (bet. Mixville & Tucker Rds.) | 203-758-7788
www.senorpanchos.com

This Mexican threesome is a "fun place to take the family", offering an "extensive" menu of "consistently good" "standard" south-of-the-border eats and "attentive" service in a "festive" setting where you can "ask the mariachis to cover Beatles tunes"; critics, though, label the fare "ho-hum" and the decor "cheesy."

Sentrista Grill *American*

▽ 21 | 20 | 24 | $43

Brewster | 512 Clock Tower Dr. (off Rte. 22), NY | 845-279-2777 | www.sentrista.net

A bit off Route 22, but "worth trying", this Brewster haven offers signatures such as osso buco and seared ahi tuna that hint at the "wide variety" of its New American menu; sage green walls with pewter accents and bay windows create a "pretty" backdrop, and "enjoyable service" and monthly wine dinners are other reasons to stop by.

Serevan *Mediterranean*

28 | 24 | 25 | $55

Amenia | 6 Autumn Ln. (Rte. 44, west of Rte. 22), NY | 845-373-9800 | www.serevan.com

Amenia gourmands "can't say enough" about "genius" chef-owner Serge Madikians and his "exceptional" Med boîte where "vegetarians, carnivores" and "even picky NYers" are kept "happy" via "memorable" meals crafted with "exotic" "Middle Eastern" touches; yes, it's a bit "expensive", but a "well-trained" staff presides over the "inviting" dining room and the "beautiful garden" come summer.

Sesame Seed Ⓢ *Mideastern*

21 | 14 | 16 | $27

Danbury | 68 W. Wooster St. (bet. Division & Pleasant Sts.) | 203-743-9850 | www.sesameseedrestaurant.com

"Wear your granny squares" to this "sorta hippie" Middle Eastern in Danbury offering "an extensive menu" of "pasta and fish dishes", as well as "wonderful vegetarian fare" that "actually feels healthy"; while a few fashionistas think the digs "could use a fresh coat of paint", others are entranced by the "sprawling collection of ephemera" that highlights the "mishmash decorating scheme" and helps take your mind off the service, which most describe as "distracted."

Shady Glen ⊘ *Diner*

23 | 16 | 21 | $14

Manchester | Manchester Parkade | 360 W. Middle Tpke. (Broad St.) | 860-643-0511

Manchester | 840 E. Middle Tpke. (bet. Lake & Westland Sts.) | 860-649-4245

"Have a malt with your sweetheart" at these Manchester "retro diners", where "people come from miles around to try" the "freshly made ice cream" and "crispy cheeseburgers"; "soda jerks in paper hats" make drinks with seltzer and syrup, and the "1950s" feel (and prices) "makes you feel like you've gone back in time to *Happy Days*."

Sharpe Hill Vineyard Ⓜ *American*

- | - | - | E

Pomfret | 108 Wade Rd. (Rte. 97) | 860-974-3549 | www.sharpehill.com

"Divine wine" "made on-site" supplements the "wonderful" New American cuisine at this "beautiful hillside vineyard" in Pomfret, where the "quaint" dining area includes two fireplaces and 18th-century antiques; it's "hard to find" and "tough to get in" (reservations required), but fans say it's "worth" it for the "wow"; N.B. open only for dinner Friday and Saturday, and lunch on Sunday.

	FOOD	DECOR	SERVICE	COST

Shell Station Continental ▽ 21 | 16 | 22 | $35

Stratford | 2520 Main St. (Broadbridge Ave.) | 203-377-1648 |
www.shellstationrestaurant.net

The "tasty" "seafood and sushi" outshines the "less than glamorous" trappings of this chef-owned Continental set in a "former train station depot"; still, "Stratford's theater crowd" and locals lured by the "unpretentious" service and "worth-the-money" meals agree it's "one of those 'hey, I gotta go there again' type of places."

Shish Kebab House of Afghanistan Afghan 24 | 20 | 22 | $32

West Hartford | 36 LaSalle Rd. (bet. Arapahoe Rd. & Farmington Ave.) |
860-231-8400 | www.afghancuisine.net

"Load up on the sides" (particularly the "addictive stewed pumpkin") at this "outstanding" West Hartford Afghan, though just about "everything" is "fresh, tasty and authentic"; "wonderful service" and "amazing decor" – including a hookah lounge – add to a "memorable" experience you'll want to repeat "again and again."

Siena ☒ Italian 25 | 19 | 22 | $49

Stamford | 519 Summer St. (bet. Broad & Spring Sts.) | 203-351-0898 |
www.sienaristorante.net

From the "inventive", "outstanding" seasonal Tuscan fare and "excellent wine selection" to the "friendly", "gorgeous waiters", this Stamford Italian may be "the closest experience to eating in Italy in Fairfield County"; the atmosphere is "lovely" and the staff "warm and welcoming", but critics carp about "expensive prices" and compare the noise level to "being in Yankee Stadium."

Solaia Champagne House Italian 22 | 18 | 19 | $52

Greenwich | Greenwich Financial Ctr. | 363 Greenwich Ave. (Fawcett Pl.) |
203-622-6400 | www.solaiaenoteca.com

Known for its "fantastic" wine list, this Greenwich go-to has recently (post-Survey) sharpened its focus on champagne, shaping its menu of mostly French and Italian dishes ("excellent pastas", "well-executed small plates") to marry well with the bubbly; opinions are divided on its subterranean space – "hip" and "comfy" to some, a "dark cave" to others – while some say that service is "too cool for school."

Solé Ristorante Italian 22 | 20 | 19 | $48

New Canaan | 105 Elm St. (bet. Park St. & South Ave.) | 203-972-8887 |
www.soleofnewcanaan.com

Boosters boast the "kitchen's got chops" (as in its signature Milanese veal) as well as "wonderful" pizzas at this New Canaan Northern Italian, where the "food never disappoints"; but some carp that the only "buzz" to the place is the room's "deafening" "noise level", and even more noisome to critics is the staff's "attitude problem."

SolToro Tequila Grill Mexican - | - | - | M

Uncasville | Mohegan Sun Casino | 1 Mohegan Sun Blvd. (bet. Rtes. 2 & 32) | 860-862-4800 | www.soltororestaurant.com

With 190 tequilas on the drinks list, it's always a fiesta at this moderately priced Mexican cantina owned by basketball great

Michael Jordan and ensconced in Mohegan Sun's Casino of the Sky; it sports brightly hued decor, whimsical cutouts around the bar and meandering mariachis, and the party continues on the plate with tacos, fajitas, enchiladas and such served up with plenty of visual appeal.

SoNo Baking Company & Café *Bakery*   25 | 17 | 17 | $19

South Norwalk | 101 S. Water St. (Hanford Pl.) | 203-847-7666 | www.sonobaking.com

"Delicious" cakes and pastries, "imaginative sandwiches" and the "daily bread offerings" will have you saying "one of each, please" at this "rock-solid" SoNo bakery/cafe started by "Martha Stewart protégé" John Barricelli; sure, "it charges a lot of dough for its dough" and its "white-tiled" decor can best be described as "sterile", but carb-cravers still "recommend the place to everyone."

Sonora *Nuevo Latino*   24 | 22 | 22 | $51

Port Chester | 179 Rectory St. (Willett Ave.), NY | 914-933-0200 | www.sonorarestaurant.net

"Everything clicks" at this "vibrant" Nuevo Latino "winner" parked in a "hard-to-find" Port Chester address, where top toque Rafael Palomino cooks up "creative", "flavor-filled" dishes that are "plated beautifully"; the bi-level setting is "calmer upstairs" and "trendier downstairs", but no matter where you sit you can expect "attentive" service, "great energy" and "pricey" tabs – though the lunchtime prix fixe is an "incredible bargain."

Sono Seaport Seafood *Seafood*   16 | 14 | 15 | $28

South Norwalk | 100 Water St. (bet. Elizabeth St. & Hanford Pl.) | 203-854-9483 | www.sonoseaportseafood.com

"Get your fried fish fix" while you "sit outside on a large deck" and "watch the boats" on Norwalk Harbor at this uber-"casual" seafooder, but it'll help if you "like picnic benches" and "paper plates"; even the "best lobsters around" come with a "reasonable" tab, but more progressive palates complain that "nothing-special" grub and "lackluster service mean that only the seagulls leave happy."

Soul de Cuba *Cuban*   ▽ 21 | 20 | 21 | $32

New Haven | 283 Crown St. (bet. High & York Sts.) | 203-498-2822 | www.souldecuba.com

"You'll have to make new friends" (the quarters are *that* "cozy") at this "undiscovered" New Haven Cuban whose "delicious atmosphere matches the delicious food", including "slow-cooked chicken that melts off the bone"; expect "friendly service", "drinks that make you dance" and little opportunity for "intimate conversation."

Southport Brewing Co. *Pub Food*   15 | 15 | 17 | $27

Branford | 850 W. Main St. (Orchard Hill Rd.) | 203-481-2739
Hamden | 1950 Dixwell Ave. (off Merritt Pkwy.) | 203-288-4677
Milford | 33 New Haven Ave. (bet. Prospect & River Sts.) | 203-874-2337
Southport | 2600 Post Rd./Rte. 1 (River St.) | 203-256-2337

(continued)

	FOOD	DECOR	SERVICE	COST

(continued)

Southport Brewing Co.

Stamford | 131 Summer St. (Broad St.) | 203-327-2337
www.southportbrewing.com

A "happy-hour favorite" serving up "decent pub grub" along with an "interesting array of beers", this microbrewery chain is also a "family-friendly" option, with a children's menu that includes "healthy options" that come with "veggies and a toy", and magicians on Sunday nights; it gets "noisy" and "crowded", and while some find it merely "serviceable", others praise it for "not trying to be more than it is."

Southwest Cafe *New Mexican* | 20 | 16 | 21 | $33 |

Ridgefield | Copps Hill Common | 109 Danbury Rd. (bet. Copps Hill Rd. & South St.) | 203-431-3398 | www.southwestcafe.com

Owner Barbara Nevins "will go to far reaches to bring back new and interesting ingredients" to her "cozy, friendly" Ridgefield New Mexican that gets a shout out for "masterpiece chimichangas", "standout green chili stews" – and now, a new small-plates menu; *compañeros* give "kudos" to the "lively music" on Thursday and Saturday nights that adds to the "cool vibe"; N.B. a patio was added post-Survey.

Spadaro Ⓜ *Italian* | 24 | 12 | 19 | $48 |

New Rochelle | 211 E. Main St. (Stephenson Blvd.), NY | 914-235-4595

There's "no menu" at this "tiny" family-run storefront Italian in New Rochelle where the "delicious" "simply prepared" dishes come "fresh from the chef's imagination" and change daily; "solicitous" service creates a "warm" atmosphere all around, though a smattering of surveyors claim they were unpleasantly "surprised" by the final bill.

NEW Spinghar Kabob *Afghan* | - | - | - | M |

Glastonbury | Griswold Plaza | 2862 Main St. (Glastonbury Blvd.) | 860-657-2757 | www.spingharkabob.com

Named for the mountain range that forms the border between Afghanistan and Pakistan, this tiny newcomer brings authentic Afghan cuisine to Glastonbury, including tender kebabs and chai served in ornate teacups; the decor's nothing fancy, but a super-friendly staff and owner make up for any lack of ambiance.

Splash *Seafood* | 21 | 23 | 17 | $49 |

Westport | Inn at Longshore | 260 S. Compo Rd. (Greens Farm Rd.) | 203-454-7798 | www.decarorestaurantgroup.com

For the "best view anywhere", nab a "table on the deck" of this "pricey" seafooder set on a "gorgeous beach" at Westport's Inn at Longshore; the culinary concept is the "same as sibling Baang" ("excellent" "dishes made for sharing"), and so is the "noise level", particularly "in the summer when there's a band" at the "awesome" Patio Bar; still, critics wish the staff would deep-six the "'tude."

Sports Page *Pub Food* | - | - | - | M |

White Plains | 200 Hamilton Ave. (Cottage Pl.), NY | 914-437-8721

The White Plains address may be Hamilton instead of Marmaroneck Avenue, but the vibe remains the same at this iconic sports bar opened in 1981 by Bob Hyland, ex-Giant, ex-Stepinac student and perennial local boy done good; its kitchen runs the same tried-and-true plays: beer, Buffalo wings and other pub classics, ranging from burgers to burritos, all served amid the flickering lights of 50 game-filled flat-screens.

Spris ⓈItalian | 21 | 20 | 21 | $40 |

Hartford | 10 Constitution Plaza (State St.) | 860-247-7747 | www.sprishartford.com

"If you can find the place", fans of this "upscale" Northern Italian in Downtown Hartford say you'll dig its "excellent" "homemade pasta" and "good wine list"; detractors cite "dull" food and "service that fails to impress", but a "nice outdoor patio" works in its favor.

Squire's Redding Roadhouse Eclectic | 19 | 22 | 21 | $39 |

Redding | 406 Redding Rd./Rte. 53 (Rte. 107) | 203-938-3388 | www.reddingroadhouse.com

Reviewers reckon this Redding outpost "has quite a following" because of its "wonderful bar" "with weekend music", as well as a "quaint New England atmosphere" that "makes you feel warm and fuzzy" "on a cold night"; "Thai flavors" enliven the "decent" Eclectic menu (including "good burgers"), which a few say "needs updating."

Stand, The Ⓢ Vegan | – | – | – | I |

Norwalk | 31 Wall St. (Commerce St.) | 203-956-5670

Notable in Downtown Norwalk for being in the vegan vanguard, this compact contender delivers "delicious juices and smoothies", as well as "prepared foods" like soups and sandwiches made from all-organic ingredients; wheatgrass-hued walls and a chalkboard listing fruits and veggies available for blending add to the crunchy vibe.

Steak Loft Steak | 18 | 17 | 19 | $34 |

Mystic | Olde Mistick Vill. | Rte. 27 (I-95) | 860-536-2661 | www.steakloftct.com

Don't get any lofty ideas about this "barnlike" steakhouse just "off I-95" near Mystic Aquarium and Seaport where "you'll have to fight tourists for a table"; still, "rib-sticking portions" of "consistent standard fare" and a "well-stocked" salad bar has made it a "perennial favorite", even if some sniff that it's merely "your basic mall restaurant minus the mall."

Still River Café Ⓜ American   ▽ | 26 | 26 | 24 | $58 |

Eastford | 134 Union Rd./Rte. 171 (Centre Pike) | 860-974-9988 | www.stillrivercafe.com

True, this 27-acre Eastford farm and its 150-year-old "restored barn" are "in the middle of nowhere", but once you sample the "brilliant" New American cuisine "you feel as if you've died and gone to paradise"; co-owners Robert and Kara Brooks share responsibilities, and kudos: he "grows most of the [organic] produce", she "turns out magic" in the kitchen with her "inspired 'trios'" (as in duck prepared three ways); pricey, perhaps, but "worth every penny"; N.B. open for dinner only Friday–Saturday, plus Sunday brunch.

FOOD | DECOR | SERVICE | COST

☑ Stonehenge ⚠ Ⓜ *Continental* 24 | 25 | 24 | $63

Ridgefield | Stonehenge Inn | 35 Stonehenge Rd. (Rte. 7) | 203-438-6511 |
www.stonehengeinn-ct.com

"Expensive but exquisite", this Continental on 11 acres in Ridgefield
is "still the queen of Fairfield County inns" according to respondents, who rave that the "indulgent service" and "beautiful" setting "will transport you to millionaires' row"; while some think
it's "passé" and no longer "matches its reputation of yester-
year", for many it's a "wonderful" experience that "warrants a
trip to the boonies."

Stone House Ⓜ *American/Seafood* 21 | 21 | 20 | $39

Guilford | 506 Old Whitfield St. (Seaview Terr.) | 203-458-3700 |
www.stonehouserestaurant.com

It "sounds counterintuitive", but some vets of this New American
seafooder near the "Guilford docks" say "skip the stuffy dining
room" in favor of the "cozy" "bar next to the roaring fire"; wherever
you perch, choose from the same "interesting" menu, including
"high-quality" fin fare and "great burgers"; P.S. outdoorsy types can
"watch the boats go by" from the seasonal Little Stone House
Café next door.

Strada 18 *Italian* 25 | 20 | 21 | $41

South Norwalk | 122 Washington St. (bet. Main & Water Sts.) |
203-853-4546 | www.strada18.com

"Everybody knows your name . . . and that you love the mussels
with a side of meatballs" at this "reasonably priced" SoNo Italian,
where the brick oven pretty much "could make a shoe taste
great"; maybe, but more credit goes to "friendly" chef/co-owner
David Raymer, whose artisanal approach (e.g. he "makes his own
mozzarella") results in "awesome thin-crust pizzas" and "superb
baked casseroles", complemented by what some call a "world-
class" wine list; N.B. takes reservations at lunch and for large parties on weeknights only.

Su Casa *Mexican* 18 | 17 | 18 | $27

Branford | 400 E. Main St. (Featherbed Ln.) | 203-481-5001

"Comfy, cozy and casual" "with killer margaritas" – that's what amigos adore about this Branford Mexican; *sí*, the food's "pretty
Americanized" ("stay away if you're an orthodox foodie"), but it's a
"step above chain" and a "fun place to go when you have a craving"
for "ok Tex-Mex."

☑ Super Duper Weenie *Hot Dogs* 22 | 9 | 18 | $11

Fairfield | 306 Black Rock Tpke. (Commerce Dr.) | 203-334-3647 |
www.superduperweenie.com

"You'd have to bark up another tree for a better dog" than the "best-
in-show" varieties at this "superior road food" joint in Fairfield,
where "fresh-cut fries" and "homemade condiments" are other reasons fawning frank-ophiles say "go out of your way to get there";
plus it's so super-duper "affordable", it ranks as Connecticut's No. 1
Bang for the Buck.

Sushi Nanase *Japanese*

27 | 17 | 21 | $67

White Plains | 522 Mamaroneck Ave. (DeKalb Ave.), NY | 914-285-5351
"Master" chef-owner Yoshimichi Takeda "rules" this "tiny" White Plains Japanese turning out "pristine" sushi "made the traditional way" for those who abide his "finicky" reservations policy that yields little grace for lateness; it's "not for amateurs" (i.e. "no California rolls") and it is "expensive", although acolytes agree such "sublime" fare is "worth every penny"; N.B. no walk-ins allowed; call ahead for the omakase.

Sushi 25 *Chinese/Japanese* (aka Hunan Taste)

- | - | - | M

New Canaan | 24 Elm St. (bet. Main St. & South Ave.) | 203-966-1009 | www.sushi25.com
This New Canaan favorite has a split personality, serving sushi on one side and Chinese on the other; Japanese offerings include udon noodles and teriyaki dishes, while the Hunan Taste menu includes Thai and Indonesian flavors; N.B. it's less expensive than Ching's Table, its better-known Pan-Asian sib just around the corner.

T&J Villaggio Trattoria Ⓜ *Italian*

23 | 10 | 20 | $31

Port Chester | 223-225 Westchester Ave. (bet. Grove & Oak Sts.), NY | 914-937-6665 | www.tandjs.net
"Everything on the menu tastes like home" at this Port Chester Italian dishing out all the "red-sauce" classics at prices that "won't break your wallet" – though the "hearty" helpings might just "break the zipper on your pants"; though the setting is "spartan", warm welcomes and a "friendly", "family-oriented" vibe overcome all.

Tandoori Taste of India *Indian*

23 | 17 | 22 | $34

Port Chester | 163 N. Main St. (bet. Highland & Mill Sts.), NY | 914-937-2727 | www.tandooritasteofindia.com
"Delicious" classics are "well prepared" and served from "traditional copper pots" at this Port Chester Indian; the digs are "pleasant" if "plain", and service is "gracious", but most are more intrigued by the "great" value, especially that "nicely priced buffet lunch."

Tango Ⓢ *Argentinean/Italian*

- | - | - | M

Glastonbury | 2935 Main St. (off Rte. 2) | 860-657-4527 | www.cttango.com
It takes two to tango – a couple of colorful culinary traditions, that is, which dance on the palate at this Glastonbury Italo-Argentine; highlights on the moderately priced menu include housemade pastas and paella, while the bar's tapas go down well with a mojito or caipirinha, all served up amid impressively trendy environs.

Tango Grill *Argentinean/Italian*

22 | 19 | 20 | $59

White Plains | 128 E. Post Rd. (Court St.), NY | 914-946-6222 | www.tangogrillny.com
A "nice change from the usual chophouse", this White Plains Argentinean "hits the mark" with "amazing steaks" and an "inspired" lineup of Italian dishes amid cherrywood accents; though

servers are "charming" and "knowledgeable", many feel stung by "stratospheric" pricing ("watch out for the specials") that feels out of step with the "cramped" setting and off-the-beaten-track locale.

Tapas *Mediterranean*   23 | 15 | 20 | $24

Bloomfield | 852 Cottage Grove Rd. (Bloomfield Ave.) | 860-882-0756
West Hartford | 1150 New Britain Ave. (Yale St.) | 860-521-4609

Tapas on Ann ⊠ *Mediterranean*

Hartford | 126-130 Ann St. (bet. Asylum & Pearl Sts.) |
860-525-5988
www.tapasonline.com

Name notwithstanding, you won't find Spanish tapas on the "inventive" menu at this "big-bang-for-the-buck" chainlet, just "hearty, tasty" Mediterranean fare "served in a welcoming atmosphere"; the "best Greek salad around" is "worth the trip" alone, and the "blackboard specials" usually include "lots of vegetarian options."

Tarantino's ⊠ *Italian*   24 | 19 | 24 | $54

Westport | 30 Railroad Pl. (bet. Franklin St. & Riverside Ave.) |
203-454-3188 | www.tarantinorestaurant.com

It's "pure *Italiano*" at this "festive" Westport "legend" "across from the train station" that's "as busy as it should be when the food is this good", including standouts like the osso buco and "homemade pasta"; however, gird yourself for "expensive" prices (though it reduced its rates at lunchtime post-Survey), and "small, close quarters" that can be "deafening" when the place is "packed."

Taro's ⊅ *Italian/Pizza*   20 | 10 | 22 | $22

Millerton | 18 Main St. (N. Center St.), NY | 518-789-6630

"Excellent" thin-crust pizzas, "tasty" pastas and other "basic" Italian dishes make this "low-key" Millerton joint the "go-to place" for both locals and weekenders; true, "it ain't fancy", but the "super-friendly" servers "work hard", and it's perfect before or after the movies, offering the "best bang for the buck in the area."

Tarry Lodge *Italian*   24 | 24 | 20 | $50

Port Chester | 18 Mill St. (Abendroth Ave.), NY | 914-939-3111 |
www.tarrylodge.com

Chef-superstar Mario Batali and partner Joe Bastianich have "knocked it out of the park" with this much-"hyped" revamp of a beloved Port Chester tavern, now showcasing their brand of "true Italian" cooking like wood-fired pizzas and "exceptionally crafted" pastas, all served with "superb" wines in a "lively" (some say "deafening") gold-hued setting; throw in surprisingly "reasonable prices", and it makes a "tempting" suburban "alternative to Babbo" – "if you can ever get in."

NEW **Taste of Charleston** *Southern*   - | - | - | M

Norwalk | 195 Liberty Sq. (Goldstein Pl.) | 203-810-4075 |
www.atasteofcharleston.net

For those seeking to satisfy Low Country cravings, this Norwalk newcomer across from Veterans Memorial Park provides some Southern exposure; expect generous portions of mudbugs (that's crawfish to you Northerners), babyback ribs and shrimp 'n' grits served up with heaps of hospitality – and though the decor is on the plain-Jane side, happily the prices are just as modest.

Taste of India *Indian*   20 | 15 | 19 | $24

West Hartford | 139 S. Main St. (Sedgwick Rd.) | 860-561-2221 | www.tasteofindiawh.com

"Don't let the sad storefront keep you out" of this "hits-the-spot" Indian in West Hartford with "reliable" chow and an interior that was refurbished a couple of years ago ("boy, did it need it"); if some surveyors suggest "turning up the heat on some dishes", few gripe about the "all-you-can-eat lunch buffet", a "great value" for $7.95.

Tavern on Main *New England*   19 | 20 | 19 | $42

Westport | 150 Main St. (Avery Pl.) | 203-221-7222 | www.tavernonmain.com

Westporters jonesing for a "quintessential New England tavern" – "tilted ceilings and floors" included – head to this "cozy" Colonial (circa 1810) proffering "solid if unspectacular" regional American cuisine like "Yankee pot roast"; in summer, those-in-the-know hit the "lovely" "covered patio" and "watch the shoppers" on Main Street, while winter finds them "near the large open fireplace", perhaps pondering, as a few do, if it's "gotten too expensive."

Tawa *Indian*   ∇ 22 | - | 25 | $25

Stamford | 211 Summer St. (bet. Broad & Main Sts.) | 203-359-8977 | www.tawaonline.com

An "attentive", "excellent" staff serves up "freshly prepared" fare, including "plenty of vegetarian options", at this Stamford Indian where the "enjoyable" $11 lunch buffet is a "real bargain" and the rest of the menu is "reasonable" as well; those who found fault with its "strip-mall setting" should appreciate that it recently relocated to new Downtown digs.

Ted's Montana Grill *American*   21 | 22 | 20 | $32

South Windsor | 500 Evergreen Way (Cedar Ave.) | 860-648-1100 | www.tedsmontanagrill.com

While the "tasty" signature bison burger may be "reason enough" to visit this South Windsor outpost of Ted Turner's "refreshing" Western-themed chain, the "diverse" menu also includes "other good takes on American classics"; sure, service can be "uneven" and there's "nothing flashy" going on ambiancewise, but it's still a "good value for the money."

Telluride *Southwestern*   21 | 20 | 19 | $48

Stamford | 245 Bedford St. (bet. Broad & Spring Sts.) | 203-357-7679 | www.telluriderestaurant.com

"Fabulous wines" "pair well" with the "diverse, adventurous menu" at this "creative" Southwestern in Downtown Stamford, where a "cozy Western motif" creates a "fresh-from-the-Rockies" feel; detractors, though, dis "mile-high prices and up-in-the-air service", with some concluding that it's a "shadow of its former self."

	FOOD	DECOR	SERVICE	COST

☒ Tengda Asian Bistro *Asian* — 23 | 18 | 19 | $40

Darien | Goodwives Shopping Ctr. | 23 Old Kings Hwy. N. (Sedgewick Ave.) | 203-656-1688
Greenwich | 21 Field Point Rd. (bet. W. Elm St. & W. Putnam Ave.) | 203-625-5338
NEW Milford | 1676 Boston Post Rd. (Woodruff Rd.) | 203-877-8888
Westport | 1330 Post Rd. E. (Old Rd.) | 203-255-6115
Katonah | Katonah Shopping Ctr. | 286 Katonah Ave. (Rte. 117), NY | 914-232-3900 Ⓜ
www.asianbistrogroup.com

"Embrace your sense of culinary adventure" at this "trendy" Pan-Asian chainlet where most say "the food crackles with flavor", from the "must-try" curry glazed rock shrimp to "creative, fresh" sushi; dissenters find it "unspectacular" and a "touch pricey", but factor in an "eclectic drink list" and "knowledgeable" service, and crowds (and "noise") are almost "inevitable."

1020 Post Oyster Bar & Bistro *French* — - | - | - | E

Darien | 1020 Post Rd. (bet. Center St. & Corbin Dr.) | 203-655-1020 | www.tentwentypost.com

This "open, airy" Darien bistro on the Post Road shares the same owners as its Rye cousin, Ruby's Oyster Bar & Bistro, along with a seafood-inspired brasserie menu including oysters, bouillabaisse, moules frites and lobster mac 'n' cheese; partisans profess it's also a "great place to go for a drink", but whether you sip or sup, know that it's fairly "expensive."

Tequila Mockingbird *Mexican* — 17 | 18 | 17 | $34

New Canaan | 6 Forest St. (East Ave.) | 203-966-2222

A place for "regular Joes" in "fashionable New Canaan", this "delightful" Mexican attracts "diners of all ages" with "above-average" fare and one of the "best selections of tequila around", served in an "eye-catching", "kid-friendly" setting at prices that "don't break the bank"; the "bustle of this place confirms its appeal" – which will be boosted when outdoor seating is added (it's planned for summer 2010).

Tequila Sunrise *Mexican* — 15 | 16 | 15 | $33

Larchmont | 145 Larchmont Ave. (bet. Addison St. & Boston Post Rd.), NY | 914-834-6378 | www.tequilasunriselarchmont.com

The "standard Mexican" menu plays second fiddle to the "festive" mood at this "roaring" Larchmont venue – a "loud" mix of "roving mariachis", "delicious margaritas" and "birthday celebrations every few minutes"; despite "Americanized" chow that's pretty "ordinary", it's quite the "popular spot" for "large gatherings."

Terra Mar Grille *American* — ▽ 21 | 25 | 19 | $47

Old Saybrook | Saybrook Point Inn & Spa | 2 Bridge St. (College St.) | 860-388-1111 | www.saybrook.com

"Ask for a window seat" at this "gorgeous" if "pricey" New American at the Saybrook Point Inn & Spa so you can enjoy "fine dining" with a "fabulous" vista of the marina, Connecticut River and Long Island Sound; "professional service" and a "great patio" add appeal, yet it still falls short for a few who fret it "relies too much on the view and not enough on the kitchen."

Terra Ristorante *Italian*

| 22 | 20 | 18 | $48 |

Greenwich | 156 Greenwich Ave. (bet. Elm & Lewis Sts.) | 203-629-5222 | www.terraofgreenwich.com

Go for the "wood-grilled chicken" and the "dependable pizzas" at this "see-and-be-seen" Northern Italian trattoria "on the avenue" in Greenwich; service draws mixed marks and the setting is "cozy" and "convivial" to some but "cramped" and "noisy" to others, which may be why cognoscenti say it's "best in the warm months on the patio."

Thai Chi Asian Bistro *Asian*
(fka Plateau)

| 22 | 16 | 20 | $34 |

Stamford | 25 Bank St. (bet. Atlantic & Main Sts.) | 203-961-9875

Although the owners remain the same at this Stamford standby, a name change and a menu revamp (which may outdate the above ratings) have given it a new Pan-Asian identity, with offerings spanning myriad curries, rice and noodle dishes like pad Thai to Chinese stir-fries and sushi, sashimi and other special rolls; white tablecloths and soft lighting add warmth to the minimalist setup, while prices remain reasonable.

Thai Pan Asian *Thai*

| ▽ 17 | 11 | 18 | $20 |

New Haven | 1150 Chapel St. (York St.) | 203-752-9898

You'll have to "overlook the sparse decor" to take advantage of the "great value" offered by this "authentic" New Haven Thai, whose "huge variety" of "mouthwatering" dishes includes Bangkok duck; vets vow it's best "before a show" or midday, when its "inexpensive lunch buffet" ($7.95) makes it a standout.

Thai Pearl *Thai*

| 19 | 17 | 18 | $30 |

Ridgefield | Copps Hill Common | 113 Danbury Rd. (Farmingville Rd.) | 203-894-1424

Tucked away in an "undistinguished strip mall" in Ridgefield, this Thai "sleeper" serves up "authentic", "richly flavorful" fare – including "distinctive curries" – that is "prepared with care and served with grace" by a "friendly" staff; it's "not fancy", but the "inviting" atmosphere and wallet-friendly BYO policy are two more reasons many consider it "well worth the search."

Thai Place *Thai*

| - | - | - | M |

Putnam | 241 Kennedy Dr. (Bridge St.) | 860-963-7770 | www.thaiplacerestaurant.net

Those seeking pad Thai in Putnam will find that this intimate standby satisfies with fresh, flavorful, affordable fare; those unimpressed with the de rigueur Asian decor (blond wood, bamboo accents, umbrellas hanging from the ceiling) can always opt for takeout.

Z Thali *Indian*

| 26 | 22 | 23 | $39 |

New Canaan | 87 Main St. (bet. East & Locust Aves.) | 203-972-8332
New Haven | 4 Orange St. (George St.) | 203-777-1177

(continued)

(continued)

Thali

Ridgefield | Ridgefield Motor Inn | 296 Ethan Allen Hwy./Rte. 7 (Florida Hill Rd.) | 203-894-1080
www.thali.com

∎ Thali Too *Indian/Vegetarian*

New Haven | Yale University campus | 65 Broadway (Elm St.) | 203-776-1600 | www.thalitoo.com

These "innovative Indians" make you "come back again" for their "wonderful variety of dishes" singing with "sensuous spices", complemented by "generous cocktails" and a "surprisingly good wine list"; the digs are "cool" and "unusual", especially in New Canaan, with its "suspended waterfall in a high-ceiling room", and while some lament that it's "expensive", the $16.95 Sunday brunch is a real "buy"; N.B. New Haven's vegetarian outlet, Thali Too, opened post-Survey.

Thataway Cafe *American*   `15` `14` `16` `$30`

Greenwich | 409 Greenwich Ave. (bet. Grigg St. & Railroad Ave.) | 203-622-0947 | www.thatawaycafe.com

A "convenient", "reliable" option "before a movie" or "after a hard day of power shopping on Greenwich Avenue", this American offers "decent salads", "good burgers" and "a bit of people-watching from its outdoor dining area"; though foes find the food "utterly average" and the service "inconsistent", pragmatists put up with it "thataway" because it "fills the need for moderate-priced dining."

∎ Thomas Henkelmann ⑤Ⓜ *French*   `28` `28` `28` `$86`

Greenwich | Homestead Inn | 420 Field Point Rd. (bet. Bush Ave. & Merica Ln.) | 203-869-7500 | www.thomashenkelmann.com

Voted No. 1 for Food, Decor and Service in the CT Survey, this "extraordinary" Greenwich New French helmed by "master" chef Thomas Henkelmann and "charming" wife/hostess Theresa is where the "incredible is the usual" – "ethereal" cuisine, "uncompromised" service and "richly textured decor" reminiscent of a "European country manor"; the prices can "intimidate", but most insist it's "worth" the "splurge" – it "doesn't get any better than this"; N.B. jacket required.

3 Jalapeños *Tex-Mex*   `17` `15` `18` `$27`

Mamaroneck | 690 Mamaroneck Ave. (Grand St.), NY | 914-777-1156 | www.3jalapenos.com

"Families" feel at home at this "casual" Mamaroneck cantina applauded for its "efficient" service and "cheerful" vibe; granted, the Tex-Mex cooking isn't four star, but most reckon it's "reasonably tasty" in light of the "fair" prices, easygoing vibe and "enormous" portions.

Tiberio's Ⓜ *Italian*   `-` `-` `-` `M`

Old Saybrook | 1395 Boston Post Rd. (bet. Schoolhouse & Tompkins Rds.) | 860-388-2459 | www.tiberiosrestaurant.com

While the space may be "odd" to some, fans say you "can't fault the food" at this Old Saybrook Italian, where the chef-owner's signature is veal scaloppine – and "plenty of it"; overall, the staff "strives to make it an enjoyable experience and succeeds surprisingly well."

	FOOD	DECOR	SERVICE	COST

Tiger Bowl *Chinese*

| 15 | 5 | 15 | $20 |

Westport | Westport Shopping Ctr. | 1872 Boston Post Rd. E./Rte. 1 (bet. Buckley Ave. & Hulls Hwy.) | 203-255-1799 | www.tigerbowlwestport.com

Fans of this "small" Westport Chinese say it's "packed for good reason" – prices for the "basic" fare just "can't be beat" ("you'll be stuffed for $20"); then again, detractors say "you get what you pay for", citing "sub-quality" food and a "plain" storefront setting "next to Walgreens."

Todd English's Tuscany *Italian*

| 23 | 22 | 22 | $52 |

Uncasville | Mohegan Sun Casino | 1 Mohegan Sun Blvd. (Sandy Desert Rd.) | 860-862-3238 | www.toddenglish.com

"Make your way through the waterfall" to this "fantasmagorical" Northern Italian "in a cavelike" setting at Mohegan Sun, where Todd English's "tasty" take on Tuscan fare "continues to impress and delight"; too bad the "noisy" cascade can "detract from a pleasant experience" (tip: "sit inside"), and some bean counters carp about "expensive" tabs; N.B. hours vary, so call ahead.

Toscana *Italian*

| 21 | 22 | 21 | $47 |

Ridgefield | 43 Danbury Rd. (bet. Grove St. & Mountain View Ave.) | 203-894-8995 | www.toscanaridgefield.com

"Tasting is believing" say supporters who declare this Ridgefield Tuscan a "winner" thanks to the "welcoming" chef-owner's "excellent" seafood risotto, "well-prepared" apps and "fun family dinners" on Sundays; the setting is "lovely", although the room can get "loud", and while the staff is "friendly", service can be "mixed."

Toshi Japanese *Japanese*

| ▽ 23 | 17 | 15 | $34 |

Avon | 136 Simsbury Rd. (bet. Fisher Dr. & Rosewood Rd.) | 860-677-8242 | www.toshirestaurant.com

Avon afishionados hit this moderately priced Japanese joint "often", as the sushi is "always incredibly fresh" (if "not as creative as others") and the "cooked dishes are decent enough"; if service can be "less than fully attentive" and the "wood setting" doesn't wow, an "excellent sake selection" helps divert attention from any shortcomings.

Town Dock *American*

| 17 | 12 | 18 | $36 |

Rye | 15 Purdy Ave. (bet. Boston Post Rd. & Purchase St.), NY | 914-967-2497

A "Rye tradition" for more than a decade, this "friendly" local "hangout" lures families with comforting American standards and seafood (think burgers, meatloaf and fish 'n' chips) served in "casual" nautically themed surroundings; it's "a little overpriced", but given the tony neighborhood, jaded sorts shrug "you expect that."

Towne Crier Cafe Ⓜ *American*

| ▽ 15 | 14 | 15 | $34 |

Pawling | 130 Rte. 22 (Fenwood Dr.), NY | 845-855-1300 | www.townecrier.com

"It's all about the music" at this Pawling venue presenting local and national bands on a "small stage", so the "simple, reliable" New

American eats ("over-stuffed burritos", burgers and "fab desserts") are almost "afterthoughts"; the "rustic room " gets crowded" and the staffers "overworked", "but they try and it shows", so go – "socialize."

Toyo Sushi *Japanese*   22 | 14 | 17 | $34

Mamaroneck | 253 Mamaroneck Ave. (bet. Palmer & Prospect Aves.), NY | 914-777-8696 | www.toyosushi.com

"Locals never tire" of this "wildly popular", well-priced Mamaroneck Japanese where "über-fresh" fish comes in "interesting specialty rolls" and "artfully arranged" platters; so "take the kids (everybody else does)", and "as for the crowds" – they "handle them as best as they can", but just "don't expect to linger."

Trattoria Carl Anthony *Italian*   23 | 16 | 17 | $40

Monroe | Clock Tower Sq. | 477 Main St. (bet. Hubbell Dr. & Stanley Rd.) | 203-268-8486 | www.trattoriacarlanthony.com

The cuisine goes "above and beyond" the already "great" expectations that Monroe Italophiles have for this "fairly priced" trattoria; however, some feel that the "cramped" conditions and sometimes "slow", "arrogant" service detract from its "excellent reputation."

Trattoria Lucia *Italian*   ▽ 16 | 14 | 16 | $39

Bedford | 454 Old Post Rd. (bet. Hollyhock Ln. & The Farms Rd.), NY | 914-234-7600

Catering to children with a *"Romper Room*-style" dining room, this Bedford Italian is where families come together to munch on mid-priced pizzas and pastas followed by housemade gelato for dessert; foes fume the food's "mediocre", and note that "even with a separate area for adults", it's "still too noisy."

Trattoria Vivolo *Italian*   21 | 16 | 23 | $41

Harrison | 301 Halstead Ave. (bet. Parsons & Purdy Sts.), NY | 914-835-6199

Chef-owner Dean Vivolo is "always there to greet you" at this "aims-to-please" Harrison Italian where the "traditional" dishes are "lovingly prepared" and conveyed by an "amiable" crew; it's set in a "small" refurbished diner, though insiders head for the greenhouse-like garden room, the "most pleasant part of the restaurant."

Tre Angelina ⊠ *Italian*   21 | 17 | 21 | $48

White Plains | 478 Mamaroneck Ave. (bet. Marion & Shapham Pls.), NY | 914-686-0617 | www.treangelinany.com

Recently (post-Survey) expanded, this "wonderful, old-style" "standby" in Downtown White Plains sets a "welcoming" tone with "complimentary bruschetta" presented alongside "traditional" Northern Italian specialties; though it's relatively "easy on the wallet", some find fault with "noisy" acoustics.

Tre Scalini *Italian*   23 | 21 | 22 | $43

New Haven | 100 Wooster St. (bet. Chestnut & Franklin Sts.) | 203-777-3373 | www.trescalinirestaurant.com

This ristorante in New Haven's Little Italy serves "rich", "old-school Italian" meals alongside an "impressive wine list"; tabs that are "fair" to some are "a bit pricey" to others, but many agree that the staff provides "polite", "flexible" service even if the "tasteful" space is "a little tight."

Trinity Grill & Bar *American*   19 | 14 | 17 | $34

Harrison | 7-9 Purdy St. (bet. Colonial Pl. & Halstead Ave.), NY | 914-835-5920 | www.trinitygrill.net

Considered a "safe" bet in the center of Harrison, this affordable outpost offers "basic" New American "comfort food" (think rack of lamb, burgers and pastas) in a "pubby", "family-friendly" setting; it's "not trying to be something it isn't" – it's just a "local place", with a busy back room that's a "nice option" for groups.

Troutbeck Ⓜ *American*   ▽ 24 | 26 | 24 | $62

Amenia | Troutbeck Estate & Resort | 515 Leedsville Rd./Rte. 2 (Rte. 343), NY | 845-373-9681 | www.troutbeck.com

Set in a "beautiful" stone manor, this Amenia inn/conference center and "wonderful retreat" offers "much to marvel at" in its "gorgeous grounds" and old English decor; add in "surprisingly good" New American fare, and it's no wonder it hosts many a "special occasion", including "weddings" galore; N.B. call ahead, as hours can vary.

Trumbull Kitchen *Eclectic*   24 | 20 | 21 | $37

Hartford | 150 Trumbull St. (bet. Asylum & Pearl Sts.) | 860-493-7417 | www.trumbullkitchen.com

"Younger and more hip" than some of its Max Group brethren, this "place to be seen" (but "not to have a quiet conversation") in Downtown Hartford "delivers good value" in "something-for-everyone" Eclectic small and large plates that "send taste buds into overdrive"; there's also a "killer bar scene" and a "great patio."

Turkish Cuisine Westchester *Turkish*   - | - | - | I

White Plains | 116 Mamaroneck Ave. (Quarropas St.), NY | 914-683-6111 | www.turkishcuisineny.com

A former partner from Mamaroneck's well-regarded Turkish Meze is behind this bright, sparsely decorated eatery on a bar-packed strip of Downtown White Plains; kebabs, gyros and other Turkish delights comprise the fare, while soft drinks and strong coffee can be augmented with BYO bottles.

Turkish Meze *Mediterranean/Turkish*   22 | 16 | 21 | $38

Mamaroneck | 409 Mt. Pleasant Ave. (Stanley Ave.), NY | 914-777-3042 | www.turkishmeze.com

"Istanbul" comes to Mamaroneck via this Med-Turk "keeper" serving "delicious" meze and other "honest food" for a "low cost"; its "people-person" owner oversees the "courteous, efficient" service, and despite "fairly dull" "Turkish bazaar" decor, it's "always busy."

Turquoise *Mediterranean/Turkish*   19 | 16 | 20 | $38

Larchmont | 1895 Palmer Ave. (bet. Chatsworth Ave. & Depot Way W.), NY | 914-834-9888 | www.turqmed.com

Something "different" near the Larchmont train station, this "solid" Med-Turk proffers "kebabs that rock" and other "tasty" items set down by a "welcoming" crew; though there's some debate about the cost – "inexpensive" vs. "on the high side" – bargain-hunters "stick to the appetizers for a well-priced meal."

Tuscan Oven Trattoria *Italian*   18 | 19 | 17 | $39

Norwalk | 544 Main Ave. (Grist Mill Rd.) | 203-846-4600 | www.tuscanoven.com

Brick-oven pizzas, "solid" pastas and other "Italian delights" come paired with "decent-enough" wines at this "midscale" Norwalk trattoria that fans find a "convenient" pick for a "client lunch" or a "casual" dinner; service is "prompt" in its Tuscan-style space, so even if some say it's "nothing spectacular", it "doesn't disappoint" either; N.B. in summer, try the patio.

Tuscany ⓜ *Italian*   25 | 18 | 24 | $48

Bridgeport | 1084 Madison Ave. (bet. Lincoln Ave. & Madison Terr.) | 203-331-9884

Recently redecorated (post-Survey), this "terrific" Bridgeport Tuscan attracts returnees for its "enticing", "high-quality" fare served by staffers who treat them "like family"; tabs alternate between "reasonable" and "not cheap" ("ask the price of the specials" before ordering), but since the setting is "small", it remains a "secret that many keep from their friends."

Tuscany Grill *Italian*   ▽ 20 | 18 | 17 | $35

Middletown | Middlesex Opera House Bldg. | 120 College St. (Main St.) | 860-346-7096 | www.tuscany-grill.com

Set in an old movie house, this Italian entertains the "Wesleyan and Middletown business communities" in a "pleasant", terra-cotta-and-gold dining room, mezzanine, bar and patio; there are "many delicious items" on the "large", moderately priced menu, but give yourself plenty of time to sample them because "service can be slow"; N.B. there's live entertainment on weekends.

Two Boots Pizza *Pizza*   21 | 13 | 15 | $19

Bridgeport | 277 Fairfield Ave. (bet. Broad & Harrison Sts.) | 203-331-1377 | www.twobootsbridgeport.com

"It musta been some trip" that inspired this Bridgeport spin-off of the New York City chain spinning "crunchy cornmeal-crusted pizza and N'Awlins po' boys" and the like in an atmosphere redolent of the "bohemian East Village"; the "innovative flavor combinations" yield some "awesome" results, and there are occasional "great bands to boot."

Two Steps Downtown Grille *Southwestern*   13 | 17 | 15 | $29

Danbury | 5 Ives St. (bet. Main & White Sts.) | 203-794-0032 | www.ciaocateringtwosteps.com

This "casual" Danbury Southwestern is "lively" and "affordable", a double draw for "locals" stepping out for "after-work get-togethers" or just looking for a spot "the kids will love"; however, "vintage" firehouse digs and "funky" decorations can't fully distract from the "wish-it-were-better" food ("salads, burgers, nachos and wraps").

	FOOD	DECOR	SERVICE	COST

☑ Union League Cafe ☒ *French*   27 | 26 | 25 | $57

New Haven | 1032 Chapel St. (bet. College & High Sts.) | 203-562-4299 | www.unionleaguecafe.com

"Despite a down economy", "sophisticated" Yalies and "high-society" types shell out "hefty" payments for "well-trained" chef Jean-Pierre Vuillermet's "perfectly prepared classic French cuisine" (augmented with "some twists, so it never bores") at this "grande dame of New Haven"; vintage stained glass, mahogany and other "elegant" appointments lend it the feeling of a "formal" "private club", while the "remarkable service" comes generally "without pomposity."

Union Street Tavern   *American*   - | - | - | I

Windsor | 20 Union St. (Palisado Ave.) | 860-683-2899 | www.unionstreettavern.com

Tipplers who've tried this American tavern say there are "enough beers on tap to please everyone", plus "a decent martini" menu to boot; furthermore, the "value"-priced fare is of real "quality", and the former firehouse setting with a restored 1920s-era bar and booths make it feel like a true "classic", all of which adds up to one "special find for Windsor."

U.S.S. Chowder Pot   *Seafood*   16 | 13 | 16 | $32

Branford | 560 E. Main St. (bet. NE Industrial & School Ground Rds.) | 203-481-2356
Hartford | 165 Brainard Rd. (Murphy Rd.) | 860-244-3311
www.chowderpot.com

"Busloads of retirees" fill "railroad-station-sized rooms" festooned with "weird" "schooner decor" at these seafooders where "rushed but pleasant" staffers ferry fish that's "dependable", if "never quite as good as you'd like"; "portions so large they can feed two people" make the "reasonable prices" seem "quite low"; N.B. live bands in Branford and dinner shows in Hartford are regularly scheduled.

☑ Valbella ☒ *Italian*   25 | 23 | 25 | $75

Riverside | 1309 E. Putnam Ave./Rte. 1 (Sound Beach Ave.) | 203-637-1155 | www.valbellact.com

The "line of BMWs" outside signals it's always a "big night out" at this "venerable" Riversider where the "amazing" Northern Italian menu is "as impressive as the wine list" – and where you may end up seated next to "regulars" like Regis or the Donald; yes, the "bill might scare even the black AmEx", but with "service equal to the food", respondents reckon it's "worth it in the end"; N.B. recent minor renovations that added more modern touches may outdate the above Decor score.

Valencia Luncheria ⚲ *Venezuelan*   27 | 10 | 18 | $19

Norwalk | 172 Main St. (bet. Catherine St. & Plymouth Ave.) | 203-846-8009 | www.valencialuncheria.com

With "breakfasts worth waking up for", "amazing lunches" ("try the heavenly empanadas") and "delicious" dinners featuring a "dizzying list of specials", this "teeny-tiny", cash-only Venezuelan "hole-in-the-wall" in Norwalk hits "extraordinary" heights; "enormous por-

	FOOD	DECOR	SERVICE	COST

tions" for "cheap" and a BYO policy make it "one of the best values" around – no wonder there's often "a long wait" for a table.

Vanilla Bean Cafe *American* | 23 | 18 | 19 | $22 |

Pomfret | 450 Deerfield Rd. (Pomfret St.) | 860-928-1562 | www.thevanillabeancafe.com

The "Harley crowd" mixes with "local granolas" at this "rustic", "funky" American in an old barn in "beautiful" "middle-of-nowhere" Pomfret; though "nothing fancy", the "fantastic selection" of "low-cost" victuals tastes "so good", especially when mixed with fresh country air on the "relaxing", "pleasant terrace."

Vazzy's *Italian* | 18 | 13 | 17 | $27 |

Bridgeport | Beardsley Park Plaza | 513 Broadbridge Rd. (bet. Hooker Rd. & Huntington Tpke.) | 203-371-8046
Milford | 157 Cherry St. (bet. Buick Ave. & Sunnyside Ct.) | 203-877-7475
Monroe | 415 Main St. (bet. Brook & Green Sts.) | 203-459-9800
Stratford | 3355 Main St. (bet. Birch Pl. & Garden St. E.) | 203-375-2776
www.vazzysrest.com

"You don't have to break the bank" for "high quality" say surveyors who rely on this "kid-friendly" quartet for "awesome pizzas" and "delicious classic Italian entrees" served in "generous portions"; however, you might want to "bring your earplugs" because the "din can be deafening", especially if you're "sitting near the bar."

Venetian Restaurant *Italian* | 22 | 17 | 22 | $41 |

Torrington | 52 E. Main St. (bet. Franklin St. & Volkman Ln.) | 860-489-8592 | www.venetian-restaurant.com

"Popular with Torrington locals" since 1921, this purposely "old-fashioned" Northern Italian "continues to provide well-prepared" fare at "good prices"; true, the "Venetian camp" decor "could use a face-lift", but it's appropriate for the genre, plus "if you're going to the nearby Warner Theater", the "attentive" servers will get you to the show on time.

Versailles *Bakery/French* | 20 | 13 | 12 | $31 |

Greenwich | 315 Greenwich Ave. (bet. Bruce & Havemeyer Pls.) | 203-661-6634 | www.versaillesgreenwich.com

Despite the "cramped layout" and "frazzled" service, "businessmen breakfast" and "ladies lunch" at this French patisserie/bistro in Greenwich; regulars say just "swallow your pride" (and the "terrific onion soup"): the fare may be "simple" but it's "priced right", and the baked goods are "absolutely killer"; N.B. a post-Survey face-lift may outdate the above Decor score.

Viale Ristorante Bar & Grille Ⓜ *Italian*   ▽ | 21 | 21 | 22 | $38 |

Bridgeport | 3171 Fairfield Ave. (bet. Davidson & Poland Sts.) | 203-610-6193 | www.vialeristorante.net

Bridgeport "garlic-lovers" are big "fans" of this "typical Italian" – indeed, they often "take the family" or "business" associates to dine in its "comfortable" digs, which are overseen by "prompt, knowledge-able" staffers; however, some connoisseurs deem it "overrated."

Via Sforza Trattoria *Italian*

`21` `21` `20` `$41`

Westport | 243 Post Rd. W. (Sylvan Rd.) | 203-454-4444 | www.viasforza.com

"Cool" environs featuring an "elaborate stone" facade, barrel-vault ceilings and rustic, wrought-iron-flecked fixtures are a fitting showcase for the "mouthwatering", "real Italian" dishes served at this "family-oriented" "happy place" in Westport; a "fine wine list", "spot-on service" and "not-out-of-sight prices" please, but the no-reservations policy sometimes makes it "tough" to get into.

Villa Del Sol *Mexican*

`18` `17` `18` `$31`

Westport | 36 Elm St. (bet. Church Ln. & Main St.) | 203-226-7912 | www.villadelsolrestaurants.com

"Snap out of a funk" at this "cheery" Westport Mexican boasting "festive" decor and "terrific" margaritas; "dependable" "basics" dot the "fairly priced" menu, many "drenched in cheese, cheese and more cheese", but just "don't go early if screeching kids annoy you."

Vinny's Backyard ◐ *Pub Food*

▽ `19` `10` `18` `$23`

Stamford | Springdale Shopping Ctr. | 1078 Hope St. (bet. Camp Ave. & Mulberry St.) | 203-461-9003

"Super-thin-crust pizza", "terrific wings" and "decent bar food" earn this Stamford Italian tavern a faithful coterie of fans that say it's both a "place to bring the kids" and a "nice" neighborhood bar where you can catch a Saturday afternoon game on one of its "big-screen TVs"; "attentive" service seals the deal.

Vito's by the Park *Italian*

`19` `19` `19` `$33`

Hartford | 26 Trumbull St. (Jewell St.) | 860-244-2200

Vito's by the Water *Italian*

Windsor | 1936 Blue Hills Ext. (bet. Day Hill Rd. & Tunxis Ave.) | 860-285-8660

Vito's Wethersfield *Italian*

Wethersfield | 673 Silas Dean Hwy. (bet. Somerset St. & Wells Rd.) | 860-563-3333
www.vitosct.com

"Located right near the Bushnell", this "classic Italian bistro" in Hartford is a smart "spot to grab a bite before the theater", while "great views" of the park from the large, windows and patio make it a "nice" warm-weather destination; its Windsor and Wethersfield siblings are equally dependable for "workmanlike" chow that may be "nothing to remember", but there's "tons" of it and it's "reasonably priced."

Viva Zapata *Mexican*

`17` `14` `15` `$28`

Westport | 530 Riverside Ave. (Bridge St.) | 203-227-8226 | www.vivazapata.com

The joint is "jumping" at this Westport Mexican where "killer" margaritas in "mason jars" fuel a "lively weekend bar scene" on the patio; foodies find the fare "mediocre" and critics fume that the staff "could care less", but thanks to the "lethal" tequila concoctions, many say "there's no place [they'd] rather be on a hot summer night."

	FOOD	DECOR	SERVICE	COST

VIVO Seasonal Trattoria *Italian* ▽ 21 | 23 | 21 | $47

Hartford | Marriott Hotel | 200 Columbus Blvd. (bet. Arch & Grove Sts.) | 860-760-2333 | www.waterfordgrouprestaurants.com

An "elegant" space inside Hartford's Marriott sets the stage for this Northern Italian's Tuscan menu, which includes a number of "unusual" offerings, as well as an "above-average breakfast" buffet spread; critics, though, find the fare "unevenly executed" and the service overly "casual", and lament that it's "not as special as it could be."

Vox Ⓜ *American/French* 21 | 19 | 19 | $51

North Salem | 721 Titicus Rd. (Peach Lake Rd.), NY | 914-669-5450 | www.voxnorthsalem.com

"Tucked away" "off the beaten path" in North Salem sits this "cozy" bistro run by "honest-to-gosh French people" and offering up a "nice mix" of Gallic–New American fare from "oysters to burgers and everything in between"; prices are "on the expensive side", but it pays off with an "elegant" white-tablecloth setting boasting "sweeping views" of the "bucolic" landscape and a patio that's "magical on a summer evening."

V Restaurant & Wine Bar *Californian* 16 | 18 | 17 | $35

Westport | 1460 Boston Post Rd. E. (bet. Maple Ave. & Mills St.) | 203-259-1160 | www.vrestaurantandwinebar.com

This "reliable" "Westport stalwart" "can accommodate kids and adults" alike with a "diverse menu" of "reasonably priced" Californian cuisine and "some terrific wines", including "exceptional" selections by the glass, which are served by an "enthusiastic staff" in a "comfortable", "spacious" setting with a vineyard motif; though cynics sniff it's "far from fine dining", the "good value" it offers keeps it "consistently crowded."

Walter's ⊄ *Hot Dogs* 22 | 10 | 14 | $10

Mamaroneck | 937 Palmer Ave. (bet. Fulton & Richbell Rds.), NY | www.waltershotdogs.com

The "Peter Luger of hot dog stands", this Mamaroneck "icon" – voted the No. 1 Bang for the Buck in the Westchester/Hudson Valley Survey – has folks "driving from afar" for its "succulent" franks griddled in butter and served up with "mouthwatering fries" and "superlative shakes"; rain or shine, a constant "lineup" 'round the "roadside pagoda" setting "is part of the package", but that's no deterrent to longtime fans who insist "it wouldn't be summer without multiple trips" here.

Wandering Moose Café *American* 18 | 14 | 16 | $27

West Cornwall | 421 Sharon Goshen Tpke./Rte. 128 (bet. Lower River & River Rds.) | 860-672-0178 | www.thewanderingmoosecafe.com

A "locals' favorite", this West Cornwall American also attracts scores of "out-of-towners" "wandering the northwest Connecticut hills" with its "reliable" American eats and "attractive" location near a "covered bridge", where moose and deer sightings are common; a few find the service "spotty" and the fare "nothing special", but most consider it a "good value" that's "worth a detour"; N.B. a post-Survey renovation may outdate the above Decor score.

Wasabi *Japanese* | 23 | 14 | 21 | $28 |

Orange | 350 Boston Post Rd. (bet. Lambert & Silverbrook Rds.) | 203-795-5856 | www.wasabiorange.com

A "wonderful find" in a "strip mall" on "busy Boston Post Road", this Orange Japanese dishes out "large" portions of "amazing" sushi and other "beautiful, creative" dishes at "reasonable" prices; while it's "not fancy" and may be "lacking in ambiance", aficionados aver the "staff couldn't be nicer."

Wasabi Chi ⓜ *Asian* | 24 | 23 | 22 | $47 |

South Norwalk | 2 S. Main St. (Washington St.) | 203-286-0181 | www.wasabichi.com

It's "always a fun night out" ("especially for dates") at Doug Nguyen's "New Age" Pan-Asian specialist showcasing "excellent, fresh sushi" and other "inventive" dishes served by a "friendly" staff in a "high-tech" space; there's a "great bar scene" and the ambiance is "out of this world", all of which contribute to a "wonderful" – if "pricey" – dining experience in South Norwalk.

Watercolor Cafe *American* | 18 | 16 | 17 | $40 |

Larchmont | 2094 Boston Post Rd. (bet. Chatsworth & Larchmont Aves.), NY | 914-834-2213 | www.watercolorcafe.net

The "food serves as a prelude to the performances" at this "casual" Larchmont cafe that's better known for its live jazz and folk music than its "competent" yet "uninspiring" New American cuisine; though some claim the "tables are a little too close for comfort" and the acoustics "noisy", it's still a "reasonable" option for a "simple meal."

Watermoon *Asian* | 22 | 18 | 17 | $39 |

Rye | 66 Purchase St. (bet. Elm Pl. & W. Purdy Ave.), NY | 914-921-8880

Rye denizens descend on this "busy" Pan-Asian where "tempting" dishes (like a "terrific" crispy red snapper) are set down in "hip", "hopping" digs sporting an indoor waterfall; prices are a "relative bargain", but the trade-offs are "uneven" service and a noise level so "deafening" you "can't hear yourself chew."

Water Street Cafe *American* | 25 | 19 | 20 | $41 |

Stonington | 143 Water St. (bet. Grand & Pearl Sts.) | 860-535-2122

"Everyone's treated like a local" at this "cozy" Stonington New American proffering a "varied menu" of "excellent" fare, including "fresh and tasty" raw bar selections and salads "to die for"; service is "accommodating" but can be "slow" say insiders, who warn that you can "expect to wait for a table", though most agree it's "worthwhile."

Westbrook Lobster *Seafood* | 18 | 13 | 15 | $32 |

Clinton | 346 E. Main St. (Bluff Ave.) | 860-664-9464
Wallingford | 300 Church St. (Main St.) | 203-265-5071
www.westbrooklobster.com

These family-run seafooders reel in fans with lobsters and other "good basic" fin fare at "affordable prices", plus the Clinton loca-

FOOD DECOR SERVICE COST

tion's attached market is a popular stop for supplying "summer clambakes" (and the Wallingford branch offers takeout too); however, there are a few crabs that carp about "average" fare, "hit-or-miss" service and "warehouse"-like decor.

West Street Grill *American*   22 | 20 | 20 | $56

Litchfield | 43 West St. (bet. North & South Sts.) | 860-567-3885 | www.weststreetgrill.net

"Don't be swayed by sightings of glitterati", it's the "seasonal" menu "using regional ingredients" that's the main attraction of this Litchfield New American; the "gracious owners/hosts" ensure a "sophisticated" experience with an "extensive wine list" and "imaginatively prepared" "comfort food" that "continues to evolve" – unlike the service, which some say can be "snotty if you're not a regular."

White Hart *American*   17 | 21 | 18 | $43

Salisbury | White Hart Inn | 15 Under Mountain Rd./Rte. 41 (bet. Conklin & Main Sts.) | 860-435-0030 | www.whitehartinn.com

Changes are afoot (which may outdate the above ratings) at this Salisbury standby set in a "lovely" 1806 inn, where a new chef is ushering in an updated menu featuring more upscale (but still Traditional American) cuisine and phasing out the "pub grub" offerings; a top-to-bottom revamp of the space is also underway, and while the "wood-paneled" Tap Room is expected to remain, the Garden Room will morph into the Hunt Room – which should please its clientele "so Waspy you need to look for something tweed to wear."

White Horse Tavern Ⓜ *American*   ▽ 15 | 19 | 18 | $42

Redding | Spinning Wheel Inn | 107 Black Rock Tpke. (bet. Barlow Dr. & Giles Hill Rd.) | 203-938-2511 | www.spinningwheelinn-ct.com

This Traditional American housed in a circa-1742 Redding inn wins praise for its "lovely setting", complete with "huge fireplaces" and antiques; still, some surveyors who judge the fare "so-so" and the ambiance "blah" lament what they see as a "waste" of "a lot of potential."

Wild Rice *Asian*   21 | 17 | 18 | $29

Norwalk | 370 Main Ave. (Merritt Pkwy., exit 40A) | 203-849-1688 | www.wildrice999.com

"You won't feel like second fiddle to the sushi crowd" at this Norwalk Pan-Asian serving not only "super-fresh" fin fare, but also "great dim sum" and other "creative" offerings; while some find service "hit-or-miss", the staff is "friendly" and the place is "always packed", "so be prepared for some elbow bumping."

Willett House *Steak*   23 | 20 | 21 | $64

Port Chester | 20 Willett Ave. (Abendroth Ave.), NY | 914-939-7500 | www.thewilletthouse.com

"Everything a serious steakhouse should be", this "longtime" Port Chester chop shop offers "top-notch" "prime-aged" cuts, "fantastic" sides and an "extensive" wine list in "clubby", brick-and-wood environs; service is "knowledgeable" and the vibe "comfortable",

FOOD | DECOR | SERVICE | COST

but for best results when the check arrives, "let someone else pay" – it is nicknamed "The Wallet House", after all.

Wilson's Barbeque Ⓜ *BBQ*

24 | 12 | 13 | $20

Fairfield | 1851 Post Rd. (bet. Bungalow Ave. & Granville St.) | 203-319-7427 | www.wilsons-bbq.com

"Get a true education in pork" from "top pit master" Ed Wilson at his "down-home" joint in Fairfield that "deserves its popularity" thanks to "beautiful, bountiful BBQ" that 'cuennoisseurs christen the "real thing"; the vibe is "friendly" and "happy", but the "tiny tables", "stools" and "cafeteria-style service" lead most to conclude that "takeout seems to be the theme" here.

Winvian Ⓜ *American*

– | – | – | E

Morris | 155 Alain White Rd. (bet. County & E. Shore Rds.) | 860-393-3004 | www.winvian.com

Inside an elegant Colonial-style former home recently opened to the public, this Traditional American eatery is part of a Relais & Châteaux resort featuring whimsically themed cottages hidden in the Litchfield Hills town of Morris; diners feast within three intimate, crackling fireplace-equipped rooms, or out on the lovely porch (at lunch only), enjoying sumptuous fare such as the signature beef duo (tenderloin and braised short rib) or frisée salad with pigeon and foie gras; N.B. the $90 three-course prix fixe seems almost economical given all the opulence.

Woodland, The Ⓜ *American/Continental*

23 | 19 | 21 | $42

Lakeville | 192 Sharon Rd./Rte. 41 (bet. Easy St. & Wells Hill Rd.) | 860-435-0578

It may be in a "secluded" Lakeville locale, but the "fresh, tasty" fare – from "seafood and sushi" to cheeseburgers and "terrific steaks" – at this "reliable" American-Continental "attracts the entire town to its door" (so "have a reservation"); "sizable portions", "top-notch wines" and a "lively bar scene" quell grumbles about service that "can be slow at times."

Wood-n-Tap ◑ *Pub Food*

19 | 17 | 19 | $24

Farmington | 1274 Farmington Ave. (bet. Brickyard Rd. & Lakeshore Dr.) | 860-773-6736

Hartford | 99 Sisson Ave. (Capitol Ave.) | 860-232-8277

Rocky Hill | 12 Town Line Rd. (bet. Mountain Laurel Dr. & Silas Deane Hwy.) | 860-571-9444

Southington | 420 Queen St. (bet. Laning & Loeper Sts.) | 860-329-0032

Vernon | 236 Hartford Tpke. (bet. Green Circle Rd. & Talcottville Rd./Rte. 83) | 860-872-6700

www.woodntap.com

For "happy hour" or a "quick bite" "with the family", this "casual" American chain has the Hartford area covered, offering "dependable" "pub grub" and a "wide tap selection" at "fair prices"; the bartenders are "friendly", the servers "energetic and youthful" and there's "nothing pretentious about it" – that said, be prepared for a "loud" scene.

	FOOD	DECOR	SERVICE	COST

Wood's Pit BBQ & Mexican Cafe Ⓜ *BBQ/Mexican*

22 | 11 | 18 | $28

Bantam | 123 Bantam Lake Rd./Rte. 209 (Roosevelt Ave.) | 860-567-9869 | www.woodspitbbq.com

"Not gourmet, just good", this "popular BBQ joint" is the "perfect spot" "before or after" taking in an "indie movie" at the Bantam Cinema next door say cineastes and others who applaud the "awesome" ribs and "better-than-ok" Mexican; "brassy but friendly waitresses" serve up the eats, and while the setting is "plain" and "rustic", few mind since the "price is right."

ⓩ Woodward House Ⓜ *American*

26 | 28 | 28 | $64

Bethlehem | 4 The Green (West Rd.) | 203-266-6902 | www.thewoodwardhouse.com

Devotees declare "yes, there is a god in Bethlehem, and he's cooking" at this "outstanding" New American housed in "everyone's dream of a picturesque 18th-century Colonial", with four small dining rooms, each "decorated in its own style" (including one "with funky Peter Max original artwork"); chef-owner Jerry Reveron's cuisine is "sumptuous", "innovative and excellent", his wife Adele is a "gracious, pleasing hostess" and both are "visibly engaged in running" things to ensure a "wonderful" (albeit "pricey") dining experience.

Yorkside ❶ *Greek/Pizza*

16 | 8 | 14 | $15

New Haven | Yale University campus | 288 York St. (bet. Elm & Wall Sts.) | 203-787-7411 | www.yorksidepizza.com

"Feeding starving grad students for longer than Yale has been in existence", this "hallowed" Hellenic "greasy spoon" in New Haven dishes out "satisfying" pizzas, "Greek salads that take two men and a boy to carry" and more; sure, some find the cooking "indifferent" and certain servers might be "as old as the pictures" that cover the walls, but most hope this "friendly" "institution" will "live long and prosper."

Zaroka *Indian*

20 | 18 | 18 | $24

New Haven | 148 York St. (bet. Chapel & Crown Sts.) | 203-776-8644 | www.zaroka.com

A "dependable" source for "classic dishes prepared well", this New Haven Indian is also a "great deal" for lunch with its "bargain" $8.95 buffet; while it may "not be much to look at from the outside", inside the "atmosphere is charming", the service is "attentive" and "the price is right"; still, some skeptics feel this spot, "one of the best known" in town, "needs to step it up" a notch.

Zhang's *Chinese/Japanese*

18 | 14 | 18 | $27

Madison | 44 Boston Post Rd. (Old Post Rd.) | 203-245-3300
Mystic | 12 Water St. (bet. New London Rd. & W. Main St.) | 860-572-5725
Old Saybrook | 455 Boston Post Rd. (Middlesex Tpke.) | 860-388-3999
www.zhangsrestaurant.com

Aficionados advise "fresh vegetables and seafood are the best choices on the menu" of this Asian trio serving a "combo of Chinese and Japanese" fare, including sushi; there's "nothing fancy" about them – some find the scene rather "gloomy" – but for fans, the "reliable" grub and "reasonable prices" are "reasons enough to eat here."

Z Zinc ☒ *American*   24 | 22 | 22 | $46

New Haven | 964 Chapel St. (bet. College & Temple Sts.) | 203-624-0507 | www.zincfood.com

"Stylish and well located right on the green" in Downtown New Haven, this "hip" New American attracts a "trendy", "black-wearing urban crowd" with chef/co-owner Denise Appel's "innovative", "Asian-influenced" cuisine emphasizing "local seasonal" ingredients and pastry chef Alba Estenoz's desserts that are "worth every single blessed calorie"; the "ultramodern" setting has a "city-chic" ambiance, and while the service is "excellent", some report a bit of "attitude", not to mention tabs that'll cost you "serious money."

Zinis *Italian*   ▽ 18 | 17 | 21 | $34

Bantam | 938 Bantam Rd. (bet. Trumbull St. & Vanderpoel Ave.) | 860-567-1613 | www.zinisct.com

"Bring an appetite" to this "cozy" Northern Italian near the Bantam Cinema, where the fare is "hearty" and the "people are incredibly accommodating"; critics, though, find the digs a bit "worn around the edges" and "wish the chef would take a trip somewhere in Italy" to bring the menu out of the "1950s."

Zitoune ⓜ *Moroccan*   20 | 21 | 20 | $42

Mamaroneck | 1127 W. Boston Post Rd. (Richbell Rd.), NY | 914-835-8350 | www.zitounerestaurant.com

For "a bit of the exotic", head to this Mamaroneck "hideout" where "dreamy" tagines and other Moroccan dishes are served "under a tented ceiling"; "lovely" service adds to the "delightful" ambiance, and a "belly dancer adds pizzazz" on weekends; N.B. check its website for prix fixe deals and tapas nights.

CONNECTICUT
AND NEARBY
NEW YORK TOWNS
INDEXES

Cuisines

Includes names, locations and Food ratings.

AFGHAN

Shish Kebab | **W Hartford**	24
NEW Spinghar | **Glastonbury**	-

AMERICAN

Adrienne | **New Milford**	24
AJ's Burgers | **New Roch**	19
American Pie Co. | **Sherman**	20
Z Apricots | **Farmington**	24
Z Archie Moore's | **multi.**	19
Ash Creek | **multi.**	18
Aspen | **Old Saybrook**	21
Aux Délices | **multi.**	23
Avon Old Farm | **Avon**	-
Azu | **Mystic**	23
Bailey's | **Ridgefield**	20
NEW Bar Americain | **Uncasville**	-
Beach Café | **Fairfield**	17
Beach Hse. Café | **Old Greenwich**	-
Bedford Post/Barn | **Bedford**	24
Bedford Post/Farm | **Bedford**	-
Beehive | **Armonk**	17
Z Bespoke | **New Haven**	24
Bistro 22 | **Bedford**	23
B.J. Ryan's | **Norwalk**	22
Blue | **White Pl**	19
Blue Lemon | **Westport**	24
Blue Pearl | **New Haven**	20
Blue Point B&G | **Stratford**	18
Boathouse | **Lakeville**	16
Bobby Valentine | **Stamford**	15
Bogey's Grille | **Westport**	16
NEW Bombay Olive | **W Hartford**	-
Boom | **multi.**	22
Z Boulders Inn | **New Preston**	22
Brazen Fox | **White Pl**	15
Brendan's/Elms | **Ridgefield**	22
Brewhouse | **S Norwalk**	16
Bull's Bridge | **Kent**	16
Burke in Box | **Ledyard**	-
Z Carole Peck's | **Woodbury**	27
Cascade Mtn. | **Amenia**	16
Chat 19 | **Larch**	18

Chatterley's | **New Hartford**	20
Z Cheesecake Fac. | **multi.**	18
Chef Luis | **New Canaan**	25
Chestnut Grille | **Old Lyme**	24
Cobble Stone | **Purchase**	15
Z Cobb's Mill Inn | **Weston**	18
Z Copper Beech | **Ivoryton**	24
Country House | **Patterson**	20
Creek | **Purchase**	17
Curtis House | **Woodbury**	16
Diorio | **Waterbury**	24
Dish B&G | **Hartford**	20
Donovan's | **S Norwalk**	-
Z Dressing Room | **Westport**	23
East-West Grille | **W Hartford**	23
Elbow Room | **W Hartford**	18
Elements | **W Hartford**	-
Eli Cannon's | **Middletown**	20
Elizabeth's Cafe | **Madison**	26
Emma's Ale | **White Pl**	-
Épernay | **Bridgeport**	-
Evergreens | **Simsbury**	25
Field | **Bridgeport**	17
Fifty Coins | **multi.**	14
59 Bank | **New Milford**	18
Z Firebox | **Hartford**	25
Foe | **Branford**	22
42 | **White Pl**	22
Foster's | **New Haven**	17
Gabrielle's | **Centerbrook**	21
Ginger Man | **multi.**	17
Globe B&G | **Larch**	15
Gnarly Vine | **New Roch**	19
Grand | **Stamford**	18
Z Grant's | **W Hartford**	25
Greenwich Tav. | **Old Greenwich**	-
Griswold Inn | **Essex**	18
G.W. Tavern | **Wash Depot**	20
Halstead Ave. | **Harrison**	18
Harborside B&G | **Stratford**	15
Hard Rock | **Ledyard**	15
Z Harvest Supper | **New Canaan**	27

Hawthorne Inn | **Berlin**	18
Heirloom | **New Haven**	-
Horse & Hound | **S Salem**	16
Inn at Newtown | **Newtown**	19
NEW Jack Rabbit's | **Old Saybrook**	-
Jeffrey's | **Milford**	23
Joe's American | **Fairfield**	16
John Harvard's | **Manchester**	19
John's Café | **Woodbury**	24
Kona Grill | **Stamford**	17
La Cuisine | **Branford**	-
Lady Luck | **Bridgeport**	-
Lansdowne | **New Haven**	-
Larchmont Tav. | **Larch**	17
NEW Le Farm | **Westport**	-
Long Ridge Tav. | **Stamford**	14
Longwood Rest. | **Woodbury**	18
NEW Lucky Lou | **Wethersfield**	-
Mango's B&G | **Branford**	19
Market | **Stamford**	23
Z Match | **S Norwalk**	24
NEW Matthew's | **Unionville**	-
Z Max Downtown | **Hartford**	27
Z Mayflower Inn | **Washington**	25
McKinney/Doyle | **Pawling**	25
Meetinghouse | **Bedford Vill**	18
Z Métro Bis | **Simsbury**	26
NEW Molly Spillane | **Mamaro**	16
Mo's NY | **New Roch**	21
Z Napa & Co. | **Stamford**	25
NEW No. 9 | **Millerton**	-
North Star | **Pound Ridge**	23
Old Lyme Inn | **Old Lyme**	20
Olio | **Groton**	24
Oliver's Taverne | **Essex**	13
Olive Tree | **Southbury**	19
121 Rest. | **N Salem**	21
121 Rest. | **Oxford**	23
Opus 465 | **Armonk**	16
Palmer's Crossing | **Larch**	18
Pantry | **Wash Depot**	25
Paradise B&G | **Stamford**	13
Pat's Kountry | **Old Saybrook**	14
Plan B Burger | **multi.**	23
Plates | **Larch**	24

PolytechnicON20 | **Hartford**	28
Pond House Café | **W Hartford**	22
Porter Hse. | **White Pl**	18
Putnam Hse. | **Bethel**	16
Rainforest Cafe | **Farmington**	11
Z Rebeccas | **Greenwich**	25
Red Barn | **Westport**	17
Rest./Water's Edge | **Westbrook**	20
River Cat Grill | **Rowayton**	22
River House | **Westport**	16
River Tavern | **Chester**	25
NEW Roasted Peppers | **Mamaro**	-
Saltwater Grille | **Stamford**	20
Sam's/Gedney | **White Pl**	17
Schoolhse./Cannondale | **Wilton**	-
Seamen's Inne | **Mystic**	19
Sentrista Grill | **Brewster**	21
Shady Glen | **Manchester**	23
Sharpe Hill/Vineyard | **Pomfret**	-
Southport Brew. | **multi.**	15
Still River | **Eastford**	26
Stone House | **Guilford**	21
Ted's Montana | **S Windsor**	21
Terra Mar | **Old Saybrook**	21
Thataway Cafe | **Greenwich**	15
Town Dock | **Rye**	17
Towne Crier | **Pawling**	15
Trinity Grill | **Harrison**	19
Troutbeck | **Amenia**	24
Union Street Tav. | **Windsor**	-
Vanilla Bean | **Pomfret**	23
Vox | **N Salem**	21
Wandering Moose | **W Cornwall**	18
Watercolor Cafe | **Larch**	18
Water St. Cafe | **Stonington**	25
West St. Grill | **Litchfield**	22
White Hart | **Salisbury**	17
White Horse Tav. | **Redding**	15
Winvian | **Morris**	-
Woodland | **Lakeville**	23
Wood-n-Tap | **multi.**	19
Z Woodward Hse. | **Bethlehem**	26
Z Zinc | **New Haven**	24

ARGENTINEAN

NEW Milonga | **N White Plains**	-
Tango Grill | **White Pl**	22

ASIAN

Asiana Cafe | **Greenwich**	20
Asian Kitchen | **Ridgefield**	22
Asian Tempt. | **White Pl**	20
☑ Baang Cafe | **Riverside**	23
Bambou | **Greenwich**	23
Bentara | **New Haven**	24
Bond Grill | **Norwalk**	18
☑ Ching's | **multi.**	24
East-West Grille | **W Hartford**	23
Euro Asian | **Port Chester**	21
☑ Feng Asian | **multi.**	26
Ginban Asian | **Mamaro**	-
Golden Rod | **New Roch**	20
Haiku | **Mamaro**	23
NEW Haiku | **White Pl**	-
Kari | **New Haven**	23
Kudeta | **New Haven**	21
Little Kitchen | **Westport**	22
Made In Asia | **Armonk**	21
Matsumoto | **Larch**	-
Mei Tzu | **E Windsor**	-
Nuage | **Cos Cob**	23
Penang Grill | **Greenwich**	23
Red Plum | **Mamaro**	-
☑ Tengda | **multi.**	23
Thai Chi | **Stamford**	22
Wasabi Chi | **S Norwalk**	24
Watermoon | **Rye**	22
Wild Rice | **Norwalk**	21

AUSTRIAN

Hopkins Inn | **New Preston**	20

BAKERIES

American Pie Co. | **Sherman**	20
Bedford Post/Barn | **Bedford**	24
Corner Bakery | **Pawling**	23
Isabelle/Vincent | **Fairfield**	-
SoNo Baking Co. | **S Norwalk**	25
Versailles | **Greenwich**	20

BARBECUE

Barnacle | **Mamaro**	-
Big W's | **Wingdale**	26
Black-Eyed Sally | **Hartford**	21
Boathouse/Smokey | **Stamford**	21
Bobby Q's | **Westport**	19

☑ Cookhouse | **New Milford**	19
NEW Flaggstead | **Farmington**	-
Jeff's Cuisine | **S Norwalk**	25
Little Mark's | **Vernon**	20
NEW Nat Hayden | **Windsor**	-
Q Rest. | **Port Chester**	20
Wilson's BBQ | **Fairfield**	24
Wood's Pit BBQ | **Bantam**	22

BRAZILIAN

Churrasc. Braza | **Hartford**	21
Copacabana | **Port Chester**	23

BURGERS

AJ's Burgers | **New Roch**	19
Blazer Pub | **Purdys**	22
Brooklyn's Famous | **White Pl**	15
Burger Bar | **S Norwalk**	24
Burgers/Shakes | **Greenwich**	-
☑ City Limits | **multi.**	18
Cobble Stone | **Purchase**	15
Donovan's | **S Norwalk**	-
NEW Flipside Burgers | **Fairfield**	-
NEW Fraîche Burger | **Bridgeport**	-
Larchmont Tav. | **Larch**	17
Louis' Lunch | **New Haven**	24
Lucky's | **Stamford**	15
Meetinghouse | **Bedford Vill**	18
Oliver's Taverne | **Essex**	13
Plan B Burger | **multi.**	23
Porter Hse. | **White Pl**	18
Prime 16 | **New Haven**	-
Red Rooster | **Brewster**	18
Route 22 | **multi.**	13
Sam's/Gedney | **White Pl**	17
Sports Page | **White Pl**	-
Town Dock | **Rye**	17
Towne Crier | **Pawling**	15

CAJUN

Black-Eyed Sally | **Hartford**	21
Cuckoo's Nest | **Old Saybrook**	18
Rye Roadhse. | **Rye**	18

CALIFORNIAN

C.O. Jones | **New Haven**	16
Gates | **New Canaan**	18
V Rest. | **Westport**	16

CARIBBEAN

Mango's B&G | **Branford** — 19

CHINESE

(* dim sum specialist)

Aberdeen* | **White Pl** — 23
Bao's | **White Pl** — -
Butterfly Chinese | **W Hartford** — 15
Chengdu | **W Hartford** — 18
NEW Chili Chicken | **Stamford** — -
China Pavilion | **Orange** — 21
David Chen | **Armonk** — 18
Forbidden City | **Middletown** — 23
Great Taste | **New Britain** — 27
Hunan Larchmont | **Larch** — 16
Imperial | **N White Plains** — 18
Jasmine | **Westport** — 15
Panda Pavilion | **multi.** — 16
Z P.F. Chang's | **multi.** — 19
Ray's Cafe | **multi.** — 19
Royal Palace | **New Haven** — 24
Sushi 25 | **New Canaan** — -
Tiger Bowl | **Westport** — 15
Zhang's | **multi.** — 18

COFFEEHOUSES

Cafe Mozart | **Mamaro** — 17
Irving Farm | **Millerton** — 20

COFFEE SHOPS/ DINERS

Brooklyn's Famous | **White Pl** — 15
Z City Limits | **multi.** — 18
NEW Eveready | **Brewster** — 19
Gold Roc | **W Hartford** — 12
Lucky's | **Stamford** — 15
Nautilus | **Mamaro** — 15
Orem's Diner | **Wilton** — 16
Shady Glen | **Manchester** — 23

CONTINENTAL

Altnaveigh Inn | **Storrs** — 24
Brass City | **Waterbury** — -
Christopher Martins | **New Haven** — 20
Drescher's | **Waterbury** — 22
Flood Tide | **Mystic** — 21
Grist Mill | **Farmington** — 24
Harvest/Pomfret | **Pomfret** — 22

Heirloom | **New Haven** — -
Jeffrey's | **Milford** — 23
Mill on River | **S Windsor** — 23
Roger Sherman | **New Canaan** — 22
Shell Station | **Stratford** — 21
Z Stonehenge | **Ridgefield** — 24
Woodland | **Lakeville** — 23

CREOLE

Rye Roadhse. | **Rye** — 18

CUBAN

Karamba | **White Pl** — 20
Latin Am. Cafe | **White Pl** — 20
Soul de Cuba | **New Haven** — 21

DELIS

Edd's Place | **Westbrook** — 22
Firehouse Deli | **Fairfield** — 21
Kisco Kosher | **White Pl** — 19
Oscar's | **Westport** — 19
Rein's NY Deli | **Vernon** — 22

DESSERT

American Pie Co. | **Sherman** — 20
Aux Délices | **multi.** — 23
Cafe Mozart | **Mamaro** — 17
Z Cheesecake Fac. | **multi.** — 18
Chocopologie | **S Norwalk** — -
Corner Bakery | **Pawling** — 23
McKinney/Doyle | **Pawling** — 25
Pantry | **Wash Depot** — 25
SoNo Baking Co. | **S Norwalk** — 25
Versailles | **Greenwich** — 20

ECLECTIC

Arch | **Brewster** — 26
Aspen Garden | **Litchfield** — 15
NEW Ballou's | **Guilford** — -
Beehive | **Armonk** — 17
Bin 100 | **Milford** — 25
Cafe Mirage | **Port Chester** — 21
Z Capt. Daniel Packer | **Mystic** — 22
Caseus | **New Haven** — -
Dragonfly | **Stamford** — 20
Flood Tide | **Mystic** — 21
Hamilton Inn | **Millerton** — 21
Manna Dew | **Millerton** — 24

Metric | **Bridgeport**	–
116 Crown | **New Haven**	23
Osetra | **Norwalk**	26
Rye Grill | **Rye**	–
Squire's | **Redding**	19
Trumbull Kitchen | **Hartford**	24

EUROPEAN

Duo | **Stamford**	23
John-Michael's | **N Salem**	25

FONDUE

Blue Pearl | **New Haven**	20
Melting Pot | **multi.**	18

FRENCH

Aux Délices | **multi.**	23
☑ Bernard's | **Ridgefield**	27
Bistro Basque | **Milford**	26
Brie/Bleu | **New London**	24
Brix | **Cheshire**	19
☑ Cavey's | **Manchester**	28
☑ DaPietro's | **Westport**	26
Isabelle/Vincent | **Fairfield**	–
☑ Jean-Louis | **Greenwich**	28
La Bretagne | **Stamford**	22
La Crémaillère | **Bedford**	26
La Panetière | **Rye**	27
Le Château | **S Salem**	25
☑ L'Escale | **Greenwich**	23
Meli-Melo | **Greenwich**	25
Nuage | **Cos Cob**	23
☑ Ondine | **Danbury**	25
NEW Rest. L&E | **Chester**	–
RSVP | **W Cornwall**	29
Schoolhse./Cannondale | **Wilton**	–
Solaia | **Greenwich**	22
☑ Thomas Henkelmann | **Greenwich**	28
Vox | **N Salem**	21

FRENCH (BISTRO)

☑ Bistro Bonne Nuit | **New Canaan**	26
Bistro 22 | **Bedford**	23
Café Routier | **Westbrook**	25
Chez Jean-Pierre | **Stamford**	24
du Glace | **Deep River**	–

Encore Bistro | **Larch**	22
Le Figaro Bistro | **Greenwich**	20
☑ Le Petit Cafe | **Branford**	28
Le Provençal | **Mamaro**	23
Luc's Café | **Ridgefield**	24
Pascal's | **Larch**	20
Pastorale | **Lakeville**	24
Rue/Crêpes | **Harrison**	15
Saint Tropez | **Fairfield**	23
1020 Post | **Darien**	–
☑ Union League | **New Haven**	27
Versailles | **Greenwich**	20

GERMAN

Drescher's | **Waterbury**	22
East Side | **New Britain**	20
Old Heidelberg | **Bethel**	20

GREEK

Eos Greek | **Stamford**	–
Niko's Greek | **White Pl**	20
Osianna | **Fairfield**	–
Post Corner Pizza | **Darien**	19
Yorkside | **New Haven**	16

HOT DOGS

☑ Super/Weenie | **Fairfield**	22
Walter's | **Mamaro**	22

INDIAN

Bangalore | **Fairfield**	23
Bengal Tiger | **White Pl**	23
Bombay | **Westport**	23
NEW Bombay Olive | **W Hartford**	–
NEW Chili Chicken | **Stamford**	–
☑ Coromandel | **multi.**	26
Jaipore Indian | **Brewster**	24
Masala | **Hartford**	–
Rangoli | **New Roch**	24
Rani Mahal | **Mamaro**	23
Rasa | **Greenwich**	20
Royal Palace | **White Pl**	20
Tandoori Taste | **Port Chester**	23
Taste/India | **W Hartford**	20
Tawa | **Stamford**	22
☑ Thali | **multi.**	26
Zaroka | **New Haven**	20

IRISH

NEW Crooked Shillelagh | **Branford** — |

O'Neill's | **S Norwalk** 18 |

ITALIAN

(N=Northern; S=Southern)

Abatino's	**N White Plains**	21
Abruzzi Tratt.	**Patterson**	21
Adriana's	**New Haven**	23
Alba's	N	**Port Chester**	22
Alforno	N	**Old Saybrook**	23
Aloi	N	**New Canaan**	24
Anna Maria's	**Larch**	18
Antipasti	**White Pl**	21
Aurora	N	**Rye**	20
Avellino's	**Fairfield**	20
Aversano's	**Brewster**	—
Bar Vivace	**Mamaro**	22
Basta	**New Haven**	20
Bellizzi	**Larch**	15
Z Bertucci's	**multi.**	16
Bin 228	**Hartford**	23
Blue Dolphin	S	**Katonah**	23
Brass City	**Waterbury**	—
Bravo Bravo	**Mystic**	24
Bricco	**W Hartford**	25
Brickhouse	**Derby**	—
Brix	**Cheshire**	19
Buon Amici	**White Pl**	19
Buon Appetito	N	**Canton**	24
Cafe Allegre	**Madison**	20
Cafe Goodfellas	S	**New Haven**	21
Cafe Livorno	N	**Rye**	20
Café/Green	N	**Danbury**	23
Café Roma	N	**Bridgeport**	22
Cafe Silvium	S	**Stamford**	—
Café Tavolini	**Bridgeport**	19
Carbone's	N	**Hartford**	25
Carrabba's	**Manchester**	19
Cava Wine	N	**New Canaan**	23
Z Cavey's	N	**Manchester**	28
Centro	N	**multi.**	19
Chef Antonio	S	**Mamaro**	16
Cinzano's	**Fairfield**	19
Colony Grill	**Stamford**	—
Z Columbus Park	**Stamford**	25

Confetti	**Plainville**	18
Consiglio's	**New Haven**	25
Coppia	N	**Fairfield**	24
Cucina Modo	N	**Westport**	—
NEW DaCapo's	**Avon**	—
Da Giorgio	**New Roch**	20
Z DaPietro's	N	**Westport**	26
DiNardo's	**Pound Ridge**	19
Diorio	N	**Waterbury**	24
Doc's Trattoria	**Kent**	21
Eclisse	**Stamford**	20
Emilio Rist.	**Harrison**	23
Enzo's	**Mamaro**	18
Ernesto	**White Pl**	21
Esca	**Middletown**	—
Ferrante	**Stamford**	20
55°	N	**Fairfield**	—
59 Bank	**New Milford**	18
First & Last	**multi.**	20
Fratelli	**New Roch**	21
Gavi	**Armonk**	17
Gervasi's	**White Pl**	—
Giorgio's	N	**Port Chester**	23
Graziellas	**White Pl**	17
Hidden Vine	**Newington**	—
Hostaria Mazzei	**Port Chester**	21
Hot Tomato's	**Hartford**	21
Iannelli's	**White Pl**	19
NEW Il Castello	**Mamaro**	—
Il Falco	**Stamford**	22
Il Palio	N	**Shelton**	23
Il Sogno	**Port Chester**	—
Z Insieme	**Ridgefield**	25
La Bocca	**White Pl**	22
Laguna	N	**White Pl**	19
La Manda's	**White Pl**	18
La Piccola Casa	N	**Mamaro**	20
La Riserva	N	**Larch**	18
La Taverna	N	**Norwalk**	22
La Tavola	**Waterbury**	—
La Villetta	**Larch**	25
La Zingara	**Bethel**	25
Le Fontane	S	**Katonah**	20
Leon's	**New Haven**	—
NEW Limoncello	**Mamaro**	—
L'Orcio	**New Haven**	23

Luca Rist. | **Wilton**	24
Lusardi's | **Larch**	24
Maestro's | **New Roch**	16
Mamma Francesca | **New Roch**	16
Mancuso's | **Fairfield**	18
Marianacci's | **Port Chester**	20
Mario's Pl. | **Westport**	19
Marisa's | **Trumbull**	18
Max-a-Mia | **Avon**	24
Max Amore | N | **Glastonbury**	23
Michael's | N | **Wallingford**	23
NEW Milonga | **N White Plains**	-
Modern Rest. | S | **New Roch**	21
Morello | **Greenwich**	-
Mulino's | **White Pl**	25
Napoli Sul Fiume | **Westport**	16
Nessa | **Port Chester**	20
Nino's | **S Salem**	18
Nino's | **Bedford Hills**	19
122 Pizza Bistro | **Stamford**	19
Osteria Applausi | **Old Greenwich**	23
☑ Paci | **Southport**	26
Papacelle | **Avon**	-
Pasquale Rist. | **Port Chester**	21
☑ Pasta Nostra | **S Norwalk**	25
Pasta Vera | **Greenwich**	21
Pazzo Italian | **multi.**	23
Pellicci's | **Stamford**	20
Peppercorn's Grill | **Hartford**	25
Peppino's | N | **Katonah**	19
Piccolo Arancio | **Farmington**	26
Piero's | **Port Chester**	23
NEW Pizzeria Molto | **Fairfield**	-
Polpo | **Greenwich**	24
Ponte Vecchio | **Fairfield**	20
Portofino Pizza | **Goldens Bridge**	22
Portofino's | **Wilton**	21
Positano's | S | **Westport**	22
Posto 22 | **New Roch**	-
Primavera | N | **Crot Falls**	23
☑ Quattro Pazzi | **multi.**	22
Ralph/Rich's | **Bridgeport**	24
Rist. Luce | **Hamden**	22
NEW Rocco's | S | **New Canaan**	-
Rraci | **Brewster**	-
Sagi | S | **Ridgefield**	-

Sardegna | **Larch**	21
Scoozzi Tratt. | N | **New Haven**	22
Siena | N | **Stamford**	25
Solaia | **Greenwich**	22
Solé Rist. | N | **New Canaan**	22
Spadaro | **New Roch**	24
Spris | N | **Hartford**	21
Strada 18 | **S Norwalk**	25
T&J Villaggio | **Port Chester**	23
Tango | **Glastonbury**	-
Tango Grill | **White Pl**	22
Tarantino's | **Westport**	24
Taro's | **Millerton**	20
Tarry Lodge | **Port Chester**	24
Terra Rist. | N | **Greenwich**	22
Tiberio's | **Old Saybrook**	-
Todd English's | N | **Uncasville**	23
Toscana | N | **Ridgefield**	21
Tratt. Carl Anthony | **Monroe**	23
Tratt. Lucia | **Bedford**	16
Tratt. Vivolo | **Harrison**	21
Tre Angelina | N | **White Pl**	21
Tre Scalini | **New Haven**	23
Tuscan Oven | **Norwalk**	18
Tuscany | N | **Bridgeport**	25
Tuscany Grill | **Middletown**	20
☑ Valbella | N | **Riverside**	25
Vazzy's | **multi.**	18
Venetian | N | **Torrington**	22
Viale Rist. | **Bridgeport**	21
Via Sforza | **Westport**	21
Vinny's Backyard | **Stamford**	19
Vito's | **multi.**	19
VIVO Tratt. | N | **Hartford**	21
Zinis | N | **Bantam**	18

JAMAICAN

NEW Elaine's Healthy | **New Haven**	-

JAPANESE

(* sushi specialist)

Abis* | **Greenwich**	18
Akasaka* | **New Haven**	17
Duo | **Stamford**	23
Edo | **Port Chester**	20
Egane* | **Stamford**	20

Z Feng Asian*	Hartford	26
Fin/Fin II*	multi.	22
Fuji Mtn.	Larch	17
NEW Haiku*	White Pl	-
Hajime*	Harrison	25
Hanami*	Clinton	-
Hunan Larchmont	Larch	16
Imperial	N White Plains	18
Jasmine	Westport	15
Karuta*	New Roch	21
Kazu*	S Norwalk	24
Kicho*	Bedford Hills	17
Kira*	Armonk	21
Kobis	multi.	19
Koji	Hartford	19
Kona Grill*	Stamford	17
Koo*	multi.	23
Kotobuki*	Stamford	23
Kujaku*	Stamford	17
Kumo*	multi.	22
Mei Tzu*	E Windsor	-
Miso	New Haven	23
Murasaki*	W Hartford	19
Noda's Steak*	White Pl	19
Nuage	Cos Cob	23
Plum Tree*	New Canaan	21
Sakura*	Westport	21
Seasons Japanese*	White Pl	20
Sushi Nanase*	White Pl	27
Sushi 25*	New Canaan	-
Z Tengda*	multi.	23
Toshi Japanese*	Avon	23
Toyo Sushi*	Mamaro	22
Wasabi*	Orange	23
Wasabi Chi*	S Norwalk	24
Zhang's*	multi.	18

KOREAN

(* barbecue specialist)

Egane*	Stamford	20
Kalbi Hse.*	White Pl	20

KOSHER/ KOSHER-STYLE

Ahimsa	New Haven	17
Claire's Corner	New Haven	19
Kisco Kosher	White Pl	19

LEBANESE

Hanna's Mideastern	Danbury	22
Layla's Falafel	multi.	23

MACROBIOTIC

It's Only Natural	Middletown	23

MALAYSIAN

Bentara	New Haven	24
Kari	New Haven	23

MEDITERRANEAN

Acqua	Westport	21
Arugula	W Hartford	24
Basso Café	Norwalk	-
NEW Café Manolo	Westport	-
Centro	multi.	19
Costa Brava	Norwalk	22
f.i.s.h.	Port Chester	21
Gates	New Canaan	18
Harbor Lights	Norwalk	20
Il Sogno	Port Chester	-
John's Café	Woodbury	24
Lusardi's	Larch	24
Med. Grill	Wilton	19
Mediterraneo	Greenwich	22
Oliva Cafe	New Preston	25
Osianna	Fairfield	-
Primavera	Crot Falls	23
River Bistro	New Milford	19
NEW Rouge Winebar	S Norwalk	-
Serevan	Amenia	28
Tapas/Ann	multi.	23
Turkish Meze	Mamaro	22
Turquoise	Larch	19

MEXICAN

NEW Besito	W Hartford	-
Chuck's Steak	Branford	18
C.O. Jones	New Haven	16
Coyote Flaco	multi.	21
Cuckoo's Nest	Old Saybrook	18
El Tio	multi.	24
Fonda La Paloma	Cos Cob	18
Gusano Loco	Mamaro	19
Kiosko	Port Chester	-
La Herradura	multi.	-

NEW Lalo's	**Hartford**	‑
Little Mex. Cafe	**New Roch**	22
NEW Lolita	**Greenwich**	‑
Los Cabos	**Norwalk**	17
Olé Molé	**multi.**	21
Señor Pancho's	**multi.**	17
SolToro	**Uncasville**	‑
Su Casa	**Branford**	18
Tequila Mock.	**New Canaan**	17
Tequila Sunrise	**Larch**	15
Villa Del Sol	**Westport**	18
Viva Zapata	**Westport**	17
Wood's Pit BBQ	**Bantam**	22

MIDDLE EASTERN

Aladdin	**Hartford**	18
Myrna's	**Stamford**	21
Sesame Seed	**Danbury**	21

MOROCCAN

| Zitoune | **Mamaro** | 20 |

NEW ENGLAND

| Tavern on Main | **Westport** | 19 |

NEW MEXICAN

| Southwest Cafe | **Ridgefield** | 20 |

NUEVO LATINO

Z Bespoke	**New Haven**	24
Pacifico	**New Haven**	23
Sonora	**Port Chester**	24

PACIFIC RIM

| Char Koon | **S Glastonbury** | 23 |

PAN-LATIN

NEW Ay! Salsa	**New Haven**	‑
Brasitas	**multi.**	‑
Karamba	**White Pl**	20

PERUVIAN

| Patrias | **Port Chester** | 20 |

PIZZA

Abatino's	**N White Plains**	21
Acqua	**Westport**	21
Aladdin	**Hartford**	18
Alforno	**Old Saybrook**	23
Angelina's	**Westport**	18
Aurora	**Rye**	20

Bellizzi	**Larch**	15
Z Bertucci's	**multi.**	16
Bru Room/BAR	**New Haven**	25
Z California Pizza	**multi.**	16
DiNardo's	**Pound Ridge**	19
Doc's Trattoria	**Kent**	21
Ernesto	**White Pl**	21
Fat Cat Pie	**Norwalk**	23
First & Last	**multi.**	20
Z Frank Pepe	**multi.**	26
Frank Pepe's/Spot	**New Haven**	26
Harry's Bishops	**W Hartford**	‑
Harry's Pizza	**W Hartford**	24
Iannelli's	**White Pl**	19
La Manda's	**White Pl**	18
Luna Pizza	**multi.**	20
Maestro's	**New Roch**	16
Mancuso's	**Fairfield**	18
Z Modern Apizza	**New Haven**	25
Modern Rest.	**New Roch**	21
Mystic Pizza	**multi.**	17
122 Pizza Bistro	**Stamford**	19
Pizzeria Lauretano	**Bethel**	26
NEW Pizzeria Molto	**Fairfield**	‑
Portofino Pizza	**Goldens Bridge**	22
Portofino's	**Wilton**	21
Post Corner Pizza	**Darien**	19
Rizzuto's Pizza	**multi.**	‑
Z Sally's Apizza	**New Haven**	26
Sal's Pizza	**Mamaro**	24
Taro's	**Millerton**	20
Tarry Lodge	**Port Chester**	24
Terra Rist.	**Greenwich**	22
Tuscan Oven	**Norwalk**	18
Two Boots	**Bridgeport**	21
Vazzy's	**multi.**	18
Yorkside	**New Haven**	16

PORTUGUESE

| Omanel | **Bridgeport** | 22 |
| Peniche | **White Pl** | 22 |

PUB FOOD

Z Archie Moore's	**multi.**	19
Blazer Pub	**Purdys**	22
Brewhouse	**S Norwalk**	16
Bru Room/BAR	**New Haven**	25

NEW Crooked Shillelagh | **Branford**	–
Eli Cannon's | **Middletown**	20
John Harvard's | **Manchester**	19
Lady Luck | **Bridgeport**	–
Lansdowne | **New Haven**	–
Larchmont Tav. | **Larch**	17
Lazy Boy Saloon | **White Pl**	17
NEW Little Pub | **Ridgefield**	–
Mackenzie's | **Old Greenwich**	15
O'Neill's | **S Norwalk**	18
Prime 16 | **New Haven**	–
Route 22 | **multi.**	13
Southport Brew. | **multi.**	15
Sports Page | **White Pl**	–
Union Street Tav. | **Windsor**	–
Vinny's Backyard | **Stamford**	19
Wood-n-Tap | **multi.**	19

SANDWICHES

Brooklyn's Famous | **White Pl**	15
Corner Bakery | **Pawling**	23
Così | **multi.**	15
Firehouse Deli | **Fairfield**	21
Harney/Sons | **Millerton**	21
Irving Farm | **Millerton**	20
Kisco Kosher | **White Pl**	19
Oscar's | **Westport**	19
Pantry | **Wash Depot**	25
Rein's NY Deli | **Vernon**	22

SEAFOOD

Z Abbott's Lobster | **Noank**	23
Barnacle | **Mamaro**	–
Beach Café | **Fairfield**	17
Beach House | **Milford**	22
Bennett's | **Stamford**	21
Bill's Seafood | **Westbrook**	19
Brickhouse | **Derby**	–
Carmen Anthony Fish. | **multi.**	21
Confetti | **Plainville**	18
Costello's | **Noank**	18
Dock/Dine | **Old Saybrook**	15
Dolphins Cove | **Bridgeport**	19
Edd's Place | **Westbrook**	22
80 West | **White Pl**	19
Z Elm St. Oyster | **Greenwich**	24

f.i.s.h. | **Port Chester**	21
Flanders Fish | **E Lyme**	20
Gervasi's | **White Pl**	–
Go Fish | **Mystic**	20
Gus's Franklin Pk. | **Harrison**	20
Harbor Lights | **Norwalk**	20
Jasper White's | **Uncasville**	21
Legal Sea Foods | **White Pl**	19
Z Lenny/Joe's | **multi.**	22
Lenny's Indian | **Branford**	20
Liv's Oyster | **Old Saybrook**	24
NEW Matthew's | **Unionville**	–
Max Fish | **Glastonbury**	24
Z Max's Oyster | **W Hartford**	25
Morgans Fish | **Rye**	24
Octagon | **Groton**	26
Osetra | **Norwalk**	26
Pacifico | **New Haven**	23
Peppermill | **Stratford**	18
Rest./Rowayton Sea. | **Rowayton**	22
Rest./Water's Edge | **Westbrook**	20
Ruby's Oyster | **Rye**	21
Sage American | **New Haven**	20
Saltwater Grille | **Stamford**	20
Saybrook Fish | **Rocky Hill**	21
Scribner's | **Milford**	23
Seamen's Inne | **Mystic**	19
Seaside Johnnie's | **Rye**	13
Shell Station | **Stratford**	21
Sono Seaport | **S Norwalk**	16
Splash | **Westport**	21
Stone House | **Guilford**	21
1020 Post | **Darien**	–
Town Dock | **Rye**	17
U.S.S. Chowder | **multi.**	16
Westbrook Lobster | **multi.**	18

SMALL PLATES

(See also Spanish tapas specialist)

Antipasti | Italian | **White Pl**	21
Bar Vivace | Italian | **Mamaro**	22
Dragonfly | Eclectic | **Stamford**	20
Gabrielle's | Amer. | **Centerbrook**	21
Gnarly Vine | Amer. | **New Roch**	19
Z Harvest Supper | Amer. | **New Canaan**	27

116 Crown | Eclectic | **New Haven** — 23

Osetra | Eclectic/Seafood | — 26
Norwalk

Osianna | Med. | **Fairfield** — –

Solaia | French/Italian | **Greenwich** — 22

Southwest Cafe | New Mex. | — 20
Ridgefield

Tapas/Ann | Med. | **multi.** — 23

Z Thali | Indian | **New Haven** — 26

SOUTHERN

Jeff's Cuisine | **S Norwalk** — 25

NEW Taste/Charleston | — –
Norwalk

SOUTHWESTERN

Boxcar Cantina | **Greenwich** — 20

Coyote Blue | **Middletown** — 23

Geronimo | **New Haven** — 17

J. Gilbert's | **Glastonbury** — 25

Salsa | **New Milford** — 23

Telluride | **Stamford** — 21

Two Steps | **Danbury** — 13

SPANISH

(* tapas specialist)
Barça* | **Hartford** — 20

Z Barcelona* | **multi.** — 23

Bistro Basque | **Milford** — 26

Costa del Sol* | **Hartford** — 25

España* | **Larch** — 20

Z Ibiza* | **multi.** — 28

La Paella | **Norwalk** — 25

Z Meigas* | **Norwalk** — 26

Meson/Españoles* | **White Pl** — 23

Olive Mkt.* | **Georgetown** — –

Patrias | **Port Chester** — 20

Peniche* | **White Pl** — 22

River Bistro* | **New Milford** — 19

STEAKHOUSES

Beach House | **Milford** — 22

Bennett's | **Stamford** — 21

Blackstones | **Norwalk** — 23

BLT Steak | **White Pl** — 23

Brickhouse | **Derby** — –

Bugaboo Creek | **Manchester** — 15

Z Capital Grille | **Stamford** — 25

Carmen Anthony | **multi.** — 22

Cedars | **Ledyard** — 21

Central Steak | **New Haven** — 23

Chuck's Steak | **multi.** — 18

Churrasc. Braza | **Hartford** — 21

Country House | **Patterson** — 20

NEW Craftsteak | **Ledyard** — –

Croton Creek | **Crot Falls** — 20

Dakota Steak | **multi.** — 18

David Burke | **Ledyard** — 27

Edo | **Port Chester** — 20

Frankie/Johnnie's | **Rye** — 23

Giovanni's | **Darien** — 20

J. Gilbert's | **Glastonbury** — 25

Joseph's | **Bridgeport** — 24

Kobis | **multi.** — 19

Marc Charles | **Armonk** — 28

Mario's Pl. | **Westport** — 19

Z Max Downtown | **Hartford** — 27

Z Michael Jordan's | **Uncasville** — 25

Mighty Joe | **White Pl** — 16

Z Morton's | **multi.** — 24

Mo's NY | **New Roch** — 21

New Deal Steak | **Westbrook** — 14

Octagon | **Groton** — 26

Z Outback Steak | **multi.** — 16

Peppermill | **Stratford** — 18

Z Ruth's Chris | **Newington** — 24

Sage American | **New Haven** — 20

Steak Loft | **Mystic** — 18

Willett House | **Port Chester** — 23

TEAROOMS

Harney/Sons | **Millerton** — 21

TEX-MEX

Mary Ann's | **multi.** — 17

3 Jalapeños | **Mamaro** — 17

THAI

Bangkok Gardens | **New Haven** — 22

Bangkok Thai | **Mamaro** — 21

Hot Basil | **W Hartford** — 21

King & I | **multi.** — 21

Kit's Thai | **Stamford** — 22

Lemon Grass | **W Hartford** — 19

Little Thai/Buddha | **multi.** — 23

Lotus Thai | **Stratford** — 20

Papaya Thai | **S Norwalk**	20
Pho Mekong | **Westport**	20
Puket Café | **Wethersfield**	-
Red Lotus | **New Roch**	20
Reka's | **White Pl**	18
Thai Chi | **Stamford**	22
Thai Pan Asian | **New Haven**	17
Thai Pearl | **Ridgefield**	19
Thai Place | **Putnam**	-

TURKISH

Turkish Cuisine | **White Pl**	-
Turkish Meze | **Mamaro**	22
Turquoise | **Larch**	19

VEGETARIAN

(* vegan)

Ahimsa* | **New Haven**	17
Bloodroot* | **Bridgeport**	21

Claire's Corner | **New Haven**	19
NEW Elaine's Healthy* | **New Haven**	-
It's Only Natural* | **Middletown**	23
Lime | **Norwalk**	23
Z P.F. Chang's* | **White Pl**	19
Stand* | **Norwalk**	-
Tawa | **Stamford**	22
Z Thali | **New Haven**	26

VENEZUELAN

Valencia Luncheria | **Norwalk**	27

VIETNAMESE

Bamboo Grill | **Canton**	21
Lotus | **Vernon**	23
Pho Mekong | **Westport**	20
Pot-au-Pho | **New Haven**	20

CT/NEARBY NY

CUISINES

Locations

Includes names, cuisines and Food ratings.

Connecticut

AVON

Avon Old Farm | *Amer.* —
🅩 Bertucci's | *Italian* 16
Carmen Anthony Fish. | *Seafood* 21
Così | *Sandwiches* 15
🆕 DaCapo's | *Italian* —
Dakota Steak | *Steak* 18
First & Last | *Italian* 20
Max-a-Mia | *Italian* 24
Papacelle | *Italian* —
Toshi Japanese | *Japanese* 23

BANTAM

Wood's Pit BBQ | *BBQ/Mex.* 22
Zinis | *Italian* 18

BERLIN

Hawthorne Inn | *Amer.* 18

BETHEL

La Zingara | *Italian* 25
Old Heidelberg | *German* 20
Pizzeria Lauretano | *Pizza* 26
Putnam Hse. | *Amer.* 16
Rizzuto's Pizza | *Italian* —

BETHLEHEM

🅩 Woodward Hse. | *Amer.* 26

BLOOMFIELD

Tapas/Ann | *Med.* 23

BRANFORD

Chuck's Steak | *Steak* 18
🆕 Crooked Shillelagh | *Irish* —
Foe | *Amer.* 22
La Cuisine | *Amer.* —
Lenny's Indian | *Seafood* 20
🅩 Le Petit Cafe | *French* 28
Mango's B&G | *Carib.* 19
Southport Brew. | *Pub* 15
Su Casa | *Mex.* 18
U.S.S. Chowder | *Seafood* 16

BRIDGEPORT

Ash Creek | *Amer.* 18
Bloodroot | *Vegan/Veg.* 21
Café Roma | *Italian* 22
Café Tavolini | *Italian* 19
Coyote Flaco | *Mex.* 21
Dolphins Cove | *Seafood* 19
Épernay | *Amer.* —
Field | *Amer.* 17
🆕 Fraîche Burger | *Burgers* —
Joseph's | *Steak* 24
King & I | *Thai* 21
Lady Luck | *Pub* —
Metric | *Eclectic* —
Omanel | *Portug.* 22
Ralph/Rich's | *Italian* 24
Tuscany | *Italian* 25
Two Boots | *Pizza* 21
Vazzy's | *Italian* 18
Viale Rist. | *Italian* 21

CANTON

Bamboo Grill | *Viet.* 21
Buon Appetito | *Italian* 24
🅩 Feng Asian | *Asian* 26

CENTERBROOK

Gabrielle's | *Amer.* 21

CHESHIRE

Brix | *French/Italian* 19

CHESTER

🆕 Rest. L&E | *French* —
River Tavern | *Amer.* 25

CLINTON

Hanami | *Japanese* —
Westbrook Lobster | *Seafood* 18

COS COB

Fonda La Paloma | *Mex.* 18
Nuage | *French/Japanese* 23

DANBURY

☑ Bertucci's	*Italian*	16
Café/Green	*Italian*	23
Chuck's Steak	*Steak*	18
Hanna's Mideastern	*Lebanese*	22
Koo	*Japanese*	23
☑ Ondine	*French*	25
☑ Outback Steak	*Steak*	16
Sesame Seed	*Mideast.*	21
Two Steps	*SW*	13

DARIEN

Aux Délices	*Amer./French*	23
☑ Bertucci's	*Italian*	16
☑ Ching's	*Asian*	24
Chuck's Steak	*Steak*	18
☑ Coromandel	*Indian*	26
Così	*Sandwiches*	15
Giovanni's	*Steak*	20
Little Thai/Buddha	*Thai*	23
Melting Pot	*Fondue*	18
Olé Molé	*Mex.*	21
Post Corner Pizza	*Pizza*	19
☑ Tengda	*Asian*	23
1020 Post	*French*	-

DEEP RIVER

du Glace	*French*	-

DERBY

☑ Archie Moore's	*Pub*	19
Brickhouse	*Italian*	-

EASTFORD

Still River	*Amer.*	26

EAST LYME

Flanders Fish	*Seafood*	20

EAST WINDSOR

Mei Tzu	*Asian*	-

ESSEX

Griswold Inn	*Amer.*	18
Oliver's Taverne	*Amer.*	13

FAIRFIELD

☑ Archie Moore's	*Pub*	19
Avellino's	*Italian*	20
Bangalore	*Indian*	23
☑ Barcelona	*Spanish*	23
Beach Café	*Amer.*	17
Cafe Lola	*French*	-
Centro	*Italian/Med.*	19
Cinzano's	*Italian*	19
Coppia	*Italian*	24
55°	*Italian*	-
Fin/Fin II	*Japanese*	22
Firehouse Deli	*Deli*	21
NEW Flipside Burgers	*Burgers*	-
☑ Frank Pepe	*Pizza*	26
Isabelle/Vincent	*Bakery/French*	-
Joe's American	*Amer.*	16
King & I	*Thai*	21
Kobis	*Japanese*	19
Layla's Falafel	*Lebanese*	23
Mancuso's	*Italian*	18
Osianna	*Med.*	-
Panda Pavilion	*Chinese*	16
NEW Pizzeria Molto	*Italian*	-
Ponte Vecchio	*Italian*	20
☑ Quattro Pazzi	*Italian*	22
Saint Tropez	*French*	23
☑ Super/Weenie	*Hot Dogs*	22
Wilson's BBQ	*BBQ*	24

FARMINGTON

☑ Apricots	*Amer.*	24
☑ California Pizza	*Pizza*	16
NEW Flaggstead	*BBQ*	-
Grist Mill	*Continental*	24
Piccolo Arancio	*Italian*	26
Rainforest Cafe	*Amer.*	11
Wood-n-Tap	*Pub*	19

GEORGETOWN

Olive Mkt.	*Spanish*	-

GLASTONBURY

☑ Bertucci's	*Italian*	16
J. Gilbert's	*SW/Steak*	25
Luna Pizza	*Pizza*	20
Max Amore	*Italian*	23
Max Fish	*Seafood*	24
Pazzo Italian	*Italian*	23
Plan B Burger	*Burgers*	23

NEW Spinghar | *Afghan*	–
Tango | *Argent./Italian*	–

GREENWICH

Abis | *Japanese*	18
Asiana Cafe | *Asian*	20
Aux Délices | *Amer./French*	23
Bambou | *Asian*	23
Z Barcelona | *Spanish*	23
Boxcar Cantina | *SW*	20
Burgers/Shakes | *Burgers*	–
Centro | *Italian/Med.*	19
Così | *Sandwiches*	15
Z Elm St. Oyster | *Seafood*	24
Ginger Man | *Amer.*	17
Z Jean-Louis | *French*	28
Le Figaro Bistro | *French*	20
Z L'Escale | *French*	23
Little Thai/Buddha | *Thai*	23
NEW Lolita | *Mex.*	–
Mediterraneo | *Med.*	22
Meli-Melo | *French*	25
Morello | *Italian*	–
Panda Pavilion | *Chinese*	16
Pasta Vera | *Italian*	21
Penang Grill | *Asian*	23
Polpo | *Italian*	24
Rasa | *Indian*	20
Z Rebeccas | *Amer.*	25
Solaia | *Italian*	22
Z Tengda | *Asian*	23
Terra Rist. | *Italian*	22
Thataway Cafe | *Amer.*	15
Z Thomas Henkelmann | *French*	28
Versailles | *Bakery/French*	20

GROTON

Octagon | *Seafood/Steak*	26
Olio | *Amer.*	24

GUILFORD

NEW Ballou's | *Eclectic*	–
First & Last | *Italian*	20
Stone House | *Amer./Seafood*	21

HAMDEN

Z Ibiza | *Spanish*	28
Kumo | *Japanese*	22

Rist. Luce | *Italian*	22
Southport Brew. | *Pub*	15

HARTFORD

Aladdin | *Mideast.*	18
Barça | *Spanish*	20
Bin 228 | *Italian*	23
Black-Eyed Sally | *BBQ*	21
Carbone's | *Italian*	25
Z Cheesecake Fac. | *Amer.*	18
Churrasc. Braza | *Brazilian*	21
Costa del Sol | *Spanish*	25
Coyote Flaco | *Mex.*	21
Dish B&G | *Amer.*	20
Z Feng Asian | *Asian*	26
Z Firebox | *Amer.*	25
First & Last | *Italian*	20
Hot Tomato's | *Italian*	21
Koji | *Japanese*	19
NEW Lalo's | *Mex.*	–
Masala | *Indian*	–
Z Max Downtown | *Amer./Steak*	27
Z Morton's | *Steak*	24
Peppercorn's Grill | *Italian*	25
PolytechnicON20 | *Amer.*	28
Spris | *Italian*	21
Tapas/Ann | *Med.*	23
Trumbull Kitchen | *Eclectic*	24
U.S.S. Chowder | *Seafood*	16
Vito's | *Italian*	19
VIVO Tratt. | *Italian*	21
Wood-n-Tap | *Pub*	19

IVORYTON

Z Copper Beech | *Amer.*	24

KENT

Bull's Bridge | *Amer.*	16
Doc's Trattoria | *Italian*	21

LAKEVILLE

Boathouse | *Amer.*	16
Pastorale | *French*	24
Woodland | *Amer./Continental*	23

LEDYARD

Burke in Box | *Amer.*	–
Z California Pizza | *Pizza*	16

Menus, photos, voting and more – free at ZAGAT.com

Cedars	Steak	21
NEW Craftsteak	Steak	-
David Burke	Steak	27
Hard Rock	Amer.	15

LITCHFIELD

Aspen Garden	Eclectic	15
Señor Pancho's	Mex.	17
West St. Grill	Amer.	22

MADISON

Cafe Allegre	Italian	20
Elizabeth's Cafe	Amer.	26
Z Lenny/Joe's	Seafood	22
Zhang's	Chinese/Japanese	18

MANCHESTER

Bugaboo Creek	Steak	15
Carrabba's	Italian	19
Z Cavey's	French/Italian	28
Z Frank Pepe	Pizza	26
John Harvard's	Amer.	19
Z Outback Steak	Steak	16
Shady Glen	Diner	23

MANSFIELD CENTER

| Coyote Flaco | Mex. | 21 |

MIDDLETOWN

Coyote Blue	SW	23
Eli Cannon's	Amer.	20
Esca	Italian	-
First & Last	Italian	20
Forbidden City	Chinese	23
It's Only Natural	Health	23
Tuscany Grill	Italian	20

MILFORD

Z Archie Moore's	Pub	19
Beach House	Seafood/Steak	22
Bin 100	Eclectic	25
Bistro Basque	French/Spanish	26
Jeffrey's	Amer./Continental	23
Scribner's	Seafood	23
Southport Brew.	Pub	15
Z Tengda	Asian	23
Vazzy's	Italian	18

MONROE

| Tratt. Carl Anthony | Italian | 23 |
| Vazzy's | Italian | 18 |

MORRIS

| Winvian | Amer. | - |

MYSTIC

Azu	Amer.	23
Bravo Bravo	Italian	24
Z Capt. Daniel Packer	Eclectic	22
Flood Tide	Continental/Eclectic	21
Go Fish	Seafood	20
Mystic Pizza	Pizza	17
Seamen's Inne	Amer./Seafood	19
Steak Loft	Steak	18
Zhang's	Chinese/Japanese	18

NEW BRITAIN

| East Side | German | 20 |
| Great Taste | Chinese | 27 |

NEW CANAAN

Aloi	Italian	24
Z Bistro Bonne Nuit	French	26
Cava Wine	Italian	23
Chef Luis	Amer.	25
Z Ching's	Asian	24
Fifty Coins	Amer.	14
Gates	Calif./Med.	18
Z Harvest Supper	Amer.	27
Plum Tree	Japanese	21
NEW Rocco's	Italian	-
Roger Sherman	Continental	22
Solé Rist.	Italian	22
Sushi 25	Chinese/Japanese	-
Tequila Mock.	Mex.	17
Z Thali	Indian	26

NEW HARTFORD

| Chatterley's | Amer. | 20 |

NEW HAVEN

Adriana's	Italian	23
Ahimsa	Vegan/Veg.	17
Akasaka	Japanese	17
Z Archie Moore's	Pub	19

NEW Ay! Salsa	*Pan-Latin*	-
Bangkok Gardens	*Thai*	22
Z Barcelona	*Spanish*	23
Basta	*Italian*	20
Bentara	*Malaysian*	24
Z Bespoke	*Amer./Nuevo Latino*	24
Blue Pearl	*Amer./Fondue*	20
Bru Room/BAR	*Pizza*	25
Cafe Goodfellas	*Italian*	21
Carmen Anthony	*Steak*	22
Caseus	*Eclectic*	-
Central Steak	*Steak*	23
Christopher Martins	*Continental*	20
Claire's Corner	*Veg.*	19
C.O. Jones	*Cal./Mex.*	16
Consiglio's	*Italian*	25
NEW Elaine's Healthy	*Soul/Veg.*	-
Foster's	*Amer.*	17
Z Frank Pepe	*Pizza*	26
Frank Pepe's/Spot	*Pizza*	26
Geronimo	*SW*	17
Heirloom	*Amer./Continental*	-
Z Ibiza	*Spanish*	28
Kari	*Malaysian*	23
Kudeta	*Asian*	21
Kumo	*Japanese*	22
Lansdowne	*Pub*	-
Leon's	*Italian*	-
L'Orcio	*Italian*	23
Louis' Lunch	*Burgers*	24
Miso	*Japanese*	23
Z Modern Apizza	*Pizza*	25
116 Crown	*Eclectic*	23
Pacifico	*Nuevo Latino/Seafood*	23
Pot-au-Pho	*Viet.*	20
Prime 16	*Pub*	-
Royal Palace	*Chinese*	24
Sage American	*Seafood/Steak*	20
Z Sally's Apizza	*Pizza*	26
Scoozzi Tratt.	*Italian*	22
Soul de Cuba	*Cuban*	21
Thai Pan Asian	*Thai*	17
Z Thali	*Indian/Veg.*	26
Tre Scalini	*Italian*	23
Z Union League	*French*	27
Yorkside	*Greek/Pizza*	16

Zaroka	*Indian*	20
Z Zinc	*Amer.*	24

NEWINGTON

Z Bertucci's	*Italian*	16
Hidden Vine	*Italian*	-
Z Outback Steak	*Steak*	16
Z Ruth's Chris	*Steak*	24

NEW LONDON

Brie/Bleu	*French*	24
Z Outback Steak	*Steak*	16

NEW MILFORD

Adrienne	*Amer.*	24
Z Cookhouse	*BBQ*	19
59 Bank	*Amer.*	18
River Bistro	*Spanish*	19
Salsa	*SW*	23

NEW PRESTON

Z Boulders Inn	*Amer.*	22
Hopkins Inn	*Austrian*	20
Oliva Cafe	*Med.*	25

NEWTOWN

Inn at Newtown	*Amer.*	19

NOANK

Z Abbott's Lobster	*Seafood*	23
Costello's	*Seafood*	18

NORTH HAVEN

Z Outback Steak	*Steak*	16

NORTH STONINGTON

Mystic Pizza	*Pizza*	17

NORWALK

Ash Creek	*Amer.*	18
Basso Café	*Med.*	-
B.J. Ryan's	*Amer.*	22
Blackstones	*Steak*	23
Bond Grill	*Asian*	18
Brasitas	*Pan-Latin*	-
Costa Brava	*Med.*	22
Fat Cat Pie	*Pizza*	23
Harbor Lights	*Med./Seafood*	20
La Paella	*Spanish*	25
La Taverna	*Italian*	22
Lime	*Health*	23

Little Thai/Buddha	*Thai*	23
Los Cabos	*Mex.*	17
Z Meigas	*Spanish*	26
Osetra	*Eclectic/Seafood*	26
Z Quattro Pazzi	*Italian*	22
Stand	*Vegan*	-
NEW Taste/Charleston	*Southern*	-
Tuscan Oven	*Italian*	18
Valencia Luncheria	*Venez.*	27
Wild Rice	*Asian*	21

OLD GREENWICH

Beach Hse. Café	*Amer.*	-
Greenwich Tav.	*Amer.*	-
Mackenzie's	*Pub*	15
Osteria Applausi	*Italian*	23

OLD LYME

Boom	*Amer.*	22
Chestnut Grille	*Amer.*	24
Old Lyme Inn	*Amer.*	20

OLD SAYBROOK

Alforno	*Italian*	23
Aspen	*Amer.*	21
Cuckoo's Nest	*Mex.*	18
Dock/Dine	*Seafood*	15
NEW Jack Rabbit's	*Amer.*	-
Liv's Oyster	*Seafood*	24
Pat's Kountry	*Amer.*	14
Terra Mar	*Amer.*	21
Tiberio's	*Italian*	-
Zhang's	*Chinese/Japanese*	18

ORANGE

Z Bertucci's	*Italian*	16
China Pavilion	*Chinese*	21
Z Coromandel	*Indian*	26
Z Outback Steak	*Steak*	16
Wasabi	*Japanese*	23

OXFORD

121 Rest.	*Amer.*	23

PLAINVILLE

Confetti	*Italian/Seafood*	18
First & Last	*Italian*	20

POMFRET

Harvest/Pomfret	*Continental*	22
Sharpe Hill/Vineyard	*Amer.*	-
Vanilla Bean	*Amer.*	23

PUTNAM

Thai Place	*Thai*	-

REDDING/ REDDING RIDGE

Squire's	*Eclectic*	19
White Horse Tav.	*Amer.*	15

RIDGEFIELD

Asian Kitchen	*Asian*	22
Bailey's	*Amer.*	20
Z Bernard's	*French*	27
Brendan's/Elms	*Amer.*	22
Fifty Coins	*Amer.*	14
Z Insieme	*Italian*	25
Koo	*Japanese*	23
NEW Little Pub	*Pub*	-
Luc's Café	*French*	24
Sagi	*Italian*	-
Southwest Cafe	*New Mex.*	20
Z Stonehenge	*Continental*	24
Thai Pearl	*Thai*	19
Z Thali	*Indian*	26
Toscana	*Italian*	21

RIVERSIDE

Aux Délices	*Amer./French*	23
Z Baang Cafe	*Asian*	23
Z Valbella	*Italian*	25

ROCKY HILL

Chuck's Steak	*Steak*	18
Dakota Steak	*Steak*	18
Pazzo Italian	*Italian*	23
Saybrook Fish	*Seafood*	21
Wood-n-Tap	*Pub*	19

ROWAYTON

Rest./Rowayton Sea.	*Seafood*	22
River Cat Grill	*Amer.*	22

SALISBURY

White Hart	*Amer.*	17

CONNECTICUT

LOCATIONS

SHELTON

Z Bertucci's	Italian	16
Il Palio	Italian	23
Kobis	Japanese	19
Z Outback Steak	Steak	16

SHERMAN

American Pie Co.	Amer.	20

SIMSBURY

Evergreens	Amer.	25
Luna Pizza	Pizza	20
Z Métro Bis	Amer.	26
Plan B Burger	Burgers	23

SOUTHBURY

Olive Tree	Amer.	19
Señor Pancho's	Mex.	17

SOUTH GLASTONBURY

Char Koon	Pac. Rim	23

SOUTHINGTON

Z Bertucci's	Italian	16
Z Outback Steak	Steak	16
Wood-n-Tap	Pub	19

SOUTH NORWALK

Z Archie Moore's	Pub	19
Z Barcelona	Spanish	23
Brewhouse	Amer.	16
Burger Bar	Burgers	24
Chocopologie	Dessert	-
Z Coromandel	Indian	26
Donovan's	Amer.	-
Ginger Man	Amer.	17
Jeff's Cuisine	BBQ/Southern	25
Kazu	Japanese	24
Z Match	Amer.	24
O'Neill's	Pub	18
Papaya Thai	Thai	20
Z Pasta Nostra	Italian	25
NEW Rouge Winebar	Med.	-
SoNo Baking Co.	Bakery	25
Sono Seaport	Seafood	16
Strada 18	Italian	25
Wasabi Chi	Asian	24

SOUTHPORT

Olé Molé	Mex.	21
Z Paci	Italian	26
Southport Brew.	Pub	15

SOUTH WINDSOR

Mill on River	Continental	23
Ted's Montana	Amer.	21

STAMFORD

Z Barcelona	Spanish	23
Bennett's	Seafood/Steak	21
Boathouse/Smokey	BBQ	21
Bobby Valentine	Amer.	15
Brasitas	Pan-Latin	-
Cafe Silvium	Italian	-
Z California Pizza	Pizza	16
Z Capital Grille	Steak	25
Chez Jean-Pierre	French	24
NEW Chili Chicken	Chinese/Indian	-
Z City Limits	Diner	18
Colony Grill	Italian	-
Z Columbus Park	Italian	25
Z Coromandel	Indian	26
Dragonfly	Eclectic	20
Duo	Euro./Japanese	23
Eclisse	Italian	20
Egane	Korean	20
Eos Greek	Greek	-
Ferrante	Italian	20
Fin/Fin II	Japanese	22
Grand	Amer.	18
Il Falco	Italian	22
Kit's Thai	Thai	22
Kona Grill	Amer./Asian	17
Kotobuki	Japanese	23
Kujaku	Japanese	17
La Bretagne	French	22
Layla's Falafel	Lebanese	23
Little Thai/Buddha	Thai	23
Long Ridge Tav.	Amer.	14
Lucky's	Diner	15
Market	Amer.	23
Mary Ann's	Tex-Mex	17
Z Morton's	Steak	24
Myrna's	Mideast.	21

Napa & Co. | *Amer.*	25
Olé Molé | *Mex.*	21
122 Pizza Bistro | *Italian/Pizza*	19
Paradise B&G | *Amer.*	13
Pellicci's | *Italian*	20
P.F. Chang's | *Chinese*	19
Route 22 | *Pub*	13
Saltwater Grille | *Amer.*	20
Siena | *Italian*	25
Southport Brew. | *Pub*	15
Tawa | *Indian*	22
Telluride | *SW*	21
Thai Chi | *Asian*	22
Vinny's Backyard | *Pub*	19

STONINGTON

Water St. Cafe | *Amer.*	25

STORRS

Altnaveigh Inn | *Continental*	24
Chuck's Steak | *Steak*	18

STRATFORD

Blue Point B&G | *Amer.*	18
Harborside B&G | *Amer.*	15
Lotus Thai | *Thai*	20
Peppermill | *Seafood/Steak*	18
Shell Station | *Continental*	21
Vazzy's | *Italian*	18

TORRINGTON

Venetian | *Italian*	22

TRUMBULL

Marisa's | *Italian*	18

UNCASVILLE

NEW Bar Americain | *American*	-
Frank Pepe | *Pizza*	26
Jasper White's | *Seafood*	21
Michael Jordan's | *Steak*	25
SolToro | *Mex.*	-
Todd English's | *Italian*	23

UNIONVILLE

NEW Matthew's | *Amer.*	-

VERNON

Little Mark's | *BBQ*	20
Lotus | *Viet.*	23

Rein's NY Deli | *Deli*	22
Wood-n-Tap | *Pub*	19

WALLINGFORD

Archie Moore's | *Pub*	19
Michael's | *Italian*	23
Westbrook Lobster | *Seafood*	18

WASHINGTON

Mayflower Inn | *Amer.*	25

WASHINGTON DEPOT

G.W. Tavern | *Amer.*	20
Pantry | *Amer.*	25

WATERBURY

Brass City | *Continental*	-
Carmen Anthony | *Steak*	22
Diorio | *Amer./Italian*	24
Drescher's | *German*	22
La Tavola | *Italian*	-
Señor Pancho's | *Mex.*	17

WESTBROOK

Bill's Seafood | *Seafood*	19
Boom | *Amer.*	22
Café Routier | *French*	25
Edd's Place | *Deli*	22
Lenny/Joe's | *Seafood*	22
New Deal Steak | *Steak*	14
Rest./Water's Edge | *Amer.*	20

WEST CORNWALL

RSVP | *French*	29
Wandering Moose | *Amer.*	18

WEST HARTFORD

Arugula | *Med.*	24
Barcelona | *Spanish*	23
Bertucci's | *Italian*	16
NEW Besito | *Mex.*	-
NEW Bombay Olive | *Amer./Indian*	-
Bricco | *Italian*	25
Butterfly Chinese | *Chinese*	15
Chengdu | *Chinese*	18
Così | *Sandwiches*	15
East-West Grille | *SE Asian*	23

Elbow Room	*Amer.*	18
Elements	*American*	-
Gold Roc	*Diner*	12
Z Grant's	*Amer.*	25
Harry's Bishops	*Pizza*	-
Harry's Pizza	*Pizza*	24
Hot Basil	*Thai*	21
Lemon Grass	*Thai*	19
Luna Pizza	*Pizza*	20
Z Max's Oyster	*Seafood*	25
Murasaki	*Japanese*	19
Z P.F. Chang's	*Chinese*	19
Plan B Burger	*Burgers*	23
Pond House Café	*Amer.*	22
Rizzuto's Pizza	*Italian*	-
Shish Kebab	*Afghan*	24
Tapas/Ann	*Med.*	23
Taste/India	*Indian*	20

WEST HAVEN

Chuck's Steak	*Steak*	18

WESTON

Z Cobb's Mill Inn	*Amer.*	18

WESTPORT

Acqua	*Med.*	21
Angelina's	*Pizza*	18
Z Bertucci's	*Italian*	16
Blue Lemon	*Amer.*	24
Bobby Q's	*BBQ*	19
Bogey's Grille	*Amer.*	16
Bombay	*Indian*	23
NEW Café Manolo	*Med.*	-
Cucina Modo	*Italian*	-
Z DaPietro's	*French/Italian*	26
Z Dressing Room	*Amer.*	23
Jasmine	*Chinese/Japanese*	15
NEW Le Farm	*Amer.*	-
Little Kitchen	*Asian*	22
Mario's Pl.	*Italian/Steak*	19
Napoli Sul Fiume	*Italian*	16
Oscar's	*Deli*	19
Pho Mekong	*Thai/Viet.*	20
Positano's	*Italian*	22
Red Barn	*Amer.*	17
River House	*Amer.*	16

Rizzuto's Pizza	*Italian*	-
Sakura	*Japanese*	21
Splash	*Seafood*	21
Tarantino's	*Italian*	24
Tavern on Main	*New Eng.*	19
Z Tengda	*Asian*	23
Tiger Bowl	*Chinese*	15
Via Sforza	*Italian*	21
Villa Del Sol	*Mex.*	18
Viva Zapata	*Mex.*	17
V Rest.	*Calif.*	16

WETHERSFIELD

Carmen Anthony Fish.	*Seafood*	21
NEW Lucky Lou	*Amer.*	-
Puket Café	*Thai*	-
Vito's	*Italian*	19

WILTON

Luca Rist.	*Italian*	24
Med. Grill	*Med.*	19
Orem's Diner	*Diner*	16
Z Outback Steak	*Steak*	16
Portofino's	*Italian*	21
Schoolhse./Cannondale	*Amer.*	-

WINDSOR

NEW Nat Hayden	*BBQ*	-
Union Street Tav.	*Amer.*	-
Vito's	*Italian*	19

WOODBURY

Carmen Anthony Fish.	*Seafood*	21
Z Carole Peck's	*Amer.*	27
Curtis House	*Amer.*	16
John's Café	*Amer./Med.*	24
Longwood Rest.	*Amer.*	18

Hudson Valley

AMENIA

Cascade Mtn.	*Amer.*	16
Serevan	*Med.*	28
Troutbeck	*Amer.*	24

BREWSTER

Arch	*Eclectic*	26
Aversano's	*Italian*	-
NEW Eveready	*Diner*	19
Jaipore Indian	*Indian*	24

Red Rooster	*Burgers*	18
Rraci	*Italian*	-
Sentrista Grill	*Amer.*	21

MILLERTON

Hamilton Inn	*Eclectic*	21
Harney/Sons	*Tea*	21
Irving Farm	*Coffee/Sandwiches*	20
Manna Dew	*Eclectic*	24
NEW No. 9	*Amer.*	-
Taro's	*Italian/Pizza*	20

PATTERSON

| Abruzzi Tratt. | *Italian* | 21 |
| Country House | *Amer./Steak* | 20 |

PAWLING

Corner Bakery	*Bakery*	23
McKinney/Doyle	*Amer.*	25
Towne Crier	*Amer.*	15

WINGDALE

| Big W's | *BBQ* | 26 |

Westchester County

ARMONK

Beehive	*Amer./Eclectic*	17
David Chen	*Chinese*	18
Gavi	*Italian*	17
Kira	*Japanese*	21
Made In Asia	*Asian*	21
Marc Charles	*Steak*	28
Opus 465	*Amer.*	16
Route 22	*Pub*	13

BEDFORD

Bedford Post/Barn	*Amer.*	24
Bedford Post/Farm	*Amer.*	-
Bistro 22	*Amer./French*	23
La Crémaillère	*French*	26
Tratt. Lucia	*Italian*	16

BEDFORD HILLS

| Kicho | *Japanese* | 17 |
| Nino's | *Italian* | 19 |

BEDFORD VILLAGE

| Meetinghouse | *Amer.* | 18 |

CROTON FALLS

| Croton Creek | *Steak* | 20 |
| Primavera | *Italian* | 23 |

GOLDENS BRIDGE

| Portofino Pizza | *Italian* | 22 |

HARRISON

Emilio Rist.	*Italian*	23
Gus's Franklin Pk.	*Seafood*	20
Hajime	*Japanese*	25
Halstead Ave.	*Amer.*	18
Rue/Crêpes	*French*	15
Tratt. Vivolo	*Italian*	21
Trinity Grill	*Amer.*	19

KATONAH

Blue Dolphin	*Italian*	23
Le Fontane	*Italian*	20
Peppino's	*Italian*	19
Z Tengda	*Asian*	23

LARCHMONT

Anna Maria's	*Italian*	18
Bellizzi	*Italian*	15
Chat 19	*Amer.*	18
Così	*Sandwiches*	15
Encore Bistro	*French*	22
España	*Spanish*	20
Fuji Mtn.	*Japanese*	17
Globe B&G	*Amer.*	15
Hunan Larchmont	*Chinese/Japanese*	16
Larchmont Tav.	*Amer.*	17
La Riserva	*Italian*	18
La Villetta	*Italian*	25
Lusardi's	*Italian*	24
Matsumoto	*Asian*	-
Palmer's Crossing	*Amer.*	18
Pascal's	*French*	20
Plates	*Amer.*	24
Ray's Cafe	*Chinese*	19
Sardegna	*Italian*	21
Tequila Sunrise	*Mex.*	15
Turquoise	*Med./Turkish*	19
Watercolor Cafe	*Amer.*	18

MAMARONECK

| Bangkok Thai | *Thai* | 21 |
| Barnacle | *BBQ/Seafood* | - |

Bar Vivace	*Italian*	22
Cafe Mozart	*Coffee*	17
Chef Antonio	*Italian*	16
Enzo's	*Italian*	18
Ginban Asian	*Asian*	-
Gusano Loco	*Mex.*	19
Haiku	*Asian*	23
NEW Il Castello	*Italian*	-
La Herradura	*Mex.*	-
La Piccola Casa	*Italian*	20
Le Provençal	*French*	23
NEW Limoncello	*Italian*	-
NEW Molly Spillane	*Amer.*	16
Nautilus	*Diner*	15
Rani Mahal	*Indian*	23
Red Plum	*Asian*	-
NEW Roasted Peppers	*Amer.*	-
Sal's Pizza	*Pizza*	24
3 Jalapeños	*Tex-Mex*	17
Toyo Sushi	*Japanese*	22
Turkish Meze	*Med./Turkish*	22
Walter's	*Hot Dogs*	22
Zitoune	*Moroccan*	20

NEW ROCHELLE

AJ's Burgers	*Amer.*	19
Z Coromandel	*Indian*	26
Così	*Sandwiches*	15
Coyote Flaco	*Mex.*	21
Da Giorgio	*Italian*	20
El Tio	*Mex.*	24
Fratelli	*Italian*	21
Gnarly Vine	*Amer.*	19
Golden Rod	*Asian*	20
Karuta	*Japanese*	21
La Herradura	*Mex.*	-
Little Mex. Cafe	*Mex.*	22
Maestro's	*Italian*	16
Mamma Francesca	*Italian*	16
Modern Rest.	*Italian*	21
Mo's NY	*Amer.*	21
Posto 22	*Italian*	-
Rangoli	*Indian*	24
Red Lotus	*Thai*	20
Spadaro	*Italian*	24

NORTH SALEM

John-Michael's	*Euro.*	25
121 Rest.	*Amer.*	21
Vox	*Amer./French*	21

PORT CHESTER

Alba's	*Italian*	22
Cafe Mirage	*Eclectic*	21
Copacabana	*Brazilian*	23
Coyote Flaco	*Mex.*	21
Edo	*Japanese/Steak*	20
El Tio	*Mex.*	24
Euro Asian	*Asian*	21
f.i.s.h.	*Seafood*	21
Giorgio's	*Italian*	23
Hostaria Mazzei	*Italian*	21
Il Sogno	*Italian/Med.*	-
Kiosko	*Mex.*	-
Marianacci's	*Italian*	20
Mary Ann's	*Tex-Mex*	17
Nessa	*Italian*	20
Pasquale Rist.	*Italian*	21
Patrias	*Peruvian/Spanish*	20
Piero's	*Italian*	23
Q Rest.	*BBQ*	20
Sonora	*Nuevo Latino*	24
T&J Villaggio	*Italian*	23
Tandoori Taste	*Indian*	23
Tarry Lodge	*Italian*	24
Willett House	*Steak*	23

POUND RIDGE

DiNardo's	*Italian*	19
North Star	*Amer.*	23

PURCHASE

Cobble Stone	*Amer.*	15
Creek	*Amer.*	17

PURDYS

Blazer Pub	*Pub*	22

RYE

Aurora	*Italian*	20
Cafe Livorno	*Italian*	20
Così	*Sandwiches*	15
Frankie/Johnnie's	*Steak*	23
Koo	*Japanese*	23
La Panetière	*French*	27

Morgans Fish	*Seafood*	24
Ruby's Oyster	*Seafood*	21
Rye Grill	*Eclectic*	-
Rye Roadhse.	*Cajun/Creole*	18
Seaside Johnnie's	*Seafood*	13
Town Dock	*Amer.*	17
Watermoon	*Asian*	22

RYE BROOK

Ray's Cafe	*Chinese*	19

SOUTH SALEM

Horse & Hound	*Amer.*	16
Le Château	*French*	25
Nino's	*Italian*	18

WHITE PLAINS/ N. WHITE PLAINS

Abatino's	*Italian*	21
Aberdeen	*Chinese*	23
Antipasti	*Italian*	21
Asian Tempt.	*Asian*	20
Bao's	*Chinese*	-
Bengal Tiger	*Indian*	23
BLT Steak	*Steak*	23
Blue	*Amer.*	19
Brazen Fox	*Amer.*	15
Brooklyn's Famous	*Diner*	15
Buon Amici	*Italian*	19
Z Cheesecake Fac.	*Amer.*	18
Z City Limits	*Diner*	18
80 West	*Seafood*	19
Emma's Ale	*Amer.*	-
Ernesto	*Italian*	21
42	*Amer.*	22
Gervasi's	*Italian*	-

Graziellas	*Italian*	17
NEW Haiku	*Asian*	-
Iannelli's	*Italian*	19
Imperial	*Chinese/Japanese*	18
Kalbi Hse.	*Korean*	20
Karamba	*Cuban/Pan-Latin*	20
Kisco Kosher	*Deli*	19
La Bocca	*Italian*	22
Laguna	*Italian*	19
La Manda's	*Italian*	18
Latin Am. Cafe	*Cuban*	20
Lazy Boy Saloon	*Pub*	17
Legal Sea Foods	*Seafood*	19
Melting Pot	*Fondue*	18
Meson/Españoles	*Spanish*	23
Mighty Joe	*Steak*	16
NEW Milonga	*Argent./Italian*	-
Z Morton's	*Steak*	24
Mulino's	*Italian*	25
Niko's Greek	*Greek*	20
Noda's Steak	*Japanese*	19
Z Outback Steak	*Steak*	16
Peniche	*Spanish*	22
Z P.F. Chang's	*Chinese*	19
Porter Hse.	*Amer.*	18
Reka's	*Thai*	18
Royal Palace	*Indian*	20
Sam's/Gedney	*Amer.*	17
Seasons Japanese	*Japanese*	20
Sports Page	*Pub*	-
Sushi Nanase	*Japanese*	27
Tango Grill	*Argent./Italian*	22
Tre Angelina	*Italian*	21
Turkish Cuisine	*Turkish*	-

Special Features

Listings cover the best in each category and include names, locations and Food ratings. Multi-location restaurants' features may vary by branch.

ADDITIONS

(Properties added since the last edition of the book)

Ay! Salsa	**New Haven**	-
Ballou's	**Guilford**	-
Bao's	**White Pl**	-
Bar Americain	**Uncasville**	-
Barnacle	**Mamaro**	-
Besito	**W Hartford**	-
Bombay Olive	**W Hartford**	-
Brickhouse	**Derby**	-
Cafe Lola	**Fairfield**	-
Café Manolo	**Westport**	-
Chili Chicken	**Stamford**	-
Craftsteak	**Ledyard**	-
Crooked Shillelagh	**Branford**	-
DaCapo's	**Avon**	-
Elaine's Healthy	**New Haven**	-
Elements	**W Hartford**	-
Eos Greek	**Stamford**	-
Esca	**Middletown**	-
Eveready	**Brewster**	19
Flaggstead	**Farmington**	-
Flipside Burgers	**Fairfield**	-
Fraîche Burger	**Bridgeport**	-
Haiku	**White Pl**	-
Hidden Vine	**Newington**	-
Il Castello	**Mamaro**	-
Isabelle/Vincent	**Fairfield**	-
Jack Rabbit's	**Old Saybrook**	-
Lady Luck	**Bridgeport**	-
La Herradura	**multi.**	-
Lalo's	**Hartford**	-
Lansdowne	**New Haven**	-
La Tavola	**Waterbury**	-
Le Farm	**Westport**	-
Leon's	**New Haven**	-
Limoncello	**Mamaro**	-
Little Pub	**Ridgefield**	-
Lolita	**Greenwich**	-
Lucky Lou	**Wethersfield**	-
Matsumoto	**Larch**	-
Matthew's	**Unionville**	-
Milonga	**N White Plains**	-
Molly Spillane	**Mamaro**	16
Nat Hayden	**Windsor**	-
No. 9	**Millerton**	-
Papacelle	**Avon**	-
Pizzeria Molto	**Fairfield**	-
Rest. L&E	**Chester**	-
Rizzuto's Pizza	**multi.**	-
Roasted Peppers	**Mamaro**	-
Rocco's	**New Canaan**	-
Rouge Winebar	**S Norwalk**	-
SolToro	**Uncasville**	-
Spinghar	**Glastonbury**	-
Tango	**Glastonbury**	-
Taste/Charleston	**Norwalk**	-
Thai Place	**Putnam**	-
Winvian	**Morris**	-

BREAKFAST

(See also Hotel Dining)

American Pie Co.	**Sherman**	20
Aux Délices	**multi.**	23
Cafe Mozart	**Mamaro**	17
☒ City Limits	**White Pl**	18
Claire's Corner	**New Haven**	19
Corner Bakery	**Pawling**	23
Così	**multi.**	15
East-West Grille	**W Hartford**	23
Irving Farm	**Millerton**	20
Karamba	**White Pl**	20
Meli-Melo	**Greenwich**	25
Orem's Diner	**Wilton**	16
Pantry	**Wash Depot**	25
Pat's Kountry	**Old Saybrook**	14
Rein's NY Deli	**Vernon**	22
Ruby's Oyster	**Rye**	21
Valencia Luncheria	**Norwalk**	27
Vanilla Bean	**Pomfret**	23
Versailles	**Greenwich**	20

BRUNCH

Arch	**Brewster**	26
Bedford Post/Barn	**Bedford**	24

Beehive | **Armonk**	17
🔒 Bernard's | **Ridgefield**	27
Brewhouse | **S Norwalk**	16
🔒 City Limits | **White Pl**	18
🔒 Cobb's Mill Inn | **Weston**	18
Dakota Steak | **Avon**	18
Gates | **New Canaan**	18
Griswold Inn | **Essex**	18
Jaipore Indian | **Brewster**	24
La Zingara | **Bethel**	25
Le Provençal | **Mamaro**	23
McKinney/Doyle | **Pawling**	25
Opus 465 | **Armonk**	16
Paradise B&G | **Stamford**	13
Red Barn | **Westport**	17
Rest./Water's Edge | **Westbrook**	20
Roger Sherman | **New Canaan**	22
Ruby's Oyster | **Rye**	21
Sage American | **New Haven**	20
Splash | **Westport**	21
Tavern on Main | **Westport**	19
Terra Mar | **Old Saybrook**	21
Thataway Cafe | **Greenwich**	15
Troutbeck | **Amenia**	24
Watercolor Cafe | **Larch**	18

BUFFET

(Check availability)

Abis | **Greenwich**	18
Ahimsa | **New Haven**	17
Avon Old Farm | **Avon**	-
Bengal Tiger | **White Pl**	23
Bombay | **Westport**	23
NEW Bombay Olive | **W Hartford**	-
Brewhouse | **S Norwalk**	16
NEW Chili Chicken | **Stamford**	-
Churrasc. Braza | **Hartford**	21
Confetti | **Plainville**	18
Copacabana | **Port Chester**	23
🔒 Coromandel | **multi.**	26
Cuckoo's Nest | **Old Saybrook**	18
Dakota Steak | **multi.**	18
80 West | **White Pl**	19
Evergreens | **Simsbury**	25
Flanders Fish | **E Lyme**	20
Flood Tide | **Mystic**	21
Griswold Inn | **Essex**	18

Jaipore Indian | **Brewster**	24
Longwood Rest. | **Woodbury**	18
Masala | **Hartford**	-
Rangoli | **New Roch**	24
Rani Mahal | **Mamaro**	23
Red Barn | **Westport**	17
Rest./Water's Edge | **Westbrook**	20
Royal Palace | **White Pl**	20
Saltwater Grille | **Stamford**	20
Spadaro | **New Roch**	24
Splash | **Westport**	21
Squire's | **Redding**	19
Tandoori Taste | **Port Chester**	23
Taste/India | **W Hartford**	20
Terra Mar | **Old Saybrook**	21
Thai Pan Asian | **New Haven**	17
🔒 Thali | **multi.**	26
Todd English's | **Uncasville**	23
White Horse Tav. | **Redding**	15

BUSINESS DINING

Abis | **Greenwich**	18
Acqua | **Westport**	21
Adriana's | **New Haven**	23
Ahimsa | **New Haven**	17
Akasaka | **New Haven**	17
Alba's | **Port Chester**	22
Antipasti | **White Pl**	21
🔒 Apricots | **Farmington**	24
Arugula | **W Hartford**	24
🔒 Baang Cafe | **Riverside**	23
Bedford Post/Farm | **Bedford**	-
Bennett's | **Stamford**	21
Bentara | **New Haven**	24
NEW Besito | **W Hartford**	-
Bistro 22 | **Bedford**	23
Blackstones | **Norwalk**	23
BLT Steak | **White Pl**	23
Brewhouse | **S Norwalk**	16
Brix | **Cheshire**	19
NEW Café Manolo | **Westport**	-
Café Roma | **Bridgeport**	22
🔒 Capital Grille | **Stamford**	25
Carbone's | **Hartford**	25
Carmen Anthony Fish. | **multi.**	21
Carmen Anthony | **Waterbury**	22

🖪 Cavey's | **Manchester**	28	
Central Steak | **New Haven**	23	
Centro | **multi.**	19	
Chez Jean-Pierre | **Stamford**	24	
Christopher Martins | **New Haven**	20	
NEW Craftsteak | **Ledyard**	-	
Diorio | **Waterbury**	24	
Drescher's | **Waterbury**	22	
80 West | **White Pl**	19	
🖪 Elm St. Oyster | **Greenwich**	24	
Evergreens | **Simsbury**	25	
Ferrante | **Stamford**	20	
Field | **Bridgeport**	17	
🖪 Firebox | **Hartford**	25	
Forbidden City | **Middletown**	23	
42 | **White Pl**	22	
Gabrielle's | **Centerbrook**	21	
Giovanni's | **Darien**	20	
🖪 Grant's | **W Hartford**	25	
Graziellas | **White Pl**	17	
Haiku | **Mamaro**	23	
NEW Haiku | **White Pl**	-	
NEW Il Castello | **Mamaro**	-	
Il Falco | **Stamford**	22	
Il Palio | **Shelton**	23	
Il Sogno | **Port Chester**	-	
🖪 Jean-Louis | **Greenwich**	28	
Jeffrey's | **Milford**	23	
Joseph's | **Bridgeport**	24	
Kobis | **Fairfield**	19	
Koo | **Ridgefield**	23	
Kotobuki | **Stamford**	23	
La Bocca | **White Pl**	22	
La Bretagne | **Stamford**	22	
La Panetière | **Rye**	27	
La Tavola | **Waterbury**	-	
Le Château | **S Salem**	25	
Le Figaro Bistro | **Greenwich**	20	
Lotus Thai | **Stratford**	20	
Lusardi's | **Larch**	24	
Marc Charles | **Armonk**	28	
Mario's Pl. | **Westport**	19	
Market | **Stamford**	23	
Max-a-Mia | **Avon**	24	
Max Amore | **Glastonbury**	23	
🖪 Max Downtown | **Hartford**	27	

Max Fish | **Glastonbury**	24	
Mediterraneo | **Greenwich**	22	
Metric | **Bridgeport**	-	
Mill on River | **S Windsor**	23	
NEW Milonga | **N White Plains**	-	
🖪 Morton's | **multi.**	24	
Mulino's | **White Pl**	25	
Napoli Sul Fiume | **Westport**	16	
Nino's | **S Salem**	18	
Octagon | **Groton**	26	
122 Pizza Bistro | **Stamford**	19	
Osteria Applausi | **Old Greenwich**	23	
Peppercorn's Grill | **Hartford**	25	
Peppermill | **Stratford**	18	
Piccolo Arancio | **Farmington**	26	
Ralph/Rich's | **Bridgeport**	24	
Rist. Luce | **Hamden**	22	
Saltwater Grille | **Stamford**	20	
Scoozzi Tratt. | **New Haven**	22	
SolToro | **Uncasville**	-	
Splash | **Westport**	21	
Tango Grill | **White Pl**	22	
Tarry Lodge | **Port Chester**	24	
Tavern on Main | **Westport**	19	
🖪 Thomas Henkelmann | **Greenwich**	28	
Trinity Grill | **Harrison**	19	
Troutbeck | **Amenia**	24	
Tuscan Oven | **Norwalk**	18	
🖪 Union League | **New Haven**	27	
🖪 Valbella | **Riverside**	25	
VIVO Tratt. | **Hartford**	21	
Willett House | **Port Chester**	23	
Wood-n-Tap | **Hartford**	19	

BYO

Bamboo Grill | **Canton**	21	
Basso Café | **Norwalk**	-	
Big W's | **Wingdale**	26	
Buon Appetito | **Canton**	24	
Burgers/Shakes | **Greenwich**	-	
Chef Luis | **New Canaan**	25	
Coppia | **Fairfield**	24	
Edd's Place | **Westbrook**	22	
NEW Flaggstead | **Farmington**	-	
Hot Basil | **W Hartford**	21	

La Cuisine | **Branford**	–
NEW Le Farm | **Westport**	–
Z Lenny/Joe's | **Madison**	22
Little Thai/Buddha | **multi.**	23
Meli-Melo | **Greenwich**	25
NEW Nat Hayden | **Windsor**	–
Olé Molé | **Stamford**	21
Penang Grill | **Greenwich**	23
RSVP | **W Cornwall**	29
Turkish Cuisine | **White Pl**	–
Valencia Luncheria | **Norwalk**	27

CATERING

Acqua | **Westport**	21
Aux Délices | **multi.**	23
Z Bernard's | **Ridgefield**	27
Blue | **White Pl**	19
Cafe Mirage | **Port Chester**	21
Z Carole Peck's | **Woodbury**	27
Christopher Martins | **New Haven**	20
Claire's Corner | **New Haven**	19
Z Coromandel | **New Roch**	26
Costello's | **Noank**	18
Elizabeth's Cafe | **Madison**	26
Firehouse Deli | **Fairfield**	21
f.i.s.h. | **Port Chester**	21
Golden Rod | **New Roch**	20
It's Only Natural | **Middletown**	23
Jeff's Cuisine | **S Norwalk**	25
Kira | **Armonk**	21
Koo | **Rye**	23
Z Match | **S Norwalk**	24
Max Amore | **Glastonbury**	23
Z Max Downtown | **Hartford**	27
McKinney/Doyle | **Pawling**	25
Olé Molé | **Stamford**	21
Omanel | **Bridgeport**	22
Opus 465 | **Armonk**	16
Pantry | **Wash Depot**	25
Plates | **Larch**	24
Q Rest. | **Port Chester**	20
Z Quattro Pazzi | **Fairfield**	22
Rangoli | **New Roch**	24
Sonora | **Port Chester**	24
Tango Grill | **White Pl**	22
Telluride | **Stamford**	21

Z Thali | **multi.**	26
Tratt. Carl Anthony | **Monroe**	23
Valencia Luncheria | **Norwalk**	27
Vanilla Bean | **Pomfret**	23
Vazzy's | **multi.**	18
Watermoon | **Rye**	22
Willett House | **Port Chester**	23

CHILD-FRIENDLY

(Alternatives to the usual fast-food
places; * children's menu available)

Abatino's* | **N White Plains**	21
Z Abbott's Lobster* | **Noank**	23
Abis* | **Greenwich**	18
American Pie Co.* | **Sherman**	20
Z Archie Moore's* | **multi.**	19
Arugula | **W Hartford**	24
Ash Creek* | **Norwalk**	18
Asiana Cafe | **Greenwich**	20
Asian Kitchen | **Ridgefield**	22
Avellino's | **Fairfield**	20
Bailey's* | **Ridgefield**	20
Beach House | **Milford**	22
Beehive* | **Armonk**	17
Bellizzi* | **Larch**	15
Z Bertucci's* | **multi.**	16
Bill's Seafood* | **Westbrook**	19
Blazer Pub | **Purdys**	22
Blue Dolphin | **Katonah**	23
Boxcar Cantina | **Greenwich**	20
Brewhouse* | **S Norwalk**	16
Brooklyn's Famous* | **White Pl**	15
Carmen Anthony Fish.* | **multi.**	21
Carmen Anthony* | **Waterbury**	22
Centro* | **multi.**	19
Chat 19 | **Larch**	18
Z Cheesecake Fac.* | **White Pl**	18
Chuck's Steak* | **multi.**	18
Z City Limits* | **multi.**	18
Claire's Corner | **New Haven**	19
Z Cobb's Mill Inn* | **Weston**	18
Corner Bakery | **Pawling**	23
Così* | **multi.**	15
Coyote Flaco* | **multi.**	21
Dakota Steak* | **Avon**	18
David Chen | **Armonk**	18
DiNardo's | **Pound Ridge**	19

Dolphins Cove* | **Bridgeport**	19
East-West Grille | **W Hartford**	23
Fifty Coins* | **multi.**	14
Firehouse Deli* | **Fairfield**	21
☑ Frank Pepe | **New Haven**	26
Frank Pepe's/Spot | **New Haven**	26
Fuji Mtn.* | **Larch**	17
Gates* | **New Canaan**	18
Golden Rod | **New Roch**	20
Gus's Franklin Pk.* | **Harrison**	20
Hanna's Mideastern | **Danbury**	22
Harry's Pizza | **W Hartford**	24
Hot Tomato's* | **Hartford**	21
Hunan Larchmont | **Larch**	16
It's Only Natural* | **Middletown**	23
Jeff's Cuisine | **S Norwalk**	25
Kazu | **S Norwalk**	24
Kit's Thai | **Stamford**	22
Kobis* | **Fairfield**	19
Laguna* | **White Pl**	19
Legal Sea Foods* | **White Pl**	19
Lime* | **Norwalk**	23
Little Kitchen | **Westport**	22
Lotus Thai | **Stratford**	20
Luna Pizza | **multi.**	20
Mancuso's | **Fairfield**	18
Mary Ann's* | **Port Chester**	17
Meetinghouse* | **Bedford Vill**	18
Melting Pot | **Darien**	18
Modern Rest.* | **New Roch**	21
Mystic Pizza* | **multi.**	17
Nino's | **S Salem**	18
Olé Molé | **Stamford**	21
Omanel | **Bridgeport**	22
Orem's Diner* | **Wilton**	16
Panda Pavilion | **multi.**	16
Pantry | **Wash Depot**	25
☑ P.F. Chang's | **White Pl**	19
Pho Mekong* | **Westport**	20
Portofino Pizza | **Goldens Bridge**	22
Q Rest.* | **Port Chester**	20
Ray's Cafe | **multi.**	19
Red Barn* | **Westport**	17
NEW Rocco's* | **New Canaan**	-
Route 22* | **Armonk**	13
Rye Grill* | **Rye**	-

☑ Sally's Apizza | **New Haven**	26
Saybrook Fish* | **Rocky Hill**	21
Señor Pancho's* | **multi.**	17
Sesame Seed | **Danbury**	21
SoNo Baking Co. | **S Norwalk**	25
Sono Seaport* | **S Norwalk**	16
Southport Brew.* | **multi.**	15
Tavern on Main* | **Westport**	19
Tequila Mock.* | **New Canaan**	17
Thai Pearl | **Ridgefield**	19
☑ Thali* | **multi.**	26
Tiger Bowl | **Westport**	15
Town Dock* | **Rye**	17
Turkish Meze | **Mamaro**	22
Tuscan Oven | **Norwalk**	18
Two Steps* | **Danbury**	13
Valencia Luncheria | **Norwalk**	27
Vazzy's* | **multi.**	18
Vinny's Backyard* | **Stamford**	19
Viva Zapata* | **Westport**	17
Westbrook Lobster* | **Clinton**	18

DANCING

Brickhouse | **Derby**	-
Chat 19 | **Larch**	18
Globe B&G | **Larch**	15
Grand | **Stamford**	18
Hawthorne Inn | **Berlin**	18
Rest./Water's Edge | **Westbrook**	20
Saltwater Grille | **Stamford**	20
Squire's | **Redding**	19
Wood-n-Tap | **Hartford**	19

DELIVERY

Abatino's | **N White Plains**	21
Angelina's | **Westport**	18
Aux Délices | **multi.**	23
Bamboo Grill | **Canton**	21
☑ Bertucci's | **multi.**	16
Black-Eyed Sally | **Hartford**	21
Boathouse/Smokey | **Stamford**	21
Bobby Valentine | **Stamford**	15
Bogey's Grille | **Westport**	16
Bombay | **Westport**	23
Brooklyn's Famous | **White Pl**	15
Coyote Flaco | **multi.**	21
Golden Rod | **New Roch**	20

Imperial | **N White Plains**	18
Jasmine | **Westport**	15
Kit's Thai | **Stamford**	22
Kotobuki | **Stamford**	23
Kujaku | **Stamford**	17
Luna Pizza | **Simsbury**	20
Modern Rest. | **New Roch**	21
Noda's Steak | **White Pl**	19
Panda Pavilion | **multi.**	16
Pellicci's | **Stamford**	20
Polpo | **Greenwich**	24
Post Corner Pizza | **Darien**	19
Royal Palace | **New Haven**	24
Royal Palace | **White Pl**	20
Thai Chi | **Stamford**	22
Thai Pan Asian | **New Haven**	17
Two Steps | **Danbury**	13
Vanilla Bean | **Pomfret**	23
Vito's | **Hartford**	19

DINING ALONE

(Other than hotels and places
with counter service)

AJ's Burgers | **New Roch**	19
Aladdin | **Hartford**	18
American Pie Co. | **Sherman**	20
Asian Kitchen | **Ridgefield**	22
Aspen Garden | **Litchfield**	15
Aux Délices | **Riverside**	23
NEW Ay! Salsa | **New Haven**	–
Bamboo Grill | **Canton**	21
Bangalore | **Fairfield**	23
Bangkok Gardens | **New Haven**	22
Basta | **New Haven**	20
Big W's | **Wingdale**	26
Bloodroot | **Bridgeport**	21
Boathouse/Smokey | **Stamford**	21
Brie/Bleu | **New London**	24
Bull's Bridge | **Kent**	16
Burger Bar | **S Norwalk**	24
Butterfly Chinese | **W Hartford**	15
Cafe Mirage | **Port Chester**	21
Café/Green | **Danbury**	23
Café Roma | **Bridgeport**	22
Café Tavolini | **Bridgeport**	19
Char Koon | **S Glastonbury**	23
Chat 19 | **Larch**	18

NEW Chili Chicken | **Stamford**	–
Z City Limits | **White Pl**	18
Claire's Corner | **New Haven**	19
Coppia | **Fairfield**	24
Corner Bakery | **Pawling**	23
Costello's | **Noank**	18
Coyote Flaco | **multi.**	21
NEW Crooked Shillelagh | **Branford**	–
Curtis House | **Woodbury**	16
David Chen | **Armonk**	18
Drescher's | **Waterbury**	22
East-West Grille | **W Hartford**	23
NEW Elaine's Healthy | **New Haven**	–
El Tio | **Port Chester**	24
Épernay | **Bridgeport**	–
NEW Eveready | **Brewster**	19
Fat Cat Pie | **Norwalk**	23
Fifty Coins | **New Canaan**	14
Fin/Fin II | **multi.**	22
NEW Flaggstead | **Farmington**	–
NEW Fraîche Burger | **Bridgeport**	–
Z Frank Pepe | **Manchester**	26
Great Taste | **New Britain**	27
Hanna's Mideastern | **Danbury**	22
Irving Farm | **Millerton**	20
Isabelle/Vincent | **Fairfield**	–
It's Only Natural | **Middletown**	23
NEW Jack Rabbit's | **Old Saybrook**	–
Jeff's Cuisine | **S Norwalk**	25
Karamba | **White Pl**	20
Kiosko | **Port Chester**	–
Kit's Thai | **Stamford**	22
Koo | **Danbury**	23
La Cuisine | **Branford**	–
NEW Lalo's | **Hartford**	–
Larchmont Tav. | **Larch**	17
Layla's Falafel | **multi.**	23
Z Lenny/Joe's | **multi.**	22
Lenny's Indian | **Branford**	20
Lime | **Norwalk**	23
Little Kitchen | **Westport**	22
NEW Little Pub | **Ridgefield**	–
Little Thai/Buddha | **multi.**	23

Louis' Lunch	**New Haven**	24
Mackenzie's	**Old Greenwich**	15
Matsumoto	**Larch**	-
Meli-Melo	**Greenwich**	25
Metric	**Bridgeport**	-
Michael's	**Wallingford**	23
Myrna's	**Stamford**	21
Mystic Pizza	**multi.**	17
Napoli Sul Fiume	**Westport**	16
NEW Nat Hayden	**Windsor**	-
Nino's	**Bedford Hills**	19
Olé Molé	**multi.**	21
Oscar's	**Westport**	19
Pantry	**Wash Depot**	25
Pasta Vera	**Greenwich**	21
Pat's Kountry	**Old Saybrook**	14
Post Corner Pizza	**Darien**	19
Pot-au-Pho	**New Haven**	20
Red Rooster	**Brewster**	18
Rein's NY Deli	**Vernon**	22
River House	**Westport**	16
Salsa	**New Milford**	23
Sardegna	**Larch**	21
Scribner's	**Milford**	23
Seamen's Inne	**Mystic**	19
SoNo Baking Co.	**S Norwalk**	25
☑ Super/Weenie	**Fairfield**	22
☑ Tengda	**Westport**	23
Thai Pan Asian	**New Haven**	17
Thai Place	**Putnam**	-
Two Boots	**Bridgeport**	21
Valencia Luncheria	**Norwalk**	27
Venetian	**Torrington**	22
Viale Rist.	**Bridgeport**	21
Wasabi	**Orange**	23
Wilson's BBQ	**Fairfield**	24
Yorkside	**New Haven**	16
☑ Zinc	**New Haven**	24

ENTERTAINMENT

(Call for days and times
of performances)

☑ Bernard's	varies	**Ridgefield**	27
Bill's Seafood	live music	**Westbrook**	19
Bobby Valentine	karaoke	**Stamford**	15

Brickhouse	varies	**Derby**	-
Harborside B&G	live music	**Stratford**	15
Luc's Café	jazz	**Ridgefield**	24
O'Neill's	varies	**S Norwalk**	18
Opus 465	bands	**Armonk**	16
Ralph/Rich's	piano	**Bridgeport**	24
Southport Brew.	varies	**multi.**	15
Squire's	live music	**Redding**	19
Thataway Cafe	varies	**Greenwich**	15
Towne Crier	varies	**Pawling**	15
Troutbeck	bands	**Amenia**	24
Watercolor Cafe	varies	**Larch**	18

FIREPLACES

Adrienne	**New Milford**	24
Alba's	**Port Chester**	22
Altnaveigh Inn	**Storrs**	24
Arch	**Brewster**	26
Avon Old Farm	**Avon**	-
NEW Ballou's	**Guilford**	-
☑ Barcelona	**New Haven**	23
Beach House	**Milford**	22
Bedford Post/Barn	**Bedford**	24
Bedford Post/Farm	**Bedford**	-
☑ Bernard's	**Ridgefield**	27
Boathouse	**Lakeville**	16
Boom	**Westbrook**	22
☑ Boulders Inn	**New Preston**	22
Boxcar Cantina	**Greenwich**	20
Brendan's/Elms	**Ridgefield**	22
Bull's Bridge	**Kent**	16
☑ Capt. Daniel Packer	**Mystic**	22
Carmen Anthony Fish.	**Woodbury**	21
Chestnut Grille	**Old Lyme**	24
Chuck's Steak	**multi.**	18
Cinzano's	**Fairfield**	19
☑ Cobb's Mill Inn	**Weston**	18
Country House	**Patterson**	20
Coyote Flaco	**New Roch**	21
Curtis House	**Woodbury**	16
Dakota Steak	**multi.**	18
Doc's Trattoria	**Kent**	21
☑ Dressing Room	**Westport**	23
East Side	**New Britain**	20
Evergreens	**Simsbury**	25

Field | **Bridgeport**	17
Ⓩ Firebox | **Hartford**	25
Flood Tide | **Mystic**	21
Foe | **Branford**	22
Fonda La Paloma | **Cos Cob**	18
Frankie/Johnnie's | **Rye**	23
Geronimo | **New Haven**	17
Gervasi's | **White Pl**	-
Ginger Man | **Greenwich**	17
Giorgio's | **Port Chester**	23
Griswold Inn | **Essex**	18
G.W. Tavern | **Wash Depot**	20
Hamilton Inn | **Millerton**	21
Hopkins Inn | **New Preston**	20
Horse & Hound | **S Salem**	16
Il Palio | **Shelton**	23
Inn at Newtown | **Newtown**	19
Irving Farm | **Millerton**	20
Isabelle/Vincent | **Fairfield**	-
J. Gilbert's | **Glastonbury**	25
John-Michael's | **N Salem**	25
La Crémaillère | **Bedford**	26
Le Château | **S Salem**	25
Lenny's Indian | **Branford**	20
Ⓩ L'Escale | **Greenwich**	23
NEW Little Pub | **Ridgefield**	-
Long Ridge Tav. | **Stamford**	14
Longwood Rest. | **Woodbury**	18
Lusardi's | **Larch**	24
Ⓩ Mayflower Inn | **Washington**	25
Mighty Joe | **White Pl**	16
Mill on River | **S Windsor**	23
NEW Molly Spillane | **Mamaro**	16
New Deal Steak | **Westbrook**	14
Old Lyme Inn | **Old Lyme**	20
Oliva Cafe | **New Preston**	25
Oliver's Taverne | **Essex**	13
Olive Tree | **Southbury**	19
Ⓩ Ondine | **Danbury**	25
O'Neill's | **S Norwalk**	18
121 Rest. | **N Salem**	21
Paradise B&G | **Stamford**	13
Pat's Kountry | **Old Saybrook**	14
Porter Hse. | **White Pl**	18
Portofino's | **Wilton**	21
Red Barn | **Westport**	17

Rest./Rowayton Sea. | **Rowayton**	22
River Bistro | **New Milford**	19
River Cat Grill | **Rowayton**	22
River House | **Westport**	16
Roger Sherman | **New Canaan**	22
Rye Grill | **Rye**	-
Sage American | **New Haven**	20
Sakura | **Westport**	21
Saltwater Grille | **Stamford**	20
Seamen's Inne | **Mystic**	19
Serevan | **Amenia**	28
Sharpe Hill/Vineyard | **Pomfret**	-
Splash | **Westport**	21
Squire's | **Redding**	19
Stone House | **Guilford**	21
Su Casa | **Branford**	18
Tango Grill | **White Pl**	22
Tavern on Main | **Westport**	19
Ⓩ Thomas Henkelmann | **Greenwich**	28
3 Jalapeños | **Mamaro**	17
Tratt. Lucia | **Bedford**	16
Troutbeck | **Amenia**	24
Tuscan Oven | **Norwalk**	18
Ⓩ Union League | **New Haven**	27
Ⓩ Valbella | **Riverside**	25
Vanilla Bean | **Pomfret**	23
Via Sforza | **Westport**	21
White Hart | **Salisbury**	17
White Horse Tav. | **Redding**	15
Winvian | **Morris**	-
Wood-n-Tap | **multi.**	19
Zinis | **Bantam**	18

GAME IN SEASON

Adrienne | **New Milford**	24
Alforno | **Old Saybrook**	23
Altnaveigh Inn | **Storrs**	24
Antipasti | **White Pl**	21
Ⓩ Apricots | **Farmington**	24
Arch | **Brewster**	26
Arugula | **W Hartford**	24
Aspen | **Old Saybrook**	21
Aspen Garden | **Litchfield**	15
Avon Old Farm | **Avon**	-
NEW Bar Americain | **Uncasville**	-

Bedford Post/Farm | **Bedford**	—
Z Bernard's | **Ridgefield**	27
Z Bistro Bonne Nuit | **New Canaan**	26
B.J. Ryan's | **Norwalk**	22
Bobby Q's | **Westport**	19
Brendan's/Elms | **Ridgefield**	22
Bull's Bridge | **Kent**	16
Cafe Lola | **Fairfield**	—
Cafe Mirage | **Port Chester**	21
Café Roma | **Bridgeport**	22
Cafe Silvium | **Stamford**	—
Z Capt. Daniel Packer | **Mystic**	22
Z Carole Peck's | **Woodbury**	27
Cascade Mtn. | **Amenia**	16
Chestnut Grille | **Old Lyme**	24
Z Cobb's Mill Inn | **Weston**	18
Coyote Blue | **Middletown**	23
NEW Craftsteak | **Ledyard**	—
Curtis House | **Woodbury**	16
Da Giorgio | **New Roch**	20
Z DaPietro's | **Westport**	26
du Glace | **Deep River**	—
Duo | **Stamford**	23
Edd's Place | **Westbrook**	22
80 West | **White Pl**	19
Emilio Rist. | **Harrison**	23
Épernay | **Bridgeport**	—
Esca | **Middletown**	—
Z Firebox | **Hartford**	25
42 | **White Pl**	22
Foster's | **New Haven**	17
Frankie/Johnnie's | **Rye**	23
Grand | **Stamford**	18
Grist Mill | **Farmington**	24
Griswold Inn | **Essex**	18
G.W. Tavern | **Wash Depot**	20
Hamilton Inn | **Millerton**	21
Z Harvest Supper | **New Canaan**	27
Hopkins Inn | **New Preston**	20
Hostaria Mazzei | **Port Chester**	21
Il Falco | **Stamford**	22
Z Jean-Louis | **Greenwich**	28
John-Michael's | **N Salem**	25
La Bretagne | **Stamford**	22
La Crémaillère | **Bedford**	26

La Panetière | **Rye**	27
La Riserva | **Larch**	18
La Zingara | **Bethel**	25
NEW Le Farm | **Westport**	—
Le Fontane | **Katonah**	20
Le Provençal | **Mamaro**	23
L'Orcio | **New Haven**	23
Z Napa & Co. | **Stamford**	25
Nino's | **Bedford Hills**	19
Z Ondine | **Danbury**	25
116 Crown | **New Haven**	23
121 Rest. | **N Salem**	21
Papacelle | **Avon**	—
Pastorale | **Lakeville**	24
Plates | **Larch**	24
PolytechnicON20 | **Hartford**	28
Z Rebeccas | **Greenwich**	25
Roger Sherman | **New Canaan**	22
Saltwater Grille | **Stamford**	20
Sentrista Grill | **Brewster**	21
Serevan | **Amenia**	28
Still River | **Eastford**	26
Z Stonehenge | **Ridgefield**	24
Tarantino's | **Westport**	24
Telluride | **Stamford**	21
Terra Mar | **Old Saybrook**	21
Z Thomas Henkelmann | **Greenwich**	28
Tratt. Vivolo | **Harrison**	21
Trinity Grill | **Harrison**	19
White Horse Tav. | **Redding**	15
Z Woodward Hse. | **Bethlehem**	26

HISTORIC PLACES

(Year opened; * building)

1640 | Grist Mill* | **Farmington**	24
1734 | Altnaveigh Inn* | **Storrs**	24
1736 | Curtis House* | **Woodbury**	16
1740 | Woodward Hse.* | **Bethlehem**	26
1742 | White Horse Tav.* | **Redding**	15
1749 | Horse & Hound* | **S Salem**	16
1750 | Long Ridge Tav.* | **Stamford**	14
1756 | Capt. Daniel Packer* | **Mystic**	22
1756 | Chestnut Grille* | **Old Lyme**	24

1757	Avon Old Farm*	**Avon**	—
1758	Harvest/Pomfret*	**Pomfret**	22
1760	Pastorale*	**Lakeville**	24
1762	Bull's Bridge*	**Kent**	16
1770	Cobb's Mill Inn*	**Weston**	18
1773	Chatterley's*	**New Hartford**	20
1774	Adrienne*	**New Milford**	24
1775	John-Michael's*	**N Salem**	25
1775	Mill on River*	**S Windsor**	23
1776	Griswold Inn*	**Essex**	18
1783	Roger Sherman*	**New Canaan**	22
1787	Lucky Lou*	**Wethersfield**	—
1789	Longwood Rest.*	**Woodbury**	18
1790	Bedford Post/Barn*	**Bedford**	24
1790	Bedford Post/Farm*	**Bedford**	—
1792	Elizabeth's Cafe*	**Madison**	26
1799	Brendan's/Elms*	**Ridgefield**	22
1799	Thomas Henkelmann*	**Greenwich**	28
1800	Gabrielle's*	**Centerbrook**	21
1800	Plan B Burger*	**Simsbury**	23
1806	White Hart*	**Salisbury**	17
1810	Tavern on Main*	**Westport**	19
1840	Old Lyme Inn*	**Old Lyme**	20
1848	Olive Tree*	**Southbury**	19
1850	G.W. Tavern*	**Wash Depot**	20
1850	La Panetière*	**Rye**	27
1850	L'Orcio*	**New Haven**	23
1850	Masala*	**Hartford**	—
1850	Vanilla Bean*	**Pomfret**	23
1852	Putnam Hse.*	**Bethel**	16
1868	Drescher's	**Waterbury**	22
1870	Paci*	**Southport**	26
1871	Emilio Rist.*	**Harrison**	23
1872	Schoolhse./Cannondale*	**Wilton**	—
1880	Donovan's*	**S Norwalk**	—
1880	Mayflower Inn*	**Washington**	25
1881	Q Rest.*	**Port Chester**	20
1882	Harney/Sons*	**Millerton**	21
1890	Boulders Inn*	**New Preston**	22
1890	Copper Beech*	**Ivoryton**	24
1890	Flood Tide*	**Mystic**	21
1890	Lime*	**Norwalk**	23
1890	Red Barn*	**Westport**	17
1890	Two Steps*	**Danbury**	13
1893	Feng Asian*	**Hartford**	26
1895	Louis' Lunch	**New Haven**	24
1898	Archie Moore's*	**New Haven**	19
1899	Basso Café*	**Norwalk**	—
1900	f.i.s.h.*	**Port Chester**	21
1900	Piero's*	**Port Chester**	23
1900	Polpo*	**Greenwich**	24
1900	Rest./Rowayton Sea.*	**Rowayton**	22
1900	Thai Pan Asian*	**New Haven**	17
1900	Union League*	**New Haven**	27
1902	Plates*	**Larch**	24
1907	Le Château*	**S Salem**	25
1910	Old Heidelberg*	**Bethel**	20
1915	Arch*	**Brewster**	26
1915	Épernay*	**Bridgeport**	—
1917	Cobble Stone*	**Purchase**	15
1919	Walter's	**Mamaro**	22
1920	Brewhouse*	**S Norwalk**	16
1920	Modern Rest.*	**New Roch**	21
1920	Troutbeck*	**Amenia**	24
1921	Aloi*	**New Canaan**	24
1921	Orem's Diner	**Wilton**	16
1921	Venetian	**Torrington**	22
1925	Frank Pepe	**New Haven**	26
1925	Frank Pepe's/Spot*	**New Haven**	26
1929	Country House*	**Patterson**	20
1930	Liv's Oyster*	**Old Saybrook**	24
1930	Route 22*	**Armonk**	13
1931	Gus's Franklin Pk.	**Harrison**	20
1932	Sam's/Gedney	**White Pl**	17
1933	Cavey's	**Manchester**	28
1933	Larchmont Tav.	**Larch**	17
1934	Blazer Pub	**Purdys**	22
1934	Modern Apizza	**New Haven**	25

1935	Colony Grill	**Stamford**	–
1935	East Side	**New Britain**	20
1936	First & Last	**Hartford**	20
1938	Consiglio's	**New Haven**	25
1938	Leon's	**New Haven**	–
1938	Sally's Apizza	**New Haven**	26
1939	Carbone's	**Hartford**	25
1940	Blue Dolphin	**Katonah**	23
1945	Hawthorne Inn	**Berlin**	18
1946	Hopkins Inn	**New Preston**	20
1947	La Crémaillère	**Bedford**	26
1947	La Manda's	**White Pl**	18
1947	Pellicci's	**Stamford**	20
1948	Abbott's Lobster	**Noank**	23
1948	Oscar's	**Westport**	19
1948	Shady Glen	**Manchester**	23
1949	Stone House*	**Guilford**	21
1950	Marianacci's	**Port Chester**	20
1955	Made In Asia*	**Armonk**	21
1960	Chef Antonio	**Mamaro**	16

HOTEL DINING

Altnaveigh Inn
Altnaveigh Inn | **Storrs** — 24

Bedford Post
Bedford Post/Barn | **Bedford** — 24
Bedford Post/Farm | **Bedford** — –

Bee & Thistle Inn
Chestnut Grille | **Old Lyme** — 24

Boulders Inn
🔁 Boulders Inn | **New Preston** — 22

Copper Beech Inn
🔁 Copper Beech | **Ivoryton** — 24

Courtyard Marriott Hotel
🔁 Napa & Co. | **Stamford** — 25

Delamar Hotel
🔁 L'Escale | **Greenwich** — 23

Elms Inn
Brendan's/Elms | **Ridgefield** — 22

Esplanade White Plains Hotel
Graziellas | **White Pl** — 17

Foxwoods Resort Casino
Burke in Box | **Ledyard** — –
🔁 California Pizza | **Ledyard** — 16
Cedars | **Ledyard** — 21

David Burke | **Ledyard** — 27
Hard Rock | **Ledyard** — 15

Griswold Inn
Griswold Inn | **Essex** — 18

Hi Ho Hotel
🔁 Barcelona | **Fairfield** — 23

Homestead Inn
🔁 Thomas Henkelmann | **Greenwich** — 28

Hopkins Inn
Hopkins Inn | **New Preston** — 20

Inn at Lafayette
Cafe Allegre | **Madison** — 20

Inn at Longshore
Splash | **Westport** — 21

Inn at Mystic
Flood Tide | **Mystic** — 21

Inn at Newtown
Inn at Newtown | **Newtown** — 19

La Quinta Hotel
Marc Charles | **Armonk** — 28

Longwood Country Inn
Longwood Rest. | **Woodbury** — 18

Marriott Hotel
VIVO Tratt. | **Hartford** — 21

Marriott Residence Inn
Aberdeen | **White Pl** — 23

Mayflower Inn & Spa
🔁 Mayflower Inn | **Washington** — 25

MGM Grand at Foxwoods
NEW Craftsteak | **Ledyard** — –

Mohegan Sun Casino
NEW Bar Americain | **Uncasville** — –
🔁 Frank Pepe | **Uncasville** — 26
Jasper White's | **Uncasville** — 21
🔁 Michael Jordan's | **Uncasville** — 25
SolToro | **Uncasville** — –
Todd English's | **Uncasville** — 23

Mystic Marriott Hotel & Spa
Octagon | **Groton** — 26

Old Lyme Inn
Old Lyme Inn | **Old Lyme** — 20

Ramada Inn
Peppermill | **Stratford** — 18

Renaissance Hotel	
80 West | **White Pl**	19
Ridgefield Motor Inn	
⚡ Thali | **Ridgefield**	26
Ritz-Carlton Westchester	
BLT Steak | **White Pl**	23
42 | **White Pl**	22
Roger Sherman Inn	
Roger Sherman | **New Canaan**	22
Saybrook Point Inn & Spa	
Terra Mar | **Old Saybrook**	21
Simmons' Way Village Inn	
NEW No. 9 | **Millerton**	–
Simsbury Inn	
Evergreens | **Simsbury**	25
Spinning Wheel Inn	
White Horse Tav. | **Redding**	15
Stonehenge Inn	
⚡ Stonehenge | **Ridgefield**	24
Study at Yale Hotel	
Heirloom | **New Haven**	–
Troutbeck Estate & Resort	
Troutbeck | **Amenia**	24
Water's Edge Resort & Spa	
Rest./Water's Edge | **Westbrook**	20
Whaler's Inn	
Bravo Bravo | **Mystic**	24
White Hart Inn	
White Hart | **Salisbury**	17

JACKET REQUIRED

⚡ Thomas Henkelmann | **Greenwich**	28

MEET FOR A DRINK

Antipasti | **White Pl**	21
⚡ Archie Moore's | **multi.**	19
Asian Tempt. | **White Pl**	20
Aspen | **Old Saybrook**	21
Azu | **Mystic**	23
⚡ Baang Cafe | **Riverside**	23
NEW Ballou's | **Guilford**	–
NEW Bar Americain | **Uncasville**	–
⚡ Barcelona | **multi.**	23
Bar Vivace | **Mamaro**	22
Beach Café | **Fairfield**	17

Beach House | **Milford**	22
NEW Besito | **W Hartford**	–
⚡ Bespoke | **New Haven**	24
Bin 100 | **Milford**	25
Bin 228 | **Hartford**	23
Black-Eyed Sally | **Hartford**	21
Blackstones | **Norwalk**	23
BLT Steak | **White Pl**	23
Blue Pearl | **New Haven**	20
Blue Point B&G | **Stratford**	18
Boathouse | **Lakeville**	16
Bobby Q's | **Westport**	19
Bobby Valentine | **Stamford**	15
Bogey's Grille | **Westport**	16
Bond Grill | **Norwalk**	18
Boxcar Cantina | **Greenwich**	20
Brazen Fox | **White Pl**	15
Brewhouse | **S Norwalk**	16
Bricco | **W Hartford**	25
Brickhouse | **Derby**	–
Bru Room/BAR | **New Haven**	25
Burger Bar | **S Norwalk**	24
Cafe Goodfellas | **New Haven**	21
Café Roma | **Bridgeport**	22
⚡ Capt. Daniel Packer | **Mystic**	22
Chat 19 | **Larch**	18
Christopher Martins | **New Haven**	20
C.O. Jones | **New Haven**	16
NEW Crooked Shillelagh | **Branford**	–
Croton Creek | **Crot Falls**	20
Cuckoo's Nest | **Old Saybrook**	18
Dish B&G | **Hartford**	20
Dock/Dine | **Old Saybrook**	15
Donovan's | **S Norwalk**	–
Duo | **Stamford**	23
Elbow Room | **W Hartford**	18
Elements | **W Hartford**	–
Emma's Ale | **White Pl**	–
Euro Asian | **Port Chester**	21
Fat Cat Pie | **Norwalk**	23
⚡ Feng Asian | **Hartford**	26
Field | **Bridgeport**	17
Fifty Coins | **Ridgefield**	14
⚡ Firebox | **Hartford**	25
First & Last | **multi.**	20

NEW Flipside Burgers | **Fairfield**	-	
Forbidden City | **Middletown**	23	
42 | **White Pl**	22	
Frankie/Johnnie's | **Rye**	23	
Geronimo | **New Haven**	17	
Ginger Man | **multi.**	17	
Grand | **Stamford**	18	
Graziellas | **White Pl**	17	
Gusano Loco | **Mamaro**	19	
Haiku | **Mamaro**	23	
NEW Haiku | **White Pl**	-	
Harbor Lights | **Norwalk**	20	
Harborside B&G | **Stratford**	15	
Hidden Vine | **Newington**	-	
Horse & Hound | **S Salem**	16	
Hot Tomato's | **Hartford**	21	
J. Gilbert's | **Glastonbury**	25	
John Harvard's | **Manchester**	19	
Kobis | **Fairfield**	19	
Kona Grill | **Stamford**	17	
Kudeta | **New Haven**	21	
Lady Luck | **Bridgeport**	-	
Lansdowne | **New Haven**	-	
Lazy Boy Saloon | **White Pl**	17	
Lenny's Indian | **Branford**	20	
NEW Little Pub | **Ridgefield**	-	
NEW Lolita | **Greenwich**	-	
Long Ridge Tav. | **Stamford**	14	
L'Orcio | **New Haven**	23	
Los Cabos | **Norwalk**	17	
Lotus Thai | **Stratford**	20	
NEW Lucky Lou | **Wethersfield**	-	
Mackenzie's | **Old Greenwich**	15	
Marc Charles | **Armonk**	28	
Mario's Pl. | **Westport**	19	
Market | **Stamford**	23	
Z Match | **S Norwalk**	24	
Max-a-Mia | **Avon**	24	
Max Amore | **Glastonbury**	23	
Z Max Downtown | **Hartford**	27	
Max Fish | **Glastonbury**	24	
Mediterraneo | **Greenwich**	22	
Melting Pot | **Darien**	18	
Mighty Joe | **White Pl**	16	
NEW Milonga | **N White Plains**	-	
NEW Molly Spillane | **Mamaro**	16	
Mulino's | **White Pl**	25	
Z Napa & Co. | **Stamford**	25	
Nino's | **Bedford Hills**	19	
Oliver's Taverne | **Essex**	13	
O'Neill's | **S Norwalk**	18	
116 Crown | **New Haven**	23	
121 Rest. | **N Salem**	21	
122 Pizza Bistro | **Stamford**	19	
Osetra | **Norwalk**	26	
Palmer's Crossing | **Larch**	18	
Papaya Thai | **S Norwalk**	20	
Paradise B&G | **Stamford**	13	
Peniche | **White Pl**	22	
NEW Pizzeria Molto | **Fairfield**	-	
Plan B Burger | **multi.**	23	
Porter Hse. | **White Pl**	18	
Putnam Hse. | **Bethel**	16	
Ralph/Rich's | **Bridgeport**	24	
Red Plum | **Mamaro**	-	
NEW Rocco's | **New Canaan**	-	
NEW Rouge Winebar | **S Norwalk**	-	
Rye Grill | **Rye**	-	
Rye Roadhse. | **Rye**	18	
Sage American | **New Haven**	20	
Saltwater Grille | **Stamford**	20	
Scoozzi Tratt. | **New Haven**	22	
Señor Pancho's | **multi.**	17	
Shell Station | **Stratford**	21	
SolToro | **Uncasville**	-	
Sonora | **Port Chester**	24	
Southport Brew. | **Hamden**	15	
Southwest Cafe | **Ridgefield**	20	
Sports Page | **White Pl**	-	
Strada 18 | **S Norwalk**	25	
Su Casa | **Branford**	18	
Tango Grill | **White Pl**	22	
Tapas/Ann | **Bloomfield**	23	
Tarry Lodge | **Port Chester**	24	
Telluride | **Stamford**	21	
Z Tengda | **Darien**	23	
Tequila Mock. | **New Canaan**	17	
Z Thali | **New Haven**	26	
3 Jalapeños | **Mamaro**	17	
Towne Crier | **Pawling**	15	
Tratt. Carl Anthony | **Monroe**	23	
Tuscany Grill | **Middletown**	20	

Two Boots | **Bridgeport**	21
Union Street Tav. | **Windsor**	–
Viale Rist. | **Bridgeport**	21
Vinny's Backyard | **Stamford**	19
Viva Zapata | **Westport**	17
VIVO Tratt. | **Hartford**	21
Vox | **N Salem**	21
Wasabi Chi | **S Norwalk**	24
Watercolor Cafe | **Larch**	18
Wood-n-Tap | **multi.**	19

MICROBREWERIES

Z Archie Moore's | **multi.**	19
Ash Creek | **Norwalk**	18
Bru Room/BAR | **New Haven**	25
Donovan's | **S Norwalk**	–
John Harvard's | **Manchester**	19
Southport Brew. | **multi.**	15

NATURAL/ORGANIC/ LOCAL

(Places specializing in organic, local ingredients)

Aspen | **Old Saybrook**	21
Basta | **New Haven**	20
Bedford Post/Barn | **Bedford**	24
Bedford Post/Farm | **Bedford**	–
Boxcar Cantina | **Greenwich**	20
Brendan's/Elms | **Ridgefield**	22
NEW Café Manolo | **Westport**	–
Z Carole Peck's | **Woodbury**	27
Z Dressing Room | **Westport**	23
Duo | **Stamford**	23
Z Elm St. Oyster | **Greenwich**	24
Épernay | **Bridgeport**	–
Fat Cat Pie | **Norwalk**	23
Ferrante | **Stamford**	20
Z Firebox | **Hartford**	25
Grand | **Stamford**	18
Harney/Sons | **Millerton**	21
Z Harvest Supper | **New Canaan**	27
NEW Le Farm | **Westport**	–
Le Figaro Bistro | **Greenwich**	20
Manna Dew | **Millerton**	24
Z Métro Bis | **Simsbury**	26
Z Napa & Co. | **Stamford**	25
Nino's | **S Salem**	18

Z Pasta Nostra | **S Norwalk**	25
Plum Tree | **New Canaan**	21
NEW Rest. L&E | **Chester**	–
Saltwater Grille | **Stamford**	20
Serevan | **Amenia**	28
Solaia | **Greenwich**	22
Stand | **Norwalk**	–
Still River | **Eastford**	26
Telluride | **Stamford**	21
Terra Rist. | **Greenwich**	22
Z Thomas Henkelmann | **Greenwich**	28
Z Valbella | **Riverside**	25
West St. Grill | **Litchfield**	22
White Hart | **Salisbury**	17
Z Zinc | **New Haven**	24

OFFBEAT

Z Abbott's Lobster | **Noank**	23
Ahimsa | **New Haven**	17
Aladdin | **Hartford**	18
Aux Délices | **multi.**	23
NEW Ay! Salsa | **New Haven**	–
NEW Ballou's | **Guilford**	–
Bangkok Gardens | **New Haven**	22
Barça | **Hartford**	20
Basta | **New Haven**	20
Bloodroot | **Bridgeport**	21
Blue Pearl | **New Haven**	20
Boathouse/Smokey | **Stamford**	21
Brie/Bleu | **New London**	24
Cafe Goodfellas | **New Haven**	21
Cafe Lola | **Fairfield**	–
Cafe Mirage | **Port Chester**	21
Z Carole Peck's | **Woodbury**	27
Cascade Mtn. | **Amenia**	16
NEW Chili Chicken | **Stamford**	–
Churrasc. Braza | **Hartford**	21
Claire's Corner | **New Haven**	19
C.O. Jones | **New Haven**	16
Drescher's | **Waterbury**	22
Egane | **Stamford**	20
NEW Elaine's Healthy | **New Haven**	–
Épernay | **Bridgeport**	–
Fat Cat Pie | **Norwalk**	23
Flanders Fish | **E Lyme**	20

NEW Fraîche Burger | **Bridgeport** _-_	Z Apricots | P, W | **Farmington** 24
Gusano Loco | **Mamaro** 19	Arch | P | **Brewster** 26
Haiku | **Mamaro** 23	Aspen Garden | P | **Litchfield** 15
NEW Haiku | **White Pl** _-_	Z Barcelona | P | **multi.** 23
Hanna's Mideastern | **Danbury** 22	Barnacle | P, W | **Mamaro** _-_
Isabelle/Vincent | **Fairfield** _-_	Bill's Seafood | T, W | **Westbrook** 19
It's Only Natural | **Middletown** 23	Bloodroot | G, P, W | **Bridgeport** 21
NEW Jack Rabbit's | **Old Saybrook** _-_	Z Boulders Inn | P | **New Preston** 22
Kit's Thai | **Stamford** 22	Brendan's/Elms | P | **Ridgefield** 22
Kobis | **Fairfield** 19	Café/Green | P, T | **Danbury** 23
Koji | **Hartford** 19	Z Carole Peck's | P | **Woodbury** 27
NEW Le Farm | **Westport** _-_	Chatterley's | P | **New Hartford** 20
Z Lenny/Joe's | **multi.** 22	Chez Jean-Pierre | S | **Stamford** 24
Lime | **Norwalk** 23	Confetti | T | **Plainville** 18
Louis' Lunch | **New Haven** 24	Coppia | G, P | **Fairfield** 24
Lucky's | **Stamford** 15	Costello's | P, W | **Noank** 18
Mango's B&G | **Branford** 19	Dock/Dine | P, W | **Old Saybrook** 15
Melting Pot | **multi.** 18	Dolphins Cove | P, W | **Bridgeport** 19
Old Heidelberg | **Bethel** 20	Edd's Place | P, W | **Westbrook** 22
121 Rest. | **Oxford** 23	Elbow Room | T | **W Hartford** 18
Pantry | **Wash Depot** 25	Eli Cannon's | P | **Middletown** 20
Z Pasta Nostra | **S Norwalk** 25	Encore Bistro | S | **Larch** 22
Pasta Vera | **Greenwich** 21	Fin/Fin II | P | **Fairfield** 22
Pat's Kountry | **Old Saybrook** 14	f.i.s.h. | P, W | **Port Chester** 21
NEW Pizzeria Molto | **Fairfield** _-_	Flood Tide | T, W | **Mystic** 21
PolytechnicON20 | **Hartford** 28	Grist Mill | P, W | **Farmington** 24
Ray's Cafe | **multi.** 19	G.W. Tavern | T, W | **Wash Depot** 20
Rein's NY Deli | **Vernon** 22	Harborside B&G | P, W | **Stratford** 15
NEW Rouge Winebar | **S Norwalk** _-_	Hopkins Inn | T | **New Preston** 20
Rue/Crêpes | **Harrison** 15	It's Only Natural | P | **Middletown** 23
Rye Roadhse. | **Rye** 18	Jeffrey's | G | **Milford** 23
Salsa | **New Milford** 23	La Zingara | P | **Bethel** 25
Scribner's | **Milford** 23	Lazy Boy Saloon | S | **White Pl** 17
Sesame Seed | **Danbury** 21	Le Figaro Bistro | P | **Greenwich** 20
NEW Spinghar | **Glastonbury** _-_	Le Fontane | G | **Katonah** 20
Stand | **Norwalk** _-_	Z Lenny/Joe's | G, P | **multi.** 22
Z Super/Weenie | **Fairfield** 22	Z L'Escale | T, W | **Greenwich** 23
NEW Taste/Charleston | **Norwalk** _-_	Longwood Rest. | G | **Woodbury** 18
Tratt. Vivolo | **Harrison** 21	Z Mayflower Inn | P | **Washington** 25
Two Steps | **Danbury** 13	Med. Grill | P | **Wilton** 19
	Mediterraneo | P | **Greenwich** 22

OUTDOOR DINING

(G=garden; P=patio; S=sidewalk;
T=terrace; W=waterside)

Z Abbott's Lobster | T, W | **Noank** 23	Z Meigas | P | **Norwalk** 26
Adrienne | P | **New Milford** 24	Mill on River | P, W | **S Windsor** 23
	Napoli Sul Fiume | P, W | **Westport** 16
	Niko's Greek | P | **White Pl** 20
	Nuage | P | **Cos Cob** 23

Old Heidelberg | G | **Bethel**	20
Oliva Cafe | T | **New Preston**	25
121 Rest. | P, T | **N Salem**	21
122 Pizza Bistro | S | **Stamford**	19
Opus 465 | P | **Armonk**	16
Oscar's | S | **Westport**	19
Pastorale | T | **Lakeville**	24
Pond House Café | P | **W Hartford**	22
Portofino's | P | **Wilton**	21
Rest./Water's Edge | T, W | **Westbrook**	20
River Cat Grill | P | **Rowayton**	22
River House | P, W | **Westport**	16
NEW Roasted Peppers | S | **Mamaro**	–
Roger Sherman | P | **New Canaan**	22
Sage American | P, W | **New Haven**	20
Scoozzi Tratt. | P | **New Haven**	22
Seamen's Inne | P, W | **Mystic**	19
Seaside Johnnie's | T, W | **Rye**	13
SoNo Baking Co. | S | **S Norwalk**	25
Sono Seaport | P, W | **S Norwalk**	16
Splash | T, W | **Westport**	21
Squire's | P | **Redding**	19
Stone House | T, W | **Guilford**	21
Tavern on Main | T | **Westport**	19
Terra Mar | P, W | **Old Saybrook**	21
Terra Rist. | P | **Greenwich**	22
Thataway Cafe | P | **Greenwich**	15
Troutbeck | T, W | **Amenia**	24
Two Steps | P | **Danbury**	13
Vito's | P | **Hartford**	19
Viva Zapata | P | **Westport**	17
Vox | P | **N Salem**	21
White Hart | P | **Salisbury**	17

PEOPLE-WATCHING

Acqua | **Westport**	21
Arugula | **W Hartford**	24
Asian Tempt. | **White Pl**	20
Azu | **Mystic**	23
Z Baang Cafe | **Riverside**	23
NEW Bar Americain | **Uncasville**	–
Z Barcelona | **New Haven**	23
Bedford Post/Barn | **Bedford**	24
Bedford Post/Farm | **Bedford**	–
Z Bespoke | **New Haven**	24

BLT Steak | **White Pl**	23
Blue | **White Pl**	19
Blue Pearl | **New Haven**	20
Boathouse | **Lakeville**	16
Bravo Bravo | **Mystic**	24
Brazen Fox | **White Pl**	15
Bricco | **W Hartford**	25
Cafe Goodfellas | **New Haven**	21
Z Carole Peck's | **Woodbury**	27
NEW Craftsteak | **Ledyard**	–
Z Dressing Room | **Westport**	23
Elbow Room | **W Hartford**	18
Euro Asian | **Port Chester**	21
Z Feng Asian | **Hartford**	26
Ferrante | **Stamford**	20
Z Firebox | **Hartford**	25
42 | **White Pl**	22
Frankie/Johnnie's | **Rye**	23
Ginban Asian | **Mamaro**	–
Ginger Man | **Greenwich**	17
Grand | **Stamford**	18
Z Grant's | **W Hartford**	25
Griswold Inn | **Essex**	18
G.W. Tavern | **Wash Depot**	20
Haiku | **Mamaro**	23
NEW Haiku | **White Pl**	–
Hot Tomato's | **Hartford**	21
Z Ibiza | **New Haven**	28
Z Jean-Louis | **Greenwich**	28
Koo | **Rye**	23
Le Figaro Bistro | **Greenwich**	20
NEW Lolita | **Greenwich**	–
Lusardi's | **Larch**	24
Market | **Stamford**	23
Z Match | **S Norwalk**	24
Z Max Downtown | **Hartford**	27
Max Fish | **Glastonbury**	24
Z Max's Oyster | **W Hartford**	25
Z Mayflower Inn | **Washington**	25
Z Michael Jordan's | **Uncasville**	25
Mighty Joe | **White Pl**	16
NEW Molly Spillane | **Mamaro**	16
Mulino's | **White Pl**	25
North Star | **Pound Ridge**	23
Nuage | **Cos Cob**	23
Oliva Cafe | **New Preston**	25

116 Crown | **New Haven**	23
2 Paci | **Southport**	26
Pastorale | **Lakeville**	24
Peniche | **White Pl**	22
NEW Pizzeria Molto | **Fairfield**	-
Polpo | **Greenwich**	24
Porter Hse. | **White Pl**	18
2 Rebeccas | **Greenwich**	25
Rist. Luce | **Hamden**	22
River House | **Westport**	16
Ruby's Oyster | **Rye**	21
Scoozzi Tratt. | **New Haven**	22
SolToro | **Uncasville**	-
SoNo Baking Co. | **S Norwalk**	25
Sonora | **Port Chester**	24
Strada 18 | **S Norwalk**	25
Tango Grill | **White Pl**	22
Tarry Lodge | **Port Chester**	24
Tavern on Main | **Westport**	19
2 Tengda | **Westport**	23
Todd English's | **Uncasville**	23
2 Union League | **New Haven**	27
Wasabi Chi | **S Norwalk**	24
West St. Grill | **Litchfield**	22
Winvian | **Morris**	-
2 Zinc | **New Haven**	24

POWER SCENES

Alba's | **Port Chester**	22
Antipasti | **White Pl**	21
2 Baang Cafe | **Riverside**	23
Bedford Post/Farm | **Bedford**	-
BLT Steak | **White Pl**	23
Boathouse | **Lakeville**	16
2 Capital Grille | **Stamford**	25
Carbone's | **Hartford**	25
2 Cavey's | **Manchester**	28
Central Steak | **New Haven**	23
Christopher Martins | **New Haven**	20
NEW Craftsteak | **Ledyard**	-
Diorio | **Waterbury**	24
2 Dressing Room | **Westport**	23
Ferrante | **Stamford**	20
2 Firebox | **Hartford**	25
42 | **White Pl**	22
Graziellas | **White Pl**	17

Il Falco | **Stamford**	22
2 Jean-Louis | **Greenwich**	28
Jeffrey's | **Milford**	23
Joseph's | **Bridgeport**	24
Koo | **multi.**	23
La Tavola | **Waterbury**	-
Lusardi's | **Larch**	24
Max-a-Mia | **Avon**	24
2 Max Downtown | **Hartford**	27
Max Fish | **Glastonbury**	24
2 Mayflower Inn | **Washington**	25
2 Meigas | **Norwalk**	26
2 Morton's | **multi.**	24
Mulino's | **White Pl**	25
Peppercorn's Grill | **Hartford**	25
Polpo | **Greenwich**	24
Ralph/Rich's | **Bridgeport**	24
Tango Grill | **White Pl**	22
2 Thomas Henkelmann | **Greenwich**	28
Tre Scalini | **New Haven**	23
2 Union League | **New Haven**	27
2 Valbella | **Riverside**	25
West St. Grill | **Litchfield**	22
Willett House | **Port Chester**	23

PRIVATE ROOMS

(Restaurants charge less at off times; call for capacity)

Acqua | **Westport**	21
Antipasti | **White Pl**	21
Bedford Post/Farm | **Bedford**	-
2 Bernard's | **Ridgefield**	27
Brendan's/Elms | **Ridgefield**	22
Bru Room/BAR | **New Haven**	25
2 Carole Peck's | **Woodbury**	27
Centro | **Greenwich**	19
Chatterley's | **New Hartford**	20
Chestnut Grille | **Old Lyme**	24
Dakota Steak | **Avon**	18
Eclisse | **Stamford**	20
Elbow Room | **W Hartford**	18
42 | **White Pl**	22
Ginger Man | **Greenwich**	17
Grand | **Stamford**	18
Graziellas | **White Pl**	17
Grist Mill | **Farmington**	24

Il Falco	**Stamford**	22
Joseph's	**Bridgeport**	24
Kujaku	**Stamford**	17
La Panetière	**Rye**	27
Max Amore	**Glastonbury**	23
🖬 Max Downtown	**Hartford**	27
🖬 Max's Oyster	**W Hartford**	25
🖬 Mayflower Inn	**Washington**	25
🖬 Meigas	**Norwalk**	26
🖬 Michael Jordan's	**Uncasville**	25
Morello	**Greenwich**	–
116 Crown	**New Haven**	23
🖬 Paci	**Southport**	26
Peniche	**White Pl**	22
Plum Tree	**New Canaan**	21
Polpo	**Greenwich**	24
Primavera	**Crot Falls**	23
Putnam Hse.	**Bethel**	16
River Bistro	**New Milford**	19
Roger Sherman	**New Canaan**	22
Ruby's Oyster	**Rye**	21
Saint Tropez	**Fairfield**	23
Scoozzi Tratt.	**New Haven**	22
Scribner's	**Milford**	23
🖬 Stonehenge	**Ridgefield**	24
🖬 Tengda	**Greenwich**	23
🖬 Thali	**New Canaan**	26
🖬 Thomas Henkelmann	**Greenwich**	28
Todd English's	**Uncasville**	23
Toshi Japanese	**Avon**	23
Tuscany	**Bridgeport**	25
🖬 Union League	**New Haven**	27
U.S.S. Chowder	**Hartford**	16
🖬 Woodward Hse.	**Bethlehem**	26

PRIX FIXE MENUS

(Call for prices and times)

Arch	**Brewster**	26
Bengal Tiger	**White Pl**	23
🖬 Bernard's	**Ridgefield**	27
Bin 100	**Milford**	25
Costa del Sol	**Hartford**	25
🖬 DaPietro's	**Westport**	26
Dish B&G	**Hartford**	20
🖬 Firebox	**Hartford**	25
Giovanni's	**Darien**	20

Halstead Ave.	**Harrison**	18
🖬 Jean-Louis	**Greenwich**	28
John-Michael's	**N Salem**	25
La Crémaillère	**Bedford**	26
La Panetière	**Rye**	27
🖬 Meigas	**Norwalk**	26
Mill on River	**S Windsor**	23
🖬 Ondine	**Danbury**	25
Pascal's	**Larch**	20
Rest./Rowayton Sea.	**Rowayton**	22
River Tavern	**Chester**	25
Shish Kebab	**W Hartford**	24
Sonora	**Port Chester**	24
Toshi Japanese	**Avon**	23
Troutbeck	**Amenia**	24
Turkish Meze	**Mamaro**	22

QUIET CONVERSATION

Ahimsa	**New Haven**	17
Aladdin	**Hartford**	18
Aloi	**New Canaan**	24
Altnaveigh Inn	**Storrs**	24
American Pie Co.	**Sherman**	20
🖬 Apricots	**Farmington**	24
Arch	**Brewster**	26
Bailey's	**Ridgefield**	20
🆕 Ballou's	**Guilford**	–
Bangalore	**Fairfield**	23
Bedford Post/Farm	**Bedford**	–
Bengal Tiger	**White Pl**	23
Bennett's	**Stamford**	21
🖬 Bernard's	**Ridgefield**	27
Bin 228	**Hartford**	23
Bistro Basque	**Milford**	26
🖬 Bistro Bonne Nuit	**New Canaan**	26
Bistro 22	**Bedford**	23
Blackstones	**Norwalk**	23
Bloodroot	**Bridgeport**	21
Blue Lemon	**Westport**	24
Bobby Q's	**Westport**	19
Brie/Bleu	**New London**	24
Brix	**Cheshire**	19
Bull's Bridge	**Kent**	16
Burger Bar	**S Norwalk**	24
Cafe Allegre	**Madison**	20

Cafe Lola | **Fairfield**	–
Cafe Mozart | **Mamaro**	17
Café Tavolini | **Bridgeport**	19
☑ Carole Peck's | **Woodbury**	27
Chef Luis | **New Canaan**	25
Chestnut Grille | **Old Lyme**	24
☑ Copper Beech | **Ivoryton**	24
Coppia | **Fairfield**	24
☑ Coromandel | **multi.**	26
NEW Crooked Shillelagh | **Branford**	–
NEW DaCapo's | **Avon**	–
David Burke | **Ledyard**	27
Diorio | **Waterbury**	24
Drescher's | **Waterbury**	22
NEW Elaine's Healthy | **New Haven**	–
Eos Greek | **Stamford**	–
Épernay | **Bridgeport**	–
Esca | **Middletown**	–
Evergreens | **Simsbury**	25
Fin/Fin II | **Stamford**	22
Flood Tide | **Mystic**	21
Foe | **Branford**	22
Gabrielle's | **Centerbrook**	21
Gervasi's | **White Pl**	–
Graziellas | **White Pl**	17
Grist Mill | **Farmington**	24
G.W. Tavern | **Wash Depot**	20
Hidden Vine | **Newington**	–
Hopkins Inn | **New Preston**	20
Il Palio | **Shelton**	23
Il Sogno | **Port Chester**	–
Inn at Newtown | **Newtown**	19
☑ Insieme | **Ridgefield**	25
Isabelle/Vincent | **Fairfield**	–
☑ Jean-Louis | **Greenwich**	28
John-Michael's | **N Salem**	25
John's Café | **Woodbury**	24
La Bocca | **White Pl**	22
La Bretagne | **Stamford**	22
La Crémaillère | **Bedford**	26
La Panetière | **Rye**	27
La Piccola Casa | **Mamaro**	20
Latin Am. Cafe | **White Pl**	20
Le Château | **S Salem**	25
NEW Le Farm | **Westport**	–
☑ Le Petit Cafe | **Branford**	28
Little Thai/Buddha | **Darien**	23
Longwood Rest. | **Woodbury**	18
L'Orcio | **New Haven**	23
Lotus Thai | **Stratford**	20
Marc Charles | **Armonk**	28
Masala | **Hartford**	–
NEW Matthew's | **Unionville**	–
☑ Mayflower Inn | **Washington**	25
Mei Tzu | **E Windsor**	–
Melting Pot | **Darien**	18
☑ Métro Bis | **Simsbury**	26
Michael's | **Wallingford**	23
NEW Milonga | **N White Plains**	–
Myrna's | **Stamford**	21
Napoli Sul Fiume | **Westport**	16
NEW No. 9 | **Millerton**	–
Nuage | **Cos Cob**	23
Old Lyme Inn | **Old Lyme**	20
Olive Tree | **Southbury**	19
☑ Ondine | **Danbury**	25
Osetra | **Norwalk**	26
Papacelle | **Avon**	–
Pascal's | **Larch**	20
Patrias | **Port Chester**	20
Pho Mekong | **Westport**	20
Pizzeria Lauretano | **Bethel**	26
PolytechnicON20 | **Hartford**	28
Puket Café | **Wethersfield**	–
Rangoli | **New Roch**	24
Rani Mahal | **Mamaro**	23
Reka's | **White Pl**	18
River Tavern | **Chester**	25
Roger Sherman | **New Canaan**	22
NEW Rouge Winebar | **S Norwalk**	–
RSVP | **W Cornwall**	29
Salsa | **New Milford**	23
Scribner's | **Milford**	23
NEW Spinghar | **Glastonbury**	–
☑ Stonehenge | **Ridgefield**	24
NEW Taste/Charleston | **Norwalk**	–
Tawa | **Stamford**	22
Thai Pearl | **Ridgefield**	19

Thai Place | **Putnam**	–
Town Dock | **Rye**	17
Troutbeck | **Amenia**	24
Turkish Meze | **Mamaro**	22
☑ Union League | **New Haven**	27
Venetian | **Torrington**	22
Watercolor Cafe | **Larch**	18
White Hart | **Salisbury**	17
White Horse Tav. | **Redding**	15
Wild Rice | **Norwalk**	21
Winvian | **Morris**	–
☑ Woodward Hse. | **Bethlehem**	26

RAW BARS

Antipasti | **White Pl**	21
NEW Bar Americain | **Uncasville**	–
Barnacle | **Mamaro**	–
Beach House | **Milford**	22
David Burke | **Ledyard**	27
Dish B&G | **Hartford**	20
80 West | **White Pl**	19
☑ Elm St. Oyster | **Greenwich**	24
First & Last | **Middletown**	20
Flanders Fish | **E Lyme**	20
42 | **White Pl**	22
Ginger Man | **Greenwich**	17
Go Fish | **Mystic**	20
Jasper White's | **Uncasville**	21
Legal Sea Foods | **White Pl**	19
☑ Lenny/Joe's | **Westbrook**	22
Liv's Oyster | **Old Saybrook**	24
☑ Max Downtown | **Hartford**	27
Max Fish | **Glastonbury**	24
☑ Max's Oyster | **W Hartford**	25
Morgans Fish | **Rye**	24
116 Crown | **New Haven**	23
121 Rest. | **N Salem**	21
Ralph/Rich's | **Bridgeport**	24
Ruby's Oyster | **Rye**	21
Sage American | **New Haven**	20
Saybrook Fish | **Rocky Hill**	21
Seaside Johnnie's | **Rye**	13
Splash | **Westport**	21
Town Dock | **Rye**	17
☑ Union League | **New Haven**	27
U.S.S. Chowder | **multi.**	16

Vito's | **multi.**	19
Water St. Cafe | **Stonington**	25

ROMANTIC PLACES

Acqua | **Westport**	21
Adriana's | **New Haven**	23
Adrienne | **New Milford**	24
☑ Apricots | **Farmington**	24
Arch | **Brewster**	26
Avon Old Farm | **Avon**	–
NEW Ballou's | **Guilford**	–
Bambou | **Greenwich**	23
Bedford Post/Farm | **Bedford**	–
Bengal Tiger | **White Pl**	23
☑ Bernard's | **Ridgefield**	27
NEW Besito | **W Hartford**	–
☑ Bespoke | **New Haven**	24
☑ Bistro Bonne Nuit | **New Canaan**	26
Bistro 22 | **Bedford**	23
Boom | **Old Lyme**	22
☑ Boulders Inn | **New Preston**	22
Brendan's/Elms | **Ridgefield**	22
Cafe Lola | **Fairfield**	–
Carbone's | **Hartford**	25
☑ Cavey's | **Manchester**	28
Chestnut Grille | **Old Lyme**	24
Chez Jean-Pierre | **Stamford**	24
☑ Cobb's Mill Inn | **Weston**	18
☑ Copper Beech | **Ivoryton**	24
Coppia | **Fairfield**	24
NEW DaCapo's | **Avon**	–
☑ Dressing Room | **Westport**	23
Emilio Rist. | **Harrison**	23
Encore Bistro | **Larch**	22
Esca | **Middletown**	–
Flood Tide | **Mystic**	21
Frankie/Johnnie's | **Rye**	23
Gervasi's | **White Pl**	–
Grist Mill | **Farmington**	24
Griswold Inn | **Essex**	18
Harbor Lights | **Norwalk**	20
☑ Harvest Supper | **New Canaan**	27
Hidden Vine | **Newington**	–
Hopkins Inn | **New Preston**	20
Horse & Hound | **S Salem**	16

Ibiza | **New Haven**	28	Stone House | **Guilford**	21
Inn at Newtown | **Newtown**	19	Tango Grill | **White Pl**	22
Isabelle/Vincent | **Fairfield**	–	Thomas Henkelmann | **Greenwich**	28
Jean-Louis | **Greenwich**	28	Tratt. Vivolo | **Harrison**	21
John-Michael's | **N Salem**	25	Tre Scalini | **New Haven**	23
La Bretagne | **Stamford**	22	Trinity Grill | **Harrison**	19
La Crémaillère | **Bedford**	26	Troutbeck | **Amenia**	24
La Panetière | **Rye**	27	Tuscany Grill | **Middletown**	20
La Piccola Casa | **Mamaro**	20	Union League | **New Haven**	27
La Zingara | **Bethel**	25	Venetian | **Torrington**	22
Le Château | **S Salem**	25	Water St. Cafe | **Stonington**	25
NEW Le Farm | **Westport**	–	White Horse Tav. | **Redding**	15
Le Petit Cafe | **Branford**	28	Winvian | **Morris**	–
Le Provençal | **Mamaro**	23	Woodward Hse. | **Bethlehem**	26
Longwood Rest. | **Woodbury**	18	Zinc | **New Haven**	24
L'Orcio | **New Haven**	23	Zitoune | **Mamaro**	20
Mayflower Inn | **Washington**	25		

SENIOR APPEAL

Meigas | **Norwalk**	26	Adriana's | **New Haven**	23
Melting Pot | **White Pl**	18	Altnaveigh Inn | **Storrs**	24
Métro Bis | **Simsbury**	26	American Pie Co. | **Sherman**	20
Mill on River | **S Windsor**	23	Apricots | **Farmington**	24
Mulino's | **White Pl**	25	Avon Old Farm | **Avon**	–
Napa & Co. | **Stamford**	25	Bedford Post/Farm | **Bedford**	–
Nessa | **Port Chester**	20	Bistro 22 | **Bedford**	23
NEW No. 9 | **Millerton**	–	B.J. Ryan's | **Norwalk**	22
Old Lyme Inn | **Old Lyme**	20	NEW Bombay Olive | **W Hartford**	–
Oliva Cafe | **New Preston**	25	Bravo Bravo | **Mystic**	24
Ondine | **Danbury**	25	Brix | **Cheshire**	19
121 Rest. | **N Salem**	21	Bull's Bridge | **Kent**	16
Opus 465 | **Armonk**	16	Burke in Box | **Ledyard**	–
Pascal's | **Larch**	20	Cafe Allegre | **Madison**	20
Pastorale | **Lakeville**	24	Café Tavolini | **Bridgeport**	19
Peppercorn's Grill | **Hartford**	25	Carbone's | **Hartford**	25
PolytechnicON20 | **Hartford**	28	Carrabba's | **Manchester**	19
Ponte Vecchio | **Fairfield**	20	Chestnut Grille | **Old Lyme**	24
Positano's | **Westport**	22	NEW Chili Chicken | **Stamford**	–
Posto 22 | **New Roch**	–	Chuck's Steak | **Branford**	18
Rist. Luce | **Hamden**	22	Cobb's Mill Inn | **Weston**	18
River House | **Westport**	16	Consiglio's | **New Haven**	25
River Tavern | **Chester**	25	Copper Beech | **Ivoryton**	24
Roger Sherman | **New Canaan**	22	NEW Crooked Shillelagh | **Branford**	–
NEW Rouge Winebar | **S Norwalk**	–		
Sardegna | **Larch**	21	Curtis House | **Woodbury**	16
Sonora | **Port Chester**	24	NEW DaCapo's | **Avon**	–
Still River | **Eastford**	26	David Burke | **Ledyard**	27
Stonehenge | **Ridgefield**	24		

Dock/Dine | **Old Saybrook**	15
Dolphins Cove | **Bridgeport**	19
Encore Bistro | **Larch**	22
NEW Eveready | **Brewster**	19
Flanders Fish | **E Lyme**	20
Foe | **Branford**	22
Fonda La Paloma | **Cos Cob**	18
Z Frank Pepe | **Manchester**	26
Giorgio's | **Port Chester**	23
Giovanni's | **Darien**	20
Go Fish | **Mystic**	20
Graziellas | **White Pl**	17
Grist Mill | **Farmington**	24
Griswold Inn | **Essex**	18
Z Harvest Supper | **New Canaan**	27
Hawthorne Inn | **Berlin**	18
NEW Il Castello | **Mamaro**	-
Inn at Newtown | **Newtown**	19
Z Insieme | **Ridgefield**	25
Kisco Kosher | **White Pl**	19
Kumo | **multi.**	22
La Crémaillère | **Bedford**	26
La Panetière | **Rye**	27
La Tavola | **Waterbury**	-
Le Château | **S Salem**	25
Z Lenny/Joe's | **multi.**	22
Lenny's Indian | **Branford**	20
Leon's | **New Haven**	-
Le Provençal | **Mamaro**	23
NEW Little Pub | **Ridgefield**	-
Long Ridge Tav. | **Stamford**	14
Longwood Rest. | **Woodbury**	18
Louis' Lunch | **New Haven**	24
NEW Matthew's | **Unionville**	-
Melting Pot | **Darien**	18
Mill on River | **S Windsor**	23
NEW Milonga | **N White Plains**	-
Mulino's | **White Pl**	25
Napoli Sul Fiume | **Westport**	16
Nino's | **S Salem**	18
Nino's | **Bedford Hills**	19
NEW No. 9 | **Millerton**	-
Old Lyme Inn | **Old Lyme**	20
Olio | **Groton**	24
Pantry | **Wash Depot**	25
Papacelle | **Avon**	-

Pascal's | **Larch**	20
Pat's Kountry | **Old Saybrook**	14
Pazzo Italian | **Glastonbury**	23
Pellicci's | **Stamford**	20
Portofino Pizza | **Goldens Bridge**	22
Portofino's | **Wilton**	21
Putnam Hse. | **Bethel**	16
Red Barn | **Westport**	17
Rest./Water's Edge | **Westbrook**	20
NEW Rocco's | **New Canaan**	-
Roger Sherman | **New Canaan**	22
Rue/Crêpes | **Harrison**	15
Seamen's Inne | **Mystic**	19
Shady Glen | **Manchester**	23
NEW Spinghar | **Glastonbury**	-
Spris | **Hartford**	21
Z Stonehenge | **Ridgefield**	24
T&J Villaggio | **Port Chester**	23
NEW Taste/Charleston | **Norwalk**	-
Tavern on Main | **Westport**	19
Tawa | **Stamford**	22
Thai Pearl | **Ridgefield**	19
Thai Place | **Putnam**	-
Z Thomas Henkelmann | **Greenwich**	28
Vazzy's | **Bridgeport**	18
Venetian | **Torrington**	22
Wandering Moose | **W Cornwall**	18
West St. Grill | **Litchfield**	22
White Hart | **Salisbury**	17
White Horse Tav. | **Redding**	15
Winvian | **Morris**	-
Woodland | **Lakeville**	23
Z Woodward Hse. | **Bethlehem**	26
Yorkside | **New Haven**	16

SINGLES SCENES

Antipasti | **White Pl**	21
Z Archie Moore's | **multi.**	19
Asian Tempt. | **White Pl**	20
Azu | **Mystic**	23
Z Baang Cafe | **Riverside**	23
Z Barcelona | **multi.**	23
Beach Café | **Fairfield**	17
Z Bespoke | **New Haven**	24
Black-Eyed Sally | **Hartford**	21

Blue | **White Pl**	19
Blue Pearl | **New Haven**	20
Blue Point B&G | **Stratford**	18
Boathouse | **Lakeville**	16
Bobby Q's | **Westport**	19
Bobby Valentine | **Stamford**	15
Bogey's Grille | **Westport**	16
Bond Grill | **Norwalk**	18
Brewhouse | **S Norwalk**	16
Brickhouse | **Derby**	-
Bru Room/BAR | **New Haven**	25
Cobble Stone | **Purchase**	15
C.O. Jones | **New Haven**	16
Cuckoo's Nest | **Old Saybrook**	18
Duo | **Stamford**	23
Elements | **W Hartford**	-
Euro Asian | **Port Chester**	21
Z Feng Asian | **Hartford**	26
Field | **Bridgeport**	17
Z Firebox | **Hartford**	25
First & Last | **multi.**	20
NEW Flipside Burgers | **Fairfield**	-
Forbidden City | **Middletown**	23
Frankie/Johnnie's | **Rye**	23
Ginger Man | **S Norwalk**	17
Grand | **Stamford**	18
Haiku | **Mamaro**	23
NEW Haiku | **White Pl**	-
Hot Tomato's | **Hartford**	21
It's Only Natural | **Middletown**	23
J. Gilbert's | **Glastonbury**	25
John Harvard's | **Manchester**	19
Kona Grill | **Stamford**	17
Kudeta | **New Haven**	21
Lady Luck | **Bridgeport**	-
Lansdowne | **New Haven**	-
Lazy Boy Saloon | **White Pl**	17
NEW Lolita | **Greenwich**	-
Long Ridge Tav. | **Stamford**	14
Mackenzie's | **Old Greenwich**	15
Market | **Stamford**	23
Mary Ann's | **Port Chester**	17
Z Match | **S Norwalk**	24
Max Fish | **Glastonbury**	24
Mediterraneo | **Greenwich**	22
Melting Pot | **White Pl**	18

Mighty Joe | **White Pl**	16
NEW Molly Spillane | **Mamaro**	16
Oliver's Taverne | **Essex**	13
116 Crown | **New Haven**	23
121 Rest. | **N Salem**	21
Paradise B&G | **Stamford**	13
NEW Pizzeria Molto | **Fairfield**	-
Porter Hse. | **White Pl**	18
Rye Grill | **Rye**	-
Sage American | **New Haven**	20
Saltwater Grille | **Stamford**	20
SolToro | **Uncasville**	-
Sono Seaport | **S Norwalk**	16
Southport Brew. | **multi.**	15
Splash | **Westport**	21
Strada 18 | **S Norwalk**	25
Su Casa | **Branford**	18
Tango | **Glastonbury**	-
Telluride | **Stamford**	21
Z Tengda | **Katonah**	23
Tequila Sunrise | **Larch**	15
Terra Rist. | **Greenwich**	22
Thataway Cafe | **Greenwich**	15
Two Boots | **Bridgeport**	21
Viva Zapata | **Westport**	17
VIVO Tratt. | **Hartford**	21
Wasabi Chi | **S Norwalk**	24
Wood-n-Tap | **Hartford**	19

SLEEPERS

(Good food, but little known)

Altnaveigh Inn | **Storrs**	24
Bambou | **Greenwich**	23
Bar Vivace | **Mamaro**	22
Brie/Bleu | **New London**	24
Buon Appetito | **Canton**	24
Café Roma | **Bridgeport**	22
Copacabana | **Port Chester**	23
Coppia | **Fairfield**	24
Corner Bakery | **Pawling**	23
David Burke | **Ledyard**	27
Drescher's | **Waterbury**	22
East-West Grille | **W Hartford**	23
Edd's Place | **Westbrook**	22
El Tio | **multi.**	24
Evergreens | **Simsbury**	25
Giorgio's | **Port Chester**	23

Great Taste	New Britain	27
Hanna's Mideastern	Danbury	22
Harvest/Pomfret	Pomfret	22
Kari	New Haven	23
Kumo	multi.	22
Lotus	Vernon	23
Louis' Lunch	New Haven	24
Marc Charles	Armonk	28
Meson/Españoles	White Pl	23
Michael's	Wallingford	23
Octagon	Groton	26
Olio	Groton	24
Omanel	Bridgeport	22
Pizzeria Lauretano	Bethel	26
PolytechnicON20	Hartford	28
Rangoli	New Roch	24
Rani Mahal	Mamaro	23
RSVP	W Cornwall	29
Salsa	New Milford	23
Still River	Eastford	26
Tawa	Stamford	22
Toshi Japanese	Avon	23
Troutbeck	Amenia	24

TEEN APPEAL

Abatino's	N White Plains	21
☒ Abbott's Lobster	Noank	23
Abis	Greenwich	18
Alforno	Old Saybrook	23
Altnaveigh Inn	Storrs	24
Angelina's	Westport	18
☒ Archie Moore's	Derby	19
Ash Creek	Bridgeport	18
Asian Tempt.	White Pl	20
Aspen Garden	Litchfield	15
Bangkok Gardens	New Haven	22
Bentara	New Haven	24
☒ Bertucci's	multi.	16
Big W's	Wingdale	26
Boathouse	Lakeville	16
Boathouse/Smokey	Stamford	21
Boxcar Cantina	Greenwich	20
Bravo Bravo	Mystic	24
Bugaboo Creek	Manchester	15
Butterfly Chinese	W Hartford	15
Chuck's Steak	multi.	18

Churrasc. Braza	Hartford	21
☒ City Limits	multi.	18
Claire's Corner	New Haven	19
☒ Cookhouse	New Milford	19
Costello's	Noank	18
Coyote Blue	Middletown	23
Dakota Steak	Avon	18
Dolphins Cove	Bridgeport	19
Eclisse	Stamford	20
NEW Elaine's Healthy	New Haven	-
Euro Asian	Port Chester	21
NEW Eveready	Brewster	19
Fifty Coins	multi.	14
Firehouse Deli	Fairfield	21
NEW Flipside Burgers	Fairfield	-
Fonda La Paloma	Cos Cob	18
NEW Fraîche Burger	Bridgeport	-
☒ Frank Pepe	multi.	26
Frank Pepe's/Spot	New Haven	26
Gates	New Canaan	18
Giovanni's	Darien	20
Go Fish	Mystic	20
Great Taste	New Britain	27
Haiku	Mamaro	23
NEW Haiku	White Pl	-
Harry's Pizza	W Hartford	24
Hawthorne Inn	Berlin	18
NEW Jack Rabbit's	Old Saybrook	-
Jasmine	Westport	15
Kobis	multi.	19
Kumo	multi.	22
La Taverna	Norwalk	22
☒ Lenny/Joe's	multi.	22
Little Kitchen	Westport	22
Little Mark's	Vernon	20
Louis' Lunch	New Haven	24
Lucky's	Stamford	15
Luna Pizza	multi.	20
Mancuso's	Fairfield	18
Mario's Pl.	Westport	19
Marisa's	Trumbull	18
Mary Ann's	Port Chester	17
Matsumoto	Larch	-
Melting Pot	Darien	18

Mo's NY | **New Roch**	21
Mystic Pizza | **multi.**	17
Nautilus | **Mamaro**	15
Noda's Steak | **White Pl**	19
Oliver's Taverne | **Essex**	13
Olive Tree | **Southbury**	19
Orem's Diner | **Wilton**	16
Oscar's | **Westport**	19
Pat's Kountry | **Old Saybrook**	14
Pellicci's | **Stamford**	20
⚡ P.F. Chang's | **White Pl**	19
Pizzeria Lauretano | **Bethel**	26
Portofino Pizza | **Goldens Bridge**	22
Portofino's | **Wilton**	21
Post Corner Pizza | **Darien**	19
Red Rooster | **Brewster**	18
Rizzuto's Pizza | **multi.**	–
Route 22 | **multi.**	13
Rue/Crêpes | **Harrison**	15
Rye Roadhse. | **Rye**	18
Sakura | **Westport**	21
⚡ Sally's Apizza | **New Haven**	26
Shady Glen | **Manchester**	23
Sono Seaport | **S Norwalk**	16
Southport Brew. | **multi.**	15
Spris | **Hartford**	21
Steak Loft | **Mystic**	18
Su Casa | **Branford**	18
⚡ Super/Weenie | **Fairfield**	22
Tandoori Taste | **Port Chester**	23
Tequila Mock. | **New Canaan**	17
Tiger Bowl | **Westport**	15
Tratt. Lucia | **Bedford**	16
Two Steps | **Danbury**	13
Valencia Luncheria | **Norwalk**	27
Vazzy's | **Bridgeport**	18
Yorkside | **New Haven**	16

TRENDY

Acqua | **Westport**	21
Ahimsa | **New Haven**	17
Antipasti | **White Pl**	21
Asian Tempt. | **White Pl**	20
Aspen | **Old Saybrook**	21
Aurora | **Rye**	20
NEW Ay! Salsa | **New Haven**	–

Azu | **Mystic**	23
⚡ Baang Cafe | **Riverside**	23
NEW Ballou's | **Guilford**	–
Bambou | **Greenwich**	23
Barça | **Hartford**	20
⚡ Barcelona | **multi.**	23
Basta | **New Haven**	20
Bedford Post/Barn | **Bedford**	24
NEW Besito | **W Hartford**	–
⚡ Bespoke | **New Haven**	24
Bin 228 | **Hartford**	23
BLT Steak | **White Pl**	23
Blue | **White Pl**	19
Blue Pearl | **New Haven**	20
Blue Point B&G | **Stratford**	18
Bond Grill | **Norwalk**	18
Bricco | **W Hartford**	25
NEW Café Manolo | **Westport**	–
Carmen Anthony Fish. | **multi.**	21
Carmen Anthony | **Waterbury**	22
⚡ Carole Peck's | **Woodbury**	27
Chat 19 | **Larch**	18
⚡ Ching's | **Darien**	24
⚡ Coromandel | **S Norwalk**	26
Costa del Sol | **Hartford**	25
NEW Craftsteak | **Ledyard**	–
Dish B&G | **Hartford**	20
⚡ Dressing Room | **Westport**	23
Elbow Room | **W Hartford**	18
⚡ Elm St. Oyster | **Greenwich**	24
Eos Greek | **Stamford**	–
Euro Asian | **Port Chester**	21
Fat Cat Pie | **Norwalk**	23
⚡ Feng Asian | **Hartford**	26
⚡ Firebox | **Hartford**	25
NEW Flipside Burgers | **Fairfield**	–
Forbidden City | **Middletown**	23
42 | **White Pl**	22
NEW Fraîche Burger | **Bridgeport**	–
⚡ Frank Pepe | **New Haven**	26
Frank Pepe's/Spot | **New Haven**	26
Geronimo | **New Haven**	17
Ginban Asian | **Mamaro**	–
Ginger Man | **S Norwalk**	17
Haiku | **Mamaro**	23
NEW Haiku | **White Pl**	–

☑ Harvest Supper	**New Canaan**	27
Hot Tomato's	**Hartford**	21
☑ Ibiza	**New Haven**	28
NEW Jack Rabbit's | **Old Saybrook**	–
Koji	**Hartford**	19
Koo	**multi.**	23
Kotobuki	**Stamford**	23
Kudeta	**New Haven**	21
Lady Luck	**Bridgeport**	–
NEW Le Farm	**Westport**	–
Le Figaro Bistro	**Greenwich**	20
NEW Lolita	**Greenwich**	–
Market	**Stamford**	23
Masala	**Hartford**	–
Max-a-Mia	**Avon**	24
Max Amore	**Glastonbury**	23
☑ Max Downtown	**Hartford**	27
Max Fish	**Glastonbury**	24
☑ Max's Oyster	**W Hartford**	25
Med. Grill	**Wilton**	19
Mediterraneo	**Greenwich**	22
☑ Meigas	**Norwalk**	26
☑ Métro Bis	**Simsbury**	26
Morgans Fish	**Rye**	24
☑ Napa & Co.	**Stamford**	25
Oliva Cafe	**New Preston**	25
116 Crown	**New Haven**	23
Osetra	**Norwalk**	26
☑ Paci	**Southport**	26
Pastorale	**Lakeville**	24
Peniche	**White Pl**	22
Piccolo Arancio	**Farmington**	26
NEW Pizzeria Molto	**Fairfield**	–
PolytechnicON20	**Hartford**	28
☑ Rebeccas	**Greenwich**	25
Red Plum	**Mamaro**	–
Rizzuto's Pizza	**multi.**	–
NEW Rouge Winebar | **S Norwalk**	–
RSVP	**W Cornwall**	29
Ruby's Oyster	**Rye**	21
Rue/Crêpes	**Harrison**	15
☑ Sally's Apizza	**New Haven**	26
Scoozzi Tratt.	**New Haven**	22
Solé Rist.	**New Canaan**	22
SolToro	**Uncasville**	–

Sonora	**Port Chester**	24
Splash	**Westport**	21
Stand	**Norwalk**	–
Still River	**Eastford**	26
Tango	**Glastonbury**	–
Tapas/Ann	**W Hartford**	23
Tarry Lodge	**Port Chester**	24
☑ Tengda	**multi.**	23
☑ Thali	**New Haven**	26
☑ Thomas Henkelmann | **Greenwich**	28
Tre Scalini	**New Haven**	23
Trumbull Kitchen	**Hartford**	24
Tuscany Grill	**Middletown**	20
Union Street Tav.	**Windsor**	–
Valencia Luncheria	**Norwalk**	27
VIVO Tratt.	**Hartford**	21
Vox	**N Salem**	21
V Rest.	**Westport**	16
Wasabi Chi	**S Norwalk**	24
Watermoon	**Rye**	22
West St. Grill	**Litchfield**	22
☑ Zinc	**New Haven**	24
Zitoune	**Mamaro**	20

VALET PARKING

Antipasti	**White Pl**	21
Arch	**Brewster**	26
☑ Baang Cafe	**Riverside**	23
Bedford Post/Barn	**Bedford**	24
Bedford Post/Farm	**Bedford**	–
Bennett's	**Stamford**	21
☑ Bernard's	**Ridgefield**	27
BLT Steak	**White Pl**	23
Blue	**White Pl**	19
☑ California Pizza	**Ledyard**	16
☑ Capital Grille	**Stamford**	25
Carmen Anthony	**New Haven**	22
Cedars	**Ledyard**	21
Christopher Martins	**New Haven**	20
☑ Cobb's Mill Inn	**Weston**	18
☑ Coromandel	**New Roch**	26
NEW Craftsteak	**Ledyard**	–
Diorio	**Waterbury**	24
Dish B&G	**Hartford**	20
☑ Feng Asian	**Hartford**	26

☑ Firebox | **Hartford**	25
Fonda La Paloma | **Cos Cob**	18
42 | **White Pl**	22
Giovanni's | **Darien**	20
Heirloom | **New Haven**	-
NEW Il Castello | **Mamaro**	-
Kona Grill | **Stamford**	17
La Bocca | **White Pl**	22
La Crémaillère | **Bedford**	26
La Panetière | **Rye**	27
Le Château | **S Salem**	25
Legal Sea Foods | **White Pl**	19
☑ L'Escale | **Greenwich**	23
Masala | **Hartford**	-
☑ Max Downtown | **Hartford**	27
☑ Mayflower Inn | **Washington**	25
NEW Milonga | **N White Plains**	-
☑ Morton's | **multi.**	24
Mulino's | **White Pl**	25
Napoli Sul Fiume | **Westport**	16
Octagon | **Groton**	26
Pellicci's | **Stamford**	20
Peniche | **White Pl**	22
Peppercorn's Grill | **Hartford**	25
Polpo | **Greenwich**	24
Positano's | **Westport**	22
Posto 22 | **New Roch**	-
Primavera | **Crot Falls**	23
Reka's | **White Pl**	18
Rest./Rowayton Sea. | **Rowayton**	22
Rest./Water's Edge | **Westbrook**	20
Roger Sherman | **New Canaan**	22
Rye Grill | **Rye**	-
SolToro | **Uncasville**	-
Sonora | **Port Chester**	24
☑ Stonehenge | **Ridgefield**	24
Tango Grill | **White Pl**	22
☑ Tengda | **Greenwich**	23
☑ Thomas Henkelmann | **Greenwich**	28
Todd English's | **Uncasville**	23
Trumbull Kitchen | **Hartford**	24
☑ Valbella | **Riverside**	25
VIVO Tratt. | **Hartford**	21
Wood-n-Tap | **Farmington**	19
Zhang's | **Mystic**	18

VIEWS

☑ Abbott's Lobster | **Noank**	23
Abruzzi Tratt. | **Patterson**	21
☑ Apricots | **Farmington**	24
Arch | **Brewster**	26
Beach House | **Milford**	22
Bill's Seafood | **Westbrook**	19
Bloodroot | **Bridgeport**	21
Boom | **Westbrook**	22
☑ Boulders Inn | **New Preston**	22
Brie/Bleu | **New London**	24
Bull's Bridge | **Kent**	16
Café/Green | **Danbury**	23
Cascade Mtn. | **Amenia**	16
☑ Copper Beech | **Ivoryton**	24
Costello's | **Noank**	18
Creek | **Purchase**	17
Cucina Modo | **Westport**	-
Dock/Dine | **Old Saybrook**	15
Dolphins Cove | **Bridgeport**	19
Edd's Place | **Westbrook**	22
80 West | **White Pl**	19
f.i.s.h. | **Port Chester**	21
Flood Tide | **Mystic**	21
42 | **White Pl**	22
Grist Mill | **Farmington**	24
G.W. Tavern | **Wash Depot**	20
Harbor Lights | **Norwalk**	20
Harborside B&G | **Stratford**	15
Hopkins Inn | **New Preston**	20
Jasper White's | **Uncasville**	21
Jeffrey's | **Milford**	23
Le Château | **S Salem**	25
Lenny's Indian | **Branford**	20
☑ L'Escale | **Greenwich**	23
Mamma Francesca | **New Roch**	16
Mill on River | **S Windsor**	23
Olive Tree | **Southbury**	19
Paradise B&G | **Stamford**	13
PolytechnicON20 | **Hartford**	28
Positano's | **Westport**	22
☑ Quattro Pazzi | **Norwalk**	22
Rani Mahal | **Mamaro**	23
Rest./Rowayton Sea. | **Rowayton**	22
Rest./Water's Edge | **Westbrook**	20
River Bistro | **New Milford**	19

River House	**Westport**	16
Sage American	**New Haven**	20
Saltwater Grille	**Stamford**	20
Seamen's Inne	**Mystic**	19
Seaside Johnnie's	**Rye**	13
Sharpe Hill/Vineyard	**Pomfret**	–
Sono Seaport	**S Norwalk**	16
Splash	**Westport**	21
Still River	**Eastford**	26
🛛 Stonehenge	**Ridgefield**	24
Stone House	**Guilford**	21
Terra Mar	**Old Saybrook**	21
🛛 Thomas Henkelmann	**Greenwich**	28
Troutbeck	**Amenia**	24
Vito's	**multi.**	19
Vox	**N Salem**	21
Wandering Moose	**W Cornwall**	18
White Hart	**Salisbury**	17

VISITORS ON EXPENSE ACCOUNT

Aloi	**New Canaan**	24
Arch	**Brewster**	26
Basta	**New Haven**	20
Beach House	**Milford**	22
Bedford Post/Farm	**Bedford**	–
Bentara	**New Haven**	24
🛛 Bernard's	**Ridgefield**	27
Bistro 22	**Bedford**	23
Blackstones	**Norwalk**	23
BLT Steak	**White Pl**	23
🛛 Capital Grille	**Stamford**	25
Carmen Anthony Fish.	**multi.**	21
Carmen Anthony	**Waterbury**	22
NEW Craftsteak	**Ledyard**	–
David Burke	**Ledyard**	27
🛛 Dressing Room	**Westport**	23
Ferrante	**Stamford**	20
42	**White Pl**	22
Graziellas	**White Pl**	17
🛛 Jean-Louis	**Greenwich**	28
Joseph's	**Bridgeport**	24
Koo	**Ridgefield**	23
La Crémaillère	**Bedford**	26
La Panetière	**Rye**	27
La Tavola	**Waterbury**	–

Le Château	**S Salem**	25
Longwood Rest.	**Woodbury**	18
Luca Rist.	**Wilton**	24
Lusardi's	**Larch**	24
Market	**Stamford**	23
🛛 Max Downtown	**Hartford**	27
Max Fish	**Glastonbury**	24
Melting Pot	**Darien**	18
🛛 Michael Jordan's	**Uncasville**	25
Mighty Joe	**White Pl**	16
🛛 Morton's	**multi.**	24
Mulino's	**White Pl**	25
Octagon	**Groton**	26
Pascal's	**Larch**	20
PolytechnicON20	**Hartford**	28
🛛 Rebeccas	**Greenwich**	25
Roger Sherman	**New Canaan**	22
🛛 Ruth's Chris	**Newington**	24
Still River	**Eastford**	26
Strada 18	**S Norwalk**	25
Tango Grill	**White Pl**	22
🛛 Tengda	**Darien**	23
🛛 Thomas Henkelmann	**Greenwich**	28
Troutbeck	**Amenia**	24
🛛 Valbella	**Riverside**	25
VIVO Tratt.	**Hartford**	21
Willett House	**Port Chester**	23
Winvian	**Morris**	–
🛛 Woodward Hse.	**Bethlehem**	26

WINNING WINE LISTS

Alba's	**Port Chester**	22
Aloi	**New Canaan**	24
Antipasti	**White Pl**	21
NEW Ballou's	**Guilford**	–
🛛 Barcelona	**multi.**	23
Beach House	**Milford**	22
Bennett's	**Stamford**	21
Bentara	**New Haven**	24
🛛 Bernard's	**Ridgefield**	27
Bin 100	**Milford**	25
Bin 228	**Hartford**	23
Bistro 22	**Bedford**	23
BLT Steak	**White Pl**	23
🛛 Boulders Inn	**New Preston**	22

Brie/Bleu | **New London**	24
Cafe Lola | **Fairfield**	-
NEW Café Manolo | **Westport**	-
Café Routier | **Westbrook**	25
Z Capital Grille | **Stamford**	25
Carbone's | **Hartford**	25
Carmen Anthony Fish. | **multi.**	21
Carmen Anthony | **multi.**	22
Cava Wine | **New Canaan**	23
Z Cavey's | **Manchester**	28
Central Steak | **New Haven**	23
Chez Jean-Pierre | **Stamford**	24
NEW Craftsteak | **Ledyard**	-
Z DaPietro's | **Westport**	26
Duo | **Stamford**	23
Z Elm St. Oyster | **Greenwich**	24
Emilio Rist. | **Harrison**	23
Enzo's | **Mamaro**	18
Esca | **Middletown**	-
Fat Cat Pie | **Norwalk**	23
Field | **Bridgeport**	17
42 | **White Pl**	22
Frankie/Johnnie's | **Rye**	23
Geronimo | **New Haven**	17
Gnarly Vine | **New Roch**	19
Hidden Vine | **Newington**	-
Hostaria Mazzei | **Port Chester**	21
Z Ibiza | **New Haven**	28
Il Falco | **Stamford**	22
Z Jean-Louis | **Greenwich**	28
John's Café | **Woodbury**	24
La Bretagne | **Stamford**	22
La Crémaillère | **Bedford**	26
La Panetière | **Rye**	27
NEW Le Farm | **Westport**	-
Le Fontane | **Katonah**	20
Z Le Petit Cafe | **Branford**	28
L'Orcio | **New Haven**	23
Luca Rist. | **Wilton**	24
Lusardi's | **Larch**	24
Max Fish | **Glastonbury**	24
Melting Pot | **Darien**	18
Z Michael Jordan's | **Uncasville**	25
Michael's | **Wallingford**	23
Z Morton's | **multi.**	24
Z Napa & Co. | **Stamford**	25
Nessa | **Port Chester**	20
Octagon | **Groton**	26
Z Ondine | **Danbury**	25
Peppercorn's Grill | **Hartford**	25
Piccolo Arancio | **Farmington**	26
Pizzeria Lauretano | **Bethel**	26
Plates | **Larch**	24
PolytechnicON20 | **Hartford**	28
Z Rebeccas | **Greenwich**	25
Rist. Luce | **Hamden**	22
River Tavern | **Chester**	25
NEW Rouge Winebar | **S Norwalk**	-
Strada 18 | **S Norwalk**	25
Tango Grill | **White Pl**	22
Tarry Lodge | **Port Chester**	24
Telluride | **Stamford**	21
Z Thomas Henkelmann | **Greenwich**	28
Tre Scalini | **New Haven**	23
Z Valbella | **Riverside**	25
Willett House | **Port Chester**	23
Winvian | **Morris**	-

THE BERKSHIRES
RESTAURANT
DIRECTORY

TOP FOOD

28 Old Inn/Green | *Amer.*
27 Wheatleigh | *Amer./French*
   Blantyre | *Amer./French*
25 Gramercy | *Amer./Eclectic*
   Elizabeth's | *Eclectic*

TOP DECOR

28 Wheatleigh | *Amer./French*
   Blantyre | *Amer./French*
27 Old Inn/Green | *Amer.*
25 Jae's Spice | *Amer./Asian*
23 Mezze Bistro | *American*

Aegean Breeze *Mediterranean*

19 | 15 | 18 | $39

Great Barrington | 327 Stockbridge Rd. (bet. Cooper & Crissey Rds.) | 413-528-4001 | www.aegean-breeze.com

Great Barrington Grecophiles breeze into this "casual", "fairly priced" Mediterranean for "luscious broiled fish" and other "delicious" "traditional" Hellenic fare proffered by a battalion of "hospitable" servers; although some find the blue-and-white taverna-style digs "uninteresting", the "attractive" patio is "pleasant" "in warm weather."

Allium *American*

22 | 22 | 19 | $46

Great Barrington | 42-44 Railroad St. (Main St.) | 413-528-2118 | www.mezzeinc.com

"Food mad" Great Barrington gets a fresh "big-city dining" experience by way of this "sophisticated" New American, a "cool sibling of Williamstown's Mezze"; the "limited" but "intriguing" market-based menu served in "chic", "modern" environs impresses most, and though the fussy fume it's "more show than go" with "erratic" service and "pricey" tabs, overall it's a "winner."

Alta *Mediterranean*

20 | 18 | 21 | $37

Lenox | 34 Church St. (bet. Housatonic & Walker Sts.) | 413-637-0003 | www.altawinebar.com

"Wonderfully nice owners" set a "friendly" tone at this "fine" Lenox restaurant and wine bar where "terrific" Mediterranean eats are matched by a "great selection" of "reasonably priced" wines; if the "informal" interior is a tad too "young and lively" (read: "noisy"), it's "lovely to eat on the outdoor porch" when weather permits.

Aroma Bar & Grill *Indian*

21 | 14 | 22 | $30

Great Barrington | 485 Main St. (bet. Maple Ave. & Pope St.) | 413-528-3116 | www.aromabarandgrill.com

A "refreshing alternative" in Great Barrington, this "traditional" Indian offers "generous portions" of "well-priced", "delicious" dishes "spiced to your taste" and served by a "conscientious" staff that "tries hard to please"; as for the decor, some call it "kitschy" and some bill it bland – but "who cares?"

Baba Louie's Sourdough Pizza *Pizza*

24 | 12 | 18 | $21

Great Barrington | 286 Main St. (bet. Elm & Railroad Sts.) | 413-528-8100 | www.babalouiespizza.com

"Waiting crowds are a testament" to the "outstanding" "crunchy", organic thin-crust pizzas purveyed at this "rockin'" Great Barrington destination; add "fresh, novel" toppings, "marvelous salads", "first-rate" Italian sandwiches, a "competent staff" and "value" prices, and no wonder it's a "family favorite."

	FOOD	DECOR	SERVICE	COST

Barrington Brewery & Restaurant *American*

| 15 | 15 | 19 | $24 |

Great Barrington | 420 Stockbridge Rd./Rte. 7 N. (Old Stonebridge Rd./ Rte. 183) | 413-528-8282 | www.barringtonbrewery.net

Though it's certainly "not fancy", the "basic" American grub at this "family-friendly" Great Barrington microbrewery "hits the spot" "after a day of leaf peeping" or skiing; "large servings for little cash" come dished up "fast" in a big, "cheerful", "lively" space with working vats on view – oh, and "the beer ain't bad either!"

NEW Berkshire Harvest *American*

| - | - | - | M |

Lenox | 55 Pittsfield Rd. (bet. Dugway Rd. & Main St.) | 413-637-9777 | www.theberkshireharvest.com

Aptly named, this Lenox newcomer relies on regional farmers, bakers, vintners and even chocolatiers to supply ingredients for its New American menu, on which surprises such as tandoori chicken turn up alongside updated comfort classics like roast turkey, mac 'n' cheese and meatloaf; all come served in a casual, sunlit dining room adorned with local photos or a spacious taproom, with affordable rates a bonus (the under-$10 daily blue-plate specials are a particular boon for the budget conscious).

Bistro Zinc *French*

| 22 | 22 | 19 | $48 |

Lenox | 56 Church St. (Housatonic St.) | 413-637-8800 | www.bistrozinc.com

It's all "trendy" "urban chic" at Lenox's "popular" "replica of a French bistro", where "young and old" gather for "delightful" fare in "sexy" surroundings that include a "cool bar"; if only the prices weren't so "steep", the service were "warmer" and the "tight room" weren't so "zoo-y" in high season (remember, "reservations are a must").

Bizen *Japanese*

| 22 | 17 | 17 | $42 |

Great Barrington | 17 Railroad St. (Rte. 7) | 413-528-4343

"Yummy", sometimes "edgy" sushi and Japanese grilled dishes make up the "encyclopedic menu" at this "rather pricey" spot in Great Barrington; a "small space" plus "bustling" "crowds" equals often "harried" staffers, so cognoscenti "sit at the bar" and "schmooze" with "knowledgeable" chef-owner Michael Marcus (he also "makes the pottery" on view) or retreat to a tatami room for the prix fixe kaiseki dinner.

Z Blantyre *American/French*

| 27 | 28 | 27 | $163 |

Lenox | Blantyre | 16 Blantyre Rd. (Rte. 20) | 413-637-3556 | www.blantyre.com

A true "grande dame", this "ritzy" hotel dining room with "a magnificent setting" in Lenox exudes the "luxury" of "a bygone era", from the "fabulous" French–New American à la carte lunches and prix fixe dinners to the "thoroughly professional", "refined staff" to "gorgeous", "romantic" environs filled with "fresh flowers" and soft piano music; yes, the whole "pampering" experience is "over-the-top", just like the "out-of-sight prices" – but this is "one splurge that's really worth the dough"; N.B. jacket and tie required; no children under 12.

	FOOD	DECOR	SERVICE	COST

Bombay ⓜ *Indian* | 23 | 14 | 19 | $30

Lee | Quality Inn | 435 Laurel St. (Rte. 20) | 413-243-6731 |
www.fineindiandining.com

"Spicy food"–favorers find "wonderful" renditions at this "festive" Lee Indian appreciated for "considerate service" and a weekend brunch buffet deemed "one of the best buys anywhere"; if the plain decor seems "peculiar", "sit at a window" and enjoy the "lovely lake view."

Brix Wine Bar ⓜ *French* | 22 | 21 | 23 | $40

Pittsfield | 40 West St. (bet. McKay & North Sts.) | 413-236-9463 |
www.brixwinebar.com

"Fine" French bistro fare and "a smart wine list" make for "a winning combination" at this "appealing" Pittsfield "hangout" where the "expensive" food tabs are tempered by "good-value flights"; an "attentive" staff works the "intimate" gold-and-burgundy room, which some say gets too "noisy" when everyone else is having too much "fun."

Cafe Adam *European* | 22 | 15 | 19 | $36

Great Barrington | 325 Stockbridge Rd. (bet. Cooper & Crissey Rds.) |
413-528-7786 | www.cafeadam.org

"Imaginative", "well-prepared" contemporary European fare is served "at reasonable prices" alongside an "amazing wine list" at this "casual", "out-of-the-way" Great Barrington cafe where toque-owner Adam Zieminski "settled down" after some swanky cheffing across the pond; diners settle in the minimalist "NY-style interior" with its black accents and matching blackboards (for specials) or nab an umbrella table on the porch when it's nice out.

Café Lucia ⓜ *Italian* | 21 | 17 | 20 | $51

Lenox | 80 Church St. (bet. Franklin & Housatonic Sts.) | 413-637-2640 |
www.cafelucialenox.com

"If you love osso buco, make a beeline" for this Lenox veteran where the "chef's signature" is the highlight of the "pricey" menu of "reliable" Italian "classics"; even admirers admit the "ordinary" interior of the 1839 house gets too "crowded" and "noisy", but they just ask the "pleasant" staff for a table on the "pleasurable" deck.

Castle Street Cafe *American/French* | 19 | 17 | 20 | $44

Great Barrington | 10 Castle St. (Main St.) | 413-528-5244 |
www.castlestreetcafe.com

"Popular with transplanted NYers and locals" alike, this "dependable" Great Barrington American-French bistro serves up "old favorites done well" in lighter preparations at the "lively" bar – which is "enhanced by cool jazz on weekends" (nightly in summer) – and "more pricey" full dinners in the "spacious" dining room; a "courteous" staff is another reason it packs an "invariably full house."

Chez Nous ⓜ *French* | 24 | 18 | 23 | $50

Lee | 150 Main St. (Academy St.) | 413-243-6397 |
www.cheznousbistro.com

"Half the time it's excellent, the other half it's out of sight" pronounce pleased "picky locals" of Gallic chef Franck Tessier's "mouthwatering"

French fare and his American wife Rachel Portnoy's "luscious desserts" (she also offers "warm welcomes" as hostess) at this "comfy", costly "country house" in Lee; there's also a "quality wine list", from which the "efficient" staff can suggest "perfect complements."

Church Street Cafe *American*   21 | 17 | 20 | $43

Lenox | 65 Church St. (bet. Franklin & Housatonic Sts.) | 413-637-2745 | www.churchstreetcafe.biz

A "tried-and-true" "standby for Lenox residents" (as well as tourists heading to Tanglewood), this "relaxed" New American employs an "accommodating staff" to deliver "delicious food" that's "a bit pricey but worth it"; patrons pick from three "peaceful" rooms, or sit on the "delightful" porch to "enjoy the scenery" "in the middle of town."

Coyote Flaco ⓜ *Mexican*   ▽ 21 | 18 | 20 | $30

Williamstown | 505 Cold Spring Rd. (Bee Hill Rd.) | 413-458-4240 | www.mycoyoteflaco.com

"Come hungry" for "real Mexican" "served with flair" advise amigos of this "family-owned" chainlet; even those who declare it "generally mediocre" find places in their hearts for "not-to-be-missed" margaritas and the occasional "mariachi serenade."

Cranwell Resort, Spa & Golf Club *American*   20 | 23 | 22 | $51

Lenox | 55 Lee Rd./Rte. 20 (Rte. 7) | 413-637-1364 | www.cranwell.com

"What a beautiful place" declare dazzled guests of Lenox's "lovely" Tudor-style mansion resort, where "attentive" staffers serve "wonderful", "expensive" New American fare in the "romantic" Wyndhurst room or Music Room Grill; the less enthused tut it's a tad "hoity-toity" and suggest "sticking to Sloane's Tavern", the home of "good burgers and shareable salads" "at moderate prices", or the spa cafe and its "fresh" light fare.

Dakota Steakhouse *Steak*   18 | 17 | 19 | $34

Pittsfield | 1035 South St. (Dan Fox Dr.) | 413-499-7900 | www.steakseafood.com

A "family atmosphere" pervades the links of this "large, popular" steakhouse chain known for its "huge menu" of "predictable", "plentiful" protein in various guises, "amazing salad bar", "magnificent" Sunday brunch and "value prices"; the "pseudo" "big-game-hunter theme" (think mounted "elk and moose heads") is "disconcerting" to some, but the "warm", "caring" service "never disappoints."

Dream Away Lodge ⓜ⇴ *American*   - | - | - | I

Becket | 1342 County Rd. (Stanley Rd.) | 413-623-8725 | www.thedreamawaylodge.com

Legendary in the Berkshires, this New American eatery/bar–cum-performance venue buried in the backwoods of Becket has hosted diverse acts from Bob Dylan to Liberace in a laid-back old farmhouse as colorful as its brothel/speakeasy past; a small affordable menu of comfort classics (think chicken, pot roast, mac 'n' cheese) is served in a comfy room, where all is so mismatched it matches, but remember, it's cash only, just weekends in winter and get good directions.

☑ Elizabeth's Ⓜ🖗 *Eclectic* — 25 | 13 | 22 | $33

Pittsfield | 1264 East St. (Newell St.) | 413-448-8244

Practically a "cult classic", this "offbeat" Pittsfield Eclectic offers a "limited", "lovingly prepared" menu of "unbelievable pastas" and "bountiful", "spectacular salads", plus one fish and one meat dish (both "amazing") per night; "foodies" "sit in the kitchen" of the "homey" space to watch "scene-stealer" chef Tom Ellis, then marvel at the final "quirk": only checks, cash "or IOU – and they mean it."

Fin *Japanese* — 23 | 13 | 18 | $38

Lenox | 27 Housatonic St. (Church St.) | 413-637-9171 | www.finsushi.com

"Tiny but tony", this Lenox "hole-in-the-wall", co-owned by Bistro Zinc's Jason Macioge and his brother, Nick, serves "inventive, yummy sushi" and other "complex" Japanese dishes "with twists"; while the "roar" and "cramped", "diner"-style digs are negatives, fans find greater comfort at the red-lacquered bar – or when they get it to go.

Firefly *American* — 17 | 17 | 15 | $39

Lenox | 71 Church St. (Housatonic St.) | 413-637-2700 | www.fireflylenox.com

Pros proclaim this "casual" "neighborhood place" in Lenox a "fine choice" for "interesting" New American fare, while cons criticize an "unfocused menu" and "disappearing servers"; however, come summer, all appreciate the "busy", "pretty bar" and "wonderful porch."

Flavours of Malaysia Ⓜ *Asian* — - | - | - | I

Pittsfield | 75 North St. (McKay St.) | 413-443-3188 | www.flavoursintheberkshires.com

Now in Pittsfield after a move from Lenox, this easygoing Asian owned by chef Sabrina Tan turns out the tastes of China, Malaysia, India and Thailand, so expect everything from dim sum to chicken satay to samosas (with a few American dishes thrown in for good measure); spacious burgundy surroundings create a warm, relaxed vibe, while inexpensive tabs keep the mood happy.

Frankie's Ristorante Italiano *Italian* — - | - | - | M

Lenox | 80 Main St. (Cliftwood St.) | 413-637-4455 | www.frankiesitaliano.com

Chef-owner Stephane Ferioli creates a classic mom-and-pop vibe at this casual Lenox Italian where family photos on red felt walls and golden ceilings fashion a cozy backdrop for traditional recipes from his *nonna* (think lasagna with spinach dough, ragout bolognese and seafood fra diavolo); spouse Molly meets and greets, and moderate tabs add another friendly note.

Gala — ∇ 21 | 24 | 23 | $41
Restaurant & Bar *American/Continental*

Williamstown | Orchards Hotel | 222 Adams Rd. (Main St.) | 413-458-9611 | www.galarestaurant.com

This Williamstown New American–Continental's "calm setting" includes "spacious" rooms bedecked with "dark-wood paneling" and

	FOOD	DECOR	SERVICE	COST

a "lovely" courtyard; an "eager staff" conveys the "beautifully presented" fare, and while it's somewhat pricey, a lighter menu is available in the bar area where "seats by the fireplace are coveted."

☑ Gramercy Bistro *American/Eclectic* | 25 | - | 23 | $40 |

North Adams | Mass MoCA | 87 Marshall St. (bet. River St. & Rte. 2) | 413-663-5300 | www.gramercybistro.com

The "thoughtfully prepared", "updated" bistro classics made with "local, artisanal" ingredients "exceed expectations" at this "welcoming" chef-owned American-Eclectic in North Adams, which is also appreciated for its "luscious desserts", "personable service" and overall "warm" vibe; it recently moved into roomier digs (the revamped former Café Latino space) at Mass MoCA up the block, and now boasts a patio for fair-weather dining.

Haven *American/Bakery* | - | - | - | I |

Lenox | 8 Franklin St. (Main St.) | 413-637-8948 | www.havencafebakery.com

This casual American cafe and bakery in Downtown Lenox serves freshly prepared fare featuring local/organic ingredients for breakfast, lunch and, occasionally in the summer, dinner; gin, rum and vodka come from a local distillery, and everything's served in simple surroundings with wainscoting and dark hardwood floors.

Hub, The ☒ *American* | - | - | - | M |

North Adams | 55 Main St. (Center St.) | 413-662-2500

Culinary couple Matthew and Kate Schilling (he chefs, she greets) create a country-diner mood at their North Adams American where the storefront space sports stools at a counter, a black-and-white-tiled floor and vintage photos on the walls; it's a convivial hub for locals looking for affordable light fare like burgers and sandwiches or heartier offerings such as the signature spicy jambalaya.

Isabella's ☒ *Italian* | - | - | - | M |

North Adams | 869 State Rd. (bet. Georgia & Hawthorne Aves.) | 413-662-2239 | www.isabellasrest.com

Professors, businessmen and families mingle merrily at this affordable North Adams Italian that's named after the daughter of chef-owner Drew Nicastro and his front-of-house spouse Leigh-Anne Jones; set inside an 1890s farmhouse, the environment includes soothing moss-green-and-khaki rooms and a summertime dining porch.

Jae's Spice *American/Asian* | 21 | 25 | 19 | $38 |

Pittsfield | 297 North St. (bet. Summer & Union Sts.) | 413-443-1234 | www.eatatjaes.com

Creating "buzz" in a "dramatic" old-department-store space in Pittsfield, this Jae Chung venture proffers the "Pan-Asian food he's famous for" as well as "mainstream" New American dishes, all at "remarkably modest prices"; the "gorgeous" decor features scattered Asian doodads and a sushi bar, and once the sometimes "disorganized" service "smoothes out", all will be "terrific."

	FOOD	DECOR	SERVICE	COST

John Andrews *American*

25	21	22	$55

South Egremont | Rte. 23 (Blunt Rd.) | 413-528-3469 |
www.jarestaurant.com

"You want classy in the Berkshires?" – this "charming", "off-the-beaten-track" South Egremont New American is it declare devotees; an "elegant" dining room sets the mood for "masterfully prepared", "sophisticated" cooking "that'll warm your heart", served by a staff that "knows how to keep fussy New Yorkers happy"; wallet-watchers who find it "on the expensive side" opt for the bar where the less expensive, "simpler menu is just as delicious."

Jonathan's Bistro *American*

–	–	–	M

Lenox | 55 Pittsfield Rd. (bet. Dugway Rd. & Main St.) | 413-637-8022
New American cooking that runs the gamut from wraps and grilled pizza to fancier fare keeps a diverse crowd coming to this midpriced Lenox spot; all nestle into bistro-style digs tricked out in shades of pumpkin with gold curtains and a copper bar or head to the patio when it's warm.

Marketplace Kitchen *American/Sandwiches*

–	–	–	I

Sheffield | 18 Elm Ct. (Main St.) | 413-248-5040 |
www.marketplacekitchen.com

An offshoot of the Marketplace, the popular specialty foods store down the road, this casual Sheffield American serves creative sandwiches, salads and soups in a sunny storefront done up in hues of coffee and butternut squash; locals pile in for cheap breakfasts and lunches and for Tuesday's family dinner, an ever-changing theme meal where a mere $20 feeds a family of four.

Mezze Bistro + Bar *American*

25	23	23	$45

Williamstown | 16 Water St. (Rte. 2) | 413-458-0123 | www.mezzeinc.com
Expect "love at first bite" at this "upscale" New American "surprise" in Williamstown, where "refined", "inventive" tastes are matched by a "superb wine list" and "professional service"; the "attractive setting", tricked out in chocolate and cream tones, is "the place to be seen", or come summer, "get an eyeful, if you're into star-watching."

Mill on the Floss Ⓜ *French*

23	22	23	$49

New Ashford | 342 Rte. 7 (Rte. 43) | 413-458-9123 |
www.millonthefloss.com

Known as an "old favorite" in New Ashford, this "time-tested" French spot offers "sophisticated", "pricey" fare in a "lovely, unpretentious" 18th-century farmhouse; sure, it's "a bit dated", but "romantics" "take comfort in the warmth" of its wood-beamed, "cozy", candlelit rooms, while "friendly, helpful service" is another reason it's an "enjoyable" standby for "special occasions."

Mission Bar & Tapas ●Ⓩ *Spanish*

–	–	–	M

Pittsfield | 438 North St. (Maplewood Ave.) |
www.missionbarandtapas.com

Perhaps this Spanish tapas specialist is kind of "arty" for Pittsfield, but "young hipsters and older couples" alike pile in for "superb" small plates, charcuterie, "tangy salads" and Iberian wines; works by local artists brighten deep red walls in the long and narrow room where "musicians playing live" add to the "mellow, unrushed" atmosphere.

Morgan House *New England* | 16 | 15 | 17 | $37 |

Lee | Morgan House | 33 Main St. (Mass. Tpke., exit 2) | 413-243-3661 | www.morganhouseinn.com

Lee locals report the newish owners are "really trying to better" this "quaint" early-19th-century inn, starting with "updating" the decor with fresh paint and a mural of the town; initially, the New England "comfort food" remained "pretty much the same" as before – however, a post-Survey menu update may have changed all that (and outdated the above Food score as well).

Napa *Eclectic* | 19 | 18 | 17 | $43 |

Great Barrington | 293 Main St. (Church St.) | 413-528-4311 | www.napagb.com

This Great Barrington eatery and wine bar offers "interesting", "well-prepared" Eclectic dishes alongside "inexpensive wines" (a contrast to the somewhat pricey fare); high ceilings, peach walls and a long bar create a "nice" setting that helps patrons overlook the "noisy sound level" and "needs-improvement" service; N.B. there's live cabaret or jazz Tuesdays, Fridays and Saturdays.

NEW Nudel Ⓜ *American* | - | - | - | M |

Lenox | 37 Church St. (bet. Housatonic & Walker Sts.) | 413-551-7183 | www.nudelrestaurant.com

Young chef Bjorn Somlo, a Berkshires native, launched this Lenox New American newcomer in the spot once occupied by Dish Café Bistro after transforming the narrow space into a bright, warm room with an open kitchen, wood floors and benches and a bar fashioned from recycled church pews; the seasonally driven, daily changing and reasonably priced menu spotlights 'nudels' (as in 'pastas') paired with innovative accoutrements.

☒ Old Inn on the Green *American* | 28 | 27 | 25 | $65 |

New Marlborough | Old Inn on the Green | 134 Hartsville-New Marlborough Rd./Rte. 57 (Rte. 272) | 413-229-7924 | www.oldinn.com

"Worth every minute of the drive" to "remote" New Marlborough, this New American "jewel" set in an "exquisite" 1760 inn is "a fabulous find" for chef-owner Peter Platt's "outstanding" cuisine, matched by "stellar service" and "wonderful wines"; the "impossibly romantic" dining rooms "lit only by candles and fireplaces" might "leave you drowsy with satisfaction", while the tabs will definitely cause your wallet to be considerably lighter – unless you've come on Wednesday, Thursday or Sunday for the "bargain" $30 prix fixe.

Old Mill *American* | 24 | 23 | 25 | $50 |

South Egremont | 53 Main St. (Rte. 41) | 413-528-1421 | www.oldmillberkshires.com

"Wonderful", "lovingly prepared" American cooking, "gracious" service and a fireside "atmosphere that makes you feel warm and cuddly" explain why this "well-worth-the-cost" "rustic charmer" in a "beautiful" 1797 South Egremont mill has been "a must" for more than 30 years; the one teeny "turnoff" is the no-rez policy for fewer than five, but even that's made up for by the "delightful bar to wait in."

Once Upon a Table *American/Continental*　| 21 | 15 | 23 | $38 |

Stockbridge | The Mews | 36 Main St. (bet. Elm St. & Rte. 7) | 413-298-3870 | www.onceuponatablebistro.com

"Simple, well-cooked" eats are the attraction at this "adorable" Continental–New American "tucked in the mews" next to Stockbridge's Red Lion; a "friendly, efficient" staff works the "pleasant" but "tiny" room, which is "great" for lunch and quickly "full at night" ("reservations are a must").

NEW Perigee *Eclectic/New England*　| - | - | - | M |

Lee | 1575 Pleasant St. (bet. Church & Willow Sts.) | 413-394-4047 | www.perigee-restaurant.com

At this midpriced Lee newcomer, New England classics meet the rest of the culinary world to create an Eclectic assemblage that the proprietors have trademarked as Berkshire cuisine; the neat brick exterior with periwinkle shutters gives way to a bistro-style downstairs with a cozy beamed bar and a quieter, softly lit, wainscoted upstairs.

Pho Saigon *Vietnamese*　| ▽ 19 | 10 | 18 | $24 |

Lee | 5 Railroad St. (Main St.) | 413-243-6288

"Traditional" "homestyle" Vietnamese comes in "good, plentiful" and cheap supply at this "authentic", owner-operated Lee spot; most don't mind that bamboo accents are the only things notable in the no-frills digs, the "cheerful" servers "hardly speak English" or the "kitchen's slow when it gets busy."

Point at Thornewood Inn 🅂🅼 *American*　| - | - | - | M |

Great Barrington | Thornewood Inn | 453 Stockbridge Rd. (Rtes. 7 & 183) | 413-528-3828 | www.thornewoodinn.com

Comfort's the point of this Great Barrington Traditional American dispensing crowd-pleasers like pork tenderloin, mac 'n' cheese, grilled salmon and a regular whimsical chicken-something, all at affordable rates; its setting in a sprawling Dutch Colonial–style inn features three dining spaces: a pubby taproom, a cozy area done up in creams and a larger environment with soft-green walls, a dance floor and Palladian windows overlooking a garden.

Prime Italian　| 20 | 20 | 20 | $57 |
Steakhouse & Bar 🅼 *Italian/Steak*

Lenox | 15 Franklin St. (Rte. 7A) | 413-637-2998 | www.primelenox.com

It may "not blow your socks off", but the menu at this "solid" Lenox Southern Italian steakhouse mixes "simple meat and potatoes" with chef-owner Gennaro Gallo's homemade gnocchi and the like; manned by a "pleasant" staff, the setting features "smoked glass" dividers on the booths, a lit-from-beneath bar and bright red banquettes.

	FOOD	DECOR	SERVICE	COST

Red Lion Inn *New England* | 18 | 22 | 21 | $45 |

Stockbridge | Red Lion Inn | 30 Main St./Rte. 102 (Rte. 7) | 413-298-5545 | www.redlioninn.com

This 1773 "quintessential New England inn" – a Stockbridge "icon" – trots out "warhorses like roast turkey" on its "fine", "old-fashioned" menu; a "courteous" staff serves in the "genteel", "high-priced" main dining room, "cozy", "less expensive" Widow Bingham's Tavern or "fun", "reasonable" Lion's Den pub, and even the debonair who decry it's "dowdy" and "stuffed with tourists" declare it's "lovely to eat in the courtyard."

Rouge ☑ *French* | 23 | 18 | 16 | $50 |

West Stockbridge | 3 Center St. (Rte. 41) | 413-232-4111 | www.rougerestaurant.com

"A charming couple" runs this "lively" West Stockbridge bistro: chef William Merelle cooks up "exceptional", somewhat pricey French fare (and "inventive" tapas, served in the bar), while spouse Maggie greets in the "homey" space; *les négatives* are "lapses in service" on "busy" nights, when it's "noisy as a Paris subway."

Route 7 Grill *American/BBQ* | 23 | 17 | 21 | $33 |

Great Barrington | 999 S. Main St. (bet. Brookside & Lime Kiln Rds.) | 413-528-3235 | www.route7grill.com

"Lip-smacking ribs, succulent pulled pork" and other "fantastic" BBQ tops a menu of "delicious" American "comfort food" at this "hopping joint" in Great Barrington; "locavores" love its "commitment to regional farmers", while everyone "gives three cheers" for the "festive", "child-friendly" vibe, "cordial" service and "reasonable" tabs; a two-sided fireplace warms up the "spare decor", and there's "a jolly bar too."

Shiro Sushi & Hibachi *Japanese* | ▽ 20 | 19 | 22 | $34 |

Great Barrington | 105 Stockbridge Rd. (bet. Blue Hill Rd. & Brooke Ln.) | 413-528-1898

NEW **Shiro Lounge** *Japanese*

Pittsfield | 48 North St. (School St.) | 413-236-8111 www.berkshiro.com

"Enthusiastic, goofy chefs" perform a "typical hibachi show" at this Great Barrington Japanese offering "fresh sushi" in addition to the "theatrical" experience; "don't overlook it" just because of its plain digs "next to a bowling alley"; N.B. post-Survey, a sports bar was erected on one side of the dining room, and Shiro Lounge, a hibachi-less, more upscale offshoot, made its debut in Pittsfield.

Siam Square Thai Cuisine *Thai* | 18 | 15 | 19 | $27 |

Great Barrington | 290 Main St. (Railroad St.) | 413-644-9119 | www.siamsquares.com

"Thai food is hard to come by" in the Berkshires, so this "reliable", "welcoming" Great Barrington "landmark" "does the trick" when "noodle cravings" hit, dispensing all "the basics as well as a few un-usual options" for "cheap"; the space is "modest and quiet", while the staff is "sweet."

	FOOD	DECOR	SERVICE	COST

Stagecoach Tavern Ⓜ *American*   ▽ 20 | 23 | 22 | $41

Sheffield | Race Brook Lodge | S. Undermountain Rd./Rte. 41
(Berkshire School Rd.) | 413-229-8585 | www.stagecoachtavern.net
The "warm hearth beckons" at this "rustic" roadside tavern in
Sheffield, where seasonal American fare made with local and organic
ingredients comes full of "flair and flavor"; its staff is "friendly", while
"inviting" decor reflects the inn's 1829 vintage with "beautiful wood"
beams and floors, candlelight and "cozy corners for quiet talk."

Sullivan Station Restaurant *New England*   ▽ 15 | 15 | 19 | $33

Lee | 109 Railroad St. (Mass. Tpke., exit 2) | 413-243-2082 |
www.sullivanstationrestaurant.com
"Weekend crowds, even off-season" confirm that Lee's "delightful"
"converted train station" is on the right track with its "variety" of
simple, "solid" New England "comfort fare" "at the right price"; it's
a "family-friendly" spot that's "literally a hoot" when the Berkshire
Scenic Railway tourist ride rolls by.

Sushi Thai Garden *Japanese/Thai*   20 | 14 | 19 | $28

Williamstown | 27 Spring St. (Rte. 2) | 413-458-0004 |
www.sushithaigarden.com
"A nice surprise in staid Williamstown", this Thai turns out "fresh",
"spicy" "standards" – and the "sushi isn't bad either"; the decor is
"typical", staff "helpful" and rates "reasonable", so no surprise it's a
"favorite of faculty and students", with just a fussy few shrugging
it's "nothing special."

Taylor's Ⓢ *American*   - | - | - | M

North Adams | 34 Holden St. (Center St.) | 413-664-4500 |
www.taylorsna.com
Housed in the storefront once occupied by Gideons, this American
restaurant in underserved North Adams offers "nicely presented"
classic steaks and seafood at moderate prices; "helpful" staffers pre-
side over the brick-walled space, which underwent a massive renovation recently, adding a new mahogany bar next to an open kitchen.

Trattoria Il Vesuvio Ⓢ *Italian*   ▽ 18 | 17 | 20 | $39

Lenox | 242 Pittsfield Rd. (bet. Lime Kiln & New Lenox Rds.) |
413-637-4904 | www.trattoria-vesuvio.com
Pros claim "you can't go wrong" with the "red-sauce" classics at this
"popular" Lenox Italian presided over by an "accommodating",
"down-to-earth" family that "appreciates your company"; cons
complain the eats are "simply so-so", but even they're pleased that
the "rustic", converted century-old stable is made "cozy" by a wood-
fired brick oven.

Trattoria Rustica *Italian*   23 | 21 | 20 | $45

Pittsfield | 27 McKay St. (West St.) | 413-499-1192 |
www.trattoria-rustica.com
"Turn on your GPS" to find this "little corner of Naples" "hidden in
the backstreets of Pittsfield", where chef-owner Davide Manzo's
"delectable", "pricey but worth-every-penny" Southern Italian

meals come via "congenial", "well-paced" service; add a wood oven and "low-lit", "romantic" ambiance in the "pretty" stone-and-brick-walled room and you've got a "winning combination."

Truc Orient Express *Vietnamese*   21 | 18 | 19 | $34
West Stockbridge | 3 Harris St. (Main St.) | 413-232-4204
"Super" Vietnamese cooking at "fair prices" keeps customers coming "year after year" to this family-run West Stockbridge "standby" that's been "doing something right" for three decades now; an "efficient", "polite" staff plus a "really nice gift shop" are other reasons it's "worth a detour", so though the digs decorated with art from the motherland are "a bit dated", it's "no matter."

Viva Ⓜ *Spanish*   ∇ 23 | 19 | 21 | $44
Glendale | 14 Glendale Rd. (Rte. 102) | 413-298-4433 |
www.vivaberkshires.com
"Finally, a real Spanish" spot in Glendale cheer those "pleasantly surprised" to find this nook near the Norman Rockwell museum; "authentic tastes" can be found in "to-die-for paella", "terrific tapas" and other "fabulous" fare in a "comfortable", casual mustard-and-terra-cotta setting jazzed up with a Picasso-esque mural.

⚡ Wheatleigh *American/French*   27 | 28 | 26 | $97
Lenox | Wheatleigh | 11 Hawthorne Rd. (Hawthorne St.) |
413-637-0610 | www.wheatleigh.com
It's "heaven on earth" avow the "wowed" at this "gorgeous" Italianate mansion in Lenox, where "truly lovely" rooms form an "elegant" backdrop for "superb" French–New American cuisine and "extraordinary", "formal service"; it strikes a few as "somewhat stuffy", but most are "left sighing" by the whole "spectacular" experience, and though you may have to "sell your house" to pay the bill, this is one "splurge" that's "worth every penny"; N.B. jackets suggested.

Xicohtencatl *Mexican*   21 | 18 | 21 | $35
Great Barrington | 50 Stockbridge Rd. (Rte. 7) | 413-528-2002 |
www.xicohmexican.com
"Upscale", "real Mexican" is the deal at this "colorful" Great Barrington cantina serving "scrumptious" "regional specialties" in "generous" amounts and for relatively "modest costs"; a "staggering selection of tequilas" ensures everyone has "a blast" in the "festive" digs, while "dining on the terrace at sunset is sublime"; P.S. don't sweat the name, just call it "'shico.'"

THE BERKSHIRES
INDEXES

Cuisines

Includes names, locations and Food ratings.

AMERICAN

Allium	**Great Barr**	22
Barrington Brew	**Great Barr**	15
NEW Berkshire Harvest	**Lenox**	-
☑ Blantyre	**Lenox**	27
Castle St.	**Great Barr**	19
Church St.	**Lenox**	21
Cranwell Resort	**Lenox**	20
Dream Away	**Becket**	-
Firefly	**Lenox**	17
Gala	**Williamstown**	21
☑ Gramercy	**N Adams**	25
Haven	**Lenox**	-
Hub	**N Adams**	-
Jae's Spice	**Pittsfield**	21
John Andrews	**S Egremont**	25
Jonathan's	**Lenox**	-
Marketplace	**Sheffield**	-
Mezze Bistro	**Williamstown**	25
NEW Nudel	**Lenox**	-
☑ Old Inn/Green	**New Marl**	28
Old Mill	**S Egremont**	24
Once Upon	**Stockbridge**	21
Point at Thornewood Inn	**Great Barr**	-
Route 7	**Great Barr**	23
Stagecoach Tav.	**Sheffield**	20
Taylor's	**N Adams**	-
☑ Wheatleigh	**Lenox**	27

ASIAN

Flavours/Malaysia	**Pittsfield**	-
Jae's Spice	**Pittsfield**	21

BAKERY

Haven	**Lenox**	-

BARBECUE

Route 7	**Great Barr**	23

CONTINENTAL

Gala	**Williamstown**	21
Once Upon	**Stockbridge**	21

ECLECTIC

☑ Elizabeth's	**Pittsfield**	25
☑ Gramercy	**N Adams**	25
Napa	**Great Barr**	19
NEW Perigee	**Lee**	-

EUROPEAN

Cafe Adam	**Great Barr**	22

FRENCH

☑ Blantyre	**Lenox**	27
Castle St.	**Great Barr**	19
Mill on the Floss	**New Ashford**	23
☑ Wheatleigh	**Lenox**	27

FRENCH (BISTRO)

Bistro Zinc	**Lenox**	22
Brix Wine	**Pittsfield**	22
Chez Nous	**Lee**	24
Rouge	**W Stockbridge**	23

INDIAN

Aroma B&G	**Great Barr**	21
Bombay	**Lee**	23

ITALIAN

(S=Southern)

Café Lucia	**Lenox**	21
Frankie's Rist.	**Lenox**	-
Isabella's	**N Adams**	-
Prime Italian	S	**Lenox**	20
Tratt. Il Vesuvio	**Lenox**	18
Tratt. Rustica	S	**Pittsfield**	23

JAPANESE

(* sushi specialist)

Bizen*	**Great Barr**	22
Fin*	**Lenox**	23
Shiro*	**multi.**	20
Sushi Thai Gdn.*	**Williamstown**	20

MEDITERRANEAN

Aegean Breeze	**Great Barr**	19
Alta	**Lenox**	20

MEXICAN

Coyote Flaco | **Williamstown** 21

Xicohtencatl | **Great Barr** 21

NEW ENGLAND

Morgan Hse. | **Lee** 16

NEW Perigee | **Lee** -

Red Lion Inn | **Stockbridge** 18

Sullivan Station | **Lee** 15

PIZZA

Baba Louie's | **Great Barr** 24

SANDWICHES

Marketplace | **Sheffield** -

SPANISH

(* tapas specialist)

Mission Bar* | **Pittsfield** -

Viva | **Glendale** 23

STEAKHOUSES

Dakota Steakhouse | **Pittsfield** 18

Prime Italian | **Lenox** 20

THAI

Siam Sq. Thai | **Great Barr** 18

Sushi Thai Gdn. | **Williamstown** 20

VIETNAMESE

Pho Saigon | **Lee** 19

Truc Orient | **W Stockbridge** 21

THE BERKSHIRES

CUISINES

Locations

Includes names, cuisines and Food ratings.

BECKET
Dream Away | *Amer.* ⎯

GLENDALE
Viva | *Spanish* 23

GREAT BARRINGTON
Aegean Breeze | *Med.* 19
Allium | *Amer.* 22
Aroma B&G | *Indian* 21
Baba Louie's | *Pizza* 24
Barrington Brew | *Amer.* 15
Bizen | *Japanese* 22
Cafe Adam | *Euro.* 22
Castle St. | *Amer./French* 19
Napa | *Eclectic* 19
Point at Thornewood Inn | *Amer.* ⎯
Route 7 | *Amer./BBQ* 23
Shiro | *Japanese* 20
Siam Sq. Thai | *Thai* 18
Xicohtencatl | *Mex.* 21

LEE
Bombay | *Indian* 23
Chez Nous | *French* 24
Morgan Hse. | *New Eng.* 16
🆕 Perigee | *Eclectic/New Eng.* ⎯
Pho Saigon | *Viet.* 19
Sullivan Station | *New Eng.* 15

LENOX
Alta | *Med.* 20
🆕 Berkshire Harvest | *Amer.* ⎯
Bistro Zinc | *French* 22
🆉 Blantyre | *Amer./French* 27
Café Lucia | *Italian* 21
Church St. | *Amer.* 21
Cranwell Resort | *Amer.* 20
Fin | *Japanese* 23
Firefly | *Amer.* 17
Frankie's Rist. | *Italian* ⎯
Haven | *Amer./Bakery* ⎯
Jonathan's | *Amer.* ⎯
🆕 Nudel | *Amer.* ⎯

Prime Italian | *Italian/Steak* 20
Tratt. Il Vesuvio | *Italian* 18
🆉 Wheatleigh | *Amer./French* 27

NEW ASHFORD
Mill on the Floss | *French* 23

NEW MARLBOROUGH
🆉 Old Inn/Green | *Amer.* 28

NORTH ADAMS
🆉 Gramercy | *Amer./Eclectic* 25
Hub | *Amer.* ⎯
Isabella's | *Italian* ⎯
Taylor's | *Amer.* ⎯

PITTSFIELD
Brix Wine | *French* 22
Dakota Steakhouse | *Steak* 18
🆉 Elizabeth's | *Eclectic* 25
Flavours/Malaysia | *Asian* ⎯
Jae's Spice | *Amer./Asian* 21
Mission Bar | *Spanish* ⎯
Shiro | *Japanese* 20
Tratt. Rustica | *Italian* 23

SHEFFIELD
Marketplace | *Amer./Sandwiches* ⎯
Stagecoach Tav. | *Amer.* 20

SOUTH EGREMONT
John Andrews | *Amer.* 25
Old Mill | *Amer.* 24

STOCKBRIDGE
Once Upon | *Amer./Continental* 21
Red Lion Inn | *New Eng.* 18

WEST STOCKBRIDGE
Rouge | *French* 23
Truc Orient | *Viet.* 21

WILLIAMSTOWN
Coyote Flaco | *Mex.* 21
Gala | *Amer./Continental* 21
Mezze Bistro | *Amer.* 25
Sushi Thai Gdn. | *Japanese/Thai* 20

Menus, photos, voting and more – free at ZAGAT.com

Special Features

Listings cover the best in each category and include names, locations and Food ratings. Multi-location restaurants' features may vary by branch.

ADDITIONS

(Properties added since the last edition of the book)

Berkshire Harvest | **Lenox**	-
Flavours/Malaysia | **Pittsfield**	-
Hub | **N Adams**	-
Isabella's | **N Adams**	-
Jonathan's | **Lenox**	-
Marketplace | **Sheffield**	-
Nudel | **Lenox**	-
Perigee | **Lee**	-
Point at Thornewood Inn | **Great Barr**	-

BRUNCH

Alta | **Lenox**	20
Bombay | **Lee**	23
Cafe Adam | **Great Barr**	22
Dakota Steakhouse | **Pittsfield**	18
☑ Wheatleigh | **Lenox**	27
Xicohtencatl | **Great Barr**	21

BUSINESS DINING

Allium | **Great Barr**	22
Cranwell Resort | **Lenox**	20
Gala | **Williamstown**	21
Jae's Spice | **Pittsfield**	21
Napa | **Great Barr**	19
Taylor's | **N Adams**	-

CATERING

Bizen | **Great Barr**	22
Bombay | **Lee**	23
Castle St. | **Great Barr**	19
John Andrews | **S Egremont**	25
Mezze Bistro | **Williamstown**	25

CHILD-FRIENDLY

(Alternatives to the usual fast-food places; * children's menu available)

Aegean Breeze | **Great Barr**	19
Baba Louie's | **Great Barr**	24
Barrington Brew* | **Great Barr**	15
Bistro Zinc* | **Lenox**	22

Café Lucia | **Lenox**	21
Castle St. | **Great Barr**	19
Church St.* | **Lenox**	21
Coyote Flaco* | **Williamstown**	21
Dakota Steakhouse* | **Pittsfield**	18
☑ Elizabeth's | **Pittsfield**	25
Marketplace | **Sheffield**	-
Morgan Hse. | **Lee**	16
Old Mill | **S Egremont**	24
Once Upon | **Stockbridge**	21
Red Lion Inn* | **Stockbridge**	18
Rouge | **W Stockbridge**	23
Route 7* | **Great Barr**	23
Shiro | **Great Barr**	20
Siam Sq. Thai | **Great Barr**	18
Sullivan Station* | **Lee**	15
Sushi Thai Gdn. | **Williamstown**	20
Tratt. Il Vesuvio* | **Lenox**	18
Xicohtencatl* | **Great Barr**	21

DINING ALONE

(Other than hotels and places with counter service)

Alta | **Lenox**	20
Baba Louie's | **Great Barr**	24
Fin | **Lenox**	23
Napa | **Great Barr**	19
Once Upon | **Stockbridge**	21
Pho Saigon | **Lee**	19

ENTERTAINMENT

(Call for days and times of performances)

☑ Blantyre | varies | **Lenox**	27
Castle St. | jazz/piano | **Great Barr**	19
Mission Bar | folk/indie rock | **Pittsfield**	-
Red Lion Inn | varies | **Stockbridge**	18

FIREPLACES

Aegean Breeze | **Great Barr**	19
Barrington Brew | **Great Barr**	15

Blantyre	Lenox	27
Cranwell Resort	Lenox	20
Dakota Steakhouse	Pittsfield	18
Dream Away	Becket	-
Gala	Williamstown	21
John Andrews	S Egremont	25
Mill on the Floss	New Ashford	23
Morgan Hse.	Lee	16
Old Inn/Green	New Marl	28
Old Mill	S Egremont	24
Red Lion Inn	Stockbridge	18
Route 7	Great Barr	23
Stagecoach Tav.	Sheffield	20
Truc Orient	W Stockbridge	21
Wheatleigh	Lenox	27

GAME IN SEASON

Allium	Great Barr	22
Alta	Lenox	20
Bistro Zinc	Lenox	22
Blantyre	Lenox	27
Brix Wine	Pittsfield	22
Café Lucia	Lenox	21
Castle St.	Great Barr	19
Church St.	Lenox	21
Cranwell Resort	Lenox	20
Elizabeth's	Pittsfield	25
Firefly	Lenox	17
Gramercy	N Adams	25
John Andrews	S Egremont	25
Jonathan's	Lenox	-
Mezze Bistro	Williamstown	25
Napa	Great Barr	19
NEW Nudel	Lenox	-
Old Inn/Green	New Marl	28
Red Lion Inn	Stockbridge	18
Rouge	W Stockbridge	23
Stagecoach Tav.	Sheffield	20
Wheatleigh	Lenox	27

HISTORIC PLACES

(Year opened; * building)

1760	Old Inn/Green*	New Marl	28
1773	Red Lion Inn*	Stockbridge	18
1797	Old Mill*	S Egremont	24

1817	Morgan Hse.*	Lee	16
1829	Stagecoach Tav.*	Sheffield	20
1839	Café Lucia*	Lenox	21
1840	Jae's Spice*	Pittsfield	21
1841	Chez Nous*	Lee	24
1852	Church St.*	Lenox	21
1890	Mezze Bistro*	Williamstown	25
1893	Sullivan Station*	Lee	15
1893	Wheatleigh*	Lenox	27
1894	Cranwell Resort*	Lenox	20
1900	Tratt. Il Vesuvio*	Lenox	18
1903	Gramercy*	N Adams	25
1924	Brix Wine*	Pittsfield	22
1945	Dream Away	Becket	-

HOTEL DINING

Blantyre
| Blantyre | Lenox | 27 |

Morgan House
| Morgan Hse. | Lee | 16 |

Old Inn on the Green
| Old Inn/Green | New Marl | 28 |

Orchards Hotel
| Gala | Williamstown | 21 |

Quality Inn
| Bombay | Lee | 23 |

Race Brook Lodge
| Stagecoach Tav. | Sheffield | 20 |

Red Lion Inn
| Red Lion Inn | Stockbridge | 18 |

Thornewood Inn
| Point at Thornewood Inn | Great Barr | - |

Wheatleigh
| Wheatleigh | Lenox | 27 |

JACKET REQUIRED

(* Tie also required)
| Blantyre* | Lenox | 27 |

MEET FOR A DRINK

Alta	Lenox	20
Bistro Zinc	Lenox	22
Brix Wine	Pittsfield	22

Castle St. | **Great Barr**	19	Bistro Zinc | **Lenox**	22
Chez Nous | **Lee**	24	Mezze Bistro | **Williamstown**	25
Gala | **Williamstown**	21		

POWER SCENES

Z Gramercy | **N Adams**	25	Bistro Zinc | **Lenox**	22
Jae's Spice | **Pittsfield**	21	Mezze Bistro | **Williamstown**	25
Mission Bar | **Pittsfield**	-		

PRIVATE ROOMS

Napa | **Great Barr**	19	(Restaurants charge less at off times; call for capacity)
Old Mill | **S Egremont**	24	

Prime Italian | **Lenox**	20	Bizen | **Great Barr**	22
Red Lion Inn | **Stockbridge**	18	**Z** Blantyre | **Lenox**	27
Stagecoach Tav. | **Sheffield**	20	Castle St. | **Great Barr**	19
		Church St. | **Lenox**	21

MICROBREWERY

Barrington Brew | **Great Barr**	15	Cranwell Resort | **Lenox**	20
		Dakota Steakhouse | **Pittsfield**	18

OFFBEAT

Barrington Brew | **Great Barr**	15	Gala | **Williamstown**	21
Z Elizabeth's | **Pittsfield**	25	John Andrews | **S Egremont**	25
		Mill on the Floss | **New Ashford**	23

OUTDOOR DINING

(G=garden; P=patio; T=terrace; W=waterside)	Red Lion Inn | **Stockbridge**	18
	Rouge | **W Stockbridge**	23

Aegean Breeze | P | **Great Barr**	19	Stagecoach Tav. | **Sheffield**	20
Alta | P | **Lenox**	20	**Z** Wheatleigh | **Lenox**	27

Barrington Brew | G | **Great Barr**	15

PRIX FIXE MENUS

Cafe Adam | P | **Great Barr**	22	(Call for prices and times)

Café Lucia | G, T | **Lenox**	21	Bizen | **Great Barr**	22
Church St. | P | **Lenox**	21	**Z** Blantyre | **Lenox**	27
Firefly | P | **Lenox**	17	Bombay | **Lee**	23
Gala | P, W | **Williamstown**	21	**Z** Old Inn/Green | **New Marl**	28
John Andrews | T | **S Egremont**	25	**Z** Wheatleigh | **Lenox**	27

Jonathan's | P | **Lenox**	-

QUIET CONVERSATION

Z Old Inn/Green | T | **New Marl**	28	**Z** Blantyre | **Lenox**	27
Red Lion Inn | P | **Stockbridge**	18	Gala | **Williamstown**	21
Rouge | T | **W Stockbridge**	23	**Z** Gramercy | **N Adams**	25
Shiro | P | **Great Barr**	20	John Andrews | **S Egremont**	25
Sullivan Station | T | **Lee**	15	Mill on the Floss | **New Ashford**	23
Tratt. Il Vesuvio | T | **Lenox**	18		
Tratt. Rustica | P | **Pittsfield**	23	Stagecoach Tav. | **Sheffield**	20
Xicohtentatl | T | **Great Barr**	21	Taylor's | **N Adams**	-
		Z Wheatleigh | **Lenox**	27

PEOPLE-WATCHING

RESERVE AHEAD

Allium | **Great Barr**	22	Bistro Zinc | **Lenox**	22
Alta | **Lenox**	20	**Z** Blantyre | **Lenox**	27
		Z Old Inn/Green | **New Marl**	28

| Once Upon | **Stockbridge** | 21 |
| **Z** Wheatleigh | **Lenox** | 27 |

ROMANTIC PLACES

Z Blantyre	**Lenox**	27
Cranwell Resort	**Lenox**	20
John Andrews	**S Egremont**	25
Mill on the Floss	**New Ashford**	23
Z Old Inn/Green	**New Marl**	28
Taylor's	**N Adams**	-
Tratt. Rustica	**Pittsfield**	23
Z Wheatleigh	**Lenox**	27

SENIOR APPEAL

Aegean Breeze	**Great Barr**	19
Cranwell Resort	**Lenox**	20
Gala	**Williamstown**	21
Morgan Hse.	**Lee**	16
Red Lion Inn	**Stockbridge**	18
Taylor's	**N Adams**	-

SINGLES SCENES

Alta	**Lenox**	20
Brix Wine	**Pittsfield**	22
Castle St.	**Great Barr**	19
Jae's Spice	**Pittsfield**	21
Napa	**Great Barr**	19
Prime Italian	**Lenox**	20
Sushi Thai Gdn.	**Williamstown**	20

SLEEPERS

(Good food, but little known)
Bombay	**Lee**	23
Brix Wine	**Pittsfield**	22
Cafe Adam	**Great Barr**	22
Fin	**Lenox**	23
Z Gramercy	**N Adams**	25
Mill on the Floss	**New Ashford**	23
Rouge	**W Stockbridge**	23
Route 7	**Great Barr**	23
Tratt. Rustica	**Pittsfield**	23
Viva	**Glendale**	23

TAKEOUT

Aegean Breeze	**Great Barr**	19
Baba Louie's	**Great Barr**	24
Barrington Brew	**Great Barr**	15

Bistro Zinc	**Lenox**	22
Bizen	**Great Barr**	22
Café Lucia	**Lenox**	21
Castle St.	**Great Barr**	19
Church St.	**Lenox**	21
Dakota Steakhouse	**Pittsfield**	18
Gala	**Williamstown**	21
John Andrews	**S Egremont**	25
Marketplace	**Sheffield**	-
Morgan Hse.	**Lee**	16
Once Upon	**Stockbridge**	21
Rouge	**W Stockbridge**	23
Shiro	**Great Barr**	20
Siam Sq. Thai	**Great Barr**	18
Stagecoach Tav.	**Sheffield**	20
Sushi Thai Gdn.	**Williamstown**	20
Truc Orient	**W Stockbridge**	21

TEEN APPEAL

Baba Louie's	**Great Barr**	24
Barrington Brew	**Great Barr**	15
Coyote Flaco	**Williamstown**	21
Dakota Steakhouse	**Pittsfield**	18

TRENDY

Allium	**Great Barr**	22
Bistro Zinc	**Lenox**	22
Bizen	**Great Barr**	22
Brix Wine	**Pittsfield**	22
Cafe Adam	**Great Barr**	22
Castle St.	**Great Barr**	19
Fin	**Lenox**	23
Jae's Spice	**Pittsfield**	21
John Andrews	**S Egremont**	25
Mission Bar	**Pittsfield**	-
Napa	**Great Barr**	19
Z Old Inn/Green	**New Marl**	28
Prime Italian	**Lenox**	20
Rouge	**W Stockbridge**	23
Xicohtencatl	**Great Barr**	21

VIEWS

Bombay	**Lee**	23
Cranwell Resort	**Lenox**	20
Route 7	**Great Barr**	23
Z Wheatleigh	**Lenox**	27

Menus, photos, voting and more - free at ZAGAT.com

VISITORS ON EXPENSE ACCOUNT

Z Blantyre | **Lenox** 27

Old Mill | **S Egremont** 24

Z Wheatleigh | **Lenox** 27

WINNING WINE LISTS

Alta | **Lenox** 20

Brix Wine | **Pittsfield** 22

Cafe Adam | **Great Barr** 22

Castle St. | **Great Barr** 19

Z Gramercy | **N Adams** 25

John Andrews | **S Egremont** 25

Mezze Bistro | **Williamstown** 25

Mission Bar | **Pittsfield** -

Z Old Inn/Green | **New Marl** 28

Wine Vintage Chart

This chart is based on our 0 to 30 scale. The ratings (by U. of South Carolina law professor **Howard Stravitz**) reflect vintage quality and the wine's readiness to drink. A dash means the wine is past its peak or too young to rate. Loire ratings are for dry whites.

Whites	95	96	97	98	99	00	01	02	03	04	05	06	07	08
France:														
Alsace	24	23	23	25	23	25	26	23	21	24	25	24	26	-
Burgundy	27	26	23	21	24	24	24	27	23	26	27	25	25	24
Loire Valley	-	-	-	-	-	23	24	26	22	24	27	23	23	24
Champagne	26	27	24	23	25	24	21	26	21	-	-	-	-	-
Sauternes	21	23	25	23	24	24	29	25	24	21	26	23	27	25
California:														
Chardonnay	-	-	-	-	23	22	25	26	22	26	29	24	27	-
Sauvignon Blanc	-	-	-	-	-	-	-	-	25	26	25	27	25	-
Austria:														
Grüner V./Riesl.	24	21	26	23	25	22	23	25	26	25	24	26	24	22
Germany:	21	26	21	22	24	20	29	25	26	27	28	25	27	25

Reds	95	96	97	98	99	00	01	02	03	04	05	06	07	08
France:														
Bordeaux	26	25	23	25	24	29	26	24	26	24	28	24	23	25
Burgundy	26	27	25	24	27	22	24	24	27	25	23	28	25	24	-
Rhône	26	22	24	27	26	27	26	-	26	24	27	25	26	-
Beaujolais	-	-	-	-	-	-	-	24	-	27	24	25	23	
California:														
Cab./Merlot	27	25	28	23	25	-	27	26	25	24	26	23	26	24
Pinot Noir	-	-	-	24	23	25	26	25	26	24	23	27	25	
Zinfandel	-	-	-	-	-	25	23	27	22	22	21	21	25	
Oregon:														
Pinot Noir	-	-	-	-	-	-	26	24	25	26	26	25	27	
Italy:														
Tuscany	24	-	29	24	27	24	27	-	25	27	26	25	24	-
Piedmont	21	27	26	25	26	28	27	-	25	27	26	25	26	-
Spain:														
Rioja	26	24	25	-	25	24	28	-	23	27	26	24	25	-
Ribera del Duero/ Priorat	26	27	25	24	25	24	27	20	24	27	26	24	26	-
Australia:														
Shiraz/Cab.	24	26	25	28	24	24	27	27	25	26	26	24	22	-
Chile:	-	-	24	-	25	23	26	24	25	24	27	25	24	-
Argentina:														
Malbec	-	-	-	-	-	-	-	-	25	26	27	24	-	

Menus, photos, voting and more – free at ZAGAT.com

Take us with you.
ZAGAT Mobile